The Rise of Puritanism

TITLE-PAGE OF JOHN DOWNAME, THE CHRISTIAN WARFARE, 1634

The Rise of
PURITANISM

Or, THE WAY TO THE NEW JERUSALEM
AS SET FORTH IN PULPIT AND PRESS
FROM THOMAS CARTWRIGHT TO JOHN
LILBURNE AND JOHN MILTON, 1570–1643

WILLIAM HALLER

UNIVERSITY OF PENNSYLVANIA PRESS

Philadelphia

To

MALLEVILLE

EIGHT OF WHOSE GREAT-AUNTS

MARRIED EMINENT DIVINES

Preface

THE studies which have led to this book were first prompted by a desire to understand the place of Milton's *Areopagitica* in its own time. I came to the opinion that one could not justly understand Milton at any point in his career without understanding his relation to Puritanism and that one could not understand Puritanism without knowledge of the teachings of the Puritan pulpit. I therefore turned to the sermons, popular expositions of doctrine, spiritual biographies and manuals of godly behavior in which Puritan preachers ever since the early days of Elizabeth had been telling the people what they must do to be saved. The result of my reading is not, I need hardly say, a history of all phases of the movement which led to the Puritan Revolution, but a sketch of Puritan propaganda before 1643. I have paused at 1643 because, with the convening in that year of the Westminster Assembly, Puritans, including Milton, thought that their long struggle for the reform of the church was about to be crowned with accomplishment. What happened after 1643 to the Puritan dream of a Utopia founded upon the word of God and what effect the shattering of that dream had upon Milton, I hope to set forth at a later time.

My interpretation of Puritanism is based directly upon my own reading of what Puritans themselves wrote. Their writings were nothing if not abundant and have for a long time been almost totally ignored. I have read many of them but not all, preferring at every point the popular sermon or tract to the learned and technical treatise. I have not been able to read them without renewed amazement at the extraordinary vitality of Puritan thought and character or without feeling that I have drawn near to the central fire which still burns in the pages of Milton. Of that vitality I hope that I have given a just and lively impression. I hope at the same time that it will not seem that I have myself undertaken to wage spiritual war either for Puritanism or against it.

Preface

There is much in the Puritan tradition from which we may well wish to be free. I learned at Amherst many years ago that there is also something which must always command respect. Professor Samuel Eliot Morison's recent account of the beginnings of New England intellectual culture as manifested at the founding of Harvard precisely confirms that respect. Sir Herbert Grierson has shown how important has been the influence of Puritanism in English poetry; he has also shown how Milton may be appreciated without being either idolized or condemned. To his *Cross Currents in English Literature of the Seventeenth Century* and to his personal counsel and encouragement I owe much of the impulse and many of the ideas which have animated this study. I take pleasure in acknowledging the debt I share with other students of Milton to Professor James Holly Hanford, to Mr. E. M. W. Tillyard and to Mrs. Tillyard for their contributions to our understanding of the poet's youth. I regret that Mr. Tillyard's most recent book, *The Miltonic Setting,* did not appear until my own work was done. To its presentation of Milton's essential Protestantism I subscribe with admiration. I also regret that Mr. A. S. P. Woodhouse's discussion of 'Puritanism and Liberty,' which he offers as an introduction to his forthcoming edition of the Clarke Papers, did not reach me sooner. If it had, some things I have said might have been said differently and with more confidence.

The Columbia University Council for Research in the Humanities has provided assistance in the preparation and publication of this work. The work could not have been done at all but for the existence of the McAlpin Collection and the patience and courtesy of the officials and attendants of the library of the Union Theological Seminary, particularly of Dr. W. W. Rockwell and Mr. D. H. Schroeder. My colleagues, Professor Harry Morgan Ayres and Professor Hoxie Neale Fairchild, have helped in the writing of this book in more ways than they have known or than I can tell. Malleville Haller has been my constant assistant and critic. The book is hers as well as mine.

WILLIAM HALLER

Barnard College
June 1, 1938

Contents

The Rise of Puritanism

For Books are not absolutely dead things, but doe contain a potencie of life in them to be as active as that soule was whose progeny they are; nay they do preserve as in a violl the purest efficacie and extraction of that living intellect that bred them. I know they are as lively, and as vigorously productive, as those fabulous Dragons teeth; and being sown up and down, may chance to spring up armed men.

—Milton, AREOPAGITICA

I

Physicians of the Soul

WHO was the first Puritan and who may prove to be the last are questions one need not try to answer. There were Puritans before the name was invented, and there probably will continue to be Puritans long after it has ceased to be a common epithet. Chaucer met one on the road to Canterbury and drew his portrait. No better and no very different picture of the kind of man we shall be dealing with in these pages was ever drawn by any of the numerous pens which attempted the task two centuries later. The parson, Chaucer says, was a learned man, devoted to teaching and caring for his people. He was poor, but 'he coude in litel thing han suffisaunce.' When sufficiently provoked, he rebuked the obstinate whether of high or low estate, but his real business was to lead men to heaven by fair words and good example. He was discreet and benign of speech, not 'daungerous ne digne.' Above all

> This noble ensample to his sheep he yaf,
> That first he wroghte, and afterward he taughte; . . .
> And this figure he added eek ther-to,
> That if gold ruste, what shal iren do?
> . . . Christes lore, and his apostles twelve,
> He taughte, and first he folwed it himselve.

The reader will meet him again in John Dod and many another. When the host calls upon him for a story, swearing 'by goddes dignitee,' he promptly snubs the fellow for his profanity. 'O Jankin, be ye there? . . . I smelle a loller in the wind,' cries Harry Bailey and bids the company stop and listen:

> For we shal han a predicacioun;
> This loller heer wil prechen us som-what.

The shipman, however, knows, as many have learned, that preachers are makers of trouble. He is a good fellow but of careless conscience.

He will listen to no sermon, 'nay, by my fader soule!' Enough for him, a good latitudinarian, that 'we leve al in the grete god.' This preacher

> . . . wolde sowen some difficultee,
> Or springen cokkel in our clene corn.

So, to stop him from talking, the shipman breaks forth into a ribald tale. But preachers are not put off forever by such tactics. The moment comes, all the other pilgrims having had their say, when the host calls upon the parson again. 'Unbokel, and shewe us what is in thy male. . . . Tel us a tale anon, for cokkes bones!' 'Thou getest fable noon y-told for me,' the parson replies. What he has in his 'male' is 'moralitee and vertuous matere,' no lewdness, no romancing, nothing but the truth. 'I can nat geste—rum, ram, ruf—by lettre,' and he cares as little for riming. He will make an end to all their fabling by telling them a tale in prose, but such a tale, 'and Jesu for his grace, wit me sende,' as will

> . . . shewe yow the wey, in this viage,
> Of thilke parfit glorious pilgrimage
> That highte Jerusalem celestial.

We need not linger over the parson's sermon.[1] We shall hear many like it before we have done. In his own way Chaucer has put the whole matter of preaching before us. In the fourteenth, as in the seventeenth, century there was the church with its sacraments and its hierarchies, and there was the preacher. His business and his opportunity was to preach, but in order to preach successfully he must preach to the people, must preach what the people—no matter what the shipman and his kind might say—would listen to and think they understood. He must preach what could be practiced, and he must himself practice what he preached. The substance of the sermon Chaucer puts into his parson's mouth was the substance of most sermons for three centuries to come. The preacher has to say that a man's chief concern should be with the welfare of his own soul, that he must not let his life be swallowed up in immediate and material affairs but must dedicate it to spiritual ends. He must begin with repentance and confession. He must persevere in struggle against the seven deadly sins. He must set forth upon a pilgrimage, make war on despair and pride, and expect thus to arrive at the heavenly city, there to dwell in triumph and glory forevermore. Whatever we may think of this, Chaucer—and there is no reason for not believing that he meant what he said—was persuaded of its truth. When he came to take leave of his readers at the end of the sermon with which he closes his book, he begged to be forgiven his 'endytinges of worldly vanitees' and gave thanks for having written his translation of Boethius, his legends of saints, and his books of devotion and morality.

With these writings of Chaucer, with the other religious writers of the fourteenth century, above all with the preachers of that time, we might logically enough enter upon the history of Puritan thought and expression. Beginning at a later date, we shall do well to remember what we cannot take time to be often reminding ourselves of, namely that Puritanism, so called, was nothing new or totally unrelated to the past but something old, deep-seated, and English, with roots reaching far back into medieval life.[2] Historic Puritanism, with which this book is concerned, was a movement for reform of religion, Puritan in spirit, begun by the successors of Chaucer's parson early in the reign of Elizabeth. In little more than a single lifetime it led to the founding of New England and the revolutionizing of English society. What is meant by Puritan in spirit, if Chaucer has not already made sufficiently clear, should become apparent as we examine the writings in which Puritans of many sorts tried to express the spirit that was in them.

From the expulsion in 1570 of Thomas Cartwright from the University of Cambridge to the calling in 1643 of the Westminster Assembly, the Puritan reformers were checked in their plans for reorganizing the church. During that period of delay, they devoted themselves to the production of a literature. In spite of the restrictions placed upon their activities, they incessantly preached the gospel and published books. Almost no one reads their writings now, but the people read them then, and no one can wisely ignore them who desires to understand what Puritanism was and what it came to mean. A consequence of the greatest importance quickly resulted from the abundant use which the Puritan preachers made of the press. The press itself prospered at such a rate and to such a degree that, from being an adjunct to the pulpit, it rapidly became a distinct organ of expression in its own right. The success of the preachers in winning adherents to the cause of reform provoked other men of reforming tempers to express themselves not only in pulpits but in conventicles, in the streets, in shops and taverns, and always sooner or later in print. By such process the propagation of Puritanism passed more and more out of the control of Puritan churchmen, becoming at the same time more and more revolutionary. When the Stuart regime collapsed, there was consequently a host of preachers, but there was also a host of other able, energetic and enthusiastic writers ready with matter to keep the printers busy. One of these latter was a political journalist of genius and one was a great poet. Even after the revolutionary state collapsed, the production of Puritan literature went on and achieved its greatest triumphs. Never did the effort to reform and edify through the medium of print move more swiftly or more clearly to so magnificent a flowering. The ensuing pages deal with the first stage in the development of that propaganda, the setting forth of Puritanism in pulpit and press up to the moment when the Puritan clergy were called upon to devise the kind of church they had so long desired—the kind of church, it turned out, which could not be brought to being in the kind of world they had helped to create.

Elizabeth came to the throne in 1558. Her father may be said to have seized the church. Her brother and sister before her had in contrary ways and with unhappy results tried to reform it. She perceived that she must govern it or be ruined. Her people were divided in faith. The majority perhaps, especially about London, were Protestant, but a considerable number were still Catholic, and of these there was no telling how many might prove hostile to her authority. There were, in addition, differences within the ranks of both parties. Practically everybody agreed that there could be but one true religion and that the church should be maintained by the state. The continuance of ordered society was as yet inconceivable without the Christian church, and the church was inconceivable except as a single comprehensive institution uniform in faith and worship. But since in fact her subjects could not agree as to what religion ought to be enforced as true, Elizabeth's policy was to maintain at least the semblance of uniformity and the framework of the church without at the same time wrecking her government. She did not question the assumptions common to her time. But it is doubtful whether she reflected much upon them and certain that she did not allow them to govern her official acts in defiance of common political prudence. What she chiefly wanted, after all, was to be queen of England and live. She had the common sense to know that her people would permit her to do this provided they also were permitted to live and go about their accustomed affairs with as little interference as might be. So, without troubling to be either logical or zealous, she made herself safe. She affirmed the independence, the Protestantism, of the English church. As head of the nation, she asserted her control over church government. She insisted that her bishops be men she could depend upon, and she saw to it that they asserted their authority and her own. She required them to bear hard upon the disobedient when disobedience seemed a menace to the successful maintenance of her rule and policy. But she seems personally to have preferred not to disturb people for the supposed good of their souls. When repressive measures seemed necessary, she made, if possible, someone else bear the onus of them. The only religious test she unfailingly insisted upon was willingness to swear allegiance to herself as the church's governor. Such practices failed to please earnest reformers, bigots and doctrinaires, but they gave her people a taste of the practical advantages of toleration and patriotism.

Naturally there were not a few to whom Elizabeth's handling of the religious problem was far from acceptable. The church had long claimed to be an independent empire of the spirit to which all men, including kings, were subject. Elizabeth made it an instrument and a symbol of royal authority within the nation. This policy was fraught with momentous implications. It meant that the common bond of her people would in future be not their religion but their nationality and that the religious loyalties of the English would express not their unity as Christians but their division upon various lines as Englishmen. In the long run it meant that the swarming English of the ensuing age, as they became divided even in nationality and blood, would retain only the community of language, literature and custom. The great queen, however, did not concern herself over such eventualities. What did concern her was the fact that two important groups of her subjects regarded her church as at best only a temporary compromise and at worst but one remove, if that, from the church of Antichrist. Catholics, who wished to restore the church to its former transcending position, could hardly acknowledge an arrangement which they were bound to regard as error and sin. Protestant reformers, no less determined to restore the church, but the church purified according to their own ideas, could not content themselves with a reformation which reformed so little. Elizabeth to their dismay did not reform the church but only swept the rubbish behind the door. The Puritan movement may be said to have sprung out of the shock of that disappointment.

The reformers or Puritans were Calvinists, but we shall fail to understand Puritanism if we conceive of English Calvinism in too narrow or rigid a sense. The dynamic Pauline doctrine of faith, with its insistence on the overruling power of God, on the equality of men before God, and on the immanence of God in the individual soul, had long appealed to the English mind, and the struggle of the English people to secure their independence from foreign power as symbolized to them by the papacy had confirmed that appeal. What Calvinism did for them was to supply a current formulation of historic doctrine in lucid, trenchant terms, strikingly supported by the success of the state which Calvin's genius had called into being at Geneva. There in Geneva English Protestant churchmen, when driven from home by the vicissitudes of domestic religious politics, had found congenial refuge. There they had seen what appeared to be Utopia founded on the word of God. Thence they had issued that English version of the word which became commonly known as the Geneva Bible and which, completed in 1560, became the Bible of the Elizabethan populace, of the Scottish Reformation, and of the New England Pilgrims. The accession of Elizabeth to the throne, which the returning exiles assumed to be the triumph of Protestantism, was inevitably expected by them to prove also the triumph of Calvinism. John Knox had gone home to impose that pattern upon Scotland. They could hope to accomplish no less in England.

This hope was not destined to be realized. There was much, to be sure, that needed to be reformed. The turmoil of the three preceding reigns had left the income, property and organization, the authority and prestige, the learning and the morality of the church in confusion and decay. But Elizabeth did little or nothing directly to attack these evils, content to let well enough alone and to consolidate her own position by asserting her authority against any attempt from within or without to disturb the structure of things as they were. The effect was presently to divide English churchmen into two camps. Some, the majority, quickly saw the wisdom of giving their support or at least their acceptance to the new regime. But others, less moderate in their desires and growing more and more impatient at halfway measures and politic compromises, drew together in opposition and demanded that the long-anticipated reforms be at once accomplished. In derision these latter were called Puritans, and the name stuck.[3] If, as it is now easy to say was never possible, they had succeeded in their purpose, the age of Elizabeth would be remembered as that in which English society became cast in the mold which was in fact fixed upon Scotland and New England.

English Puritanism, that spiritual outlook, way of life and mode of expression which eventually flowered so variously and so magnificently in Milton, Bunyan and Defoe, was in the first instance the result of the conditions imposed by Elizabeth upon the reform movement within the English church. The Puritans throughout her reign were firmly held in check, but they were not crushed or completely thwarted. They had always powerful sympathizers at court, who at least found them useful in keeping the political balance among conflicting interests in the state at a working equilibrium. Thus the very policy which prevented them from securing control of the church permitted them within measure to continue advocating their ideals and even their program. An overzealous professor or fellow of a college might now and then be expelled. A too outspoken preacher might from time to time be silenced. A luckless fanatic might upon occasion be imprisoned or hanged. The government, when its own interest was thought to be at stake, could be expected to fall with as little compunction upon a Puritan as upon a papist. But there was no systematic or sustained effort to stamp Puritanism out. Thus the Puritan reformers gained time and opportunity to develop their characteristic thought, their propaganda, their code and not least important their full complement of differences, inconsistencies, compro-

mises and extravagances such as revolutionary movements seem always
the more likely to incur the longer their consummation is delayed.

Popular unrest was the soil in which the Puritan movement arose,
but its formal and conscious inception took place not among the
populace but among members of the academic intellectual class. At
the Reformation, Cambridge had taken the lead over Oxford as the
center of theological learning and intellectual activity. Among the
leaders of Protestant thought who had taken refuge at Geneva during
the Marian eclipse and who had returned upon Elizabeth's accession
full of zeal for reform, her sons were the most numerous and active.
It was, therefore, at Cambridge that impatience with Elizabeth's
failure to satisfy the most extreme Protestant hopes found its earliest
and most explicit statement. With historic appropriateness, indeed,
that statement came from the Lady Margaret Professor of Divinity,
who in 1570 put forward in his lectures a program for reform and
opposition so definite and far-reaching that it could not possibly be
mistaken or ignored.

Thomas Cartwright was a thoroughly representative Cambridge
reformer.[4] Born of yeoman stock, he came to Clare Hall as a sizar
in 1547 at the age of twelve. Three years later he was received at St.
John's as a scholar. Upon Mary's accession in 1553, he did not, young
as he was, go into exile, but graduating B.A., left the university for
the study of law. When five years later Elizabeth came in, he returned
and was made fellow, first of St. John's, then of Trinity. In 1567 he
was elected a university preacher and in 1569 Lady Margaret Professor. As preacher his sermons were of such effect that 'the Sextone
was faigne to take down the Windows' of St. Mary's, so great was
the crowd that came to hear.[5] It is a fair surmise that he voiced in
some fashion the chagrin and displeasure of the more zealous of his
party at the conclusion of ten years of hope deferred. Certainly in
his divinity lectures, Cartwright made their position plain.[6] God had
revealed his will in the scriptures. The scriptures laid down a rule of
church government. That rule was not episcopacy as set up by Elizabeth in the English church but presbyterianism as conceived by Cartwright and his sympathizers upon the model of the Calvinist church
at Geneva. According to the Elizabethan settlement, the ministry of
the English church remained under the control of bishops appointed

by the crown. According to the scheme which Cartwright proposed, ministers were to be chosen by the people. The issue between the rulers of the church and the Puritan reformers could not have been more clearly drawn. Cartwright was promptly expelled from his professorship and from the university. He left Cambridge to become the advocate-in-chief of a cause, unsuccessful but never wholly defeated. He proved indeed to be the perfect model of the high-minded doctrinaire, sticking to his dialectic through all the vicissitudes of unavailing agitation. His writings consisted chiefly of politico-theological polemics directed against his episcopal opponents. The most important statement of the proposals of his party for church reform was a famous manual, commonly called *The Book of Discipline* and associated with the name of Walter Travers. The Latin text of this was circulated in manuscript, criticized and amended in Puritan circles in the years following 1583; the English translation was not published until 1644.[7] This work became the textbook of all those who sought presbyterian reform of church government. The rulers of the church, led by Whitgift and Bancroft, were kept busy for years in refuting it and in circumventing its authors and disciples. In order to offset its effect and the general influence of its authors, Richard Hooker, the rival of Travers at the Temple, was led to supply the intellectual basis for Anglicanism in his great treatise *Of the Laws of Ecclesiastical Polity*. Yet in spite of everything, though all overt attempts to put presbyterianism into practice were suppressed, the ideal of the church expressed in the *Book of Discipline* kept and extended its hold upon English Protestantism and remained uppermost in the minds of most of the men called by the Long Parliament to the Westminster Assembly in 1643.

The implications in Cartwright's conception of church government were, indeed, dangerous to existing institutions. He and his followers did not propose to divide or abandon the historic church. If anything, they sought to make its authority even more far-reaching and all-embracing. In advocating reform they had not the slightest intention of permitting any deviation whatsoever from presbyterian doctrine and discipline once established. Their ideal was the Augustinian and Calvinistic ideal of the church as the city of God, the kingdom of Christ on earth, the divinely inspired organ of spiritual life in human society, having reciprocal relations with the rulers of this world but acting in complete independence of their authority. Its task was to render men obedient first to God and then under God to Caesar, whose first duty also was to obey God as his church might direct. The church in its obedience instructed both rulers and subjects in theirs. Before God all men were equal in sin, equally deserving of damnation. If any were raised above the rest in this world, it was God's doing, not theirs. This equality was the condition of all government in church or state. In the church, the people without distinction of person must choose by whom they were to be taught and served. Parish by parish they should elect their elders and ministers, and the church as a national body should be knit together by a graduated series of representative assemblies drawn from the parishes. Such a scheme would in practice have enervated, if it did not abolish, episcopacy. It would above all else have made the ministers supreme, since they alone were the final interpreters of scripture, from which these arrangements and every other rule of life could be by them infallibly deduced. That any act which sinners could conceive or execute would have been privileged from criticism and correction by these keepers of God's word was not human to suppose. They would have gained direction and control of public opinion, and public opinion would have been directed and controlled as never before. The conduct of government itself would have been subjected to continuous review by the people, or rather by the preachers as a privileged caste telling the people what to think and tolerating no dissent.

Queen Elizabeth naturally did not relish such a prospect. She had recently had a taste of what it might mean to let preachers have free rein in the pulpit. Edward Dering,[8] a friend of Cecil himself, a Christ's College man and fresh from the Lady Margaret preachership, was acknowledged to be one of the ablest and most learned men in the English church. He was not one to bridle his tongue even before majesty. Early in 1570 he preached before the queen and told her in plain terms of the disappointment such men as he felt at her failure to satisfy their expectations of reform. Well-chosen images from scripture did not dull the force or meaning of the instructions he gave his sovereign for performance of her duty. A ruler, 'whether he be Prince or Emperor, Duke, Earle, Lord, Counsellour, Magistrate whatsoever . . . must feed Gods people in Jacob, and his inheritance in

Israell.'[9] This duty Elizabeth had, in his opinion, taken no steps to accomplish, and Dering gave her in specific terms an account of the resulting evils and of the remedies she must forthwith apply. He gave, incidentally, a vivid picture of the circumstances that were helping to make Puritans out of bright young men who were beginning to swarm out of the colleges of Cambridge, looking for jobs. Dering pointed first to the condition in which the benefices of the church were being permitted to remain, 'defiled with impropriations, some with sequestrations, some loaden with pensions, some robbed of their commodities.' Patrons sell them, farm them out, give them to boys, to servingmen, to their own children, seldom to learned pastors. The present incumbents are often 'Ruffians,' 'Hawkers and Hunters,' 'Dicers and Carders,' some even still 'Morrowmasse Priests.' They are 'blind guides, and can not see . . . , dumb dogs and will not bark,' that is to say, preach. Far from gathering the people together in the net of the gospel, these men are usually occupied in contending with them and with one another, 'The Parson against the Vicar, the Vicar against the Parson, the Parish against both, and one against another, and all for the belly.' 'And yet you,' he tells Elizabeth to her face, 'in the meane while that all these whordoms are committed, you at whose hands God will require it, you sit still and are carelesse, let men doe as they list.' What ought she to do? The images of imprecation come from the preacher, tumbling over one another. They all lead to this: take away authority from the bishops and set a truly learned preaching ministry over the church. 'I tell you this before God . . . : amend these horrible abuses, and the Lord is on your right hand, you shall not be removed for ever. Let these thinges alone, and God is a righteous God, hee will one day call you to your reckoning.'[10]

Elizabeth was not a ruler to take kindly to such barking from the pulpit, but her treatment of Dering exemplified that baffling opportunism which kept her safe by letting minorities live, yet which at the same time kept them from going too far or too fast. Dering was a person of some consequence. He was forbidden to preach again, but he was not forbidden to return to Cambridge, whence he was soon writing to Cecil in Cartwright's behalf. Two years later, he was back in London preaching at St. Paul's and publishing a catechism. Again he was suspended, but when arraigned before Star Chamber, he was leniently treated and presently allowed to go back to his pulpit. He died soon after, but his published works enjoyed wide circulation in the decade or so after his death. Such was the devious tolerance of Elizabeth, which allowed the Puritans to bark as long as there was no immediate danger lest they bite. Much has been made of the heroism of those who under Elizabeth and her successor suffered persecution for conscience sake, but considering the almost universal prevalence of belief in the necessity for some sort of religious uniformity and at the same time the condition of violent disagreement among Englishmen as to just what religion ought to be enforced, the wonder is that so many Puritans went unpersecuted, went so nearly undisturbed about the business of undermining the existing structure of society.

But though Puritanism was not harried out of the land—far from it!—its consummation was delayed, and delay by fostering the tropic efflorescence of the Puritan spirit proved fatal to presbyterianism. Elizabeth's policy was, wherever possible, to deal with opposition by ignoring, dividing and disarming it, and the more Puritanism was winked at the more it spread, spread, however, by developing differences within its own ranks. The key to Calvinistic reasoning was that the Bible gave a rule to be followed in church and state as in all other affairs in life. Cartwright's party asserted their scheme to be that rule. Delay in its adoption, however, exposed it to criticism and variation based upon scripture itself. The theory was that truth in scripture when brought to bear upon conscience by the force of reason would lead men to early agreement unless they chose wilfully and maliciously to resist the light. The fact was, as experience was to demonstrate, that scripture, which had more poetry in its pages than law, worked upon men of uncritical minds, lively imaginations, differing temperaments and conflicting interests not as a unifying but as a divisive force. Elizabethan policy, waiving consistency and ignoring variations of opinion when politically harmless, gave scope for all sorts of men to search the scriptures, to fall in love with their own strange ideas, to espouse fantastic dreams, to collect bands of earnest souls, in short to go and eat forbidden fruit so long as they did not try to upset the apple cart. But the reformers could hardly have been expected to foresee that such and not uniformity of belief and opinion was destined to become the accustomed English way.

Thus it came about that in course of time the church reformers who had begun by demanding presbyterianism found themselves merely the right wing of a party of opposition extending farther and farther to the left. This process of continued fission, this feathering-out of the reform movement into an increasing host of sects and factions, though abundantly deplored and usually accompanied by the most acrimonious recriminations among the very authors of it, sprang from one of the very vital principles of Puritanism itself. The presbyterians and the sects alike generally asserted that there was but one form of church government revealed in scripture and that this should and eventually would prevail. But they also believed that for discovering the truth as revealed in scripture the divinely appointed instrument was the minister or ministers whose gift of interpretation was sealed by the acknowledgement of the people. Circumvented by royal policy, they failed to secure official acceptance and adoption of this principle. Toleration was, however, accorded in sufficient degree to permit individual ministers to begin acting upon it. That is, though the sporadic efforts to organize more or less clandestine synods and classes were quickly put down, Puritan preachers were not effectually prevented from spreading their beliefs, from seeking proselytes, or from assuming the leadership of such bands of disciples as they were able to convert and hold together. Thus English Puritanism, denied opportunity to reform the established church, wreaked its energy during a half century and more upon preaching and, under the impetus of the pulpit, upon unchecked experiment in religious expression and social behavior.

The result has been that it has proved extremely difficult for later generations to gain a clear view of the make-up and true character of the Puritan movement up to the outbreak of revolution, and one reason for this has been that we have been too much preoccupied with the endeavor to distinguish and trace the rise and growth of definite sects and parties. The real energy of the movement was supplied by the preacher, whatever his party or sect. He might not sever himself from the church at all, but whether as lecturer or parson he might preach the word from the pulpit of a parish, fearing his bishop but still hoping for some sort of gradual reform. If he were a man of more than usual force or egotism or eccentricity, he might dare to go farther and lead a flock of personal adherents out of the church into some byway suggested by scripture to his intense but uncritical mind. The generally accepted doctrine that only those elected by God's grace could be saved induced individual groups and their leaders with fatal ease to the suspicion, if not the firm conviction, that only those who participated in the true belief and way, which they inclined to think was their own peculiar way, could surely be identified as godly and admitted into the communion of the faithful. It soon became impossible to limit the function of interpreting the word to the educated and ordained. When two interpreters of something like equal gifts arose in a given group, it split in two. The inevitable conclusion to such conditions was that the congregation of elect souls following its heaven-sent teacher came more and more to regard itself as a law to itself, a conclusion the more acceptable since it served to express and aggrandize the power of the preacher, though at the expense of unified action both in the church and in the reform movement at large. If Cartwright could have had his way in 1569, all these centrifugal tendencies in Puritanism would never have been allowed to develop. But the rejection of presbyterian church government at that moment, followed by toleration, gave the preachers their heads, and the Bible did the rest. Consequently, the more the Puritan clergy avoided direct collision with authority and merely preached the word, the more they grew in numbers and influence and the more luxuriant grew the crop of non-conformists within the church and of dissenters without.

Disregarding for the moment the chronology of their development, we shall find it useful to distinguish the general types of non-conformity and dissent into which in course of time the entire movement fell. The main body of the Puritan preachers, it is important to remember, never surrendered the hope of taking over the establishment and running it according to the scheme of the *Book of Discipline*. These men became known in time as the presbyterians and composed the majority of the Westminster Assembly. They presently engendered, however, a minority of their own which sought to limit church membership more strictly to approved saints and to allow greater freedom within the church to individual preachers and congregations. These were the independents or congregationalists, some of whom finally betook themselves to Massachusetts Bay and others of whom appeared as the 'dissenting brethren' among the godly divines of the Westminster Assembly. To the left of this faction were all those who, too impatient to wait for the slow processes of internal church reform, plumped for the true church at once and set up some completely independent congregation or other. These were the Brownists, Barrowists and separatists of all sorts. A distinctly moderate congregation of separatists achieved the settlement of Plymouth in New England. A left wing grew out of separatism into the baptist congregations, which fell into heresy upon the doctrine of election itself. Beyond these arose in time still further sects, baptist for the most part in provenience and even more wildly heretical in doctrine: millenarians, seekers, ranters, quakers, Muggletonians and what not.[11]

No denunciations were more bitter or more complete than those which these bodies upon occasion leveled at one another, but we should not permit the differentia of the Puritan sects to confuse our understanding of Puritanism. They marked the origins of important Protestant communions of a later day. Their proliferation was a major factor in the rapid peopling of North America by Englishmen. Much has been made in the spirit of historical piety of the effort of each group to establish its separate identity and of the contribution of each to aspects of the common life regarded by later generations as admirable. Yet the importance of all this can easily be misunderstood if not greatly exaggerated. The disagreements that rendered Puritans into presbyterians, independents, separatists and baptists were in the long run not so significant as the qualities of character, of mind and of imagination, which kept them all alike Puritan. Coming revolutions commonly thrust forward a numerous vanguard of pioneers, rebels, cranks, martyrs, saints and heroes. Some of these organize parties, sects and juntas. Some publish programs and manifestoes, or start demonstrations, parades, riots and secessions. They are the devoted band who would save the world without delay and build Jerusalem in their own time. The activity of not a few of the early Puritan leaders and factions was of this description. We do not detract from the honor due them when we suggest that perhaps they were less the authors than the symptoms of a disturbance that at its own pace under the impulsion of more patient men, aided by circumstance, was slowly but surely breaking up the ancient pattern of English life. The force of revolutionary movements most truly shows itself in the gradual transformation of the imaginative ideals, of the habits of thought and expression, of the moral outlook and modes of behavior of whole classes of people. Puritanism was such a movement. It was, then, more than an affair of church government, more than the logomachy of churchmen and schismatics. It was a new way of life, overrunning all the divisions which from time to time seamed its surface and threatening in each of its manifestations to disrupt the existing society. Eventually it was to subdue English civilization to an attitude of mind, a code of conduct, a psychology, a manner of expression, the vitality of which far outran the particular forms of religious life which sprang up from time to time in the course of its irresistible advance.

The preachers were the true authors of that advance, and among the preachers those were far from being the least influential who mainly devoted themselves to setting forth the Puritan way of life by precept, image and example in pulpit and press rather than to agitation against the existing government or to the effort to erect separate churches in defiance of law. They and not the doctrinaire controversialists or the martyrs of persecution were the men who did most in the long run to prepare the temper of the Long Parliament and to spread among their countrymen the characteristic Puritan version of the age-old epic of man's spiritual striving. The history of the struggle for reform of government in church and state in the seventeenth century is well known. So also is the history of the important sectarian communions which arose out of that struggle. We are concerned here with recapitulating only so much of that history as may help us to understand what has not yet been adequately understood, the work of the preachers in preparing that state of mind of which the civil wars, the Puritan Commonwealth, the Westminster Assembly and all the pullulating sects, not to mention *Paradise Lost, Pilgrim's Progress* and much else, were the eventual expression. The presbyterian program as presented by Cartwright in 1569 was rejected, and all later attempts to secure its general acceptance failed. But Puritanism was far more than a scheme of church government, and in this larger sense it continued uninterrupted to strengthen and extend its hold upon the English imagination.

Cartwright left behind him at Cambridge friends and disciples who, nothing daunted by their failure to purify church government, devoted their energies more and more to the task of indoctrinating the people in Puritan ideals and of training them in the Puritan way of life. Queen Elizabeth and her bishops would not permit them to transpose Calvinism directly into legal enactment, but did not prevent them from converting country gentlemen, lawyers, merchants, and steadily increasing numbers of humbler folk to godliness. Now and then a Puritan preacher would be drawn off into partisan activity, either direct attack upon the rulers of the church or open secession from it, but by far the greater part of them were content to devote themselves under cover of the law to preaching the doctrine of faith and the sacred epic of man's fall and redemption. Behind them they had the long tradition of the popular pulpit. At hand were the opportunities provided by the new conditions, by the movement of population to the towns, by the increase and diffusion of wealth, by the crowds, by the printing presses and the Bibles of the new era. Elizabeth at the beginning of her reign frowned upon prophesying and tried to limit preaching to the customary homilies. But there was no way, as time would demonstrate, by which government in those days could silence either pulpit or press. Preaching grew in popularity, was more and more resorted to by all parties and under James became fashionable. Increase in the circulation of the Bible kept pace with preaching. Even the Catholics put forth a translation, while the bishops set up one to compete with that of the Geneva exiles, and finally the church with King James's approval prepared the authorized version. Calvinistic doctrine, though reaction was beginning both among the Anglicans and the radical sects, prevailed in all quarters. What distinguished the Puritan preachers even more than their doctrinal position was the manner and purpose of their preaching. Discountenanced by those in authority but bent upon saving the world through religious revival and ultimate ecclesiastical reform, they were compelled to seek support wherever it might be found among the people. They asserted, as did others, that man could be saved by faith alone. They endeavored to do this, however, in terms that common men might understand, in expressive images that would move men to repent, believe and begin the new life at once under the leadership of the preacher.

Preaching of this type soon came to be called 'spiritual' in contradistinction to the 'witty' preaching of the more conservative churchmen. It sprang up at Cambridge about the time of Cartwright's expulsion. It was greatly encouraged by the founding of two new colleges, Emmanuel in 1584 by Sir Walter Mildmay, who was no less a personage than chancellor of the exchequer, and Sidney Sussex in 1596 by the Countess of Sussex, aunt to Sir Philip Sidney. Both were established expressly for the purpose of training up a preaching ministry. Fuller gives us the story that when Elizabeth quizzed her chancellor upon his erecting a 'Puritan foundation,' Sir Walter replied, 'No, Madam, far be it from me to countenance any thing contrary to your established laws, but I have set an acorn, which when it becomes an oak, God alone knows what will be the fruit thereof.'[12] From Cambridge, thus fostered, the spiritual preachers issued in steadily increasing numbers to occupy the posts which a steadily rising public interest found ways of making open to them. Consequently, long before Laud came to power the spiritual preachers were the dominant figures in the pulpits of London, Cambridge and not a few provincial centers and country parishes. Steadily winning more and more converts to the Puritan way of life, extending their influence by the publication of their sermons and by the example of their own conduct, they thus undoubtedly became the chief animating force for the spread of Puritanism among all classes in society. Individuals among them participated now and then in the effort to organize opposition in the church or in parliament. Some broke away into separatism. None could be depended upon to conform strictly to all the prescribed observances. But the majority of them, certainly the most important of them, did not as a rule engage in open hostility to the establishment. Rather, they generally professed loyalty to the regime, and were as loud as any, even louder, against papists, Arminians and antinomians, to say nothing of witches, blasphemers and atheists. The more conservative were hardly less loud against Brownists, anabaptists and familists. They asked for nothing but freedom to preach the word, and that, under the anomalous conditions of the time, they were given without serious interference until it grew too late to stop them without wrecking everything. Not until Laud took measures to silence them by law did the spiritual preachers in any considerable numbers openly refuse to conform. They could afford to wait. They had their pulpits and the increasing support of men of wealth and influence. From that vantage ground they could work at the erection of a popular morale which would in the end prove to be of more effect than any premature departure from the existing frame of things. Wedded, they quite sincerely thought, to no program but to breed followers in the Lord, they could generate a temper in the people which would turn out to be stronger than respect for bishops or even for the crown, a moral atmosphere in which governments would presently find certain things impossible to enforce and others impossible to deny.

Inevitably the Puritan preachers exercised an incalculable influence on the development of popular literary taste and expression, an influence no less great for having been ignored by critics and historians.[13] Because they spoke in a form soon to be outmoded and for a cause destined to be discountenanced, oblivion overtook them after the Restoration. Literary culture, though offered as a goal of prime importance for the spiritual strivings of the middle and lower classes in later times, has been associated in the tradition of taste with Anglicanism and with all that that implies. Did not the apostle of culture to the Philistines solemnly assure the subjects of Queen Victoria that Milton himself could never have written the poetry he did if he had not had the good fortune at least to be born within the established church? Hence, though the Puritan preachers prepared the way for *Paradise Lost*, *Pilgrim's Progress* and *Robinson Crusoe*, they have been largely forgotten. Milton and Bunyan alone raised reputations above the night which descended upon the rest of the earlier literature of dissent. Yet even Milton's eminence, when it did not appear almost necessarily deplorable, seemed awful and apart, surprising and requiring to be explained. As for Bunyan, he slipped into the canon of English classics, like the tinker he was, by the back door, none knowing whence he came. Literary history in the genteel tradition, when it has considered early seventeenth-century preachers at all, has reserved most of its attention and practically all its praise for the men who represented the Anglican ideal of the church and of the religious life. The position of the Anglican churchmen at the Reformation required that they defend the separation from Rome. Their subsequent position as spokesmen for the religion established under Elizabeth required that they develop the historic catholic tradition of the church in a direction consistent with the spirit of national independence but opposed to social revolution. Taking the middle way between Catholic and Puritan, they defended the church established under the crown, an attitude their enemies attacked as Erastian. In doctrine they moved steadily away from orthodox Calvinism with its disturbing equalitarian implications toward a theology of elastic compromise and continuous adjustment between divine law and human nature, toward a rationalism which supported public security while conceding the desirability of so much change as might in the process of time prove itself to be unavoidable and relatively painless. This was the Arminianism of the church which, along with the antinomianism of the Puritan left wing, ultimately disrupted the ranks of militant orthodox Calvinism. The philosophic principles of Anglicanism were defined by Hooker at the close of the sixteenth century and brilliantly carried forward on the eve of the revolutionary crisis by Chillingworth. The first great representative of Anglicanism in the pulpit was Lancelot Andrewes; the greatest genius, but one who born in other circumstances might well have found his place among the forerunners of Milton and Bunyan, was John Donne. The themes of Anglican preaching were the divinely established authority of church and crown, the classic loci of the sacred epic hallowed by catholic Christian tradition, and the virtues and vices defined by the historic dialectic of medieval moral science. A place for the Anglicans in the developing tradition of literary taste was assured to them from the start, but this was not alone by reason of their abilities and accomplishments. They drew upon sixteenth-century humanism as well as upon the Christian fathers. They carried into the pulpit the stylistic methods of contemporary literary fashion. They delighted particularly, like other writers of the time, in conceit and wordplay. They too exploited that arresting combination of dramatic emotionalism with flashing intellectuality—of poetic with realistic imagination—which was the distinguishing characteristic of metaphysical wit. Their sermons were elaborately tessellated with allusions to classical, patristic and medieval writers, punctuated by sudden descents into the familiar and the bizarre. Too often they merely coruscated laboriously with recondite erudition and verbal ingenuity. In an age when attendance upon sermons was a popular diversion as well as a devotional practice and an intellectual stimulation, these men also had their audiences, but, measured by the extent to which their sermons circulated in print and

by the number and vigor of their imitators and disciples, their influence upon the popular mind steadily diminished before that of their
Puritan rivals.

The difference between the preaching of the Anglicans and that of
the Puritans, between witty and spiritual preaching so-called, between
'the Wisdom of Words' and 'the Word of Wisdom,' was not merely
one of style.[14] As a matter of conviction and of convention, the Puritans
professed to disapprove the citation of human authors and to depend
solely upon scripture. They even held up a perfectly arid and schematic
dialectic as the ideal mode of discourse—knowing better, it must be
said, than to practice it upon every occasion. The truth was that from
the beginning they shared fully the Elizabethan love of witty phrase
and poetic image, and far from abandoning such devices developed
them in their own way, sometimes to extravagant lengths. Literary
allusions, conscious Euphuism, far-fetched metaphysical metaphors,
these they laid aside in favor of homely similes, parables, exempla,
moral emblems and the like. The result was a modified but not less
imaginative style arising naturally out of medieval and Elizabethan
practices in response to the needs and tastes of the audience upon which
the preachers depended for personal support as well as for the eventual
triumph of their cause. The preachers, if they wished to survive, had
to find means to stir imaginations, induce emotional excitement, wring
the hearts of sinners, win souls to the Lord, in other words make themselves understood and felt. That necessity determined the nature of
their stylistic method. They would not have been the children of their
age had they not supplied theological science appropriate to their ends,
telling themselves that, when all the godly were gathered in and the
ungodly controverted and confounded, nothing but syllogisms would
be needed. But until that glorious time should come they granted to
the limitations of carnal minds the most unblushing exploitation of the
dramatic images of temptation, struggle and triumph which the newly
popularized Bible put into their hands.

Scrutiny of the lists of English printed books from the close of the
sixteenth century to the outbreak of the revolution shows that it was
the Puritan writers who probably did more than any others of the time
to keep the printers and booksellers busy and the common public supplied with reading matter.[15] The nature and extent of this literature

may be more particularly seen in the classified bibliography which John Wilkins, the grandson of John Dod and brother-in-law of Oliver Cromwell, recommends for a preacher's library in his *Ecclesiastes, or a Discourse concerning The Gift of Preaching* of 1646.[16] It abounds, needless to say, in technical and polemical writings, the inevitable accompaniment to the increasing tension of the age, but these things probably never commanded for long the attention of large numbers of people. The tall folios and thick quartos in which scripture was exegetically eviscerated in the light of Puritan dogma, the controversial tracts in which was endlessly debated the great question—what type of church government had been prescribed by the Holy Spirit and practiced by the apostles—these early began to find the road toward manifest futility, the top shelf and the dustbin. Puritanism, though it could not help begetting such books, did not grow by them or express its essential vitality in them. The preachers would never have made the headway they did with the people if they had not known how to be prophets and poets as well as technicians and polemicists. Fortunately we have no less an authority than Richard Baxter to help us sift out of the mass of books represented by Wilkins' bibliography those which came especially to be esteemed for their popular appeal. Writing, to be sure, years later but at a time when every effort had to be made to keep the old godliness alive, Baxter drew up a list of authors who, he thought, should be found in 'the poorest or smallest library that is tolerable.'[17] It is the five-foot shelf of popular Puritan literature. First comes the Bible with a concordance, a commentary and a catechism or two. Then Baxter recommends four of the 'soundest English books which open the doctrine of grace,' and concludes by urging upon his readers 'as many affectionate practical English writers as you can get.' He names no less than fifty-eight such authors, ranging in date from the closing years of the sixteenth century to his own day. The works of many of them had already been sent across the ocean to form part of William Brewster's library[18] as well as of that library which John Harvard bequeathed to the college which was to bear his name at the New England Cambridge.[19] Supplementary lists of technical and controversial works Baxter also supplied, but every man was expected first to feed his mind and stiffen his resolution upon the 'affectionate practical English writers.'

These writers were called practical because they taught men what to believe and how to act. They were called affectionate because they appealed through the imagination to men's emotions. They were all primarily preachers who with few exceptions wrote popular sermons or works of edification directly derived from sermons. Their aim was to arouse every man to ask and then to answer for himself the ancient question which the keeper of the prison asked of Paul and Silas, 'Sirs, what must I do to be saved?' Their method of attaining this end was to make every man see himself under the eternal images of the pilgrim and the warrior. For at least a century such was a chief mode of stimulating popular imagination, and we must therefore fix attention upon the men who so freely used it if we are to understand the rise of the Puritan epic and of the way of life it did so much to promote. The earliest names mentioned by Baxter are Richard Greenham, John Dod, Arthur Hildersam, Henry Smith and Richard Rogers. Dod and Hildersam were destined to live far into the next century and to take so important a place in the subsequent development of Puritan preaching that they may be more fittingly discussed at a later point. They were, however, like the other men just mentioned, except Henry Smith, among the friends and sympathizers of Cartwright at Cambridge in 1570.[20] Greenham was one of the signers of two petitions sent to Cecil in 1570 in the reformer's behalf. But, though they favored Cartwright's views of church government, they did not, after his expulsion from Cambridge, follow him into the paths of ecclesiastical agitation and public controversy. They proceeded instead by the usual academic courses to ordination and the cure of souls. At the same time, they endeavored to conduct their lives and spiritual ministrations according to what they considered a purer and more godly plan. They proposed, that is, within the church and under the conditions of the society around them, to try the experiment of living according to a self-imposed discipline which they derived from Paul, Augustine and John Calvin. The attempt in each case flowered in a book which, accompanied as it was by popular legend about the author, became in the next generation a classic of Puritan edification. Of no less importance was the fact that there also grew up about these men something like a school and a succession of preachers and writers devoted to following their example.

Richard Greenham[21] may fairly be called the patriarch of Baxter's 'affectionate practical English writers.' His personality and career foreshadow those of many a subsequent Puritan teacher. In 1559 he was matriculated at Cambridge. In 1570 he passed from a fellowship at Pembroke to the rectory of a poor parish at Dry Drayton near-by in Cambridgeshire. There he labored for twenty years, preaching also upon occasion at St. Mary's in Cambridge itself. For a brief period at the close of his life, he 'lectured' from various pulpits in London. His sermons, which he himself took no pains to publish, drew many hearers, were frequently taken down in church and widely circulated in numerous written copies among the people. Immediately upon his death, which occurred about 1594, 'some respecting gaine, and not regarding godlinesse, attempted forthwith to publish some fragments of his workes, to the griefe . . . of many loving friends, which have long desired and expected the impression of all his workes.'[22] The fulfilment of this desire was presently undertaken by Greenham's friend Henry Holland and completed by Stephen Egerton, predecessor of the famous William Gouge in the pulpit of Blackfriars. The former supplied a eulogistic sketch or character of the author, possibly the earliest of the long series of spiritual portraits of Puritan divines and others of the elect which were to play so important a part in Puritan propaganda. The nine-hundred-page folio, appearing first in 1599, seems to have reached a fifth edition before 1612 and found honored mention in the margins of no one knows how many similar volumes of the next hundred years.

Greenham, it is plain, conscientiously avoided controversy and the trouble it entailed. He was once cited for non-conformity, but quickly let off. He was said to have disapproved of the Marprelate tracts because they made sin ridiculous rather than, as it should be, odious. Holland no doubt reflects Greenham's attitude when he observes that, though there might be some profit for the church in the confutation of the adversaries of the gospel, 'yet in very many, these bookes helpe little to godlines, but rather fill the heads and hearts of men with a spirite of contradiction and contention.' Greenham set himself 'to edifie the heart and conscience, . . . and to quicken affections to embrace true godlinesse.' Moreover, he also eschewed the current literary, especially the stylistic, affectations of the learned and soon to become fashionable pulpit. His editor takes pains to agree with Roger Ascham; it is the devil that 'feedes daintie eares with choise of words, and uncleane hearts with the unchaste and wanton love-songs of Italian Poetrie.' He himself complains that sermons in his day are becoming 'glassie, bright and brittle . . . so cold and so humane, that the simple preaching of Christ doth greatly decay.'[23] 'They whose knowledge is in swelling words and painted eloquence of humane wisdome, being but a doctrine of the letter, in their death they are as if they knew nothing of Christ crucified: and whereof comes it, that there is so much preaching and so little learning? but because men preach and delight to heare plausible novelties, to please the eare rather then the simple power of the word to pearce the heart: they take the bone, and refuse the marrow: they are content with the shell, but want the kernell.'[24]

It is not difficult to believe that in that age of perplexing change many men and women, many of lowly position and simple understanding but also not a few neither simple nor humble, were racked by anxiety for their future here and hereafter. It was a period of storm and stress seldom equalled and probably never surpassed. Consequently the 'spirituall weepers' who, in the words of William Whately,[25] required cheering up seemed well-nigh numberless. There was little comfort for such in the dialectical rustlings of controversialists or in the stylistic fireworks of literary pulpiteers, and this lack the spiritual preachers of the type of Greenham set themselves to supply. It would be a mistake to suppose that they were inferior in education or in literary scholarship to their rivals. They merely made a point of laying their learning aside in order to win, or at least to make a show of seeking, the ear and the confidence of all men in order the better to address themselves with whatever gifts of mind they might possess and with whatever knowledge of the human heart their science gave them to the sympathetic treatment of the troubles, call them spiritual or psychological, by which men in their time were actually beset. Their function was to probe the conscience of the downhearted sinner, to name and cure the malady of his soul, and then to send him out strengthened and emboldened for the continuance of his lifelong battle with the world and the devil. 'Let his owne words,' says Holland of Greenham, 'testifie the good desires of his heart: for by a special occasion he speaketh of himselfe on this manner. He hath had a long time a setled disposition (as he trusteth) of God, to studie the cases of conscience, to succour the perplexed in them.'[26] The concrete results of this desire were gathered up and published under the title 'Grave Counsels.'[27] Greenham describes the spiritual complaints which the sick in mind have laid before him and the remedies which his knowledge of God's will as revealed in scripture had taught him to apply. He informs us of the doubts, despairs, fears, yieldings of the creature, seizures of weakness and of pride, which assailed the men who were trying to adjust themselves to the difficulties of that time. He also enables us to perceive, if we have imagination, by what means and with what success the preacher resolved these evils of the spirit into faith.

An important manifestation of Greenham's desire to minister to minds diseased was his effort to win others to the same work 'that hereby hee might traine up some younger men to this end, and communicate his experience with them.' Young men came to live with him at Dry Drayton, forming a kind of school, the members of which devoted themselves to the searching of the scripture and of one another's hearts. He became in this way 'the speciall instrument . . . to bring many, both godly and learned, to the holy service of Christ.' His eulogist assures us that God made use of him, in addition, 'to reduce not a few from schisme and error, striving alwaies to retaine such in obedience of lawes, and pretiouslie to esteeme and regard the peace of the Church and people of God,' but this statement, which is perhaps not quite ingenuous, requires a grain of caution in the taking.[28] The spiritual preachers were in their own way well enough aware that they were treading close to danger, that in stirring up the people's hearts they ran the risk of encouraging them to overflow the limits of the law. Consequently they were quick to claim credit for the numbers of their followers who had not caused trouble to the authorities, in order, perhaps, to disencumber themselves of responsibility for those who had. One of Greenham's pupils was Robert Browne, notorious as the father of Brownism.[29] In him we see separatism starting from the very side of the movement for reform initiated by the Cambridge preachers and intellectuals. He left Cambridge shortly after Cartwright's expulsion, but after a few years doubts and other difficulties sent him back. 'He ther had dealing,' he tells us, 'with M.

Greenham of dreiton, whoe of all others he hard sai was most for-
warde, & thought that with him and by him he should have some
stai of his care, and hope of his purpose. Wherefore, as those which
in ould tyme were called the prophetes & children of the prophetes,
& lived together, because of corruption among others, so came he
unto him.'[30] Whether Browne gained 'some stai of his care and hope
of his purpose' from Greenham, we do not really know, but the next
thing was that he was preaching at Cambridge without a license, re-
fusing to be ordained, and attacking the authority of bishops. He was
one of those who are never content with gradual processes of reform
but must go the nearest way about the business of making the world
over.

Henry Smith[31] was an Oxford man, born in 1560, the son of a
wealthy squire of Leicestershire. His stepmother was sister to Lord
Burleigh. Thomas Nash tells us that he wrote poetry before he
turned to preaching,[32] and Joshua Sylvester translated some Latin
Sapphics of his.[33] Soon after leaving Oxford about 1583, he like
Browne went to live and study with Richard Greenham and to become infused with the latter's principles. In 1587, recommended to
Burleigh, the patron of the parish, by Greenham and other godly
preachers, he became the lecturer at St. Clement Danes. When Aylmer, Bishop of London, took steps to silence him for preaching without license, Burleigh intervened in his behalf. He was called to the
pulpit of St. Clement's by the election of the minister and the congregation, and his stipend was paid by voluntary contribution.
Two years later upon the death of the incumbent, the parish re-
quested that its preacher be regularly presented to the living. Among
the signers of the petition to Burleigh were 'the two churchwardens,
the one a grocer, the other a locksmith, and a good number besides
of ordinary tradesmen, as smiths, tailors, saddlers, hosiers, haber-
dashers, glaziers, cutters, and such like.'[34] Most of them are said to
have signed by setting their marks. The significance of all this was
that Smith held his place, for a time without the bishop's official cog-
nizance, as the special stipendiary and the idol of zealous grocers,
locksmiths and other tradesmen, his listeners. In other words, the
mendicant preacher, whether as prophet or as demagogue—one could

never be sure—was back upon the English scene in the person of the Puritan lecturer.

Smith's preaching met with instant popular success. Fuller calls him silver-tongued, 'but one mettall below St. Chrysostom himself.' 'His Church was so crouded with Auditors, that Persons of good quality brought their own Pues with them, I mean their legs, to stand there upon in the Allies. Their ears did so attend to his lips, their hearts to their ears, that he held the rudder of their affections in his hands, so that he could steer them whither he pleased.'[35] Fuller was not the man to perceive or record the full effect of such eloquence, but the one reputed effect which caught his fancy is not without interest for those who remember a later and far more famous prophet. So moving were Smith's words, says Fuller, that fashionable women were persuaded by him that it was sinful not to suckle their own offspring, and many forthwith summoned their babies back to their bosoms from wet nurses in the suburbs. After three or four years, the preacher retired and died young. His sermons, promptly printed, frequently reprinted, and finally collected and edited by Fuller himself, became something like a household book for Sunday reading.[36]

Puritan or spiritual preaching, though not quite fully developed in the published sermons of Greenham and Smith, was nevertheless effectually launched by them. Perhaps a momentary stylistic uncertainty is suggested by a remark of the latter at the opening of a discourse called 'The True Trial of the Spirits.' The speaker complains on the one hand of the excessive simplicity of those who, perhaps carrying reaction against wit and learning too far, 'shroud and cover every rustical and unsavory and childish and absurd Sermon under the name of the simple kind of teaching.' Yet he immediately goes on to say that in truth to preach simply is without rudeness, ignorance or confusion 'to preach plainly and perspicuously, that the simplest man may understand what is taught, as if he did hear his name.'[37] These sentiments, almost to the very phrases, were soon to be echoed and re-echoed by numerous successors. Smith's own sermons, like those of his master Greenham, are 'plain and perspicuous' in that they are composed in straightforward lucid sentences not without wit but avoiding preciosity and the ostentation of erudition. Their substance, however, still plainly shows the influence of medieval tradition. For centuries preachers had been analyzing the moral life into such categories as pride, envy, lust, avarice and their opposites. They diagnosed spiritual morbidity by identifying the species of sin with which the soul might be infected. Their method was to make war on wickedness by attacking its several varieties. They treated sinners by showing them how to detect each sin in the abstract under the infinite disguises which evil knew but too well how to assume. They taught the differentiating marks of pride and humility so that the one could be avoided and the other practiced. This often led the preacher—in the sixteenth and the seventeenth, as in the fourteenth, centuries—to more or less realistic description of actual manners and morals as well as to elaborate systematic allegorization of moral abstractions. Not infrequently he ventured to attack particular persons or classes. On the other hand he also devoted his talents to the creation of allegorical types of human nature or of typical portraits and 'characters' representing moral qualities. Thus he came to depict the miser or the hypocrite instead of, or in addition to, defining or allegorizing the sins they embodied. Eventually he found it natural to portray social types, the country fellow, the townsman, the gallant, the apprentice and the milkmaid, even the preacher himself.

Such devices and conventions are present in the sermons of Greenham and Smith as they are also in varying degrees in those of other Calvinists and Puritans of the time. Thomas Adams, for instance, singled out for praise by nineteenth-century critics as the Shakespeare of the Puritan preachers, was no Shakespeare but a late and extreme though brilliant example of the persistence of these traditions. Of far greater significance than their use of conventional devices was the fact that Greenham and Smith showed their contemporaries how the pulpit might strike out upon new paths in response to new conditions. Though the familiar abstractions and invectives appear with some frequency in the printed pages of these men, they are giving way to something recognized at the time as novel, and one suspects that there were relatively fewer of them in the actual work of their authors among the people. The people were ready to respond to something different, and it was the people's tastes, their state of mind and spiritual condition, by which the Puritan lecturer dependent upon their favor was governed when he stood up to preach before them. Edward Topsell, whose exhortations were an excellent example of clerical railing in the older manner, asked a pertinent question in his *Times Lamentations* of 1599. He was inveighing—a favorite theme with men of his cloth—against popular neglect of moral instructions. 'Must our gallant youthes,' he exclaims, 'and proper servingmen, whose heads are hanged with haire, as if they would fright away both Christ and his ministers . . . come from the taverns, from gaming-houses, from the play-houses, from the Ale-houses, from the whoore-houses . . . to be ratled up for their follies by preaching, & forsake their fashions of the world to be new fashioned in their minds?'[38] Obviously the preacher thought they should, but the fact was that the gallant youths and proper servingmen were not likely to come and have their minds new-fashioned unless what was offered to them in church were made equally as exciting as what they were hearing in the haunts of sin. The grocers, locksmiths and other virile illiterates, also the persons of quality, who flocked to St. Clement's to hear Smith, were, we must remember, the very men for whose attention Marlowe and Shakespeare were competing. The preachers no less than the playwrights had to give the Elizabethan and Jacobean public something approaching what it wanted. That public, as the rapid developments of the marvellous decade of 1590 in the theatre testify, was more than ready to drop old conventions and abstractions and to thrill to the poetic and dramatic representation of individual human character and experience. This was what the preachers, like the playwrights, were now to discover. They were to discover that their listeners, still keeping undiminished their zest for wit and rhetoric, took a livelier interest in sin itself than in its categories, in the psychology of spiritual struggle than in the abstract analysis of moral behavior or even the satirical exposure of vice and folly. Who that saw Tamburlane, Faustus and Richard on the boards was more concerned with edifying identification of the sin of pride than with the proud souls of Tamburlane, Faustus and Richard? Who that could enjoy the two-hour traffic of the stage with such figures, though he no doubt had his own private fears for the welfare of his soul, could be any longer inclined to see his own moral life adequately reflected in the seven deadly sins of medieval moral science? Men knew what it was to be sinners. They longed to know what they must do to be saved. The opportunity that presented itself to the preachers was to minister to troubled minds and cleanse stuffed bosoms. So they set out to describe the warfare of the spirit, to portray the drama of the inner life, to expound the psychology of sin and redemption. This, they found, was what the people would come to hear, and the more actively they responded to ever-increasing audiences the more they gave up abstractions in order to mirror the individual consciousness of spiritual stress, to convince the individual of sin in order to persuade him of grace, to make him feel worse in order to make him feel better, to inspire pity and fear in order to purge him of those passions. No longer content to be analysts, moralists, satirists and stylists, they would make themselves physicians to the soul.

The preachers were, of course, confronted by their own peculiar artistic problem, a problem in rhetoric and poetic, in thus undertaking to treat the souls of men. Had they but known it or been capable of admitting it, precisely such a mirror was being held up to nature in the theatres, though not with quite the same intention or effect. They, however, were of necessity bound by the traditions and conventions of their own instrument and medium. They must do their work in the pulpit and by adaptation of the materials and methods of the pulpit. For them the ancient Christian images of spiritual struggle were the thing wherewith to catch the conscience of the common man. The history of Puritan literature, in large measure of Puritanism itself, is the record of their success in accomplishing just this end. How it was to be accomplished in the ensuing age, how the Christian myth was in their hands to take on new shape and vitality, is nowhere better illustrated at this early date than in the passage of a sermon on Matt. 27:1-4 in which Henry Smith describes the pangs of an afflicted conscience:

If there be any hell in this world, they which feel the Worme of conscience gnaw upon their hearts, may truly say, that they have felt the torments of hell. Who can express that man's horror but himselfe? Sorrowes are met in his soule at a feast: and fear, thought, and anguish divide his soule between them. All the furies of hell leaps upon his heart like a stage. Thought calleth to Fear; Fear whistleth to Horrour; Horrour beckoneth to Despair, and saith, Come and help me to torment the sinner: One saith, that she cometh from this sinne, and another saith, that she cometh from that sinne: so he goeth thorow a thousand deaths, and cannot die. Irons are laid upon his body like a prisoner. All his lights are put out at once: he hath no soul fit to be comforted. Thus he lies upon the racke, and saith that he beares the world upon his shoulders, and that no man suffereth that which he suffereth. So let him lye (saith God) without ease, untill he confesse and repent, and call for mercie. This is the godly way which the Serpent said would make you Gods, and made him a Devill.[39]

Nothing could more clearly point the direction in which the spiritual preachers were about to lead the imagination. The seven deadly sins are once more whistled up, but from being dialectical abstractions they have become furies leaping upon the heart of the sinner as upon a stage. The scene enacted upon that stage is henceforth to be the focus of all attention. It is to be the drama of sin and grace, of the war between Christ and Satan, experienced immediately in the soul. The sinner himself is to be hell, and none but he, or perhaps we should say none but the preacher who has made himself one in sympathy and thought with him, can express the horrors he is to suffer. He bears the world as his burden, lies prisoner to despair, passes through a thousand deaths. He must be made to repent and call for mercy, or he will die. The men and women crowding the aisles of St. Clement's in the Strand near Temple Bar on a day in 1590 or thereabouts are asked to see themselves as Adam and Eve hearkening to the serpent in the garden. And we as we listen with them to the preacher's eloquence may catch a forward glimpse of the Puritan legend of the wayfaring, warfaring Christian, of the Puritan epic of the fall and redemption of man.

In Greenham and his pupils, Browne and Smith, we see the Puritan mind at the early stage of its development turned outward in exhortation and agitation. These men give us no record of their own inner strivings, save such as we may infer from the sermons and pamphlets in which they addressed the world. It was, however, of the essence of the preacher's function that the war of the spirit to which he urged others he himself should first and continuously experience. His was but the more sensitive and imaginative mind, feeling more keenly the storm and stress of the age and endeavoring the more self-consciously to control it and put it into words. The formulas of Paul and Calvin, it seemed, offered the key to the problem of government not alone in church and state but also in man's inner life. This in effect was what they told men from their pulpits. It was also what they told themselves in their hearts and in their own households.

Fortunately we are not left merely to infer this in respect to the sixteenth-century preachers. Among the affectionate practical English divines of Cartwright's generation at Cambridge was one who left a private journal as well as sermons and treatises for us to read. Richard Rogers[40] was the son of a joiner at Chelmsford in Essex. In 1566 he was sent, no doubt by some wealthy patron, as a sizar to Christ's College, and he experienced at Cambridge the excitement that attended Cartwright's expulsion. After proceeding M.A. in 1574, he returned to Essex to become 'Preacher of Gods Word,' perhaps also to act as curate, in the village of Wethersfield. Externally his career followed quite exactly the pattern of the Puritan parson of that time. Stephen Egerton, his editor as well as Greenham's, testifies that he 'long laboured the conversion and confirmation of many other; but especially the mortification and quickning of his owne soule and conscience: one, whom indeed I have ever esteemed another Greenham.'[41] Rogers was the author of a daily rule of life, first devised for himself and then presented in preaching and in writing for the guidance of others. He also participated in the effort to establish a presbyterian 'classis' at Dedham, organized meetings in his neighborhood for prayer and spiritual conference, and like Greenham kept a school in his house for young men destined for Cambridge. Paul Baynes, a famous preacher of the next generation, was in all probability one of his pupils. Rogers married twice, and his children, stepchildren and sons-in-law continue to be met with among seventeenth-century Puritans. He never engaged in active open opposition to authority, and though always fearful of and sometimes subjected to interference, he invariably got off without serious trouble. Sympathetic gentlemen of the vicinity, among whom were numbered the Riches and the Barringtons, no doubt helped to see to that. By one means and another, he kept on with his experiment in godly living and preaching, yet at the same time did not fail to prosper moderately in worldly goods and reputation. He was an excellent representative of the kind of man by whose example and teaching Puritanism was permitted under Elizabeth to live and spread among the people.

Richard Rogers' writings illustrate equally well the scope of the typical preacher's expression in discourse. The perfect intellectual fruition of the life which such a man made for himself through spiritual struggle was thought to be attained in the production of an elaborate and detailed commentary on scripture or some portion of it, painfully dissected text by text. The preacher was by profession a technician possessed not only of a divinely bestowed gift but also of a special and acquired skill at deducing from the holy book rational justification for his faith and view of life. That his supposed science was less science than sciolism or, at best, imaginative intuition masked by an apparatus of logic made it seem to him none the less irrefragable. Rogers fulfilled his duty by turning out a folio on Judges and by leaving commentaries on other parts of the Bible for his son to publish. Little of this matter, however, found its way into print. What won for him his place among the writers of books practical and affectionate was his *Seven Treatises, Containing Such Direction as is gathered out of the Holie Scriptures, leading and guiding to true happines, both in this life, and in the life to come: and may be called the practise of Christianitie. Profitable for all such as heartily desire the same: in the which, more particularly true Christians may learne how to leade a godly and comfortable life every day.*

Published in 1603 with commendation from three other preachers, Stephen Egerton, Ezekiel Culverwel and Francis Marbury, reissued seven times before 1630, supplying material for the widely circulated *Garden of Spirituall Flowers*, the *Seven Treatises* was the first important exposition of the code of behavior which expressed the English Calvinist, or, more broadly speaking, the Puritan, conception of the spiritual and moral life. As such it inaugurated a literature the extent and influence of which in all departments of life can hardly be exaggerated. To the modern mind, judging hastily and with animus irrelevant to the facts, the sixteenth-century Puritan may seem a morbid, introspective, inhibited moral bigot and religious zealot. To the common man of the time this was not so. The Puritan preacher proffered to a multitude in his own age what seemed enlightenment and a new freedom. He proffered the means to a more active and significant life, a means of overcoming fears, a counsel of courage, a vision of adventure for courage to undertake, a program of self-discipline for making adventure a success, a prospect of success certain to be attained sooner or later. Rogers in the language of his day states this clearly in the 'Entrance into the Booke, or Preface to the Reader.' He wrote the book, he says, because he knew of no writer who had set before men's eyes 'as in a glasse' the infinite, secret and deceitful corruptions of their own hearts whence arise the evils of this life. Neither did he know any writer who had drawn up directions for daily use which would enable men to govern their own hearts and so overcome the wants, infirmities, rebellions, hindrances and other discouragements by which they are afflicted. 'And therefore, not to be as men that have no such priviledges,' none such, that is, as God grants to his elect, not to be men 'either cast downe with needeles feare, or possessed with an earthly or vaine rejoycing, or destitute of incouragement to walke forward in an heavenly course: But that they may be mery in the Lord, and yet without lightnes; sad and heavie in heart for their owne sins, and the abominations of the land, and yet without discouragment or dumpishnes . . . And that the ungodly may see how such are blessed in comparison of other, and what they themselves goe voyde of which they might inioy, and therefore may seeke how to become not almost, but altogether Christians with them.' Rogers' sentence structure may be muddy, but his point is clear. He is laboring to utter the 'profitable' lesson that, if his reader will but live 'a godly and comfortable life every day,' he may feel assured of nothing less than 'true happines both in this life and in the life to come.'

The rigors of the godly comfortable life, when Rogers himself underwent them, were still so novel and its rewards here and hereafter so little tested by experience that we must in fairness forgive the man for agonizing so self-consciously as he does over what was for him an experiment in living fraught with perilous possibilities. As time went on, men grew more confident in practicing, or at any rate more facile in stating, the Puritan code. Rogers, coming early, could anatomize the soul from moment to moment of the godly day only with the verbosity of the full heart. Ezekiel Culverwel, his old friend and neighbor, wished that readers of the book could have seen its author's practice with their own eyes and heard his doctrine with their own ears.[42] That after a fashion we are now enabled to do by the diary which Rogers kept while writing his *Seven Treatises* and which has only recently been put into print. Nothing extant written at this date throws more light on the nature of the struggle to which the Puritan soul committed itself in its effort to find satisfying expression in action and discourse. As we see him outside the pages of his diary, Rogers differs in no important respect from other Puritan preachers. If he seems a shade more humorlessly zealous, surely they are his nearest rivals in solemn earnestness. The inference is inescapable that, if men like Greenham, Dod and Hildersam had kept diaries, or if the diaries that no doubt some of them did keep had been preserved for us to read, we should have found them much the same in tone and content as his. This is in fact true of Samuel Ward's diary, a more meagre record written some eight years later by a less vigorous character.[43] We must be careful as we read such things not to argue too confidently from what we over-hear a man say at confession that he has a less healthy mind or religion than we ourselves. The diary like the autobiography, of which it was the forerunner, was the Puritan's confessional. In its pages he could fling upon his God the fear and weakness he found in his heart but would not betray to the world. Rogers, therefore, must not be set down too promptly as a morbid introvert, aesthetically insensitive, intellectually incurious, abnormally moralistic. His diary is enough to show that such is far from being the whole truth. It was obviously written as a religious exercise and for psychological relief by a man who had to be continually snatching for time in which to do the things he most wanted to accomplish. He regarded it as his duty to meditate, study and write at the same time that he carried on no less con-scientiously the activities of a householder, a farmer, a figure in the countryside, a preacher, a pastor, a reformer, a head of a boarding school, a husband and a prolific begetter of children. Such a man could hardly help becoming at least intermittently neurotic, but he so often indulged in, and of course repented, wandering, light-minded, carnal thoughts that we may fairly suppose that he was generally what we should call quite normal and healthy. The Puritan preacher was no Rousseau. He was a professional intellectual more or less consciously preparing himself and his generation for a revolution. When he fell weary of the coil of business, discouraged by external difficulty, by the sense of his own failure, and by the futility of his own effort, he retired to his study and poured his heart out in his diary. At such moments, the healthiest mind seems morbid. Rogers' morbidity—and the same holds for the seeming morbidity of many another man of his type and time—was merely that of a hard-working idealist momentarily over-wrought but the next moment recovering from his lassitude to be again energetic, eloquent and courageous according to his lights.

The sixteenth- or seventeenth-century churchman, Anglican or Puritan, found it hard to forget the social chaos from which he had himself in many instances but recently and narrowly escaped. He was one of the sensitive, imaginative, articulate men such as constitute the tingling nerve of a society under stress. Thus to Rogers, writing at twenty years' remove, his native village seemed to have been 'a doungehil of abhominacion' where, if he had married and settled, he must have been 'undone both in body and soule.'[44] A sizar's place at Cambridge had been for him as for many another a way out into a life of intellectual activity and self-expression. A little more or less one way or another and he would, of course, have sought his fortune as a wit in London. He remained, however, in the path more customary to the impecunious intellectual. In former times it should have led to dignified security within the church, but times had changed and the church had on the old terms much less to offer. Its wealth, its authority, its prestige had grossly diminished. The ruin Henry had made had not been remedied by Edward and Mary and only arrested rather than repaired by Elizabeth. Thus the usual way of the poor scholar was rendered especially hard in the church just at the time when social conditions were bringing forward a host of young men whose poverty, whose abilities and whose ambition spurred them to seek careers in that walk of life toward which such men had been in the habit of addressing themselves. They were encouraged by the very persons who had recently been enriched at the expense of the church. The landed gentry, growing into something like a party conscious of interests it had to protect and extend, grew active in assisting promising youths to obtain education, education which in the ordinary course would lead them to the service of religion, that is to say into the work of guiding and forming the public opinion of a new day. Hence new life flowed into the universities, rich patrons even setting up new colleges to receive the youths they sent up to be educated.[45] What to do with the increasing host of graduates soon became a serious problem with implications far-reaching and little realized. Berths within the establishment could be found for some. But the number and value of livings in the church had been greatly depleted, and the wealthy gentlemen who sent young men to Cambridge and Oxford were not as a rule inclined to restore to the church the means necessary to employ them afterward. There arose in consequence a steadily growing body of able, earnest, ambitious intellectuals, trained in the universities to do the work of an institution which lacked means if not inclination to provide them with recognized and secure positions in its service. The men did not go unprovided, but they had more and more to provide for themselves under conditions which could not but affect the whole direction and purpose of their thought and expression. They could not confidently expect security. They could, however, undertake with some hope of success to live by the exercise of their abilities. It was a much more precarious and exciting, though not, as it turned out, a less profitable, kind of career. They soon made the happy discovery that their talents could open the purses as well as melt the stony hearts of sinners. The Puritan intellectual, that is, discovered that he could get along—could get along actively and well—by becoming what was essentially a mendicant preacher. As a 'lecturer' he could flourish upon the support, carnal as well as spiritual, which audiences and patrons would give for the services he rendered. The time was coming when one such man would prefer a popular lectureship even to a bishopric.

Not the least important effect of all this was that more and more of the professional intellectual class were thus led by the circumstances of their positions as well as by their convictions to become the critics and opponents of authority, of custom, of accepted ideas and vested interest. To the discussion of this development we shall return at a later point. Rogers lived before the great order of Puritan mendicants had attained the influence which eventually enabled them to challenge the hierarchy itself. He could but regard himself as a poor preacher of the word of God, lacking countenance or regular support in the church, directly indebted to the people he served, and embarked upon an untried way wherein there was no knowing for certain what might befall him.

Confidence, therefore, was his most essential daily need, and this fact together with the self-discipline by which he taught himself to have courage was what he chiefly revealed in his diary. The lesson he thus learned he codified for the instruction of others in his *Seven Treatises*. The first step in his method, however grotesque the terms may seem in which he conceived it, was psychologically sound enough. It was frankly to acknowledge to himself that the prime danger in a life full of danger was fear. Fear, weakness, self-deception, overconfidence, irresolution, the slackening of attention and will, these were the things that must first be faced and overcome if evil were to be deprived of its power. They were, Rogers would have said, the consequences of Adam's fall, the abominations of man's sinful heart. They were the work of the devil. The preacher kept a diary not as a diversion but as a tactical maneuver against the adversary within. He could get the better of discouragement and nervous depression by thus driving his black moods out into the forefront of consciousness. Satan grew powerless when looked squarely in the eye.

The world supplied Rogers with plenty of occasions for fear. There was first of all poverty to escape and cupidity to overcome. The son of the Chelmsford joiner, as things turned out, did fairly well for himself and his family, but not without giving more attention to the matter than he enjoyed or approved. It would be hard to say that he was more intent upon money than other men, even other preachers. Nevertheless he had frequently to confess 'that the love of worldly th[ings] cleaveth so neer to my hart that I must purge it out strongulier than yet it hath been.'[46] His chief annoyance, indeed, he says upon one occasion, is 'from that common eye-sore, p[rofit], wherein I would I were able to shame my self, or to fear my hart from such unsetlednes as breaketh out that way so often.'[47] He wishes he might be more like his fellow preacher, John Knewstubs, who seemed to him to have freed himself from such temptations, 'litl account makeing of any thinge that he hath, or keepinge any stock.'[48] Knewstubs left no diary to reveal what self-accusing admiration he may have felt for Rogers. Matrimony, needless to say, also brought its trials to the spirit. It was Barbara Rogers' lot to be always on her way to or from childbed in the intervals of managing a household that included not only her husband and children but her husband's pupils and their tutor. The man had his part, to provide, to teach, to catechize, but naturally his wife and her part also invaded his mind, often without his leave. 'Wandringe thoughtes against my will,' runs one entry, 'with some likeing of them about b.'[49] Hardly has he ventured to rejoice 'that the lorde had so inlardged mine hart as that mine olde and accustomed dreames and fantasies of thinges belowe were vanished and drowned,' when suddenly he is taken off his guard: 'I began to waxe colde, the which grew uppon me by reason of lingring [in his thoughts] after ba[rbara].'[50] Marriage had its moments of exaltation when the hearts of husband and wife flowed sweetly together toward God, but it also had its moments when Richard to his shame lost his temper. Might it be after all that celibacy was more compatible with godliness? 'And this is a veary comon thing with good men that when thei come to have dealinges, occupyeinges, and families much of their delight is imployed uppon them which was wont to be geven to the lord.'[51] Yet when the wife fell to ailing, her time for giving birth again drawing near, the husband grew distracted at the thought of losing her, hardly less distracted at the thought of having to take another woman. He considered 'how many uncomfortablnesses the lord had kept from me hitherto by those which I then saw must needes come if he should part us.' First of those 'uncomfortablnesses' was the fear of 'marying againe, daungerous as 2 mar[riages] are,' and next the 'Want of it in the meane while.' But there were also to be thought of the loss of so fit a companion, the 'Losse and decay of subst[ance]', the 'Care of houshold matters cast on me', 'Neglect of study', and finally 'Feare of looseing freendship among her kinred'.[52] When at last, not upon this but upon a later occasion, Barbara made her bed in the grave, her husband remarried, taking the widow with the several children of another preacher.

In addition to such fears, which, after all, he shared with other men, there also hung over the non-conformist preacher the fear of persecution. The stirs of the Reformation in England were still too recent to let one hope that they were over and done with. The fires of Smithfield might be kindled again, the Spaniard threatened war, and no one could tell what manner of husband Elizabeth might bestow on her subjects or who would be her successor if she died. Meanwhile the church remained unpurified and papists lurked everywhere. The very conception of toleration, let alone belief in it, existed in few minds. Enforced uniformity was the common ideal, and persecution was regarded as a normal necessary practice, to be deplored only when directed against the truth. The Puritans had no doubt that their faith was true, but the average Puritan could hardly have hoped with much confidence for a toleration such as he certainly was not prepared to grant, if he had the power, to others. The fact was that, thanks to the politic opportunism of Elizabeth's government, such a man as Rogers was reasonably safe, but though that fact may seem apparent to us it was not so to him. He could not at any rate know how long his safety would last. Rogers was forbidden to preach by Archbishop Whitgift in 1583. He was relieved from this prohibition by the intervention of an influential gentleman of the neighborhood but had no assurance that it would not from one quarter or another be at any time renewed. Again and again he received or was threatened with a summons that might terminate his activity and his livelihood. In 1589 he had again to be rescued by personal influence, this time from the Court of High Commission. Less fortunate non-conformists, separatists and papists, to be sure, went to gaol and some to the scaffold. It is not difficult to understand what led Rogers while on a trip to London with his wife in the spring of 1588 to go view the prisoners at Bridewell. He went home much disturbed in mind and remained for some time 'troubled in thincking I am like to loose my liberty.'[53] He had in him, it is plain, little of the martyr or of the controversialist. He gives few details and none of the arguments relating to the occasions when he was compelled to defend himself. What occupies him as he sits at his diary is the effort to quiet his apprehensions, draw back his wandering thoughts, recapture and hold more firmly his religious mood, fight off the distractions caused by such troubles. 'I love and wish,' he writes in 1587, 'allwayes to be free and at liberty to delight in that wherin I may boldly delight without repent[ance], and that is, to be allwayes doeing or seekeing occasion to doe some good. And whither my liberty be taken from me utterly which thing I feare, or whither I may inioy it, I would that my lif in my family guiding and with the people and espec[ially] to mine owne self warde might be a paterne of good . . . to others.'[54] In 1589, when suspension from preaching seemed imminent, he 'saw it veary necessary to stay upp my weaknes with some strenghth of perswasions to rest contented and thanckful to god under it.' So he draws up under twelve heads the lessons of godliness to be learned from the affliction hanging over him. But a few days later his mind is 'not so cheerful nor of so good courage as to be readily disposed to duty, and that by reason of my great liklihood of suspension, I did this morn[ing], fall to further consideracion with my selfe how to frame my mind wil[lingly] to goe under it, though in itself most unwelcome.'[55]

The Spanish Armada sailed into the English Channel in the middle of July 1588. Wethersfield was only some twenty miles from the sea. Neighbors of Rogers were called suddenly to march away to the coast, 'never seeing wif nor takinge ordre about their goodes and busines.' This excitement did not fail to put another severe strain upon the preacher's composure. 'This weeke I have been wrapped in, I know not how, in foolish busyinge my selfe in the world.' There was some broil about assessing him as a clergyman to supply armor for the fighting men. He was sure that God had some dreadful affliction in store for England. 'We are now in peril of goodes, liberty, life, by our enemies the Span[iards], and at home papistes in multitudes ready to come uppon us unawares.' The more reason, of course, why he should stir himself up 'to the continual and earnest medit[ation] of a godly life.' So he tries to take firm grip upon his nerves, to study, meditate, pray and keep up the regimen of Puritan saintliness. He has a sermon to write, but never has he found it more difficult to concentrate on spiritual matters. For one thing, the storms of that summer, so disastrous for the Armada, made wet weather in Essex, which made it hard for Rogers to get in his hay. 'One day this while I was sodainly overtaken with hardnes of hart because of the ra[in] . . . I was then to study for my sermon, and nether could I goe about that with such unsetlednes of hart, and yet not to goe about it, my sorrow was the more to be idle.' The next day he felt better and was able to go back to his God and his work. But some days later the weather, still bad, 'troubled me againe as before, and unsetled me at study for the good part of the day.' He worried first lest 'thinges would be deare,' and then he worried all that night and into the next morning that he 'should thus roave after profit, who had so litle cause.' May he not grow to resemble the bishops and 'great clarckes' who 'did never seeme grosely to have departed from god till thei grew in wealth and promotion?' Yet in less than a week he was repenting again that 'a little hay, which we have, hath more letted me this month, takeing up my time, my hart, and troubling me, for that it hath been neer lost by the weather.' Strange indeed are the ways of the human spirit, subtle, Rogers would have put it, the wiles of Satan. Here he was 'trifling out . . . time thus, whiles troubles are so great as we are evry day and hour fearing them comeing uppon us.' Where are the cheerfulness and courage, he asks himself, that formerly enabled him to teach others, where the ability he should have 'to stirre upp either our selves or the soldiers, to whome I would goe if I felt meet to doe them good?'[56]

It would be a mistake to suppose that Rogers' days were chiefly devoted to reverie. The man turned to introspection from time to time in the course of a life full of uncertainties but also busy with the responsibilities of an exacting lot. He had to face and down his discouragements, maintain cheerfulness and courage, in order to get his work done. The preacher's task, as he conceived it, was to put the human heart in order so that the human will should accomplish what God required. The specific task which Rogers set himself, over and above the necessary occupations of his household, his land, his office and his neighborhood, was to study and plan how to do this. He desired to get the meaning of life as he conceived it expressed not only in the performance of daily duties but in discourse, in sermons and treatises. All his melancholy, indeed, might be described as nothing more than the ordinary spiritual malaise of authorship, of the creative imagination laboring to shake off the inhibitions and impediments to full expression. Rogers set himself a rule of life, a regimen covering every hour of the day. This was to be practiced, also no doubt preached, but certainly to be written up. There were regular hours for prayer, for meditation, for study, and obviously an inadequate allowance of time for other obligations and for the interruptions of ill-health and sleep. The purpose of it all was to enable Rogers to do what he thought was the work of the Lord. Naturally the intrusions of boys, bishops, wife, the hay and the rain were discouraging and annoying. But in spite of them all and with the relief that came from going to confession now and then in his diary, he got his sermons, his commentaries on scripture and, most important of all, his rule of Christian life written. In December 1587 he with the other ministers at one of their 'classis' meetings 'determined to bringe into writinge a direction for our lives, which might be both for our selves and others.'[57] The result, published four years later, was his *Seven Treatises*.

The Puritan code, as presented by Rogers and a succession of other writers following immediately after, will be discussed in a later chapter. At this point it is enough to note that the first generation of Puritan preachers had helped by their preaching and writing to launch the movement which engulfed English society in the next century. We are accustomed to think of the literature of the English Renaissance, of Shakespeare, Spenser and the rest, as the first literary expression of what was to be the modern spirit. It was fully as much the last expression of medieval culture, flaring up in perhaps its grandest outburst on the eve of its final extinction. Certainly the society that blazed out so brilliantly in the closing years of Gloriana was far from stable or sure either of its foundations or its direction. The structure of medieval society lay all about in ruins. Outwitted at first and then overawed by the bewildering woman whom chance had set over them, in amazement first and then almost in a kind of deference, men paused for a moment before plunging into the crucial task of constructing the new society. In that moment, the old culture flowered. But the great queen was not long in her grave when the conflict out of which came modern civilization began.

The lines of that conflict had, of course, been slowly forming all through her long reign. Puritan and Catholic in their various gradations had been all along squaring off for a battle which had been arrested by the consummate political adroitness which balanced one against the other. But the equilibrium between those hostile forces was too unsteady to be maintained indefinitely. The causes pressing toward conflict and change were too old and too deep-seated for political measures—at any rate for those Elizabeth's successors had the wit to apply—to keep much longer from wreaking their full effect. The church had once furnished a complete spiritual setting for the people to live within, a culture, a scale of values, a mode of expression, a discipline, a satisfying ideal image and rational statement of the meaning of life. The decadence of the church under the stress of change had begun at least as early as the end of the fourteenth century. Henry did more than separate from Rome; he gave the church a blow from which it could but bleed to death. When such momentous changes occur, however, men find it difficult to realize what has happened or how final the alteration may be. Attempt after attempt is sure to be made to return to the old faith and forms as the only possible remedy for the very evils which have been as much the cause as the effect of their ruin. Thus Mary and Edward in their several ways endeavored to restore what their father had destroyed. Where they had failed, Elizabeth was too clever even to try. Enough for her politic purposes to retain the mere site and shell of the church, if only to prevent anyone else from aggravating her difficulties by attempting what she was too shrewd or too timid herself to undertake. But despite the brilliance with which she evaded the problem, the problem remained. The attempt to reconstruct and revitalize in one form or another the great central institution of spiritual existence was bound sooner or later to be made again. It was bound to be made because the need for something to perform under the new conditions for the new society the function which the medieval church had performed for the old was inevitable and imperative. That the organ or organs of man's spiritual existence on earth might take in future no single comprehensive form, or any forms not necessarily or predominantly religious and ecclesiastical, was beyond the power of most men to conceive. Neither was it conceivable by many that the Anglican church as constituted by Elizabeth was, thanks in large part to its very limitations, the only kind of church which at the moment the majority of Englishmen would accept or at any rate would not too violently disagree about. It did indeed fall far short of satisfying the needs of the Elizabethan populace for education, for moral guidance, for spiritual comfort, for the awakening of the imagination to things beyond the daily round, for adequate expression of the common man's sense of the mysteries of life. To the Puritan reformers, largely supported by the lately risen gentry, all this seemed patent. Equally patent, too, it seemed to them that in the Calvinist type of church organization lay the hope of restoring the church to the people and the people to the church. Hence the agitation led by Cartwright and so repeatedly balked by Elizabeth's government. Hence, too, in spite of that defeat, the sustained effort of preachers like Greenham and Rogers to effect by preaching and by the example of their own lives that moral and religious reform which they could not for the time being accomplish by direct control over the establishment. The success of their effort was presently apparent in the steadily increasing number of their disciples. Before long Puritan preachers would grow sufficiently numerous and influential to form something tantamount to a new order or brotherhood within the English church.

II

The Spiritual Brotherhood

THE accession of a king who had been reared in the church of John
Knox gave the Puritan reformers fresh hope. They prepared once
more to advance their cause by frontal attack. James had not been long
across the border when he was confronted by a petition from several
hundred Puritan ministers begging that the reorganization of the
church, which, they thought, had been too long delayed, be at once
consummated. In the first flush of his new-found prosperity, James
promised to listen to their proposals. What their spokesmen proposed
at the Hampton Court Conference in 1604 pointed toward such a
scheme of church government as would have put the religious life of
the people, and so in large measure the public opinion of the nation, in
the uncontrolled hands of the preachers. But the Scottish king knew
what it was to be browbeaten by godly divines. He continued, vain as
he was of his theological learning, to adhere to orthodox Calvinism,
but he had had more than enough of presbyterianism. So, after giving
himself the pleasure of chopping logic for a few days with the Puritan
leaders, he spoke some foolish words about harrying them out of the
land and confirmed the bishops in their authority. Prelacy under his
predecessor had become the means of upholding the position of the
monarch as the supreme governor of the church, a position which
James thought himself appointed by God to keep.

If the success of Elizabeth in maintaining herself in that position had
been due to tacit recognition of the expediency of toleration, the ill-
success of the Stuarts was to be due in large measure to their failure to
realize the inexpediency of intolerance ineffectively applied. James
rebuffed the reformers at Hampton Court, deprived numbers of non-
conformists of their posts in the church, even egged on ecclesiastics to
the burning of two heretics, the last to be so treated in England. By
such tactics he prevented the Puritans from putting their ideas of
church government into effect. But nothing now could have silenced

them completely except persecution of a ruthlessness such as James, assuming that he had the power, lacked the wish, let alone the backbone, to enforce. He agreed with the Puritans on most theological points. What he chiefly accomplished against them was to persecute their preachers just enough to make enemies of them and to heighten their personal prestige. Unwary non-conformists might now and then be haled before an ecclesiastical tribunal, deprived of their livings and commanded to be silent. But the preachers as a whole kept the support of patrons, continued in their Cambridge fellowships and their lectureships here and there, and went on issuing their sermons, tracts and commentaries in print. The chronicles of non-conformity, of course, still ring with indignation at the tyranny of the first two Stuarts, but the truth is that no persecutors probably ever won so evil a reputation by doing so little harm to the cause of the persecuted and so much to their own. Puritan hopes and efforts for immediate reform of church government diminished, but the setting forth by precept and example of a moral temper and a way of life profoundly incompatible with Stuart pretensions did not. Rather, the preachers under James increased in number and influence faster than before, finding a growing audience ever more willing to listen.[1]

For James made the fatal error of alienating the pulpit at a time when he was alienating a public which was already habituated to turning to the pulpit for inspiration and guidance. The Gunpowder Plot, though it made certain the loyalty of the people to the crown, only exacerbated their hatred of Romanism. They deplored the death of Prince Henry, who was thought to be a staunch Protestant. They bitterly disapproved the project of a Spanish marriage for Prince Charles and the protracted bungling which made of that project a humiliating fiasco. They complained of the failure to support Protestantism on the continent. Members of the nobility whose families had risen to greatness under the Tudors, often on the ruins of the church, did not look with favor on the elevation of new favorites at court or the intrusion of churchmen into high political office. The gentry and the lawyers, defenders of the common law, who had a long-standing quarrel with the great men of the church, shared this jealousy. All classes were animated more and more by a passion for getting on in the world, for escaping poverty, making money, rising as they had seen others rise to affluence and respectability. At the same time the number steadily grew of those who viewed with disapproval what they regarded as the extravagance and corruption of the court, the insolence of upstart favorites, the pride of prelates, the venality of judges, the extortionate practices of monopolists, each and all subservient to the crown. Step by step the Stuarts and their creatures alienated subjects of all classes. Englishmen were becoming ever more aggressively English. That meant that they hated Spain, despised France, dreaded the Pope and embraced Protestantism with the greater fervor the more these historic enemies seemed to menace England. Consequently the more the church fell under the control of the prelates, the more the prelates identified the church with the crown, and the more royal policy fell into popular disfavor, so much the readier became all elements in the population to listen to the Puritan preachers.

Better soil in which to plant the doctrine of faith could not have been found. The nature of the case, considering the habits of the time, provoked a certain amount of tilting by theological technicians against one another, but the vital function and opportunity of the pulpit was to give comfort and courage to all those who grew dissatisfied with things as they were. The preachers could make themselves strong by winning converts, by fashioning minds, by rousing imaginations, whether of peers, squires, merchants, lawyers, ploughmen, artisans, shopkeepers, apprentices or laborers. For this purpose, the most effective instrument was not polemic directed against opponents, though that too had its usefulness in propaganda, but persuasion lavished upon possible adherents and disciples. The people wished to know what to do to be saved. The preachers told them to trust in Jesus Christ and put on the whole armor of God. Yet behind the thinning veil of doctrine and image the Puritan Revolution was gathering momentum.

With the successive checks administered to overt reform of the church, the number of men who devoted themselves to spiritual preaching grew in the next fifty years to be well-nigh legion. To recount their several careers would be a task beyond the scope of the present study and would not of itself contribute to our understanding of the essential character of the Puritan movement. They are remembered in such chronicles of non-conformity as those of Neal, Brook, Barclay and Dexter. The lives of many are recorded in the Dictionary of National Biography. Their published works were listed by Crowe, Wilkins and Baxter and fill up the pages of the Short Title Catalogue. Those who, whether of separatist or non-separatist leanings, took part in launching New England, have been accorded much attention by American historians. What has not been so clearly told is the manner by which the Puritan party in the English church, from which Puritanism in all its aspects sprang, advanced its cause in the pulpit and the press. Our first task, therefore, must be to describe the organization and spread of spiritual preaching prior to the Westminster Assembly. We may then proceed to examine the character of Puritan pulpit literature both as to its immediate effect and as to its more general influence upon thought and expression.

We can best begin by centering attention upon certain leading spirits who, especially after their discomfiture at the Hampton Court Conference, made themselves a kind of nucleus for the promotion of preaching throughout the country. Within the purlieus of the church, making use of Cambridge as its seminary, the reform party under the primacies of Bancroft, Abbot and Laud built up for itself what can fairly be called a kind of Puritan order of preaching brothers. The members sprang as a rule from the gentry or merchant class or had immediate connections with that class. A few went to Oxford, but for most of them a Cambridge education culminating in a Cambridge fellowship was the starting point of their careers. As a rule they accepted ordination, though as time went on they tended to avoid formal undertaking of the cure of souls, in other words regular appointment as parish priests. That too often involved responsibility for strict performance of observances which presented difficulties to their consciences. When they did accept presentation to a living, it was generally at the hands of a sympathetic patron from among the Protestant nobles and squires and with some show of agreement consistent with presbyterian principles on the part of the parish. Often they found support and the opportunity to preach as chaplains or tutors in great households, but the post which characteristically they found most congenial and, we may add, remunerative was that of lecturer or special preacher to a congregation, for which the ordinary and prescribed services were performed by a regularly invested parson. The lecturer in such cases might or might not succeed in time to the incumbency, according as the congregation might be able to prevail upon the patron. As we have seen, Henry Smith held a lectureship at St. Clement Danes and Walter Travers at the Temple. Richard Rogers probably began by holding such a post at Wethersfield, and Richard Greenham at the close of his career lectured in various London pulpits. The lecturer was not as a rule, though he might be, designated or approved by the patron of the parish, nor did he enjoy the revenue from tithes vested in the regular incumbent. He was selected to preach by the congregation, or by some member or group of members, or by some wealthy adherent, any of whom might undertake the expense of his support. His ministrations might be sought out by people of many parishes round about. His duty was to lecture upon the Bible, that is to preach, on Sundays at times other than those of the usual services and in most instances upon weekdays as well. He was supposed to be licensed by the bishop or other proper authority in the church, to whom he was accountable under pain of being silenced. Acceptance of a formal benefice by the lecturer made no essential difference in his manner of performing his duties. Whether as lecturers, as university fellows or professors, as private chaplains, or as parsons of parishes, all preached the word of God in the same spirit and felt themselves to be members of a brotherhood bearing, as we now see, obvious resemblances to the older preaching orders of the church and presenting to those in authority similar problems. With their activity and success the number of their wealthy and influential as well as of their popular adherents steadily grew, and so also did the number of preaching posts available to them. These the leading spirits or, if such they may be called, generals of the order were ever ready to supply with their pupils and disciples. Eventually they became so strongly organized and so bold in this work that some of them endeavored to establish a permanent specially endowed foundation for planting preachers wherever throughout the kingdom there might be people to be reached by the word. All this, we must remember, was done or attempted primarily within the church, and with no admitted intention save to inspire and reform the people through the church. Independency and separatism in all their organized forms developed only as the authorities at successive stages placed more and more serious impediments in the way of the reformers' efforts.

The brotherhood of spiritual preachers never, let us make plain, entered upon anything like formal corporate organization. It was at no time anything more than an association of ministers of the church united by personal ties and common purpose. Starting from Cambridge among Cartwright's sympathizers, it spread along the lines of personal relationship and friendship. The beginnings of this development we have already seen in the careers of Greenham and Rogers, whose early place in our discussion is due chiefly to the fact that they were the first of the spiritual preachers to achieve full expression in writing. Among their contemporaries or immediate successors at Cambridge who are also to be reckoned among the reformers, three especially stand out by reason of the greater length of their careers and the correspondingly greater reach of their personal influence. These were Laurence Chaderton, Arthur Hildersam, and John Dod. The two last named were appointed by Cartwright to take charge of his papers after his death. All three survived far into the next century: Chaderton until 1640, Hildersam until 1632, Dod until 1645. They were regarded, so to speak, as the patriarchs of the spiritual brotherhood, and Hildersam and Dod eventually found their place in Baxter's list of practical and affectionate English divines.

Chaderton,[2] though he lived almost if not quite a hundred years, published little and is now the most shadowy figure of the three. He came from a wealthy family, by whom he was 'nuzled up in Popish Superstition'[3] and then disinherited when he betook himself from the Inns of Court to Puritan Christ's College at Cambridge. He was fellow of Christ's when Cartwright was expelled. He was lecturer for fifty years at St. Clement's Church at Cambridge. He was one of the Puritan representatives at the Hampton Court Conference in 1604, notwithstanding which fact he was appointed one of the translators of the authorized version of the Bible. He married into the noted Puritan family of the Culverwels, and so became the uncle by marriage of William Gouge. He launched John Dod on his career as a preacher, and when he finally gave up his lectureship at St. Clement's, forty clergymen begged him to continue, alleging that to him they owed their conversion. Fuller tells us that 'he had a *plain* but *effectual* way of *Preaching*.'[4] Once, when he had held forth for two hours and then proposed to trespass no longer on his hearers' patience, 'the Auditory cryed out, (wonder not if hungry people craved more meat) *For God Sake Sir Go on, go on.*[5] Perhaps most important of all for establishing Chaderton's influence was the fact that Sir Walter Mildmay chose him in 1584 to be master of his newly founded college at Cambridge. Thus for nearly forty years Chaderton presided over Emmanuel, that breeding ground of preachers, and retired, an octogenarian, only in order that he might make way for John Preston. Practically nothing has come to us in print that might show the secret of Chaderton's power,[6] but there can be no question that he perhaps more than any other man was responsible for the steadily increasing stream of men who went forth from Emmanuel to preach the word in plain English to the plain people.

Arthur Hildersam[7] entered Christ's College in 1576, while Chaderton was still a fellow there. His origins illustrate the close relations that existed between many of the Puritan preachers and the members of the Tudor ruling class. His mother was the niece of Cardinal Pole, and tradition has it that Queen Elizabeth once called him cousin. Breaking away from the Catholic faith of his parents, he was supported at Cambridge by his distant kinsman Henry Hastings, Earl of Huntingdon. For some reason he was refused a fellowship at Christ's, but he was vested by his noble relatives with the impropriated tithes and later with the benefice of the parish of Ashby-de-la-Zouch. When the Millenary Petition was on foot, he, with Stephen Egerton, was one of the principal agents in securing the support of the Puritan clergy. The bishops silenced him now and then, but for the better part of forty years his voice was heard by the people of Leicestershire, and his encouragement inspired many younger men to proclaim the word. He befriended William Bradshaw, a graduate of Emmanuel, who became one of the first fellows of Sidney Sussex and, as author of *English Puritanisme*, published in 1605, one of the intellectual fathers of independency. Among Hildersam's numerous disciples and admirers were William Gouge, John Preston and John Cotton, of whom we shall have much more to say presently. It is for his undoubted influence upon such men as these that Hildersam now requires mention. To the modern reader, his sermons and commentaries, published relatively late, are rather more than commonly dry. But his disciples saw in him their ideal spiritual physician, one who was always willing 'to instruct the ignorant, to satisfie the doubtfull, to settle the wavering, to comfort the dejected, and to encourage all sorts in the exercises of Religion.'[8] Preston praised his writing for its strength and succinctness.[9] Cotton, in a preface to Hildersam's *Lectures upon the Fourth of John*, 1629, which is addressed 'To the Godly Reader, whether Minister, or Private Christian,' praised him as a teacher for all sorts of men. Preachers, he says, should take him as a pattern of method and style. Others might observe in his book what was, as Cotton summed it up, the perfect compendium of sound and useful doctrine:

The scornefull vanity of corrupt Nature, the lothsomenesse and desperate danger of sinne, the wonderfull power of Gods Grace in the conversion of a sinner, the tryall of a mans owne deceitfull heart, the amiable life of Gods Grace in the regenerate, the comfortable benefit of afflictions, sundry sweet consolations of a troubled spirit, the vanitie of Popery, the necessity of a faithfull Ministry, the beauty of Gods Ordinances holily administered, and the resolution of sundry cases of conscience fitting these times.

To the imaginations of successive generations of the godly, John Dod[10] was probably a more vivid embodiment of such principles than Hildersam. Picturesque, gifted with racy utterance, long-lived, Dod became the chief holy man of the spiritual brotherhood. He died at ninety in the same year, 1645, as Laud, 'no less esteemed,' says Fuller, 'amongst men of his own persuasion.'[11] The younger son of a country gentleman, he came from Cheshire to Jesus College, Cambridge, just after the excitement caused by Cartwright. While he was still in but a 'natural'—that is, unconverted—state of soul, he flew into such a rage at the college steward for accusing him of not paying a debt that he fell into a fever. But then suddenly 'his sins came upon him like armed men, and the tyde of his thoughts was turned' to repentance and the grace of God.[12] Thus he entered upon the new life. The steward was shortly placated, remembering that the debt had after all been paid. From that point on, Dod's history is one with the growth of the spiritual brotherhood. The list of his personal connections and adherents reads like its beadroll. He married the stepdaughter of Richard Greenham. He found a second wife with the help of Stephen Egerton, the friend of Richard Rogers, and he was married to her by Egerton's successor at Blackfriars, William Gouge. With Hildersam, we have seen, he took charge of Cartwright's papers after the reformer's death, and he preached the sermon at his funeral. He was a friend of Richard Sibbes, the great preacher at Gray's Inn and Master of Catherine Hall, for a volume of whose sermons he wrote a commendatory epistle.[13] He and Hildersam were frequent visitors in John Preston's chambers at Cambridge. John Cotton consulted him before leaving for New England. These were but a few of his acquaintances in Puritan circles. Job Throckmorton of Marprelate fame and John Preston, both in the same year foreseeing their rapidly approaching ends, went down to Northamptonshire in order to have John Dod beside them when they died. Even Archbishop Ussher is reported to have said that, notwithstanding their doctrinal differences, he desired that his soul might rest with Dod's.[14]

At Cambridge, where he remained until 1585, Dod rose to be fellow of Jesus and University Preacher. He was so 'facetiously solid' at a certain commencement disputation that some 'Oxford-men there present courted him home with them,' but without avail.[15] Godly people in Ely had him over to preach to them every week. He was in the habit of meeting frequently to read and expound scripture with William Fulke, Master of Pembroke and a man who had a stormy career as an advocate of reform; Laurence Chaderton, soon to be Master of Emmanuel; and William Whitaker, soon to be Master of St. John's. In 1585 Sir Anthony Cope asked Chaderton to name a man for the vacant living of Hanwell in Oxfordshire. Chaderton named Dod, who soon won the support of Sir Anthony, of the neighboring ministers, and of the people, and so continued to preach, to catechize, and to live the spiritual life in that place for twenty years. With four other preachers he also set up a lectureship in Banbury. When he was silenced by the bishop in 1604, he helped his successor, Robert Harris, to gain the people's confidence and then found another pulpit for himself first at Fenny Compton in Warwickshire and then at Canons Ashby in Northamptonshire.[16] He now had the favor of Sir Erasmus Dryden, grandfather of the poet. Silenced again, this time by command of King James himself, he had to wait until the end of the reign in 1625 before he could again preach publicly. Later another sympathetic squire, Richard Knightley, came to his aid. This gentleman was the successor to the Sir Richard Knightley who had given shelter to the Marprelate press at Fawsley in Northamptonshire, and was himself on terms of intimacy with such other members of the Puritan squirearchy as Eliot, Pym, Hesilrigge and Hampden. It was at Fawsley that he settled John Dod, and there the preacher held his pulpit until the end of his long life.

Dod was a character of an authentic Anglo-Saxon type. He was always himself. He had the English gift of humor and the knack of salty speech. His religious faith was sound and warm but chiefly evinced in a morality practical, forthright and earnestly held. He was the kind of man men of his race like to quote and imitate. No one probably did more than he to fix by personal influence and example the way of life and style of preaching followed for generations by the rank and file of the Puritan ministry. Cartwright is quoted as authority for the statement that John Dod was 'the fittest man in the Land for a Pastoral function, . . . able to speak to any mans capacity . . . and never out of the Pulpit.'[17] 'All his discourses,' says one of his disciples, 'were Sermons, and that with such a mixture of delight, as would take with any man . . . so facetious and pithy that . . . If all his Apopthegmes were collected, they would exceed all that Plutarch in Greek or others in Latin since have published.'[18] No one more able than he at putting into plain English for the plain people the meaning of the book which had so recently been given them to puzzle over. Consequently they came to him, not without stirring the envy of less gifted parsons, from parishes all about the places where he preached. 'Poor simple people that never knew what Religion meant, when they had gone to hear him, could not choose but talk of his Sermon. It mightily affected poor creatures to hear the Mysteries of God . . . brought down to their own language and dialect.' Moreover, he made it easy for them to seek him out for private conference in their difficulties. His habit was to use the church edifice itself for his pastoral study 'that he might have room to walk in, (being troubled with the stone).' There perplexed souls would find him, and 'if he thought them bashfull, he would meet them, and say, Would you speak with me? And when he found them unable to state their question, he would help them out with it, taking care to find the sore: But would answer and deal so compassionately and tenderly, as not to discourage the poorest soul from coming again to him.' He also bore in mind Paul's injunction to be hospitable. Twice on Sunday he would preach and once during the week, and after every sermon his wife opened her house to all comers. 'He brought in many with him to dinner, besides his four or six constant Widows [women who helped him in his pastoral cares]: If his Wife began to doubt of her provision at sight of so many, he would say, Better want meat than good company, but there is something in the house, though cold.' Eating little himself but bidding the rest fall to, he would go on talking. He had plenty to say, and 'it was no great matter to pay money when one had it.' 'And when he was faint, he would call for a small glass of Wine and Beer mixt, and then to it again till night.'[19]

Really to silence such a man was, of course, possible for no bishop. Death itself, which was so slow in overtaking him, was slow too in silencing his fame. 'I am sure,' says Fuller, 'Master Dod, when his mouth was shut, (prohibited preaching), instructed almost as much as before by his holy demeanour and pious discourse.'[20] His 'plaine and familiar' expositions of the Ten Commandments, of Proverbs and of the Lord's Prayer, which will require our attention when we come to speak of the Puritan code, went everywhere among the populace. But what chiefly served to make Dod the figure he became in popular tradition was the flavor of personality which he added to pious edification and the picturesque anecdotes and pungent sayings into which it was distilled. The Dod legend in its earliest authentic form is brought to us by Samuel Clarke, the compiler of Puritan saints' lives, and by Robert Harris, Dod's successor at Hanwell and the Master of Trinity College, Oxford, under the Commonwealth. Fuller both in his *Church History* and his *Worthies* adds slightly to the picture. After the Restoration, 'old Mr. Dods sayings,' drawn from Clarke and from oral tradition, how authentic it is impossible and not important to say, became a regular article of commerce for the hawkers of popular broadsides.[21] A hundred years after their author's death they could still be found pasted on cottage walls. Granger reports in 1769 that an old woman of his neighborhood told him she would have gone distracted for the loss of her husband, if she had been without Mr. Dod's sayings in the house.[22]

The apothegms attributed to Dod by Clarke and others have the familiar ring of Anglo-Saxon homely wisdom, the characteristic mingling of common sense, humor and moral feeling. He is, for illustration, reported to have said that the difference between the rich and the poor was that 'for poor Christians their Father kept the purse, but the rich Christians keep the purse in their own hands,' and perhaps the purse was better off in the father's hands than in the child's. Dod told a friend who had come into a great estate to remember, that, whether it be upon a little boat or upon a great ship, 'while we are in this world, we are upon the Sea.' When invited to inspect the famous mansion of Sir Christopher Hatton, he chose rather to sit in the garden looking at a flower, saying: 'In this flower . . . I can see more of God than in all the beautiful buildings in the world.' Upon another occasion he remarked "if we should come in to a house, and see many Physick-boxes and Glasses, we would conclude somebody is sick; so when we see Hounds, and Hawks, and Cards, and Dice, we may fear that there is some sick soul in that Family.' When someone complained at the length of his sermons, his rejoinder was that if 'Gentlemen will follow hounds from seven in the morning till four or five in the afternoon, because they love the cry of dogs, . . . we should be content though the Minister stood above his hour.' And he added, 'methinks it is much better to hear a Minister preach than a kenell of hounds to bark.'[23]

How long the reputation of Dod persisted is illustrated by the once-famous anecdote of his sermon on malt.[24] The story, which turns up in several forms in the eighteenth century, was that some Cambridge boys in skylarking mood once encountered the preacher on a lonely road and thought to have sport at his expense. He had recently preached at the university against drunkenness. Nothing would satisfy the lads but he must get down from his horse, mount a stump beside the way and preach them a sermon on the word malt. Unabashed, Dod complied, beginning with 'Beloved, I am a little man, come at a short warning, to deliver a brief discourse upon a small subject to a thin congregation, and from an unworthy pulpit.' The rest is a mock homily, combining parody on the conventional form of the sermon with warning against the evils of drink. The thing is doubtless in whole or part apocryphal, but serves, perhaps all the better, to illustrate the role which Dod played in popular imagination.[25]

Far more significant evidence, however, of Dod's position in the spiritual brotherhood as the patriarchal utterer of memorable wise sayings is to be found among the records of John Cotton's flight from England. The leaders of the Puritan movement, not only Cotton but such others as Baynes, Preston, Goodwin, Davenport and Hooker, turned frequently to Dod for counsel and encouragement. Naturally his fame traveled in due time across the Atlantic. In a letter written from New England in 1634,[26] Cotton undertook to explain why he and Hooker had fled to the new world instead of remaining to bear witness to the truth under persecution at home. Before departing, he said, they had 'conferred with the chief of our people' on this very point, had in fact offered to continue preaching in England in spite of the certain danger of punishment. But their friends advised them to go and carry the word into the wilds of America. That, they said, was the part for young men, while the older generation should stick to their posts. 'Whilst Peter was young,' Cotton wrote, 'he might gird himself and go whither he would; but when he was old and unfit for travel, then indeed God called him rather to suffer himself to be girt of others, and led along to prison and to death.' The letter concludes with the tender of 'my dear affection' to several preachers at home, 'especially to Mr. Dod.'

This story is repeated more briefly but with more direct allusion to Dod in the life of Cotton written by his successor, John Norton.[27] 'Mr. Cotton,' we there learn, being informed of the steps taken against him by the High Commission, went into hiding 'conformably to the advice of many able heads and upright hearts (amongst whom that holy man Mr. Dod of blessed memory had a singular influence),' and presently fled not 'from the profession of the Truth but unto a more opportune place for the profession of it.' This account was incorporated verbatim into the sketch of Cotton which Clarke abstracted from Norton for publication in 1662.[28] Samuel Whiting, whose independent contemporary life of Cotton did not appear in print until the nineteenth century, adds nothing of significance to the matter.[29] But in Cotton Mather's account[30] of his great-grandfather's preparations for leaving England, the story has grown. Whether or not the author of *Magnalia Christi Americana* represents the facts as they occurred, we may safely say that he probably reports them as they were handed down in his family. John Dod is now the chief counselor of Cotton's flight. Moreover, the figure of the two Peters is put directly into his mouth, followed by a new touch, a characteristic homely similitude. 'Mr. Dod upon the whole, said thus unto him: I am old Peter, and therefore must stand still and bear the brunt; but you being young Peter, may go whether you will, and ought, being persecuted in one city, to flee unto another.' Then, to still the murmurs of those of Cotton's people who chose to stay behind in old Boston, he added: 'That the removing of a minister, was like the draining of a fish pond: the good fish will follow the water, but eels, and other baggage fish, will stick in the mud.'

The legendary character and the homely quality which we find in the stories about Dod is sustained in numerous parallel stories of other Puritan preachers who made their way into country districts before the revolution. We learn, for example, that everybody who went to see John Carter[31] and his wife 'would say, they had seen Adam and Eve, or some of the old Patriarchs.' They lived and dressed as plain as Jacob and Sarah, and had only utensils of wood, earth, pewter and brass, no plate. The wooden salt-dish had grown black with age and use. The 'House was a little Church.' Thrice a day the scriptures were read and the children and servants catechized and instructed. All comers were welcome. There was always a 'wholsome, full, and liberal Diet . . . and all fared alike: He and his wife did never think that his children and servants and poor folk did eat enough.' It was a merry saying among the godly that, 'If they would be a Cow or a Horse or a Hog or a Dog, they would choose Master Carter for their Master.' Samuel Crook[32] and his wife were almost equally famous for their hospitality. To Julines Herring's[33] sermons the people came from twenty towns and villages, flocking like doves. They came in the morning and stayed till night, 'some bringing their victuals from home with them and others going to a three-peny ordinary provided purposely for the refreshing of strangers.' Samuel Clarke[34] gives an equally charming picture of his own activities while preaching in Cheshire. Since there were few constant preachers in the neighborhood and yet enough 'Christian Purses' to maintain him by voluntary contribution, the godly came to him from six or seven miles about, 'Young and Old, Men and Women, Wet and Dry, Summer and Winter, to their very great pains and labor.' Between sermons they would spend the time repeating what the preacher had taught them, singing psalms and conferring upon the word. Once in three weeks 'all the Professors, both Men and Women, out of all the Country' gathered for a general conference 'by turns at all the richer mens Houses.' The procedure at these meetings is worth noting in full:

In the Morning when they first met, the Master of the Family began with Prayer, then was the question to be conferred of read, and the younger Christians first gave their answers, together with their proofs of Scripture for them; and then the more experienced Christians gathered up the other answers which were omitted by the former; and thus they continued until Dinner time, when having good provision made for them by the Master of the Family, they dined together with much chearfulness; after Dinner, having sung a Psalm, they returned to their Conference upon the other questions (which were three in all) till towards Evening; at which time, as the Master of the Family began, so he concluded with Prayer, and I gave them three new questions against their next Meeting; which being appointed for time and place, everyone repaired to his own home.

The material we have just been reviewing was not put into print until after 1640 and must obviously be taken not as a literal record of fact but as a representation of what, as time went on, the preachers and their people wished to believe had happened. Of its general veracity there can be little question. Of the effect of such teaching upon the popular mind, aside from any specific religious results, there can also be little doubt. The people were brought together. They learned to read, to use a book, to exchange ideas and experiences, to confer intellectually after their own fashion upon common problems, to partake of the exhilaration of discussion and self-expression. The perplexities of the individual were the focus of attention, but the individual got the relief which comes from bringing perplexities into the light and so discovering that they are but the common lot, for which, peradventure, there might be a common remedy. That the authorities should have come to regard such activities as dangerous to the status quo was not surprising. But their influence upon popular taste, imagination and modes of thought was in the long run to be no less important than the immediate disturbance they caused in the matter of government.

Inspired by the unobtrusive tutelage of Chaderton and by the example of such patriarchs as Hildersam and Dod, more and more of the oncoming generation of Cambridge youths were captivated by Puritan doctrine and the ardors of a preacher's life. Chief among these younger men was William Perkins,[35] whose writings exercised such an important influence upon the whole fraternity of spiritual preachers that we must reserve them for special attention at a subsequent point in our discussion. At this time, however, we must not fail to note Perkins' strategic significance, coming when he did, a man of brilliant intellect and potent speech, in the building up of the spiritual brotherhood. He entered Christ's College from Warwickshire in 1577 and probably took his Puritan bias from Chaderton, still one of the fellows of that foundation. He himself was elected fellow of Christ's about the time when Chaderton moved on to Emmanuel. At any rate, to him fell Chaderton's spiritual mantle in that, the most Puritan of the colleges up to that time. Tradition later invested his youth with the customary legend of wickedness before conversion. He was, it was remembered, profane, reckless and addicted to drink down to the day when he heard a woman in the street say to her fretful child, 'Hold your tongue, or I will give you to drunken Perkins yonder.'[36] That made him repent and turn to God. He was an able scholar, coursing swiftly through folios and mastering the intricate subtleties of theological science in a fashion that dazzled his fellows.[37] But he soon displayed no less a gift and passion for preaching. The mere sound of the word 'damn' uttered by him from the pulpit was enough to make men tremble for their sins. He began his career by holding forth to the condemned prisoners in the castle. So powerful and searching was he that he made one hardened lusty fellow come down from the very ladder to have his conscience probed and his soul converted before he should mount finally and step off into what he was, of course, assured in the nick of time would be an eternity of bliss. Naturally others besides the prisoners came to be edified by such performances, and Perkins was soon translated to the pulpit of Great St. Andrews. Thither both townspeople and university men flocked to hear the preacher. Voluntary contributions from the congregation and gifts from gentlemen of the neighborhood provided him with an income. Though he had to vacate his fellowship when he married, and though the authorities occasionally called him to account, he was able, by careful avoidance of controverted questions in his public discourse, to keep his pulpit undisturbed until his death at forty-four in 1602. When that as yet unregenerate Trinity undergraduate, John Cotton, heard the bell tolling for the great preacher's departure, his sinful heart secretly rejoiced that that voice would no longer trouble his conscience.[38] More brilliantly than any before him, Perkins displayed in his sermons those qualities which the spiritual brotherhood found most effective and tried most earnestly to emulate. He spoke as one having authority, and yet he made the word of God seem clear. No one could impeach his erudition, and no one could fail to understand what he said. 'In a word,' says Fuller, 'the Scholar could heare no learneder, the Townsmen plainer Sermons.'[39]

His pen, moreover, was as diligent and as skillful as his tongue. He kept the university printer busy while he lived, and after his death his disciples, numbering among them such figures as Samuel Ward, Thomas Draxe and Thomas Taylor, gathered up for publication or republication three tall volumes of his polemics, treatises and sermons. What he wrote in Latin they translated into English, and his English works Draxe turned into Latin for the enlightenment of foreigners. No books, it is fair to say, were more often to be found upon the shelves of succeeding generations of preachers, and the name of no preacher recurs more often in later Puritan literature. 'As for his Books,' Fuller observed half a century later, 'it is a miracle almost to conceive how thick they lye.'[40]

After Perkins, the stream of spiritual preachers rapidly rose to flood. Paul Baynes, another Christ's College man and probably a former pupil of Richard Rogers,[41] immediately succeeded him at Great St. Andrews. Though he lived only until 1617, this man was long remembered as 'holy Baynes.' He engaged in a controversy, famous for a day, with Bishop Downame on the vexed question of the divine right of prelacy,[42] but his real service to the Puritan cause was performed in the pulpit. Once he was accused before a bishop of keeping a conventicle, and some one in the court called out 'Speak, speak for yourself.' He spoke, and to such effect that 'a Noble-Man stood up and said, He speaks more like an Angel than a Man, and I dare not stay here to have a hand in any Sentence against him.'[43]

Richard Sibbes,[44] the son of a wheelwright in Suffolk, was sent in 1595 as a sizar to St. John's. He was, though just when we do not know, converted by Baynes, and rose to be a fellow and then in 1609 the preacher at his college. The following year he was invited by the minister and people of Trinity parish, Cambridge, to be their lecturer. Of the subscribers to the fund raised for paying Sibbes, some, it appears from the parish record, could sign only by making their mark. Yet from now on this Trinity lectureship in the town of Cambridge was to figure importantly as a stronghold of spiritual preaching in rivalry with the academic pulpit of St. Mary's. Sibbes suffered the loss of it and of his fellowship as well in 1615, but the reputation he had made there was such as at once to open for him a still more influential pulpit. The lawyers had long since learned to have no love for prelacy. By the favor of one of them, Sir Henry Yelverton, Sibbes was without delay made lecturer at Gray's Inn. In 1626 he assumed, in addition to his lectureship, the post of Master of St. Catherine's Hall at Cambridge. He also became perpetual curate of Trinity parish at Cambridge when Thomas Goodwin was forced to resign the lectureship at that church which Sibbes himself had formerly held. Sibbes's ability, his single-mindedness, his tact and resourcefulness won for him at Gray's Inn an audience of greater importance in the world than any of the brother-hood, except perhaps William Gouge, had yet attained. Lawyers, rich citizens and gentlemen, not to mention a multitude of common church-goers as well, were his adherents. His sermons were freely taken down, passed about and printed, early becoming something like classics of popular edification. Baxter as a boy was converted by one of them, bought by his father from a pedler at the door.[45] Izaak Walton bequeathed a copy of one to his son and of another to his daughter.[46] Needless to say, Sibbes's converts, the most famous being John Cotton and Hugh Peters, were many. He also kept up constant close communication with the other leading preachers of London, Cambridge and the country. The habit early arose among these men of editing one another's sermons for publication or at least of writing prefaces and testimonials for them, and Sibbes was as active as any in such offices of friendship and propaganda. Significant of the close cohesion of the whole group was the fact that, when John Preston's meteoric career came to its premature end, Sibbes and John Davenport in London and Thomas Goodwin and Thomas Ball in Cambridge collaborated in gathering up his recorded or reputed sermons, rejecting those they considered spurious and issuing the remainder to the press with dedications to various distinguished patrons and admirers. Of Sibbes's own sermons those contained in *The Bruised Reed and Smoaking Flax* appear to be the only ones published in his lifetime, but his death in 1635 was the occasion for Thomas Goodwin and Philip Nye, for John Sedgwick and Arthur Jackson, and no doubt for others to issue volume after volume within the next three or four years. Also significant of Sibbes's importance was his association with Davenport, Gouge and others, including certain lawyers and wealthy merchants, in the effort to establish a kind of corporate body for the purpose of raising funds to promote spiritual preaching throughout the kingdom. Though firm beneath his suave saintliness, he was such a sweet-natured man that Walton wrote of him

> Of this blest man, let this just praise be given,
> Heaven was in him before he was in heaven.[47]

He died just before chaos began.

During his years of preaching at Gray's Inn, Sibbes did not lack colleagues close at hand. The number of Puritan preachers in and about London steadily increased. The greatest of them at the time were, besides Sibbes himself, William Gouge and John Preston, both Cambridge men and both high in the councils of the spiritual brotherhood. Gouge[48] was, indeed, a Levite of the Levites. His mother was a daughter of a merchant named Nicholas Culverwel. Her brothers Samuel and Ezekiel were eminent divines. Her two sisters were married, the one to William Whitaker, Regius Professor of Divinity at Cambridge, Master of St. John's, Cambridge, and Chancellor of St. Paul's Cathedral; the other to Laurence Chaderton. His father was a wealthy gentleman of Stratford Bow, from whom he inherited a considerable fortune. In 1595 he went from Eton to King's College, Cambridge. He distinguished himself as a prodigy of learning and an 'Arch-Puritan,' and proceeded to the usual fellowship in 1602. A few years later the parish at Blackfriars in London found itself 'destitute of a preaching minister,' the incumbent being the aged Stephen Egerton, whom we have already encountered as the friend and editor of Richard Greenham. At this juncture 'Mr. Hildersham, a pious and powerfull Preacher, being in company among some of the better sort of Blackfriars, told them that there was one who lived in Stratford-

Bow and had no charge.'[49] Whereupon some of the good citizens of Blackfriars went down and heard Gouge of a Sunday, preaching, as he frequently did, for no pay in his native place. They chose him unanimously to be their lecturer and sometime later their regular minister. He remained with them from 1608 until his death in 1653.

At his first coming the parish had no church of its own, 'but by means that he used, the Church, the Church-porch, the Ministers house, and Church-yard (all which they had before upon courtesie) were purchased.'[50] Then by collections taken at his lectures and among his friends, he set about raising 1500 £ for rebuilding and enlarging the edifice. It is noted that no appeal was made to the sovereign for 'briefs' or letters patent authorizing these collections. Gouge knew how to raise the money he needed by his own unaided efforts. Multiply 1500 by at least four, and one may form some notion of the carnal wealth which he was able to tap by his pious and powerful preaching.

More room for Gouge at Blackfriars was clearly needed. Except for an annual vacation in the country, he preached habitually for thirty-five years, twice on Sunday and once every Wednesday forenoon. So great was the confluence of his hearers that 'he was wont (before he began his Sermons) to observe what Pues were empty and to command his Clark to open them for the ease of those who thronged in the Isles.'[51] The godly from his own and other parishes, and the unenlightened as well, thronged to Blackfriars: young ministers, ministers of other city churches, 'pious and juditious Gentlemen of the Inns of Court, besides many well-disposed Citizens.'[52] 'When the godly Christians of those times came out of the Country unto London, they thought not their businesse done unlesse they had been at Blackfriars lecture.'[53] He even courted danger by admitting to the communion service with his congregation 'the old godly Puritanes . . . who could not either at all, or at least purely (in regard of Superstitious gestures, genuflexions, etc.) enjoy that ordinance at home.'[54] Married but once, he had out of thirteen children eight who lived to grow up, and 'all his sons he brought up to learning, desiring that they might have all been imployed in the Ministery.'[55] More important still, God was said to have made him 'an aged Father in Christ, and to beget many Sons and Daughters unto righteousnesse, for thousands have been converted and built up by his Ministry.'[56] Thus we derive from the contemporary accounts of Gouge, even when we discount the exaggeration of a funeral sermon and a filial biography, our most detailed picture of a Puritan pastor and preacher among his people. He engaged in the other activities of the spiritual brotherhood as well. Like Sibbes he helped to usher into print the edifying works of other preachers. In his holidays he wrote great tomes for the instruction of those seeking the light, more arid on the whole than those of some of his colleagues but taking an honored place in the literature of godliness. As the scheme for financing the pentecostal planting of godly ministers throughout the land took shape, he was, of course, to be found with Sibbes on the board of trustees, and in due time he also took his place among the divines of the Westminster Assembly.

Nine years younger than Gouge, John Cotton[57] went to Trinity College in 1598 and progressed rapidly to be fellow and head lecturer at Emmanuel. He is reported to have testified that the preaching of William Perkins worked strongly upon him but that he resisted the stirrings of his heart and was not converted until sometime later when he heard Sibbes preach on regeneration. His sermons won a reputation at Cambridge, as occasion offered for him to preach at St. Mary's, for 'Invention, Elegancy, Purity of Stile, Ornaments of Rhetorick, Elocution, and Oratorious beauty of the whole,' but of this he soon repented. Invited again to the pulpit of St. Mary's, 'his speech and preaching was not with the enticing words of man's wisdom but in the demonstration of the Spirit and of power.' The throng of students, whom 'an Athenian Itch after some new thing as to the Ornaments of Rhetorick and abstruser notions of Philosophy' had brought flocking to hear him, was obviously disappointed with the change the Spirit and the influence of Sibbes had worked in Cotton, and the preacher retired to his chamber, feeling, it would seem, rather flat. 'But lo . . . Master Preston knocks at his door, and coming in, acquaints him with his spiritual condition, and how it pleased God to speak effectually unto his heart by that Sermon.'[58] Cotton's other services to the cause in England require little notice here. The story of his twenty-year ministry at Boston in Lincolnshire, whither he went from Cambridge in 1612, of his effect upon the people there, particularly upon that remarkable and later on so troublesome follower, Mrs. Hutchinson, has been made familiar by the historians of the beginnings of Massachusetts. We may note here merely the evidence of his intimate relations with other members of the brotherhood of which he was regarded as a shining light. Like the rest, he reverenced John Dod. John Preston recommended his pupils to finish their studies under Cotton and himself frequently visited him in Lincolnshire. Following the direction in which Preston was pointing at the time of his death, he veered away from orthodox Calvinist doctrine and, in company with such men as Thomas Goodwin, Philip Nye and John Davenport, from strict presbyterian notions of church government. When finally he fled from his post at Boston rather than conform to Laud's regulations, he took shelter for a time with Davenport and others of the brotherhood in London and then sailed for America in the same ship with Thomas Hooker and Samuel Stone, also Cambridge men, eminent in the fellowship of the spirit. They preached to one another and the ship's company all the way to Massachusetts. They found more of their Cambridge friends, Roger Williams among them, when they arrived on the other side of the water. Davenport and Hooker made their way to Connecticut, Williams to Rhode Island, and Cotton settled in the Cambridge which presently arose in the new world.

John Preston[59] was a convert of no mean consequence. Brilliant, ambitious, extremely energetic, poor but of good family, he was the kind of man likely to make his mark not in the church but in the world. He entered King's in 1604 as a sizar. But 'these Prestons though removed from their native soil and much impaired in their revinue retained yet the garb and metal of their Ancestors, they carried themselves and were accounted Gentlemen; something there was in this young Prestons spirit that was not vulgar.'[60] He soon improved his position by shifting to Queen's where, only five years after his entrance to the university, he was elected a fellow. While a 'Junior Sophister,' he 'looked high, and grew acquainted with those that were Gentile, and fancied state affairs and Courtship, . . . thought it below him to be a Minister, and the study of Divinity a kind of honest silliness.' For a brief time it seemed as though he might find sufficient backing to be a merchant; that failing, he returned to his studies, resolved, however, that if he must be shut up to the muses, 'to be no ordinary Servant to them.' He plunged into natural philosophy, making himself perfect in all the dark untrodden paths of Aristotle's physics and metaphysics: 'what broke others teeth was nuts to him.' He was busy with medicine and astrology when about 1611 he heard Cotton preach at St. Mary's and found his footsteps led as it were by the Holy Spirit to the preacher's chamber door. His low opinion of the ministry and his worldly ambition suddenly vanished. 'For he saw an over-ruling gravity and Majesty in that Sermon, that he thought had been impossible to Pulpits . . . For these were higher things that now were offered to him, concernments of eternal influence, which nothing could divert that he had studied hitherto.' So he resolved to be a preacher like Cotton and flung himself into the study of divinity, reading 'Master Calvin, whose very stile and language much affected him,' reading also Aquinas even on the barber's stool—if hair fell upon the page, he blew it off and read on. About the same time an incident occurred to test his new-made resolution, an incident such as only that age could have produced. King James in his character of learnedest fool in Christendom visited his university in Cambridge in 1615 and sat in judgment upon a disputation arranged especially in his honor concerning the question whether or not dogs reason. The appointed disputants were Preston and Matthew Wren, a future bishop destined in less happy days to receive a full broadside from Prynne.[61] In the course of the performance, Preston turned what seemed a position of disadvantage in the argument into a triumph of logic-chopping that tickled exquisitely the ribs of King Solomon. James loved his dogs, and a man who loves his dogs is always persuaded of their more than human intelligence. Preston converted his case into an irrefutable demonstration of the wit of the king's own pack. The breath-taken bystanders suddenly saw in Preston a made man. Stranger things were happening in that strange court. 'It was easie to discern that the King's Hound had opened a way for Master Preston at the Court, if he were willing,' and many of the great ones present were eager in their offers of assistance. The astute Fulke Greville gave him a pension.

Yet, though courtiers might wonder that he 'did not bite,' Preston would not be diverted from the pulpit to the court. Had he not felt the overruling gravity and majesty of spiritual preaching? He launched, consequently, upon an extraordinary career of proselytizing and wire-pulling in the interests of the Puritan cause. Nothing could have demonstrated more vividly the influence of the unacknowledged brotherhood of spiritual preachers over the uneasy public of the sixteen-twenties. Preston, though faithful in all respects to the cause he espoused, never abandoned for a moment his penchant for political chess-playing and took every possible advantage of the access to favor which his dashing flattery of the King had opened up to him. The occasion was timely, since the rising Villiers chose to play for Puritan support and was willing to use Preston for the purpose. He had as well other favorers among the great: some who leaned toward the Puritans like Fulke Greville, presently Lord Brooke, or the Earl of Warwick or Lord Saye and Sele; others like the Marquis of Hamilton, who probably thought merely that Preston might be a coming man worth weaning from the popular side. At all events, the fellow of Queen's advanced with dazzling rapidity by tactics that did not escape the notice of many and eventually the sarcastic comments of Thomas Fuller. He was promoted from post to post at Cambridge. He was consulted at court on questions of religion—or perhaps we had better say of religious politics. The Marquis of Hamilton did not succeed in persuading James to take Preston for one of his royal chaplains, but the monarch condescended to hear him preach and made him chaplain to the Prince of Wales. He was with the prince and the Duke of Buckingham at the time of the king's death in 1625, and rode up from Theobald's with them in a closed coach, 'applying comfort,' says Fuller, 'now to one now to the other on so sad occasion.'[62] He was, it is plain, a far more clever man than either, for when all was done he had used them for his purpose and had not submitted to theirs.

For Preston made his personal influence count for the advance of preaching while at the same time devoting the major part of his extraordinary energy to the pulpit. By a quick maneuver, a ride to London and a call on the right people, he got his candidate, Davenant, made Master of Queen's in 1614. He himself became dean and catechist. His sacrifice of worldly ambition helped his reputation with the godly. He grew acquainted with Dod and Hildersam. 'Men thought him meet for to be trusted with the care of youth; and many had their eyes upon him for their Sons or Friends.' Fuller pictures his chamber buzzing with pupils.[63] He undertook to 'go through a body of divinity' in the college chapel, and some honest townsmen dropped in one day to listen. The next day there were more, and soon so many, both 'Townsmen and the Scholars of other Colleges,' that the fellows when they arrived would find the place full. The result was a complaint to the vice-chancellor: 'it was not safe for any man to be thus adored and doted on, unlesse they had a mind to cry up Puritanisme, which would in a short time pull them down.' So a stop was put to the attendance of outsiders at Queen's, and the scholars were ordered to attend only at St. Mary's. But Preston took to reading divinity to his students at three o'clock in the afternoon both Sundays and weekdays, and again both townsmen and scholars of other colleges wanted to hear him. For their accommodation, he began holding forth at St. Botolph's, and the tempest thus aroused reached even the ears of the king. Nevertheless, he was considered for the Lady Margaret divinity professorship, but declined that honor because, it is said, John Dod persuaded him that 'English preaching was like to work more and win more souls to God.'

The task of persuasion could not have been difficult, considering the opportunity that presently came to him. He was offered in 1622 the post of lecturer at Lincoln's Inn. 'It suited with him to have an opportunity to exercise his Ministery in a considerable and intelligent Congregation, where he was assured many Parliament men and others of his best acquaintance would be his hearers.' The chapel of the Inn was enlarged after his coming to provide for the numbers that came to hear him. Foundations, observes his biographer, were laid 'that will not easily be ruined.' But he desired to continue at the same time to preach at Cambridge; 'a preacher in the University doth *generare patres*, beget begetters.' There followed an academic intrigue which effected the retirement of Chaderton and the election of Preston, who still retained his lectureship at Lincoln's Inn, as Master of Emmanuel. There was, to be sure, a statute of the college which required the continuous residence of the master unless prevented by necessity, but all agreed that the compulsion upon Preston to be absent in London a good part of the time was an act of God. Meanwhile, the townsmen of Cambridge had not forgotten him. Two years later, in 1624, they proposed to offer him the lectureship at Trinity once held by Sibbes, 'and great care was taken to increase the stipend from fourty or fifty pounds *per annum* unto four score.' Influential persons at court so disliked this proposal that, it is said, the promise of a bishopric or any other preferment he might wish was held forth to Preston if he would decline the election. But he preferred to preach at Trinity, and by the influence of Buckingham, who was still wooing the Puritans, he was confirmed in his lectureship. Thus flying from pulpit to pulpit in London and Cambridge and taking his due turns preaching at court, Preston burned out the last two or three years of his life. 'As he had a short race to run, so he made speed and did much in little time.' In 1628, the victim at forty-one of 'a consumption,' he betook himself to Northamptonshire to die near John Dod.

The posthumous history of Preston's sermons was hardly less indicative than the man's personal career of his influence, his reputation and the devotion and close association of the spiritual preachers. Except for a treatise on *Life Eternall,* the manuscript of which he gave to his friends Goodwin and Ball when he was dying, he had small time while he lived to prepare anything for the press. He spoke as a rule extemporaneously, and his sermons were taken down by auditors in church to be copied, recopied and circulated in the widening circles of the converted. Immediately upon his death these began to appear in print. Preston left to his disciples, Thomas Goodwin and Thomas Ball, the duty of seeing to the publication of sermons of his that were extant in manuscript about Cambridge, and to Richard Sibbes and John Davenport those circulating about London.[64] These editors complained more than once 'of the injurious dealing of such as for private gaine have published what they can get, howsoever taken,'[65] without consulting the author's representatives, and they urged all persons possessing copies of sermons supposed to be Preston's to bring them in for authoritative editorial judgment. In 1648 it seemed worth William Jemmat's while to publish for popular use a condensed version of the whole. Fugitive and spurious pieces continued to appear as late as 1658 and as far away as Edinburgh. Of the acknowledged works, edition after edition, in one instance as many as twelve, were put forth in the dozen years between Preston's death and the Long Parliament, each with a dedication addressed to some nobleman or other honorable person deemed friendly to the author and his cause. The patrons chosen by Preston's editors, such men as the Earl of Warwick, the Earl of Pembroke, Lord Saye and Sele, Henry Lawrence, Sir

Richard Knightley, form an impressive list, significant of the support which the preachers were able to evoke and ominous for the future. Oliver Cromwell was a student at Sidney Sussex and Milton at Christ's in Preston's time.

Of all Preston's disciples—and he appears to have had many—the most important was Thomas Goodwin, the friend of John Cotton, the most decisive figure and the great disturber of the Westminster Assembly, the author of an autobiography worthy in its way to be compared to the most notable self-revelations of the Puritan soul.[66] The story Goodwin gives us of the inner struggles of his youth permits us to see what must have been the effect of Puritan teaching upon more than a few sensitive, imaginative boys in the Cambridge of the early decades of the seventeenth century. At the age of six, he says, he began to feel the workings of the spirit in him and to weep for his sins. A servant in his grandfather's household in Norfolk saw to it that the torments of hell were made known to him by the time he was seven. In 1613, a twelve-year-old child, he was sent to Christ's College, Cambridge, to prepare for the church. There were in the college, he found, 'six Fellows that were great Tutors, who professed Religion after the strictest sort, then called Puritans,' and who explained 'Ursin's Catechize' to their godly pupils 'on Saturday-night with Chamber-Prayers.' 'Besides, the Town was then filled with the discourse of the Power of Mr. Perkins his Ministry, still fresh in Mens Memories,' though Perkins was already ten years in the grave, 'and Dr. Ames . . . not long before my time had by the Urgency of the Master been driven both from the College and University.' Sibbes was preaching at Trinity parish church, 'whose lecture the Puritans frequented.' Most important for the boy, however, 'was the powerful and steady Example of one of those godly Fellows in the College, Mr. Bently,' and of 'Mr. Price, who then was of the University.' The strivings of spirit which under these influences led to the lad's conversion can be clearly followed. At Easter in his fourteenth year he was admitted to his first communion, and immediately began making great preparations for taking the sacrament again at Whitsuntide. He went to hear Sibbes. He read Calvin's *Institutes*, 'and O how sweet was the reading of some Parts of that Book to me!' He looked upon the holy men of Christ's College, 'and how affected was I, that I should go to Heaven with them!' He thought that, if he could but receive the sacrament at the approaching Whitsunday, 'I should be so confirm'd that I should never fall away.' The day came and he was in his place in the college chapel, but unluckily he was a little fellow, 'the least in the whole University then and for divers Years.' Before the service began, his tutor, Mr. Power, noticing his presence, sent him out before the whole college, much ashamed.

Goodwin's later judgment no doubt approved what Mr. Power had done. He was not only too young, but he was as yet insufficiently tried and not yet effectually called. His decisive temptation and true regeneration were still to come. The precise form they took was probably colored somewhat in Goodwin's recollection by later convictions and preoccupations. What wiles could Satan more appropriately apply to one who, it turned out, became the great independent of the Westminster Assembly and a pillar of the most orthodox non-conformity than first the temptation to trust natural reason rather than revealed grace and second the temptation to seek worldly preferment by the cultivation of an ornate pulpit style instead of the service of God in the preaching of plain English? Dashed, as he well might be, at the disappointment inflicted by his tutor, he gave up looking for God. He left off praying, went no more to hear Sibbes, ceased studying sound divinity, fell back into hardness of heart and profaneness. Not that he took to 'the common Sins of Drunkeness or Whoredom, whereunto I had Temptations and Opportunities enough'; the lust that attracted him was 'the Ambition of Glory and Praise.' If God would but give him the pleasure, the credit and the preferment he desired and only not damn him at last, 'let him keep Heaven to himself.' In this mood, Goodwin turned from the lectures at Trinity Church to the 'flaunting' discourses, so much applauded at the moment, of Richard Senhouse, 'the eminentest Farrago of all sorts of Flowers of Wit, that are found in any of the Fathers, Poets, Histories, Similitudes, or whatever has the Elegancy of Wit in it.'[67] He set himself to such studies as would enable him to preach after this mode and win glory and praise. They might talk of their Puritan powerful preaching, but he would like to see the man who could trouble his conscience. Lusting thus after vainglory, he fell into Arminian vain confidence in human will and reason.

He thought he did not need to wait for God's imperious call to be saved. He could repent when and as often as he wished and so lay hold on salvation at his convenience. But the will of God was not to be so easily evaded. God was lying in wait for Goodwin. One day as the boy was going to be merry with his companions at Christ's College, whence he had removed to St. Catherine's Hall, he heard the bell at St. Edmund's tolling for a funeral. One of the lads with him pressed him to enter and hear the sermon. He hung back 'for I lov'd not preaching, especially not that kind of it which good Men used.' Nevertheless, seeing many scholars entering, he went in. Besides, the preacher was Thomas Bainbridge, Master of Christ's, 'a witty Man.' He spoke of repentance, and at his words the real change in the heart of the young man commenced. The date is carefully noted in his autobiography, 'Monday the second of Octob. 1620 in the Afternoon.' Preston soon finished what Bainbridge had begun by convincing the lad that Senhouse's way of preaching was vain and unedifying.

Before this time, Goodwin says, 'God was to me as a wayfaring Man, who came and dwelt for a Night and made me Religious for a Fit but then departed from me.' 'In a great Frost you shall see where the Sun shines hot, the Ice drops, and the Snow melts, and the Earth grows slabby; but 'tis a particular Thaw, only where the Sun shines, not a general Thaw of all things that are frozen.' Natural reason had so far enabled him to discover his 'grosser Acts against Knowledg,' but the light now suddenly vouchsafed him 'gave discovery of my Heart in all my Sinnings, carried me down to see the Inwards of my Belly (as Solomon speaks) and searched the lower Rooms of my Heart, as it were with Candles.' What he saw there was, of course, sin, the innate propensity of all flesh to evil, the original corruption of man's nature. It was, he said, 'as if I had in the heat of Summer lookt down into the Filth of a Dungeon, where by a clear Light and a piercing Eye I discern'd Millions of crawling living things in the midst of that Sink and liquid Corruption.' Thus suddenly his sins came before him and would not be put out of mind. He was in the hands of a greater power than himself or any man, a power, however, which revealed to him thus suddenly the hell within in order as suddenly to save him from it. God 'saith of and to my Soul, Yea live, yea live I say.'

The Word of Promise which he let fall into my Heart, and which was but as it were softly whisper'd to my Soul; and as when a Man speaks afar off, he gives a still, yet a certain sound, or as one hath expressed the Preachings of the Gospel by the Apostles; that God whispered the Gospel out of Sion, but the sound thereof went forth over the whole Earth: So this speaking of God to my Soul, altho it was but a gentle Sound, yet it made a noise over my whole Heart, and filled and possessed all the Faculties of my whole Soul. God took me aside, and as it were privately said unto me, do you now turn to me, and I will pardon all your Sins tho never so many, as I forgave and pardoned my Servant Paul, and convert you unto me as I did Mr. Price who was the most famous Convert and Example of Religion in Cambridge.

Goodwin's vocation was now sealed. He trusted no longer to natural reason, and he lived to argue against free will with his namesake, John Goodwin. He lusted no more after vainglory, 'casting down all those childish Imaginations of Preferment, such as Scholars do generally aim at and promise to themselves, and to attain which they make their Aim and the Card of their Life they sail by.' All these fell, and, concludes this scorner of vain ornaments of speech, 'like Bubbles broke and vanish'd to Air.' Senhouse soon became a bishop and lived just long enough to preach King Charles's coronation sermon. Goodwin remained fellow of Catherine Hall while making a reputation in and about Cambridge as a preacher of power worthy to be compared to Preston himself. When the latter died, Goodwin succeeded him as Trinity lecturer.

In the light of later events, the choice Goodwin made seems, even for an ambitious man, let alone a saint, probably not unjustified. He became one of the most active preachers and publishers of sermons. Conscience made him surrender his post at Trinity in 1634 rather than conform to Laud's will. After a few years of obscurity,[68] he settled as pastor to the English congregation at Arnheim in Holland. In 1640 he was back in an English pulpit, preaching to a 'gathered congregation' at St. Dunstan's-in-the-East. He had become, perhaps persuaded by John Cotton, a believer in the independent 'way.' Parliament put him into the Westminster Assembly. There, when the ranks of the preachers divided fatally on the question of presbyterian versus independent church government, he was to be found holding the fort of debate for independency until the triumph of Cromwell and his army settled the issue. In 1650 he was made president of Magdalen in a purified Oxford.

With Thomas Goodwin we may conclude this account of typical leaders among the Puritan preachers. It would have to be very much extended if it were to include all the Cambridge men, not to mention the Oxonians, whom Chaderton, Perkins, Baynes, Sibbes, Preston and the rest inspired to go forth and live the life of saints, to preach, mend broken souls, convert sinners, write and print books. High on the list would come John Downame, author of popular expositions of Puritan doctrine which won esteem not far below that accorded to Perkins. Richard Bernard and Thomas Taylor are of particular interest for their exploitation of images of the spiritual life in the manner that Bunyan was to follow. Important too were those intellectual fathers of independency, William Bradshaw and William Ames. William Bridge, Sidrach Simpson, Jeremiah Burroughs and Philip Nye, an Oxford man, are of interest for the part they took in standing with Thomas Goodwin for independency in 1643. Closely allied with these men were the members of the brotherhood who followed Cotton to America, Thomas Hooker, Richard Mather, Samuel Stone, John Davenport and, by no means to be omitted, Roger Williams and Hugh Peters. That gadfly of the more orthodox brethren, John Goodwin, and that strange genius, part poet and part whirling dervish, John Saltmarsh, were in their beginnings also of the fraternity. Neither can we exclude the initiators of separatism, such men as Robert Browne, Francis Johnson, John Robinson and John Smyth, all of whom sprang from the same spiritual stock at Cambridge which produced the most godly divines of the presbyterian and the independent factions. As for the 'mechanick' preachers, the Muggletons, Bunyans and George Foxes, they came forward only later as part of the whirlwind sown by their better-educated predecessors.

The contributions of these men and others like them to the development of Puritan thought and expression will receive attention later in these pages. Those whose careers and personal connections have just been described were the immediate spiritual and intellectual begetters of the Puritan revolution. One final evidence of their address and resourcefulness in advancing their cause must be mentioned before we pass on to consider the literature which they produced or inspired. After the fiasco of the Hampton Court Conference, they took no direct steps of any importance toward gaining control over the administrative machinery of the church. But as their actual control over preaching advanced, they sought to give to that control something like corporate organization in order to secure for it permanent financial support. This attempt took shape in the form of a society led by William Gouge and Richard Sibbes for raising funds and establishing a kind of foundation for the regular extension of Puritan preaching throughout the country. The chiefs of the spiritual order saw in the existing badly distributed provision for popular religious instruction both a scandal and an opportunity. The distribution of churches and parishes went back to far older times and different conditions. Social changes and the shifting of population left large numbers of people, particularly in towns, ill supplied with the services of religion. The endowed livings of the church, because of the prevailing system of appointing clergymen to the cure of souls, were in many cases—at any rate in the opinion of the Puritan reformers—in most improper hands. The persons in whom the right of presentation was vested did not as a rule find it to their interest to institute changes that would seriously alter the terms of the patronage at their disposal. Moreover, in more than a third of the parishes the income drawn from the glebe lands and the tithes was diverted to extraneous purposes.[69] Some of this went to the support of bishops, cathedrals and colleges, but a considerable proportion had been impropriated to laymen. Consequently, as the spiritual preachers looked about them, they saw many hungry sheep unfed by the word. In prosperous and aroused communities, something might be done through the willingness of patrons or the establishment of lectureships, but this would not suffice for all. The result was that a group of reformers in London set themselves up in 1626 as a kind of committee, adjudged finally to be an illicit corporation, for the purpose of buying in the lay impropriations and of using the income of those endowments for their own purposes.[70] The committee or society consisted of twelve 'feoffees,' four clergymen, four lawyers, and four citizens. The clergymen, in addition to Gouge and Sibbes, were John Davenport, Vicar of St. Stephen's in Coleman Street, later of New

Haven, Connecticut, and Charles Offspring, for over forty years rector of St. Antholin's. Of the lawyers two were from Lincoln's Inn, one from Gray's Inn, and one from the Middle Temple. The citizens were, according to Fuller, men 'who commanded rich coffers.'[71] Until they were suppressed in 1633, the twelve actively busied themselves upon a project which was aimed in effect to secure for the spiritual brotherhood control of an important part of the patronage of the church. Within seven years they raised some five or six thousand pounds by contributions from the faithful and loans from themselves. With this money they bought up thirteen impropriations. They did this, as they professed and as the representatives of authority bitterly complained, not to restore the use of the funds thus secured to the parishes from which they were drawn but, as Gouge's biographer said, 'to plant a powerfull Ministery in Cities and Market-Towns here and there in the Country for the greater propagation of the Gospell.'[72] Fuller cites Heylyn as saying that 'having bought an Impropriation, they parcelled it out into annual Pensions of 40 or 50 l. *per annum*, and therewith salaried some Lecturers in such Market-Towns where people had commonly less to do and consequently were more apt to Faction and Innovation, . . . it being observed in England that those who hold the Helm of the Pulpit alwayes steer the peoples hearts as they please.'[73]

The authorities, when finally aroused by Laud, became justly alarmed at all this. It was estimated that within fifty years the feoffees would have secured all the impropriations available for purchase. They insisted that they appointed only such preachers as under license from the given bishop were conformable to the regulations of the church. But Laud, not without reason, apprehended that the 'end was to take away the right of patronages from the Church, to make those Ministers they preferred independent on the Bishops & dependent wholly on them, and to engross most Ecclesiasticall preferments into their own hands.'[74] If Gouge, Sibbes and their associates had been permitted to continue this work uninterrupted, it is possible, if not highly probable, that the English church, which had so long successfully resisted Puritan reform, would have been reformed by the spiritual brotherhood from within, bishops or no bishops. Such indeed, at least down to the Restoration, continued to be the hope of the majority of the Puritan clergy.

The causes within Puritanism itself which rendered all such hopes in the end vain need not concern us at this point. We saw at the beginning of the last chapter how, although the general imposition of Puritan discipline from Whitgift's time to Laud's was prevented, nevertheless Puritan preaching steadily extended itself from pulpit to pulpit. It began quietly enough among such contemporaries of Cartwright's at Cambridge as Greenham and Rogers, men who were content to preach the word as they might find freedom so to do and who chose not to fight against the government. Of course, the brotherhood of preachers bred its agitators and radicals. But it continued to grow chiefly under cover of the law through the work of such men as we have seen. The nearer 1640 approached the more numerous the pulpits these men filled with their proselytes. The university at Cambridge was largely dominated by their influence. Through the system of lectureships and with the support of powerful patrons, they commanded the most strategic preaching posts in and about London. By their society for buying up impropriations, they were laying foundations for setting up new posts wherever there might be found people to be persuaded. Yet, important as all these activities were, there was still another of even more far-reaching consequence. The spiritual preachers were converting their hearers not only to godliness but also to the appetite for reading godly books, which the preachers were not slow to supply to the booksellers or the booksellers to the public. Thus they were nursing the pulpit's greatest rival, the press, by providing it with an ever-growing market for its products and at the same time with an apparently inexhaustible supply of marketable material. By 1640 the number of books circulating among the people had increased and accumulated beyond anything that had ever been known in England before, and a prodigious amount of that material came from the pens and brains of the Puritan preachers. Truly the spiritual brotherhood from Greenham and Dod through Chaderton and Perkins to Gouge and Goodwin had not reformed the church, but they had accomplished something of perhaps even greater consequence. They had created a literature in English setting forth to an increasingly restive populace a doctrine of faith and courage and a way of life calling for self-expression, self-confidence and self-exertion.

III

The Calling of the Saints

WITHIN two generations of the time when Thomas Cartwright was
expelled from Cambridge for his advocacy of reform, the Puritan
preachers had so increased in numbers and influence that the ruling
powers in church and state had either to suppress them or give way
before them. What is the explanation of their rise? Discontent in all
classes of society, aggravated by the political incompetence of the first
two Stuarts, supplied opportunity which the preachers knew how to
turn to the advantage of their cause. But this fact, though important,
does not by itself account for the role which Laud found the press and
the Puritan pulpit so freely exercising when he rose to the primacy
in 1633. The preachers could have made little of their opportunity if
they had lacked ideas or the skill to persuade their public that their
ideas offered sure remedy for the troubles of life. We must therefore
next inquire what it was the preachers preached, how they preached
and with what effect. In no other way can we truly understand the
Puritan Revolution or those forces of thought and imagination and
that way of life which have so long prevailed among English-speaking
people.

First of all we must endeavor to grasp the meaning of the central
dogma of Puritanism as it applied to the life of men in the seventeenth
century.[1] This was a conception of an all-embracing determinism,
theologically formulated as the doctrine of predestination. It is a conception which, especially in its postulates of an absolute human depravity and a purely arbitrary human redemption, has often seemed absurd
to the common sense and abhorrent to the humanitarian sentiment of
later generations. In these pages we are not concerned with such reac-
tions. Believing in predestination, the Puritan preachers persuaded our
forefathers to trust in nothing but God and the spirit within themselves
and to defy the devil and all his minions. In doing this, they were not
fools or clowns or bigots or pedants but academic intellectuals trained
in the approved science and the accustomed arts of their time and

addressing themselves to what they took to be the supreme need of the people of their time. With what ideas they could command they confronted the confusion and demoralization of a society which had been racked by the tremendous changes of the preceding century, and with what skill and force of character they possessed they attempted to implant courage, discipline and order. They took the doctrine of predestination as their dialectical weapon because it seemed to them to offer the most rational assurance for restored confidence in the future of mankind.

That Puritan doctrine was indebted to Calvin hardly requires to be said, but we have proceeded only a little way toward understanding the Puritan preachers when we have said that they were Calvinists. As Englishmen, they were Calvinists with a difference. In Geneva and in Scotland, as compared to England, the triumph of the Calvinist reformers had been quick and complete. Hence in those countries they soon gained a relatively free hand to impose their formula upon the whole social structure. No such opportunity to re-establish order throughout the church fell to the English Calvinists. Uniformity of belief and discipline was actually obtainable in England only within the sect or independent congregation and at the price of separation from the rest of society. The non-conformists and dissenters, though too weak and few to enforce their will upon others, did manage precariously to get their way among themselves, and those of them who were able to escape to New England were able to protect themselves from disunion if they wished by again handing heretics over to the secular arm or by turning them out into the wilderness. Thus in Geneva, in Scotland, in Massachusetts, and under peculiar limitations among the English sects, Calvinists of one type or another were able to achieve a reformed society in which differences of opinion were checked and uniformity maintained. But throughout England, except under the handicap of persecution, they were permitted to do nothing of the kind. There they had to accommodate themselves year after year as best they could to that peculiar condition which had been set up by the politic Elizabeth and which compelled Englishmen, the more surely the longer it endured, to the maintenance not of religious uniformity but of some sort and degree of toleration as the sine qua non of political security and economic prosperity. The reformers, then, unless they were willing to risk ostracism, exile or persecution, had to refrain from too directly assailing the government or their fellow subjects. They were in no position to suppress the people who did not fall in with their ideas, and had to advance their ideas as best they could by the peaceful arts of persuasion. Hence the English Calvinists found that all they could do to advance their cause, though they were for some two generations permitted to do that, was to plead for it by the help of whatever gifts of mind and utterance they happened to possess. Under such conditions they produced, at any rate prior to 1640, no great public leaders, lawgivers and theologians of the stature of Knox and Calvin, but a host of popular propagandists who exploited as never before the potentialities of pulpit and press. Thus Calvinism in England did not lead to a swift reconstruction of the church but to the creation of a literature which expressed a way of life that eventually far transcended all ecclesiastical and even all religious bounds.

The history of Puritan thought in England is primarily the history of the setting forth of the basic doctrine of predestination in terms calculated to appeal to the English populace. It is at the same time necessarily a history of the effect of popular reaction upon the doctrine itself and upon the modes of its presentation. Strictly speaking, English Puritanism in the large may continue to be called Calvinistic chiefly as a matter of historical reference. Actually, the preachers, Calvinist though they were in varying degrees, referred as often to St. Augustine as to the author of the *Institutes* but were chary on principle of citing any merely human authorities whatsoever. The French reformer's positive, clear, dogmatic intelligence supplied them with ideas but not on the whole with a model of discourse which they chose to imitate when they mounted the pulpit. The nature of the task to which they addressed themselves is exactly set forth by John Downame in his appropriately entitled *Guide to Godlynesse*:

I could find no one part of Divinity more profitable, in these times . . . then that which consisteth more in experience and practice, then in theory and speculation; and more principally tendeth to the sanctification of the heart, then the informing of the iudgement and the increasing of knowledge; and to the stirring up of all to the practice of that they know in the duties of a godly life, and in bringing foorth the fruits of faith in new obedience; then to fit them for discourse.[2]

Calvin's most important effect upon the preachers was to send them posting back to scripture, particularly to the epistles of Paul, to Paul's life as recorded in Acts, and so to the gospels and to the rest of holy writ. Consequently there is less of the manner and spirit of Calvin in the preachers' lives and writings than of the apostle to the Gentiles. They were following the latter's example in essaying to adapt their teaching to the spiritual condition of all men who felt themselves excluded, aggrieved, hampered and oppressed by the special privileges, the vested interests, the class prejudices of the existing order. They offered to all such the comfort that he offers in every age to the unrecognized and disallowed. There is no respect of persons, Paul said, with God, no real difference between Jew and Gentile. This spiritual equalitarianism, implicit in every word the preachers spoke, seized upon the imaginations of men who, no matter what their social rank, had reason to be discontented with the Stuart regime in church and state, and it thus became the central force of revolutionary Puritanism. Over against the inequalities of an indurated social system and an obsolete form of government, the people learned from preachers inspired by Paul to bear in mind the equality of all men before God and presently to draw the obvious practical inference that God before whom all men are leveled is sure in his own time to uplift the low and humble the great.

The famous doctrine of predestination, of salvation by faith alone, was for the Puritan classes but the rationalized statement of this sentiment, a clear dogma answering with irrefutable logic to men's emotional need for something by which to be convinced. The modern mind, inexpert in such modes of reasoning, turns away from the intricate dialectic by which the logic of predestination was upon occasion presented, and we may well do the same here. The preachers themselves asserted again and again that only so much doctrine was important to be understood as could be understood by men of least knowledge and capacity when set forth in plain English. What, therefore, is important for us to understand is less how learned doctors argued among themselves than what they succeeded in conveying to the people, not what their doctrine was but what it meant and did. Let us then disregard the technical treatises and systems of divinity, numerous though they were, and fasten our attention upon the popular sermons and tracts which the preachers offered to the common public in even greater abundance. First of all, we must note, they urged the people to base their understanding of the word of God upon Paul's Epistle to the Romans. If one began one's study of scripture at that point, William Perkins advised, and then went to the gospel of John, one had the key to the whole.[3] Thomas Draxe is still more specific and more eloquent. The Epistle to the Romans, he says, is like to nothing less than paradise itself, enclosing 'the Quintessence and perfection of saving Doctrine,' and the eighth chapter, he goes on to say, is like a conduit conveying the waters of life; rather it is the tree of life in the midst of the garden.[4]

Instructed by William Perkins, by Thomas Draxe, by John Downame, whose devotion to practical teaching we noted a few pages back, or by any one of a great number of eminent divines whom we shall have presently to consider, what did men learn from Paul? They learned that the will of God was revealed in the Bible, in the human heart and in nature. 'For the invisible things of him from the creation of the world are clearly seen, being understood by the things that are made, even his eternal power and Godhead.' The first revelation of God's will was in the law, and so long as man obeyed the law, he was happy. Disobeying it, he was inevitably and justly damned forever. No man from that time forth, since all are members one of another, could be justified under the law in the eyes of God. 'For all have sinned, and come short of the glory of God.' 'There is none righteous, no, not one,' and nothing that any man of his own motion is able to do can avail under the law to remove the universal imputation of sin. But now comes grace. By sin man surrendered his freedom, and so left it solely to God whether to save him or not as He might freely choose. God chose to do so in the person of his Son who, taking upon himself the nature of man, atoned once and for all for the sin of man. 'Wherefore, as by one man sin entered into the world, and death by sin; and so death passed upon all men, for that all have sinned, . . . even so by the righteousness of one the free gift came upon all men unto justification of life.' Therefore, though the old Adam is still present in us imputing sin to our members, so also may the new Adam be present imputing righteousness. We are saved, if we are saved, not by satisfying the law, for that, which we could not do for ourselves, Christ accomplished for us, but by receiving Christ into our spirits, by believing in him and in the sufficiency of his righteousness without help from us to atone for all our sins, no matter how many or how black.

But this led to a question of the utmost concern to the individual human soul. Is every sinner therefore saved? If not, then who are the elect and who are the damned, and on what ground are they chosen or rejected? What can a man do to be saved, and how can he win the assurance of grace? Tremendous debates expressing differences of thought that have long continued to trouble us under other terms raged over these points. Even the devils in Milton's hell occupied their leisure in disputes over 'fixed fate, free will, fore-knowledge absolute.' To the orthodox the answer seemed clear. Not all men were saved. Multitudes were eternally damned. God alone determined from the beginning who these should be. 'For whom he did foreknow, he also did predestinate to be conformed to the image of his Son, that he might be the firstborn among many brethren.' These alone and for no cause but God's free grace were predestined to be one with the redeemer. The rest remained under the law in the flesh, dead in spirit, at enmity with God. The manifestation of grace in the elect was faith. Those destined to be saved in Christ believed in his power and willingness to redeem. Those who believed evinced to themselves their faith and their redemption by making incessant war on sin in their own members. It was not that they could do no evil. They sinned again and again. But the evil which they did they hated. 'For I delight in the law of God after the inward man: But I see another law in my members, warring against the law of my mind.' The saint was a fighting, not an innocent, soul. He put on the whole armor of God and went forth to war against the sin that dwells in all flesh. This, so long as he kept it up, was the evidence of his election. The outcome need never be in doubt. He who never ceased fighting was sure to triumph in the end. That was predestined. 'We are more than conquerors through him that loved us.' Fascinated, the Puritan mind hung endlessly upon the facile but inscrutable phrases of the eighth chapter of Romans: 'Moreover, whom he did predestinate, them he also called: and whom he called, them he also justified: and whom he justified, them he also glorified.' Or as more diffusely stated by John Downame:

Whosoever therefore are predestinate to salvation, they also are effectuallie called, that is, separate from the world, and ingrafted into the bodie of Christ; and this they attaine unto by diligent and attentive hearing of the word. Whosoever are effectually called, are also justified; and therefore have attained a true and lively faith. Whosoever are justified are also sanctified, that is, die unto their sinnes, and rise againe to newnes of life; and consequently whosoever are still meer worldlings and no true members of Christs bodie (as all those are who make no conscience of hearing Gods word diligently, reverentlie, and attentively, nor of treasuring it up in their hearts) they are not truly called; whosoever have not Christs righteousnesse and obedience imputed and applied to them (which none have that are destitute of a true and fruitful faith) are not justified; whosoever live in their sinnes, without repentance, without any earnest desire and hearty endevour of serving the Lord in holinesse and righteousnesse of life are not sanctified; and whosoever are not called, justified and sanctified, shall never be saved; for the end and the meanes tending thereunto are joyned together in Gods predestination. So that where the one is, there the other is; where the one never is, there the other shall ever be wanting. And therefore as by our sanctification, justification, and vocation, we may certainely conclude that we are elected and shall be saved; so if we be without these, we may as certainely inferre that we are rejected, and shall be condemned if we live and die in this state.[5]

The persuasive strength of the doctrine of predestination, as the Puritan preachers presented it, sprang not from its metaphysical but its moral validity. It could, men believed, be proved by inexorable logic out of scripture, but what really convinced them was its fruitfulness when applied to their own living situation. It was supremely apposite. It supplied a basis both practical and ideal for decision. It suggested an attitude and a line of conduct. Put to the test of experience, it applied and it worked. The concept of universal depravity, by leveling all superiority not of the spirit, enormously enhanced the self-respect of the ordinary man. If none were righteous, then one man was as good as another. God chose whom he would and the distinctions of this world counted for nothing. The concept of free grace still further heightened his confidence. If the only real aristocracy was the aristocracy created by God, then nothing really counted but character and inner worth. Only they were Jews who were Jews inwardly, and the true circumcision was not that of the body. If election were manifested not by outward conformity to an imposed law but by the struggle of the spirit within against the weakness and disobedience of the flesh, then any man might find reason for hope within his own breast. If all this was predestined, then there could be no fear concerning the issue of life's ordeal. 'If God be with us, who can be against us?' The triumph of the saints was foreordained. Therefore nothing they could desire was impossible for them to attain. Heaven was theirs already, and if presently they demanded possession of the earth as well, that was no more than human. We are, says Richard Sibbes, like the child that lives and strives for a time blindly in the womb, but

in this dark life of ours, there is a divine instinct, power, and faculty . . . that nothing here can suffice: which shewes . . . that there is a condition which shall make a man fully happy; there must be a better life, which is, this spirituall life: for this life which wee live in the flesh, is a thing of nothing. . . . A Christian furnished with this spirituall life, can see Christ, and glory beyond all the things of this life; he can look backwards, make use of all things past, see the vanity of things so admired of others, hee can taste things nature doth not relish, he hath strength of reasons beyond all the apprehensions of reason: he is a man of strong working.[6]

Election, vocation, justification, sanctification, glorification, here was the perfect formula explaining what happened to every human soul born to be saved. It explained what happened to Paul, what might happen at any time to the very sinners who sat at the preacher's feet. The preacher could, of course, prove the formula to his own satisfaction beyond shadow of rational doubt. He could deduce it, that is, by an intellectual method which few of his hearers knew enough to question from premises which few men alive could critically examine. But it was far less important for his purposes to prove the formula than to demonstrate from observation and experience of life, as seen in himself, in the people about him and in the poetic narrative of scripture, precisely how it worked. In sermons and popular treatises almost beyond number, the Puritan preachers described the psychological pattern which exemplified the working of the formula, which all the saints were supposed to have exemplified and which every man who desired to be saved must hope would be exemplified again in his own case. As in later times men were taught to follow with patient observation the least workings of natural law in the external universe, men in the Puritan age were taught to follow by intense introspection the working of the law of predestination within their own souls. Theoretically, there was nothing they could do but watch, nothing they could of their own will do to induce or further the process of regeneration. They were only the witnesses of a drama which moved to its predetermined end according to a law they could do no more than marvel at. But the theatre of that drama was the human breast, and their own fate right up to the deathbed scene hung upon its outcome. They watched its unfolding, therefore, with the most absorbed attention. With the most anxious curiosity, they looked into their own most secret thoughts for signs that the grace of God was at its work of regeneration, and what they so urgently looked for they naturally saw. Seen by the light of the word, as they read it in the holy book and heard it expounded from the pulpit, their own lives fell under their gaze into the pattern set by Paul.

For their further prompting a flood of books soon came pouring forth from the shops of enterprising printers and booksellers. The teachings of the first flight of Puritan preachers, Greenham, Dering, Rogers, Smith and others have already been discussed. At the turn of the century by far the most important Puritan writer was William Perkins, whom we have already seen as fellow of Christ's and lecturer of St. Andrew's in Cambridge exercising a profound personal influence on the men who were to fill up the ranks of the spiritual brotherhood and make the power of the pulpit feared by reactionary rulers. That influence was widely extended by his numerous writings, published before and after his death in 1602. Perkins apparently had it in him to become a notable doctor of the schools and to fill great tomes with irrefragable technical demonstration of Calvinist doctrine. 'He had,' said Fuller, 'a capacious head with angles winding, and roomthy [sic] enough to lodge all controversiall intricacies;'[7] he did, as a matter of fact, write a famous polemic against the papists, not to mention lesser works in the same vein. Preaching, however, 'diverted him from that way,' and Fuller, though no Puritan himself, gives us a portrait of Perkins to exemplify the character of 'the faithful minister.' 'What was said of Socrates, that he first humbled the towring speculations of

Philosophers into practice and morality; so our Perkins brought the schools into the Pulpit, and unshelling their controversies out of their hard school-terms, made thereof plain and wholsome meat for his people . . . An excellent Chirurgeon he was at joynting of a broken soul, and at stating of a doubtfull conscience.'[8] He was indeed a kind of sixteenth-century William James. He did not so much prove the doctrine of predestination as analyze and depict the human soul with the help of it. He set forth in his *Golden Chaine*, in other weighty volumes, and in numerous shorter treatises what may best be called the descriptive psychology of sin and regeneration. In lucid and eminently readable prose he set forth the process by which, as anyone might observe, God converts the sinful soul into a state of grace, the technique by which man comes to be born again. In the *Golden Chaine* he even supplied a graphic chart or diagram of all the steps by which man mounts to heaven and in a parallel column those by which he may descend to hell. These writings no doubt represent the substance of Perkins' lectures to his students at Cambridge. Composed and first published in Latin, they were soon put out by his pupils in English translations. Similar in theme and purpose, though more imaginative and hortatory in style, were the numerous sermons which he himself chose to publish or which, again, his disciples published after his death from copies taken down in church. The titles alone of some of these things are sufficient to indicate the preacher's aim: *How to Live and That Well; A Graine of Mustard-Seed; The True Gaine: More in Worth than All the Goods in the World.* His influence was particularly felt by other preachers. From him probably, more than from any other, the members of the brotherhood learned to transpose the abstract doctrine into a rule of practice, into a method of spiritual self-help which they could set forth in sermon, tract and treatise for common men to apply to their own lives. In a few years, a whole literature appeared on the bookstalls for the purpose of teaching the people how to dissect and physic their souls.

John Downame's *Christian Warfare*, Samuel Hieron's *Doctrine of the Beginning of Christ*, Robert Bolton's *Discourse about the State of True Happinesse*, Daniel Dyke's *Mystery of Selfe-Deceiving*, Paul Baynes's *Holy Soliloquies*, William Whately's *The New Birth*, Ezekiel Culverwel's *Treatise of Faith*, William Gouge's *The Whole-*

Armor of God, John Preston's *The New Covenant* and *The Breast-Plate of Faith and Love*, Richard Sibbes's *The Bruised Reed and Smoaking Flax*, these books went through edition after edition and yet were only a few among the many which in the half-century before the Long Parliament traced for the unlearned reader the stages he must expect to travel on the road which, he might confidently expect, would lead to the heavenly city.

Thus the Puritan reformers, balked of their ambition to rule the church but permitted to preach and minister to those they could induce to have them do so, also took to writing books. The fruit of their efforts eventually became a new version of the sacred epic of the fall and regeneration of man. But before we arrive at the epic, we must note how its roots sprang from the personal experience of its creators. Election-vocation-justification-sanctification-glorification was more than an abstract formula. It became the pattern of the most profound experience of men through many generations. From this deep and personal experience grew both the epic and the varied forms in which it was expressed. In the last chapter, we traced the worldly activities of the preachers in organizing and extending the work of the spirit in the world. We must now look at the work of the spirit itself within the preachers and within those whom they persuaded to become one with them in the spirit. This is a task for which they have themselves left us abundant materials. William Perkins in his treatise *Of the Calling of the Ministerie* demands how one can 'declare the reconciliation betwixt God and Man' who is himself not reconciled. 'Dare he present another man to Gods mercy for pardon, and never yet presented himselfe? Can he commend the state of grace to another, and never felt the sweetnesse thereof in his own soule? Dare he come to preach sanctification with polluted lips, and out of an unsanctified heart? . . . dare any man presume to come into this most high and holy presence of the Lord, untill he have mortified his corruptions, and cast off the unrulinesse of his affections?'[9] The business of the preacher was to help others along the way into which God had already directed him. The spirit in him, reaching out to the spirit of the sinner still struggling in the darkness, helped it into the light. But first he must himself have been called out of the dark. The conversion he sought to effect he must first have experienced. He could do no less and little more than offer himself as experimental proof of his own teaching. The regenerate testified to the unregenerate, saying, as it were, 'I too was a great sinner like Paul and like you, but God having elected me to believe in him, the scales have fallen from my eyes as they may from yours.'

All this can perhaps be most clearly illustrated by the case of Thomas Goodwin, partly because his career was so typical of its kind as well as so important in its day and partly because the extant materials relating to the man are for our purpose so complete. Goodwin's disciples, Thanckful Owen and James Barron, in the eulogy they published in 1681 said that 'that Person is the best Interpreter, who (besides other Helps) hath a Comment in his own heart; and he best Interprets Paul's Epistles, who is himself the Epistle of Christ written by the Spirit of God. He best understands Paul's Epistles, who had Paul's Sense, Temptations, and Experience.'[10] As we saw in the last chapter, there could be no doubt that Goodwin by the time he reached the age of twenty had undergone an experience patterned upon Paul's. 'He had,' say Owen and Barron, 'the happiness of an early and more than ordinary Conversion, in which God favoured him with a marvellous light.' For a long time afterward his thoughts remained so intent upon that experience that 'he kept a constant Diary, of which,' his son and biographer tells us, 'I have above an hundred Sheets wrote with his own hand of Observations of the Case and Posture of his Mind and Heart toward God, and sutable, pious, and pathetical Meditations.'[11] Goodwin also left behind him an autobiography, which chiefly consists of a vivid account of its author's youthful strivings of soul, rounded out by a brief record of later events down to the period just after the Restoration. This was not published until 1704, when Thomas Goodwin, Junior, incorporated it in the biographical sketch which he supplied for the fifth volume of his father's works. One strongly suspects that the significant portions of this confession, those relating to the writer's conversion, must have been penned shortly after that event and at the same time as the diary. The usual practice of the saint was to begin his new life by setting down on paper an account of his spiritual rebirth, which account also he frequently continued in the form of a daily written record of his subsequent spiritual struggles.

Be that as it may, certain it is that when Goodwin began preaching in and around Cambridge about 1620 the religious experience he had just enjoyed formed the basis of what he had to teach in the pulpit. His extant sermons of this period, published in 1636, though preached, he says, eight years before, are not explicitly autobiographical.[12] They do, however, deal, now doctrinally and abstractly, now symbolically and imagistically, with that struggle of the soul out of the darkness of nature into the light of faith which had been and still was occupying the preacher. Even more to the point is Goodwin's own statement, made in the autobiography, of the personal basis of his preaching. He has just described how his effectual calling was finally confirmed by direct communication from God himself. God, we have seen, took him aside and said to him privately, 'Do you now turn to me, and I will pardon all your Sins tho never so many, as I forgave and pardoned my Servant Paul.' Hearing himself called, Goodwin of course believed, and presently told his good fortune to his friend 'Mr. Price . . . most famous Convert and Example of Religion in Cambridge.' He told it to other men as well, 'I know not how often.' In fact, he told it to everybody who would listen, for what were his sermons but a repetition in the sublimated idiom of the pulpit of the epistle written in his heart by the Holy Spirit? 'And I remember that I preaching at Ely two Year after, urged to the People the Example of Paul . . . as an Example to win others, in having in my Eye and Thoughts the said Experience of God's dealing with me in the same kind; and that the Examples of such are to be held forth by God as Flags of Mercy before a Company of Rebels to win them in.'[13]

'That God pardon'd such a Man in such a Condition is often brought home unto another Man in the same Condition.' The most powerful and lasting effect of the popularization of Pauline doctrine by such men as Goodwin was to arouse the most active widespread interest in the inner experience of every individual human being and an almost equally active and widespread activity in giving expression to that interest. Every man was either a convert or susceptible of conversion, and the inner life of any man, once converted, was fraught with daily possibilities for struggle and adventure. It followed that every man's state of spiritual health was the subject of acute concern to the man himself and of sympathetic curiosity to others. Naturally this gave occasion to the reporting and comparing of individual case histories, to the endless retailing of confession, reminiscence and anecdote. Out of such, shall we say, spiritual gossip arose a body of legend and a type of popular literature which was soon found to be quite as edifying and certainly as fascinating as the more formal tracts and sermons. The conditions for the development of such a form of expression were perfect—a generally accepted pattern and opportunities as abundant as life for variations upon a common theme. The devout Puritan turned his back on stage plays and romances, but only in order to look in his own heart and write what happened there. Speaking from the pulpit, the preacher did not as a rule supply explicit personal details, though his teaching was presumed to reflect personal experience. But outside the pulpit, the preacher—and of course common saints were encouraged to follow his example—was free to talk about himself and other people as much as he wished. Not only that, but he very generally kept a journal of his transactions with God and the devil or at least left written record of his conversion. The diary, as we have already seen in the case of Richard Rogers, became the Puritan substitute for the confessional, and though few diaries have actually been preserved intact, the substance of many and the fact of their having been kept are apparent in the·mass of biographical writing which rapidly accumulated as the Puritan movement progressed.

For an understanding of the nature and purpose of these diaries, we can best turn to a little treatise, called *The Journal or Diary of a Thankful Christian*, published in 1656. It is by John Beadle, himself a preacher who had been 'watered by the droppings of that great Elijah, that renowned man of God in his generation, Reverend Mr. Thomas Hooker.'[14] The state, says Beadle, has its 'diurnals' of affairs, tradesmen keep their shop books, merchants their accounts, lawyers their books of precedents and physicians theirs of experiments, wary heads of households their records of daily disbursements and travelers theirs of things seen and endured. But Christians, who like stewards or factors must one day give strict account to their Lord, have even more to gain by keeping a journal. The godly man should 'keep a strict account of his effectual calling.' If possible, he should 'set down the time when, the place where, and the person by whom he was converted.' He should make note of all the men and means that God has at any time used for his good, especially the services of parents, schoolmasters and patrons. He will find it singularly useful to put into his diary 'what

Times we have lived in, what Minister we have lived under, what Callings we were of, what Wealth was bestowed on us, what places of Authority and Command were committed to us.' Most important of all, the Christian should record all the mercies of Providence, all the answers vouchsafed by God to his prayers. 'Indeed what is our whole life, but a continued deliverance? We are daily delivered, either from the violence of the creature, or the rage of men, or the treachery of our own hearts; either our houses are freed from firing, or goods from plundering, or our bodies from danger, or our names from reproaches, or our souls from snares.' The Puritan faith invested the individual soul, the most trivial circumstances of the most commonplace existence, with the utmost significance. Why should not a man keep a record of matters in which God took so active an interest as he did in the petty moods and doings of any common sinner?

The greatest diary sprung from the Puritan confessional was begun some four years after John Fuller published Beadle's book. Pepys may or may not have read that work. But the conventions of the spiritual diary had been long established and known when Beadle wrote about them, and many a journal of self-revelation, though none of such a self as Pepys revealed, was being written before and during Pepys' time. Those of Richard Rogers and Samuel Ward, the manuscripts of which happen to have been preserved, are but early examples. No doubt others are still yellowing and gathering dust in attics and store-rooms of both Old and New England. The diary was not published, but in many instances after its author's decease it was used, supplemented by personal reminiscence, as material for an account of his life in the faith. Again and again the preacher who wrote the biography or preached the funeral sermon tells us with high approval how the departed saint kept a daily record of the state of his soul. A few instances will suffice to illustrate this practice. John Janeway 'kept a Diary in which he did write down every evening what the frame of his spirit had been all the day long.'[15] Edmund Staunton kept 'a Journal or Diary of Gods mercies.'[16] John Carter 'kept a constant Diary, or day book, in which every day he set down Gods extraordinary dispensations, his own actions, and whatsoever memorable things he had heard, or read that day.'[17] John Machin 'kept a Diary of his Life which he wrote in Characters,' probably, that is, in a shorthand cipher.[18] Lord Harington, when he had prayed after supper with his servants, 'withdrew himself into his study, where he kept a Diary or Day-book, wherein he recorded what he had done that day; how he had offended, or what good he had done; what temptations he had met with, and how he had resisted them: . . . and for such failings as were fit to be known onely to God and his own soul, he wrote them down in a private Character, which none could read but himself, and then betook himself to his rest.'[19] Samuel Fairclough's diary, which he kept from the age of twenty, was written partly in Greek and partly in 'elegant Latine.'[20] Richard Blackerby, a schoolmaster, 'kept three Diaries of his Life, one in Greek, another in Latin, a third in English.'[21] Even when we are not told that the subject of an edifying memoir kept a diary, it is obvious that the son or disciple or pastor has some such material before him as he writes his commemoration of the departed saint. Not otherwise could we have had such vivid and detailed accounts of the inner religious experiences of such persons as John Bruen and his sister Katherine Brettargh, of John Cotton, of John Rowe, of Catherine Clarke, of Elizabeth Wilkinson, and of others too numerous to mention here. If we seem to be straining a point in suggesting that a certain clerk of the Admiralty at the Restoration owed to Puritan tradition something of his impulse to record in 'character' personal matters such as men generally conceal even from themselves, it may be appropriate to call attention to the fact, conveyed to us by no less a person than Bishop Burnet, that the Lord Chief Justice of England under Charles II, Sir Matthew Hale, had also been a wild young man who repented, forsook vain company, turned abruptly to religion, and commenced a diary in which he set down the plan of each day's duties.[22] As time moved on, the Puritan spirit and way of life were destined to spread far beyond the limits of that which in the narrow sense came to be known as Puritanical.

The psychological function of the Puritan autobiography and diary was primarily the same as that of auricular confession. This should not be for us obscured by the fact that, owing to the circumstances of English life, the Puritan confession was imparted to paper and so sooner or later to one's friends and even to the general public in something which finally attained what can only be called literary form. The doctrine of salvation by faith alone became implanted in spiritual experience by a method of self-discipline the effect of which was to build up the self-respect and courage of the individual. When a man or a woman desired to be received into the outward communion of the elect, he or she had to make open acknowledgment of repentance and change of heart. Naturally there was satisfaction to be received and to be given in a specific account of full personal particulars. The life of Elizabeth Wilkinson, coming when Puritanism had reached its highest point, gives a clear and complete picture of the typical Puritan saint's experience. This lady, born probably in the sixteen twenties or thirties and dying in 1654, first became concerned about her soul at about the age of twelve. She was then presently assailed by atheistical doubts. These were banished from her mind by Calvin's *Institutes*, but were followed by despair lest she had committed the sin against the Holy Ghost. These fears were in turn allayed by Scudder's *Christians Daily Walk*, 'by the hearing of such Sermons and reading such Books as came closest unto the conscience,' and particularly by the communication of her condition to her friends. The upshot of her struggle was that she wrote out a 'particular account of Gods gracious dealing' toward her and sent it to Robert Harris, then Master of Trinity, Oxford, begging him to admit her to communion. He granted her request; she entered upon the life of a saint, kept a diary, and when she died, the story of her spiritual progress was published by Edmund Staunton, the preacher chosen to pronounce the sermon at her funeral.[23]

The test of the saint's conversion was, of course, to be seen in his perseverance in the faith, and faith must be continually active. Each day one sinned, each day one must repent, each day one must be reconciled afresh to God, and each day one must—or at any rate it was advised that one should—enter these circumstances in one's diary. It was of the very essence of Puritan self-discipline that whatsoever thoughts and actions the old Adam within had most desire to keep hidden, the very worst abominations of the heart, one must when one retired to one's private chamber at night draw forth into the light of conscience. To set them down in writing, albeit in secret 'character,' was a great help in this. They were the devil incarnate in man and could drag him down to hell. It was also of the essence of Puritan discipline that one should remember and record the good things that happened. These showed the saint that, bad as he was, God had not forsaken him, that God was still taking an intimate and loving interest in his affairs even when bestowing afflictions upon him. Having thus balanced his spiritual books, he could go to bed with a good conscience, sleep sound and wake with courage. Some of the biographies are nothing if not explicit in stating the point and in making plain the profit to be derived from such daily posting of one's accounts with God. The Reverend John Rowe tells us of his father that 'usually at the close of every day, after the casting up of his accounts, & humble and fervent prayer, the Lord made it out to him, . . . that All was pardoned . . . so that he walked in the light of Gods countenance from day to day.'[24] Every evening John Janeway took note

What incomes and profit he received in his spiritual traffique; what returns from that far-country; what answers of prayer, what deadness and flatness, and what observable providences did present themselves, and the substance of what he had been doing; and any wandrings of thoughts, inordinancy in any passions; which, though the world could not discern he could. . . . This made him to retain a grateful remembrance of mercy, and to live in a constant admiring and adoring of divine goodness; this brought him a very intimate acquaintance with his own heart; this kept his spirit low and fitted him for freer communications from God; this made him more lively and active; . . . this made him speak more affectionately and experimentally to others of the things of God: and . . . left a sweet calm upon his spirits, because he every Night made even his accounts; and if his sheets should prove his winding-sheet, it had been all one: for, he could say his work was done; so that death could not surprize him.[25]

'The examples of such are to be held forth by God, as Flags of Mercy before a Company of Rebels to win them in.'[26] Thus arose the hagiology of Puritanism. It fell in, of course, with the rising popular interest in all sorts of biographical and historical writing and with the traditional notion that the purpose of such writing was to teach by the use of examples. Biography and history appealed, however, with particular force to the Puritan mind and took from Puritanism a special character. Many a preacher found occasion to point out the peculiar force of the reported examples of others in winning the unregenerate to repentance. The best complete statement of their view of the matter

came finally from Richard Baxter. Baxter commends history much as
humanist critics like Sidney had praised poetry, for being both 'useful'
and 'delightful.' Young people, he says, 'before they can Read much
of Theological Treatises with understanding or delight,' are inclined
by nature to enjoy the reading of history. Here then is a way by which
those who would educate youth may sugar profitable instruction to
youth's appetite. But Baxter does not mean such histories as those
which recount the conquests of Alexander, Caesar and Tamerlane,
'poppit-plays' merely 'where there is much stir to little purpose, till
the Play be ended.' 'The report of one Souls Conversion to God, and
of the Reformation of one Family, City, or Church, and of the noble
Operations of the blessed Spirit, by which he brings up Souls to God,
and Conquereth the World, the Flesh, and the Devil; the Heavenly
Communications of God unto Sinners, for their Vivification, Illumination, and holy Love to God, and to his Image, are as far better than
the Stories of these grand Murderers, and Tyrants, and their great
Robberies, and Murders called Conquests, as the Diagnosticks of
Health are than those of Sickness.'[27]

When Baxter wrote these words in 1672, there was no lack in
England of the kind of historical writing he so highly recommends.
There was, indeed, a very considerable body of such literature which
had been accumulating in oral tradition, in manuscript and in print for
at least a century, and the formal history of which it will be well to
summarize before describing the part which the preachers played in
creating both it and the popular taste for it. The custom was among the
godly, when a saint of any consequence died, to engage a preacher to
pronounce a sermon at the funeral. This generally dealt quite imper-
sonally with some more or less appropriate text and concluded with
a brief biographical appendix or, as one preacher called it, a 'lean-to.'[28]
The preaching of such sermons, frequently followed by their publication, was a source of revenue as well as a professional opportunity for
the preacher. It also frequently became an occasion for embarrassment
if not abuse. Conscientious modesty or perhaps some less worthy
motive sometimes made a man forbid any such preaching when he
should come to be buried. Nevertheless the number of funeral sermons
with biographical 'lean-to's' was well-nigh legion. The reader who
is curious concerning them can do little better than turn to Θρηνοίκος,

The House of Mourning, issued in 1640 and again in 1660. This is a
kind of anthology of funeral sermons collected from such eminent
preachers as Featley, Sibbes, Preston and Thomas Taylor. It would
appear to have enjoyed wide popularity. The 'lean-to' sketch appended
to such performances frequently extended itself, when some notable
saint was the subject, into an independent work, sometimes published
with or without a sermon and sometimes remaining and perhaps circulating more or less widely in manuscript. Always and everywhere in
Puritan circles oral tradition extensively supplemented the written
hagiology. If the saint had kept no diary, he had at any rate unbosomed
himself to his friends. If his friends committed no memorial of him to
writing or print, or if their memorials of him became lost, tales of his
spiritual experience were still, sometimes for many years, conveyed by
legend, reminiscence and anecdote.

Not a little of this material, its original unction somewhat acidu-
lously reduced, found its way into the pages of Thomas Fuller, to
whom we are especially indebted for his account of William Perkins.
But for the assembling and preservation of the most considerable
amount of Puritan biographical writing and for evidence as well of
the value set upon it in the generation after the civil wars, we are
indebted to Samuel Clarke. Hugh Clarke, his father, a contemporary
of Dod and Hildersam, was a powerful preacher in Warwickshire for
over a generation, a Boanerges to the wicked but a Barnabas to the
humble and broken in spirit.[29] He sent his son, born in 1599, to study
at Emmanuel under Thomas Hooker. Samuel followed in the path
thus marked out for him.[30] He had the protection of the Earl of Warwick and of young Robert Greville, Lord Brooke. During many
troublesome years he held and lost one pulpit after another. Baxter,
at whose marriage he officiated in 1662, was his great friend. It was not
as a preacher, however, that he won fame but as a compiler of books of
biographical and historical information suited to the taste of the
Puritan public. He was an earnest, industrious, uninspired but not in-
competent writer. His method was to ransack the printed sources available to him for the lives of famous kings, martyrs, reformers and the
like and to reduce them all to the somewhat flat idiom of pious edification. But from the first, he also included lives drawn from the Puritan
hagiology. He did not invent the spiritual biography, nor in the ordi-

nary sense was he the composer of many of the biographies he printed. But he was shrewd enough to fasten upon material he found ready for his use and for which there was a going demand. From funeral sermons, from independently printed accounts, from unprinted manuscripts sent to him for the purpose, from information supplied by friends and relatives of his subjects, he drew together between 1650 and 1683 an extensive gallery of Puritan saints who had flourished in the preceding generation, or who carried on the faith into the unhappy years after 1660. Thus, though his books are relatively late in date, they represent the activity in life-writing of the older Puritans, who had established the conventions of spiritual biography, and they completely ignore the work of contemporary sectarians and lay preachers like Bunyan and other baptists, like George Fox and the quakers, or like the riffraff of ranters and their likes such as Muggleton and Clarkson, all of whom were vigorously exploiting, though repudiated by men like Clarke and Baxter, the forms of expression as well as the religious enthusiasms of the older, more academic and more respectable Puritans.

The earliest of Clarke's compilations illustrating Puritan biography appeared in 1650 and was republished in 1654 and 1675. Its title suggests its character: *The Marrow of Ecclesiastical Historie, conteined in the Lives of the Fathers, and other Learned Men, and Famous Divines, which have Flourished in the Church since Christs Time, to this present Age.* It included, along with a great deal of matter of more general edification, the lives of five preachers of the preceding age who exemplified more particularly the experience of the Puritan saint. Clarke abstracted the life of William Perkins with additions from Fuller's *Holy State*, published eight years earlier. The life of William Cowper was taken from his autobiography, published in 1619 and republished in several editions of Cowper's works. The life of Robert Bolton was taken from a life by Edward Bagshaw, originally published in 1633 in *Mr. Bolton's Last and Learned Worke of the Foure last Things*. The life of William Whately was taken from the life by William Scudder prefixed to the edition of Whately's *Prototypes* of 1640. The life of Andrew Willet was taken from the life by Peter Smith prefixed to the fifth edition of Willet's *Synopsis Papismi* of 1634. A second part of the *Marrow*, also published in 1650, included, along with 'Lives of Christian Emperors, Kings, and Soveraign Princes,' the lives of certain 'Christians of an Inferiour Rank.' These were not preachers but lay saints who, though inferior in spiritual rank, had nevertheless already been remembered in print. When Katharine Brettargh was buried in 1601, two funeral sermons were preached for her, one by William Harrison, the other by William Leygh. These were at once published with a life of the lady annexed, and were several times republished. The life had also appeared separately in at least three editions and must, therefore, have enjoyed considerable circulation before Clarke reprinted it again. Katharine Brettargh's brother, John Bruen, was no less a saint, though much longer-lived. When he died in 1625 William Hinde wrote his 'Holy Life and Happy Death,' and this too Clarke appropriated. In the case of Lord Harington of Exton, Clarke proceeded by a different method. When Harington died in 1614, Richard Stock preached his funeral sermon and published it 'Together with a patterne of Piety . . . expressed in his life and death.' Henry Holland included a notice of him in his *Herwologia Anglica*, a collection of brief, impersonal notices of English worthies which appeared in 1620. Clarke, to paraphrase his own words, 'collected' his life of Harington partly out of Stock's sermon, partly out of Holland, and 'partly out of my own knowledge.'

The *Marrow* was quickly followed by another and similar compilation from the same hand: *A general Martyrologie, containing a collection of all the greatest persecutions which have befallen the Church of Christ from the creation to our present times. Whereunto are added the Lives of sundry modern Divines.* The lives of sundry modern divines in this volume were twelve in number and supply interesting evidence concerning the nature of the material Clarke found to work upon and of the manner in which he worked it up. Seven of the twelve men had died within the past dozen years, and Clarke had probably known most of them personally. Of the remaining five, one was his own father and the others had left sons or disciples who were friends of Clarke's. Thus Clarke secured for publication Stanley Gower's account of Richard Rothwel (died 1627) and Thomas Ball's life of John Preston (died 1628), neither of which had been previously printed. Materials for the life of Arthur Hildersam (died 1632) were, Clarke says, furnished by Hildersam's son 'from his father's papers'; for the life of John Ball, by several friends of the deceased. John Dod, who had only recently died (1645), was almost certainly known to Clarke, who in writing his account must have drawn both upon personal knowledge and upon the rich body of picturesque anecdote which gathered about so famous and patriarchal a figure. From Dod, who was Cartwright's literary executor and who preached his funeral sermon (Cartwright died in 1603), or from members of Dod's circle must have come the facts for Clarke's sketch of the noted reformer. From similar sources which cannot now be traced must also have been derived the biographies of the remaining preachers in the *General Martyrologie* of 1651, namely Barnaby Potter (died 1642), Richard Sedgwick (died 1643), Julines Herring (died 1644), Robert Balsom (died 1647) and Herbert Palmer (died 1647).

The indefatigable compiler was ready the very next year, 1652, with still another collection of precisely the same character, this time *A Martyrologie, Containing a Collection of all the Persecutions which have befallen the Church of England since the first plantation of the Gospel to the end of Queen Maries Reign*. For the fuller edification of English Protestants, Clarke added *the lives of Jasper Coligni . . . slain in the Massacre of Paris And of Joane Queen of Navarre, who died of Poyson a few days before that bloody Massacre*, and then to make up good measure he also added ten more *English Divines, famous in their Generations for Learning, Piety, Parts, and for their Sufferings in the Cause of Christ*. Among these, in addition to rather perfunctory accounts of John Colet, Miles Coverdale and Edwin Sandys, churchmen not directly within the 'spiritual' tradition, we now find such well-known Puritan preachers of the former generation as Greenham, Baynes, Bradshaw, Stock, Sibbes, Thomas Taylor and Chaderton. These, it would seem, were men not so well known to Clarke, and consequently he draws more largely from printed sources, supplemented, however, from personal tradition. For Richard Greenham (died 1594?) he drew somewhat upon Henry Holland's preface to Greenham's *Workes*. For Paul Baynes (died 1617) he drew upon William Ames' preface to Baynes' *Diocesans Tryall* (1621?). Thomas Gataker furnished the life of William Bradshaw (died 1618) from information supplied by Hildersam's son, Samuel, and by Bradshaw's son, John. Gataker also contributed the account of Richard Stock (died 1626) which had already appeared in print (1627) together with the sermon Gataker preached 'at the Funerall of that worthy servant of Christ.' Clarke's rather meager notice of Richard Sibbes (died 1635) sounds like the biographical 'lean-to' of a sermon, but this has not been found. Zachary Catlin wrote a more extended but not very spiritual life of Sibbes in which he says 'and if anything here recorded, may seem convenient for His purpose, who is (as I am informed) about to publish the Lives of some Worthyes lately deceased, I shall think my labour well bestow'd.' A marginal note refers to 'Mr. Clark of London,'[31] but Clarke made no use of Catlin's manuscript, which remained unpublished until the nineteenth century. Clarke's life of Thomas Taylor (died 1633), also rather slight, shows a close relationship to the sketch published the following year, 1653, in Taylor's *Works*. For his life of Laurence Chaderton (died 1640), Clarke refers to the funeral sermon and 'commendation' by Richard Holdsworth.

Enough has been said to show that, when Samuel Clarke compiled his *Marrow* and his two martyrologies in the years 1650 to 1652, he found the Puritan spiritual biography ready to his hand. The way of life exemplified by the preachers had already found its appropriate expression in legend and literature. There can be little doubt that Clarke's labors of compilation and popularization assisted in the further spread both of godly living and of the writing of godly lives in the Puritan manner. His later publications give more and more space to such matter. In 1662 he came out with *A Collection of the Lives of Ten Eminent Divines*, namely John Carter, Samuel Crooke, John Cotton, Thomas Hill, William Gouge, Thomas Gataker, Jeremiah Whitaker, James Ussher, Richard Capel, and Robert Harris. The life of Carter (died 1635) had been sent in by his son with a request for its publication. The others concerned some of the most noted Puritan divines of the sixteen thirties and forties and were adapted, if not taken in their entirety, from the usual sort of written and printed sources. An interesting feature of this volume was that Clarke was now able to include the lives of 'some other Eminent Christians,' not churchmen but, like some of the persons included in his *Marrow*, less gifted folk—four of the six being women—who had been eminent for godliness and had provided both examples and materials for the by this time conventional biographical treatment. In 1677 Clarke combined the lives of his preceding collections, not including the *Marrow*, and appended them to his *General Martyrologie*. In 1683 was published the most extensive of his collections devoted solely to spiritual biography. This was called *The Lives of Sundry Eminent Persons in this Later Age*. There was now surely no lack of matter and no lack of collaborators for such a book. Eminent divines whom Clarke had formerly omitted, 'Several English Nobility and Gentry Eminent in this Later Age,' 'Several Excellent Ladies and Gentlewomen,' among whom are included both Baxter's wife and Clarke's own, and finally, the book being published posthumously, Clarke himself in his autobiography, are all enshrined in this last issue of the golden legend of Puritan saints.

In the preface to this final grand installment of his life's work, Clarke tells the 'Christian and Candid Reader,' 'I have been encouraged to make this Collection, and now to Publish it, finding that my former Labours in this kind have been accepted with the Saints and in the Church of Christ; which is apparent, for that they have been Printed four times in a few years space and yet never less than a Thousand at a time.' Clarke was not a brilliant writer. He was, however, an editor equal to his particular task. The material that came to his hands, he frequently condensed or cut to its advantage, to the advantage, that is, of its 'spiritual' character and to the exclusion of irrelevant factual matter. Thus he no doubt helped to conventionalize the form. As for style, he gave his readers what they wanted, plain undistinguished prose which they could read without effort, believing that what they read they read because it was truth unadorned and not because it was well written. Thomas Fuller says, referring to 'Master Samuel Clarke, with whose pen mine never did, nor shall interfere,' that 'as the flocks of Jacob were distanced three days journey from those of Laban, so (to prevent voluntary or casual commixtures) our styles are set more than a Months journey asunder.'[32] This, of course, did not prevent Thomas from making an occasional raid on the facts of Samuel in order to carry off whatever he might require. Clarke could afford to serve his wine without sparkle. He enjoyed the commendations of the godly. He had also the full approval of his friend Baxter. 'Some Enemies,' the latter observed, 'deride him for Writing

Lives with no more Art: But I take that to be his Commendation; He did not make the Histories, but take them made by faithful acquaintance of the dead.'[33] That is to say, an important element in the convention of these spiritual biographies was that they should seem to possess no art but the art of the holy spirit, which was simply to report the facts. The spirit working in the saint transpired in his life and impressed itself upon his acquaintances, who needed not to invent a tale or adorn a eulogy but merely to state the truth. Needless to say the spirit was more generous at some times than at others in supplying full and lifelike details, but as a rule it was inclined to select the most telling facts and facts all of a kind. Thus the spiritual biography developed its convention of theme and plot conveyed by artless realism.

The pattern to which, under the formula given by Paul in the eighth chapter of Romans, the life of the elect conformed was exemplified by the preachers and set forth in the story of their lives. 'I riding with him unto Tunbridge Wells,' says Simeon Ashe of Jeremiah Whitaker (died 1654), 'he was pleased to give me the History of his life . . . Oh how often, and with what meltings hath he poured forth his heart unto my bosome, in reference to all concernments, personal, relative, private, publick, comfortable and uncomfortable, which have deeply affected him!'[34] Not every feature of the common story appeared full blown in every instance, but the story was characteristically supposed to begin with an account of the horrid sins or scarcely less deplorable dry indifference from which the soul destined to be saved was called and after terrific struggle converted, generally by the reading of some godly book or by the influence of some powerful preacher. Then followed the chronicle, which might be more or less extended according to the circumstances, of the saint's lifelong war against the temptation to despair and the other abominations of his heart, lightened by the encouragements vouchsafed to him by God in the form of good fortune and of worldly and spiritual success. The last scene was the deathbed, one last terrific bout with Satan and then triumph and glory forever after. How the lives of leading members of the spiritual brotherhood, such as Perkins, Dod, Cotton, Preston and Thomas Goodwin, fitted this pattern, the reader may perceive by turning back to the preceding chapter. It will be useful to instance a few others at this point to illustrate the many variations that were played upon the common theme.

Richard Rothwel (1563?-1627), a Lancashire man, was apparently, in the Puritan succession, an early example of the type of enthusiastic preacher bred in the north country.[35] 'He was called the Rough Hewer.' When he preached the law, men trembled and cried out. When he preached the gospel, he was another Barnabas. After Cambridge, he entered the church and served as a chaplain with Essex in Ireland, after which he returned to his native country. His conversion came only after he had been some years a clergyman. 'Which,' says his biographer and disciple, Stanley Gower, 'because it was famous, and he himself afterwards proved the meanes of the Conversion of so many, I shall set it down as I remember I have heard him speak it.' 'He was tall, well set, of great strength of body and activity, of a stern countenance, of invincible courage, of approved valour, and of a very goodly and majestick presence: Grief; nor any misery could ever break him, but joy would presently melt him into tears.' But alas, for many years all these powers were but as weapons in the hands of a madman. Rothwel, notwithstanding his cloth, gave himself up to hunting, bowling and shooting, to swearing 'Faith and Troth' and to even greater blasphemies. He poached upon deer parks and fishponds, often robbing one gentleman to give to another. Caught red-handed by a gamekeeper one day, he strung the fellow up by his thumbs and left him. Then on a certain Saturday, Master Midgley, a minister of the neighborhood of greater godliness though far inferior in parts and learning, found him playing at bowls amongst papists and other vain gentlemen and told him what a pity it was that a man of his gifts should be so disporting himself when he ought to be preparing for his next day's duties. Rothwel at first slighted the good man's words, but after he got home, they began to work, and the next day he went to hear Master Midgley preach. Thus he was brought home to Christ. The devil assaulted him many times after that, but he never lost his assurance and was able himself to bring the same comfort to many others. Lady Bowes, who 'gave about one thousand pounds per annum to maintain Preachers where there were none, nor any means for them,' supported him for many years in his work in Lancashire and Nottinghamshire. Gower reports in full the spirited debate he conducted with the devil that possessed a poor fellow near Mansfield. The triumph which the preacher enjoyed upon that occasion did not, however, prevent Satan from assailing 'bold Rothwel' on his own sickbed, witnessed and also duly reported by the biographer.

Robert Bolton (1572-1631) attained great learning at Lincoln and Brasenose, Oxford; he was but a mean scholar in Christ.[36] He despised Puritans and thought Master Perkins, whose 'plaine but very sound and substantiall preaching' he heard upon a visit to Cambridge, 'a barren empty fellow.' He loved stage plays, cards and dice, Christmas merrymaking, boon companions, Sabbathbreaking and horrible swearing. Then God smote him to the ground, 'not by any soft and still voice, but in terrible tempests and thunder, the Lord running upon him as a gyant, taking him by the necke and shaking him to peeces.' Edward Bagshaw, whose tutor he had been at Oxford, and who wrote his life, tells us that the anguish of his spirit at this time often roused him from his very bed at night. Many and foul were the temptations which for many months drank up his spirit. 'Yet God gave him at length a blessed issue,' as it was reported he had done to Luther in a like case. From the very severity of his spiritual birth pangs, he gained, as was to be expected, 'an invincible courage and resolution for the cause of God' and 'a singular dexterity in comforting afflicted and wounded spirits.' A wealthy gentleman presented him to a living in Northamptonshire where he labored and preached and wrote edifying books for twenty-two years. His wife took all worldly care off his hands. He begot many children in the Lord. He was a son of thunder and consolation.

The account of Samuel Fairclough (1594-1677), one of the longest and most detailed of the spiritual biographies, was probably compiled by one of his four sons, all preachers, from abundant materials left by their father at the end of his long life.[37] Fairclough was himself the son of a clergyman, born in Suffolk. His soul was awakened early as the result of an indulgence in the same sin that St. Augustine had lived to repent and record. One day he and another boy had robbed an orchard, filling 'their Pockets as well as their Bellies with the spoils of a Mellow Pear Tree.' The next week he heard Samuel Ward preach on the duty of making fourfold restitution for theft. 'This was as a dart directed by the hand of God to the heart of our young Schoolboy.' That night he never slept, and the next morning went to his companion and told him he was going to carry twelvepence to the owner for the threepenny worth of pears he had stolen. The other boy, who could already feel the tingling of the cane, replied, 'Thou talkest like a fool, Sam, God will forgive us ten times; sooner than old Jude will forgive us once.' But neither this common sense nor the fact that the good man refused his money and forgave him had any effect upon Fairclough. He went to Ward, 'opened to him the whole state of his Soul,' had the wine and oil of the doctrine of grace poured into his wounds, was converted, and 'dedicated and devoted himself to his Saviour and Redeemer all the days of his life after.' At Queen's College, Cambridge, he became a favorite of Preston, and refused to play, even before King James, the part of an old woman in *Ignoramus*. After Cambridge, he lectured here and there in Suffolk and other counties until a rich gentleman, Sir Nathaniel Barnardiston, put him into an excellent living. 'He had a rare faculty in prescribing to the ease and cure of wounded Spirits . . . He had experience of the things he spake, and those Lessons that come from experience usually make great impressions upon others.' His publications, which included a funeral sermon on his patron, were not extensive, but he kept his vigor in the pulpit for many years until deprived at the Restoration. 'The blade was metal to the back, and although it was much worn, yet it kept its keenness to the last.'

We need not further multiply illustrations of the way in which the spiritual preachers lived their lives and also turned them into pious legend. Of no less importance is it to note that they composed according to the same pattern the lives of people they converted. Thus the experience of the commonest men came also to be dignified by the spirit into literary material no less worthy and interesting than that concerning the preachers themselves. It is, indeed, in some of the spiritual biographies of lay persons that we see even more clearly than in those of the preachers the implications that point toward the future developments which were to come from such writing. We have already noted in the case of Elizabeth Wilkinson a typical example of the life of a female Puritan saint. The account of Katherine Brettargh (1579-1601) is the picture of an almost incredibly perfect Puritan child and wife.[38] 'The Sabbath day was always dear and welcome to her, and though many times she went far for it, yet she would not be without the Ministery of the Word: And her heart was so tender, and full of compassion, that oftentimes she was perceived to hear Sermons, read, pray, and meditate, with tears.' Married at twenty, she was the model helpmeet, bountiful to the poor, faithful to her program of daily prayer, reading and meditation. In two years she died, and her biographer spares us none of the horrors of her deathbed temptation, concluding though they do, as always, in the victory of the spirit.

In 1625 John Bruen (born 1560), her brother, died, and another preacher, William Hinde, wrote his life.[39] It is a particularly rich and vivacious account of a Puritan Squire Allworthy, a pillar of the faith in the countryside and a benefactor of the faithful, painful preachers. In youth he was much given to 'hawking, hunting, and such carnal delights.' But he soon repented and then none more earnest than he in the good life. Early and late, in heat and cold, he would ride to hear sermons and bring home copies of what he heard. No wonder that, after thirty-six years of such practice, 'he left to the heirs of his Family so many Volumnes of Manuscripts set up orderly in his Study, as is scarce credible.' Naturally he also set up godly preachers in his neighborhood, even at his own expense, 'honoring God with his substance, by giving maintenance to such as were the Lords Labourers in his harvest.' He ordered the painted windows which darkened his chapel with superstitious images to be torn down and the windows glazed again. He brought in so many preachers that 'the Pipers, Fidlers, Bearwards, Players and Gamesters,' who had been infesting the town of Tarvin on Sundays, fled and the place was filled instead by 'multitudes of wel-affected people.' To be sure he fed solid creature meals to the godly upon these occasions, 'so that at one of these times, he spent in his house a fat Beef and a half in the space of three dayes.' He was much given to hospitality. 'His house was the common Inn of Gods children that came neer him.' There was no waste permitted, but a bountiful sufficiency obtained at his table, furnished as it was from 'a great flight of Pigeons, a Warren of Conies, delicate Fishponds, besides other ordinary provision.' Thus, especially in the 'deer years,' he filled the bellies of multitudes. But he was truly admired for his practice of religion, 'insomuch that divers Gentlmen of the best rank desired to sojourn in his house, for their better information in the way of God.' His servants profited no less. He employed only such as set their faces toward heaven, and he treated them as brothers in Christ. Consequently he had no man or maid who was idle or unprofitable. He was especially devoted to one old fellow, who, though he could not read, 'had a good gift in prayer,' knew the Bible, and kept a leather girdle he had invented as an aid to memory, 'long and large, which went twice about him.' It was divided into parts, one for each book, with points and thongs for chapters and knots for verses. 'This he used instead of pen and ink in hearing Sermons.' His master went often to barn or hopyard to confer with him, fed him from the high table when he grew old, and when he died kept his girdle, 'and would merrily call it the Girdle of verity.' Thus John Bruen lived his life according to the rule the preachers set, earned their gratitude, made a properly edifying end and left to one of them the materials with which to write a biography for the encouragement of other godly inclined gentlemen. He had many imitators and successors among those who had it in their power likewise to further the work of the Lord.

The preachers by no means, however, confined themselves, when it came to writing spiritual biographies, to wealthy benefactors. Among the many lives of humbler persons which they ushered into print, two, one of a woman and one of a seaman, may be especially instanced not only for their own sake but also for what they suggest toward the future literary development of form and theme. In 1622 or earlier died Mary Gunter.[40] She had been born and reared a papist, and in the household where, being orphaned, she had been placed, she had committed childish thefts at the expense of her benefactress. But a good minister awakened her conscience, not only to remorse for stealing but to fear lest she had also committed the sin against the Holy Ghost. Satan began to 'reach at her with strong and violent temptations' to despair, even to thoughts of suicide. At last, however, God brought her to the resolution that, 'though there was much in the Bible which shee did not understand, yet . . . if shee would diligently read and search the Scriptures, with earnest prayer to God for a good understanding in them, shee should attaine thence a measure of knowledge, sufficient to bring her to heaven.' Satan troubled her no more. She became one of those prudent saints who memorized whole chapters so that, in case persecution should rage again, they would not be utterly deprived of the means of grace. 'Shee kept a Catalogue of her daily slips, and set downe even the naughty thoughts which shee observed in her selfe.' Satan finally beset her again on her deathbed, but she worsted him and died rejoicing. The account of her experience was ostensibly penned by her husband, but Thomas Taylor probably stood beside him as he wrote, and published the life along with the sermon he himself preached for the funeral. This was called *The Pilgrims Profession*, a description of the life of a Christian as a wayfarer through this world to the next. We shall have to refer to it later when we consider the Puritan allegory of spiritual pilgrimage.

The great William Gouge was called upon in 1638 to preach a sermon upon the strange case of Vincent Jukes.[41] This Shropshire man was apprenticed to a cook and then sent to sea. On a voyage to Genoa, his ship was captured by the Turks, and he was sold in slavery to a blackamoor. In peril of his life, he apostatized, but later escaped and made his way to England. On his next voyage, this time to Greenland, 'hee was much troubled night and day, and . . . could not well sleepe through horrour of conscience for denying his Christian faith.' Falling into proper hands on his return, he was of course restored to grace and readmitted to the church. Gouge preached upon the occasion. The story had value at the time as news, a fact of which the preacher showed himself aware. He made haste to have his sermon printed in order to forestall 'the publishing of other copies taken at the Preaching thereof by such as have skill in Brachygraphie or short-writing.' Moreover, in presenting this extraordinary evidence of the power of the spirit to work upon the heart under the most difficult conditions, he laid aside his customary pulpit manner and simply told what had happened with an exactness that would have become Defoe himself.

This is not the place to do more than glance at the later development of the spiritual biography. Launched by the Puritan preachers early in the seventeenth century, it continued in their hands without much change of tone far beyond the Restoration, reaching its highest point in the autobiography of Richard Baxter. Perhaps, however, the greatest practitioner that might be claimed for the art was Milton, who, at his own remove and with his own lofty idiosyncrasy, also set forth his own spiritual experience, figuratively in *Comus* and *Lycidas* and explicitly in more than one autobiographical passage of his controversial tracts. But in one important respect, Milton's use of personal confession differs from that of the Puritan clergy and resembles that of the lay preachers who were to flourish in such abundance after 1640. Milton did not wait for his experiences to be put into print after his death, but printed them himself as a kind of certification of the spirit for his right to challenge the prelates and to instruct parliament and people in their duties and responsibilities. Precisely similar, though upon a different level, were the practice and the aim of the tub-preachers who sprang up on every hand in the revolution, imitating at the same time that they confounded their betters and begetters. The vulgar prophet, having no diploma more academic in origin, put forth his own account of his spiritual struggle and conversion as a kind of diploma from the Holy Ghost. Hence came not only the *Grace Abounding* of the baptist tinker, John Bunyan, but a flood of such confessions from other baptists and from the ranters, seekers, quakers, Muggletonians and the other enthusiasts who continued to awaken the spirit in the lower classes after 1650. None were more emphatic, of course, in condemning such manifestations of the Puritan spirit than the successors of those reformers within the church and the clerical caste who had been primarily responsible for initiating them. Neither Bunyan nor any of the other unlearned sectarians could be admitted by Clarke into his gallery of saints, and by the same token we must forego consideration of their part in the development of Puritan expression in order to return to the literature in which, not realizing what its full effect would be, the spiritual brotherhood set forth the way of life which its members were deriving from the formulas of Paul and Calvin.

What the preacher said in the pulpit was supposed to be but one expression, though the crowning one, of the spirit which breathed through all his acts. A man might, conceded Thomas Gataker, 'be like . . . a stonegutter (saith Augustine) that conveigheth water into a garden, but receiveth no benefit thereby itselfe; . . . or like to the baptisme water (saith Gregory) that helpes men to Heaven ward, and goeth after downe to the sinke itselfe.'[42] But not much good is done where there is no consent between lip and life. A man must preach first to himself. The new life to which he was born was a new way of life.

His whole career must be a sermon, precisely as, according to Milton,
the poet's must be a poem. He must, like John the Baptist, be 'all
voice: a voice in his habit, a voice in his diet, a voice in his dwelling, a
voice in his conversation, as well as in his preaching.'[43] He must be
none of those of whom it was said that when they were in the pulpit
men wished them never out and when they were out wished them
never in.[44] 'Wood,' said William Perkins, 'that is capable of fire doth
not burne, unlesse fire be put to it: and he must first be godly affected
himselfe, who would stirre up godly affections in other men.'[45] All
who saw him should see, as it were, religion embodied.[46] Again and
again the changes were rung on the phrases, 'as he taught, he wrought:
His doctrine and his practice concurred.'[47] 'His good works were unan-
swerable Syllogisms, invincible Demonstrations to convince his Neighbours, whereby he drew their Hearts, and engaged their Affections
after the Beauty of Holiness. He practised what he preached, and did
what he taught.'[48]

Such praise was not mere commonplace. It arose from a fervently
held and essential part of Puritan doctrine and practice. The preachers,
though they had failed to win official recognition as leaders of public
opinion, set themselves to gain the support of public opinion by living
according to their principles in the public eye. Faith, we must remember, was the consequence not the cause of God's calling the soul to come
out of sin. When faith was real, it manifested itself in the saint's
persistence every hour of every day in every word and act of his life.
He dwelt ever in his great taskmaster's eye.

But how in particular, the unenlightened needed to know, do saints
behave? The answer to this question the preachers dramatized in their
own actions and then reduced to a code which they spread abroad in a
hundred printed forms. The unloveliness of this code in some of its
later manifestations should not blind us to its positive and bracing
effect upon common life in Stuart times. The merry England doomed
by Puritan asceticism was not all cakes and ale, maypole dancing and
frolics on the village green. We have but to turn to the picture which
Baxter gives us of conditions in Cheshire and at Kidderminster to
guess at the social chaos and moral corruption of many a swollen town
and decaying country neighborhood. To the Puritans it seemed that
the church was being used simply as a bulwark to protect privilege

against reform. The traditional services, even when performed with dignity and beauty, appeared to them inadequate for the spiritual guidance of the people. Christian morality as well as Christian worship needed to be revitalized. This was what the preachers were endeavoring to effect, and the only question that can be raised is not as to the fact of their sincerity but as to the efficacy of their methods. They were endeavoring to adapt Christian morality to the needs of a population which was being steadily driven from its old feudal status into the untried conditions of competition between man and man in an increasingly commercial and industrial society under a money economy. They seized upon the opportunities for communication afforded by the gathering of people in towns, by the rise of the press, and by the consequent spreading of literacy. That is, they had the pulpit and they had an audience which had the Bible. The humanitarian idealism of the gospels was, of course, not neglected in their sermons. But of even more practical application was the Hebrew code of conduct, interpreted and reinforced by the trenchant epitomizing genius of Paul. The preachers, consequently, recast for their own age Paul's digest of the laws of Moses, giving prominent place to the indispensable duties of Bible-reading and attendance upon sermons. Thus they offered a regimen which answered to a genuine longing on the part of many of the people for a more decent, more self-controlled and self-respecting existence.

Along with the sermons and treatises in which they anatomized the spiritual life and with the diaries and confessional biographies in which they and their proselytes depicted the workings of grace in particular cases, the preachers also took to setting forth the pattern of daily existence which the saint should follow. We have already seen that Richard Rogers and the preachers of his neighborhood, even while the Armada loomed off the Essex shore, were much occupied with the attempt to draw up a rule of life for their own and others' guidance. The results emerged in 1603 in the publication of Rogers' *Seven Treatises*. 'I propound,' says the author, 'to helpe the frailtie of Gods children, . . . by setting before their eies as in a glasse, the infinite, secret, and deceitfull corruptions of the heart: from whence . . . sore and dangerous evils doe arise.'[49] But along with this, he proposes to give them a rule which will enable them to overcome and escape these dangers. He desires 'to intreate and to aide my poore neighbours and brethren . . . if by any meanes I may be able hereby, to make the Christian way anything more easie and pleasant unto them, then many finde it: and to bring it into more price, then the most doe value it at.' The saints have knowledge of 'their wants, their infirmities, their corruptions, rebellions, hindrances & other discouragements.' He will soon show them 'how they may every day in the best manner, remedie, or at least wise weaken and diminish them, and that they may also behold their liberties and prerogatives, which they have by Christ.' Other writers, he says at the conclusion to his book, have set forth many good things for the instruction of their fellows. None has heretofore done what he has done, namely 'driven at this one particular of daily directing a Christian.'

It takes Rogers in the *Seven Treatises* just short of six hundred large quarto pages to depict all the perils and to prescribe all the duties of the Christian day. He writes plainly and not without abundance of homely illustration and particular application, but he has not yet learned that men can weary even of the plainest and most wholesome instruction if too long protracted. This lesson, however, was not wasted on the preachers. Many were the short and easy expositions of the Puritan code published by Rogers' successors. A typical example, one of the most frequently reprinted, was *A Garden of Spirituall Flowers*. This little manual was made up of brief plain statements of doctrine and of practical directions for godly living, culled and condensed from the writings of Rogers himself, from Richard Greenham, William Perkins and two less-known men. It tells one how to act like a saint and so rest assured that one has grace. It passes from 'Short Rules sent by.Master Richard Greenham to a Gentlewoman troubled in minde' to 'A short Direction for the daily Exercise of a Christian, both on the Sabbath day, and also on the week dayes.'

Let us glance for a moment at the ideal day of the elect, as described in *A Garden of Spirituall Flowers* and the many other popular presentations of the Puritan code.[50] The saint is told to awake with God and pray. 'And let this bee done solemnely upon thy knees (and not as many doe, lazing upon their beds) that it may bee done with a humble, pure, and sincere devotion.' If he is the head of a household, he should be stirring early to call his family together for morning prayers. After breakfast he may betake himself to his ordinary calling and business, seeing that his family does likewise. There are 'Rules for the behaving of [himself] Christian-like in imployment about [his] worldly businesse, and enjoying the benefit of the same.' He must keep close watch upon his heart, words and deeds, and see that his time is not idly, carelessly or unprofitably spent. He must mind his own business and let other men mind theirs. 'Be not a Tale-berer, nor a Tale-receiver: deale justly & uprightly with all men: let thy conversation be without covetousnesse, and without prodigalitie: serve the Lord in singlenesse of heart: be doing good, and abstaine from all appearance of evill.' In the same spirit he is told how to bear himself in company and in solitude, in prosperity and in adversity. He is not to shun prosperity nor yet to set his heart upon it. If it comes, it will come as God's free gift and is to be used as such. He is not to fear the adversity which God may bestow for the strengthening of his spirit. Business done, he goes home and concludes the day by gathering his household once more about him. He reads to them from scripture, catechizes them, sings psalms and prays with them. Then he goes to his chamber to meditate and, as we have seen, to balance his spiritual accounts. And so to bed. For Sundays, he is given special directions. In church, whither he proceeds in the morning at the head of his family, he must keep his eyes fixed on the preacher, so that thoughts may not wander. He is advised to mark the speaker's text, observe how it is 'divided,' note the handling of each division, find the places in scripture alleged for proof, fold down the leaf at the appropriate passages so that he may review them at leisure. Then home again to discuss the sermon with the family after dinner and back again to church to repeat the whole performance in the afternoon. If such a program seem preposterous to the man of the present day, he should remember that his forefathers even in the conduct of this world's business were concerned about their consciences. Perhaps the desire of later generations to escape from Puritanism has been at least in part a desire to do business with less hindrance from a scheme of life so insistent upon keeping the individual forever in mind of his moral responsibilities.

Of all the books written for the promulgation of the Puritan code, probably the most widely circulated and the most important were those which came from John Dod. In 1603, soon after Rogers' *Seven Treatises*, Dod published *A Plaine and Familiar Exposition of the Ten Commandements*, and followed this in later years by similar works upon Proverbs and the Lord's Prayer. He had the assistance of Robert Cleaver, of whom we hear little except that he was a 'solid Textman.'[51] The popularity of Dod's commentary on the decalogue—it earned for its author the title Decalogue Dod—is evident in the fact that the book appears to have been issued eighteen times in the thirty years after its first appearance. This success was no doubt in part due to public interest in the subject, but in still larger measure it was owing to the fact that Dod interpreted the ten commandments as general rules underlying a definite way of life, the particular duties of which he proceeded to set down. The Puritan code of godly behavior in all the relations of family, household, business, church and state was never more exactly stated or carefully worked out. Dod does not occupy himself with the anatomy of sin or the drama of spiritual war. His purpose is the practical utilitarian one of directing behavior to moral ends, and this he attempts in plain straightforward prose, neither eloquent nor inspiring but apt and well salted with pithy maxims and homely analogies.

The duties of husband and wife and of the family in general occupied, naturally, a large place in the code. Puritanism has had to bear much blame for the limitations put upon woman in the society of the last three hundred years. But the peculiar Puritan attitude, which was less peculiar than it seems, was not a simple manifestation of masculine tyranny, and the emancipation of woman has involved more than the simple rejection of 'he for God only, she for God in him.' The code, much though it owed to Paul in other respects, was completely innocent of anything like an ascetic or suspicious attitude toward marriage. The saints married early and as often as mortality gave occasion, and they begot children without restraint. Like all other activities to which men might be called, marriage was an opportunity for spiritual effort, something to be sanctified by the spirit. Needless to say the code was based upon the patriarchal conception of the family as conveyed by scripture and custom. The Puritan exaltation of the family could serve only to make the godly hold to that conception the more earnestly. But Puritan individualism also had its effect and must be taken into account. Though the wife must be subordinate to the husband, woman must also be regarded as equal to man in her title to grace and in her independent responsibility before God. She too had to go on spiritual pilgrimage and make spiritual war, and she had to go on her own feet and fight her own battle. She was the weaker vessel, of course, but subject to the same law, with this advantage to compensate for her frailty: that she might have a husband to guide her. She was less than he but not alien. She should adhere to the spirit of godliness in him, being a glory to him, as he should adhere to God, being God's glory. Their marriage then, and no other marriage could truly take place, would be a union of two souls of differing capacities but of the same kindred, sharing the same freedom, the same enterprise and the same responsibility.

Certain features of this conception have always displeased not a few women and some men. But the preachers made plain that, if the wife must bow to God in the husband, the husband must take the wife to his spiritual care as God takes man. She was not his body slave but the companion of his soul. He must cherish her as such, respecting her spiritual integrity and affording her the same freedom for spiritual effort which he himself enjoyed. Thus William Gouge in his seven-hundred-page exposition of 'domesticall duties'[52] dwelt at great length on the proper subjection of wives to husbands, not without provoking some murmurs among the females of his flock, but he also labored the point that husbands should exact less strict obedience than good wives might be willing to grant. John Dod also has much to say on the same subject in his book on the decalogue, saying it, as usual, more pithily than most and with his characteristic blending of common sense and racy speech. Marriage for him is a spiritual union, but a spiritual union bringing with it many practical advantages for wives as well as husbands. The man who is truly benevolent toward his wife, Dod observes, should 'marke and observe the gifts of wisedome, and government, or what ever else God hath graced her with, that he may set them on work.' Thus he will show his love and confidence in her, and thus too she will be kept from discouragement and idleness: 'besides, it will turne to the great good and profit of the familie.' How much worse, he exclaims, is the practice of those foolish husbands, busybodies, who 'wil have all come through their own hand; and then indeed nothing goes well through any hand.' Dod was noted for being 'plain and perspicuous' in his style, but he did not abstain from the use of pat illustrations for driving home his points. 'If the Pilot,' he says, 'would both holde the sterne, and hoyse up the sayle, & be upon the hatches, and labour at the pumpe, and do all himselfe, it must needs go ill with the ship.' So he concludes with the reiteration of the injunction that husbands trust their wives and reap the increase of their talents: 'those gifts that God hath given the wife, the husband must see them put to the best use: and then she shall be a fellow helper to him, & bring a blessing upon the family, by her labour.'[53] That a lumpish wife's failure to awaken to the divine spark in her husband should be taken as just grounds for turning her away does not enter into Dod's calculations, though it was obviously a logical enough corollary to his principles.

The fullest and most important statement of the position of woman and the nature of marriage under the Puritan code was to come from Milton in his divorce tracts, as the finest expression of Puritan idealization of woman and the family was to come in *Paradise Lost*. These works fall outside the scope of the present volume, but the subject is one of such far-reaching importance that we must stop a moment here to note what the notions of such men as Dod and Gouge implied. Perhaps the most far-reaching influence which has come to us from medieval life and letters has been the romanticizing of woman and the passion of love.[54] Romantic love, however, as presented in medieval literature, was characteristically associated with extramarital relations. But there were exceptions, and with no diminution of romantic feeling the exceptions were destined to become the rule. In Spenser the woman idealized by the lover is the woman he is to marry. Any other love is evil. There is no other kind of marriage. Milton was the disciple of Spenser. But he was also the disciple of the Puritan preachers like Dod and Gouge. Medieval romantic idealizing of woman, which Spenser transposed to the sphere of marriage, was combined by Milton with Puritan religious idealizing of marriage and of woman as wife to produce the classic picture of Puritan wedlock in *Paradise Lost*. Why the idealization of love within the field of marriage should, as Milton perceived, require an altered and extended conception of divorce, and how

premarital romantic courtship came to fill so much of later literature,
are not matters to be discussed here.

One further aspect of the Puritan conception of the good life remains to be presented before we undertake to discuss the saga of the
spiritual life set forth in the sermons. The preachers endeavored by
precept and example to show how the elect, while living according to
the code of saintliness, must use their gifts and opportunities in this
life. The Puritan code was much more than a table of prohibitions. It
was the program of an active, not a monastic or contemplative, life.
The saints stripped themselves for battle, and only as the battle waxed
hot and desperate did they degenerate into the fanatical iconoclasts of
familiar tradition. Milton's lady scorned not the gifts that Comus
offered her but the giver. 'Worldly things,' according to Sibbes, 'are
good in themselves, and given to sweeten our passage to Heaven,' even
to sweeten our 'profession of Religion.' We must use the world as our
servant, not our master, take comfort in it but not set our hearts upon
it or let ourselves be made 'drunke with the cares below.' All is, in
other words, as we have grace to use it. 'This world and the things
thereof are all good, and were all made of God, for the benefit of his
creature.'[55] John Dod, gathering his flock about him, opening his
doors to all comers, sitting down at the head of a full table, talking
himself thirsty, and calling for a draft of wine and beer mixed, was no
bigoted ascetic, though he did disapprove of stage plays, dancing and
card-playing. The saint had no reason to fear the world or run away
from it. Rather he must go forth into it and do the will of God there.
Rogers scorns the suggestion that, if men live according to the godly
rule, they will neglect their necessary affairs 'and so poverty grow
upon the land.' On the contrary, he says, he who goes about his work,
not first attending upon God by faith, 'goeth about it preposterously,
& shal find his successe answerable.' 'He riddeth not most worke, who
goeth to it most early, when his instruments which he should use in
the performance of the same be blunt and dull.' 'Godlinesse hinders
not mens labours, neither decaies the Common-wealth.' There is a
'godly thrift,' a 'Christian gaining' and a 'lawfull prospering' which
come to him who goes to work 'with a minde which is at peace with
God.' Who cannot see that by the labor of such men 'the Common-

wealth . . . should flourish much more, having a certeine promise of blessing?'[56]

The saint knows that he need not fear to lose a penny while he stops to say his prayers. He knows that whatever he has and whatever he gains in the course of business comes from God. His prime piece of capital, he knows, consists in the abilities and opportunities which God has bestowed upon him for doing the business of the world. They are his talent, and he never forgets by whom this was given or by whom and on what terms it will be exacted in return. This doctrine comes, of course, directly from the parable of the talents, 'wherein,' to use the words of Gabriel Powell, 'is shewed, that no man, of what state or condition soever hee bee, is Lord of his owne riches or substance, but the steward and disposer of it, accountable unto God for all things.'[57] It is the theme of Milton's sonnet concerning the one talent which is death to hide. Our individual abilities are not given us as rewards to be enjoyed—no sinner merits any favor from God. Nor does God grant them as necessary means to ends of his own—'God doth not need either man's work or his own gifts.' They are bestowed as unconditioned occasions for service upon such as truly love their maker. Those who put their gifts to work, or, as Milton would have it, merely stand ready and waiting to do so, may feel assured that they please him. Those who do not may expect one day to hear the master chide. For, to quote Powell once more, 'we must be accountable for the least farthing which we have received of God; after what manner we came by it, how and to what use we have bestowed and spent it.'

No part of the Puritan code was more weighted with practical significance than this. Nothing in the postulates of Puritan doctrine up to this point was inconsistent with the stopping of Puritanism at mere pietism within self-centered groups of believers, and such pietistic groups did in fact spring up within the Puritan movement as among Protestants on the continent. But by insistence upon the moral aspects of the doctrine of the talent the preachers opened a wide door through which they drove their flocks out into the world to have their fill of experience. To be specific, they gave in this way to the general doctrine of God's calling a definite application. When God called his elect to repent and believe, he also called upon them to act. The gifts and opportunities, no matter how humble and narrow, with which the saint

was invested were also part of his commission from God. Whatsoever
we undertake in the exercise of our talents and in the spirit of faith is
good. It is what God has called us to do. Woe unto us if we do not do
it, and happy the man who responds to the vocation of his own abilities.
God is strict about his business, but just. 'They which are furnished
with gifts for their callings, namely aptnesse and willingnesse, and are
thereunto called or set apart by men' may rest assured that they are
called by God.[58] Moreover, when they walk in a calling lawful in
itself and suited to their capacities, they are walking in his presence and
under his special protection. This was a conviction destined to have
disturbing results when authority attempted to rule that it was not
lawful for a Milton to exercise his talent for instructing his fellow
countrymen or a Lilburne his for trading in pamphlets, wool or soap.
For the doctrine of the talent also taught that all 'offices & callings
which serve to preserve the good estate of any family, Church or
common wealth, are lawfull & of God.' Was not every man, since all
were equal under the law of God, required to believe 'that the calling
in which he is; is the particular calling in which God [would] bee
served of him?'[59] Any common man needed but to know in his heart
that what he did he did sincerely as God's own work, and it followed
that what he did was what God would have him do. His own conscience was the judge of his own conduct. 'Common actions are as the
doer is affected. A sincere man . . . is commanded to serve God in his
calling as well as in the Church, and therefore he will not,' indeed he
cannot, 'doe it negligently . . . He will not do it falsely, he will not
prophane his calling.' Common actions thus performed 'with an eye to
God' were all 'good, and religious actions. For the Grace of God is a
blessed Alcumist, where it toucheth it makes good, and religious.'[60]

The alchemy of God's grace was nowhere more charmingly set forth
than in Richard Bernard's *Ruth Recompense*, the full title of which
shows that Samuel Richardson's heroine was not the first to exemplify
the theme of virtue rewarded: *A Commentarie upon the Book of
Ruth: Wherein is shewed her happy calling out of her owne Country
and People, into the fellowship and society of the Lords Inheritance:
Her vertuous life and holy Carriage amongst them: and then, her
reward in Gods mercy, being by an honourable Marriage made a
Mother in Israel*. Ruth, we know, was placed by circumstances in an

equivocal position, a position, that is, which would have been equivocal had she not been a child of grace. Being such, she may, nay must, under the code obey her calling even though it be to court a rich man to marry her. Boaz shows how riches too may be sanctified.

Riches well used bring grace in estimation before men, for they inable men to shew forth godlinesse, & to passe on their time with more comfort, and to countenance and defend their poore Christian brethren in well-doing. Therefore if grace and goods goe together, thou hast great cause to blesse God: for it is a most happy estate, to bee rich towards the world, and to God too, to bee rich body and soule: But although this is a very rare estate, yet we see that they may meete together: and therefore we may not thinke that he which is rich, can not be religious. True it is, that it is hard for a rich man to enter the Kingdome of heaven; but it is not impossible.[61]

What was true for men in other occupations was no less but no more true for the preacher, though his task was the harder. He should, said Rogers, follow the rule laid down for every believer, and then he must also follow his special calling, which was to preach. He must have the gift for admonishing, exhorting, comforting and instructing others. He must demonstrate his possession of the gift by securing acknowledgment of its presence in him from those he would serve. He must be able to inspire his hearers to put their own talents to use. His lot was, indeed, not an easy one. Preachers must have more capacious souls than ordinary men since their work was both more difficult and more important, but they had therefore greater trials and temptations to endure.

Though it must be granted, that they have many more helps in regard of their ministery then private men; yet . . . their troubles and crosses are manie more & greater . . . for they are more shot at by Sathan and his instruments, they have many discouragements, unkindnesses offered them, and hatred for their good will and for doing of their duty.[62]

Such assertions of the special duty and the special danger of preachers in the exercise of their special gift are almost as numerous in the preachers' sermons as the sermons themselves. According to the doctrine of the talent, the only responsibility that could possibly equal theirs was that of the magistrate. These two, in fact, the vocation of the one to preach and of the other to rule, were the poles about which the truly godly state revolved. This principle was presently to be the basic contention of Milton when he took up the argument for Utopia. John Downame presented it much earlier and with admirable clearness. 'Princes and Magistrates,' he says, perform their services to God 'by enacting good lawes, and seeing them duely executed, making their owne lives (as it were) rules of that obedience which they require of the people, and lively examples and patternes for their imitation.' Preachers serve 'by leading those which are committed unto their charge, in the waies of truth and godlinesse, not onely by their preaching and writing, instruction, admonition, perswasion and exhortation, but also by practizing those duties which they teach others, and shining before them in the light of a godly life.' It will follow, if each has exercised his talent in the fear of the Lord, that the people will also strive to please God, 'by yeelding their cheerefull obedience to the godly lawes of Governors, and by imbracing the sound and profitable doctrine, and imitating the Christian and religious examples of their godly Teachers.'[63] Thus did the preachers link the doctrine of the talent with their conception of the dual state, one part carnal, the other spiritual, the two complementary. They were, perhaps, dreaming of such a theocracy as indeed they achieved for a time in New England, but they were also, certainly without intention, preparing for a society in which popular education and the free play of public opinion would become the conditions under and by which government must operate.

We have now traced the course of Puritan preaching from its beginning at Cambridge after the expulsion of Cartwright to the time when the spiritual brotherhood had attained a position of power which the rulers of state and church could not let go unchallenged. We have seen how the preachers transposed the teachings of Paul and the doctrine of Calvin into a psychological pattern and a code of behavior for all men to follow. As their work prospered, the godly Utopia again began to dazzle their vision, but before they could reach the New Jerusalem they had to go a long journey and fight many battles.

IV

The Rhetoric of the Spirit

EVERY Puritan saint in believing himself chosen by God to be saved knew that he must give witness to the grace that had befallen him by living a saintly life. He must put his abilities to work in the spirit of faith for the glory of God. This was as true for the preacher as for other men, except only that the preacher, being entrusted with a greater gift, was burdened with a greater responsibility. His talent, and therefore his service, was to utter as well as to enact godliness. He had the gift of discourse, a gift, to the Puritan way of thinking, of a peculiar sanctity and power.

The authorized version of 1611 was the culmination of the effort of a long succession of English churchmen to put the word of God into the vernacular. Versed though they were in the learned tongues and reared in the tradition of letters, the translators did not do their work upon the level of academic Latinized English. Neither, on the other hand, did they English the Bible upon the everyday or vulgar plane. They turned their learning and skill to the task of developing out of the familiar common speech an English appropriate to the lofty matter they had in hand and yet moving and intelligible to the plain, unlearned reader. The result was the marvellous idiom of the English Bible. The Puritan preachers were churchmen, indistinguishable in respect to social origin and intellectual attainments from others. They had, of course, earnestly supported the enterprise of placing the scriptures within reach of the people, and some of the more eminent among them had taken part in the actual work of translation. Preaching was for them but the natural carrying on of the holy endeavor to popularize the sacred book and the science of understanding and applying its lessons. The motive they acknowledged was zeal for the saving of souls, but we must not forget that they had also to fill their bellies. They were mendicants and had like the wits and playwrights to coin their gifts and learning in order to live. Their evangelical zeal, from this point of view, was but the convention of their art, the condition under which on their stage, in their theatre, they could hope to win the imagination and also the support of the crowd. Other conventions followed upon this. The preachers, moved by the spirit of godliness, professed to appeal not at all, like other wielders of words, to imagination but to absolute truth in scripture and the inescapable facts of human experience. What they said was not rhetoric or poetry but science and law. It owed nothing essential to human device or invention but proceeded directly from the word of God, as anyone who could read English was supposed to be able to see for himself. We need not accept these assumptions in order to perceive their results on the development of the art of English words. The immediate effects varied. The preacher might practice the studied artlessness we have observed in William Gouge's account of the reconversion of Vincent Jukes. He was often prompted to compile technical treatises, complicated, interminable and arid in the extreme. By the initiated, these things were no doubt read and pondered. By the general run of godly folk, they were regarded with respect. But for the common public they were as a rule too expensive to buy, too dull to read and too difficult to understand. To be sure, such methods of discourse, prevalent as they were in controversial writing, intruded more or less frequently into the pulpit, but there they were regarded by the best judges as distinctly out of place. Sermons, as Robert Harris said, should not be divinity lectures,[1] and such for the most part they were not. The auditory liked to think that behind the sermon were ranged inexhaustible learning and irrefragable logic but lent its ears most willingly to something else.

We can well afford to do as the great majority of common men of that age did, neglect the divinity lectures and fasten attention upon the sermons and other works of edification which the preachers produced for the illumination of the multitude. The style they chose to adopt was nothing if not consciously devised for a definite purpose. It was in the first place a deliberate reaction away from the style which was growing fashionable in the orthodox Anglican pulpits. It was asserted to be by contrast 'plain and perspicuous,' 'English' and 'spiritual.' Actually it was an intensely imaginative hortatory prose. It adapted traditional medieval conventions of popular preaching to the great themes of Puritan doctrine. It adapted also to the same end the style of the English Bible, which was repeatedly and insistently alleged to be the perfect model of discourse, offered to the use of man by no less a writer than the Holy Spirit himself. John Downame's statement of this may be taken as typical, expressing as it does the preacher's general aim as well as his belief in divine authority for his stylistic practice.

For whereas men in their writings affect the praise of flowing eloquence and loftiness of phrase, the holy Ghost . . . hath used great simplicitie and wonderfull plainesse, applying himselfe to the capacitie of the most unlearned . . . and under the vaile of simple and plaine speech, there shineth such divine wisdome and glorious majestie, that all the humane writings in the world, though never so adorned with the flowers of eloquence, and sharpe conceits of wit and learning, cannot so deeply pearce the heart of man, nor so forcibly worke upon his affections, nor so powerfully incline his will either to the imbracing of that which is good, or avoiding of that which is evill, as the word of God . . . [The scriptures] speake in the same manner, and injoyne the like obedience, to prince and people, rich and poore, learned and unlearned, without any difference or respect of person . . . and therefore, howsoever the Lord in the profunditie of wisdome could have written in such a loftie stile as would have filled even the most learned with admiration, yet he useth a simple easie stile fit for the capacity of all, because it was for the use of all, and necessarie to salvation to bee understood of all sorts and conditions.[2]

The primary rules in this democratic rhetoric of the spirit were found in the fourteenth chapter of Paul's first epistle to the Corinthians. 'Let all things be done unto edifying,' says the apostle. To be able to speak strange tongues is good, but 'except ye utter by the tongue words easy to be understood, how shall it be known what is spoken?' For the end of preaching is to make manifest to the unlearned stranger the things of his own heart. 'In which words,' remarks William Perkins in his *Treatise of the Duties and Dignities of the Ministrie*, 'observe an admirable plainnesse and an admirable powerfullnesse.'[3] That must be plain by which an unlearned man is enabled to perceive his own faults. That must be powerful which moves the unregenerate conscience to exclaim 'Certainely God speaks in this man!' Perkins elaborates the advice of Paul still more explicitly in his

Art of Prophecying. The minister must so frame his preaching 'that all, even ignorant persons & unbeleevers may judge that it is not so much he that speaketh, as the Spirit of God in him and by him.' This, Perkins frankly states, required some care. It was the enthusiasts of a later generation who cherished the delusion, or at any rate avowed the theory, that the spirit spoke from their mouths without their having to take any pains with style. The earlier preachers were advised by Perkins that they must themselves contrive to make their speech 'spirituall and gracious,' 'simple and perspicuous, fit both for the peoples understanding, and to expresse the Majestie of the Spirit.' To this end they must note that 'Artis etiam est celare artem; it is also a point of Art to conceale Art.' The preacher should have the 'arts, Philosophy, and variety of reading' at command in preparing his sermon, but in the preaching of it 'Humane wisedome must be concealed.' There must be no indulgence in 'Greek and Latine phrases and quirkes.' John Dod's saying that 'so much Latine was so much flesh in a Sermon' was often quoted. Perkins objected that learned allusions distracted the people's attention, hindered understanding and made it hard to 'fit those things which went afore with those that follow.'[4] Beyond that, he 'that lookes to live by his ministerie' must beware of attempting 'to feede his auditorie with Philosophie, or fables, or lying Legends,' and he is also warned 'not to preach poeticall fictions, Thalmudical dreams, Schoolmens quiddities, Popish decrees, or humane constitutions, or to tickle the itching eares of his auditorie with the fine ringing sentences of the Fathers.'[5]

How John Cotton and, following his lead, Thomas Goodwin and John Preston scorned the flaunting wit and rhetoric of such men of their time as Richard Senhouse, we have already seen. Reaction against the style of the orthodox Anglicans was an important element in the preacher's conversion, and the account of his 'plainness and powerfulness' became almost as conventional a part of the legend of him as conversion itself. Certainly no group of men ever labored more earnestly or self-consciously to make themselves understood by their audience as they found it. Richard Stock spoke so 'that both the learnedest might receive satisfaction from him, and the very meanest and dullest might also reap benefit by him.'[6] God gave Richard Rothwell 'great in-let into the hearts of men,' 'great Dexterity in Communicating his mind to another, and speaking to his understanding.'[7] Samuel Crook was not like one of those 'who for want of wares in their shops, set up painted boxes to fill up empty shelves,' nor did he feed his flock 'with airy dews of effeminate Rhetorick . . . nor yet with the jerks, and quibbles of a light spirit, which he ever abhorred as the excrementitious superfluities of frothy brains, and unhallowed hearts.' Rather he spoke always in the words 'which the Holy Ghost teacheth,' knowing 'very well how to set forth καινὰ, κοινῶς abstruse points plainly, and how to manage κοινά, καινῶς plain truths elegantly.'[8] Richard Capel would stoop to speak to country people in 'their own proper dialect,' and had special skill in making deep mysteries plain to shallowest capacities.[9] Richard Mather aimed 'to shoot his Arrows not over Peoples Heads but into their Hearts and Consciences.'[10] Robert Harris 'could so cook his meat that he could make it relish to every pallate: He could dress a plain discourse, so as that all sorts should be delighted with it. He could preach with a learned plainness, and had learned to conceal his Art. He had clear Notions of high Mysteries, and proper language to make them stoop to the meanest capacity.'[11] John Dod, finally, was pre-eminent in this as in the other virtues of the Puritan minister. All the favorite eulogistic terms were applied to his style; it was plain, powerful, perspicuous, pithy. His preaching so searched the hearts of sinners that some said he must have had spies and informers at work for him. His reply was a perfect expression of the ideal of the whole brotherhood: 'he answered that the Word of God was searching, and that if he was shut up in a dark Vault, where none could come at him, yet allow him but a Bible and a Candle, and he should preach as he did.'[12]

We should not take too literally the boast of plainness in the sermons of the spiritual preachers. At any rate, a plain style did not mean for them a colorless or prosaic style. They and many of their auditors were quite capable of wielding and of understanding the erudition and the rhetoric of the metaphysical and witty preachers. But there were others unable to do so whom it was important to please by reason of their growing wealth and influence. To these people, rendered literate and articulate as never before by the help of the popularized Bible, the learning and the language of the orthodox Anglican pulpit seemed alien, newfangled and pretentious. No longer inclined to accept with resignation the imputation of ignorance and of intellectual inferiority, they made implicit demands which offered an opportunity to the preachers similar to that which had come to the playwrights and translators. The style in which the spiritual brethren chose to address the new vernacular public was called plain English not because it was unimaginative or in the larger sense unliterary but because it was designed to be intelligible and moving to plain people who were very conscious of being English. In the same spirit, Milton a little later would finally abandon Latin in order to address himself to his fellow citizens in the mother dialect. The literary quality of the dialect the preachers actually used was, of course, affected in part by the fact that they were themselves thoroughly conversant in the high intellectual culture of their time. But of incalculable importance also was the fact that the mother dialect had its own traditions of no mean power in the art of expression which the cultivated skill of the preachers enabled them to utilize and develop. The English folk were a people accustomed to the life of the countryside, the household, the market town and the sea. Their language was still racy of that life, readier for concrete and consequently for suggestive and imaginative expression than for abstract, intellectual and polite. The zeal for Latin elegance had not yet subdued in the vernacular the flavor of the Anglo-Saxon soil. Moreover the common people had their own background of imaginative experience through the medium of speech. Humanistic culture reached them in some degree through translations and adaptations on the stage or in print. But this influence, at any rate for the Puritan classes, was in large measure overlaid by the preponderant influence of the Bible. The truth was that the life and poetry of Israel were easier to naturalize in common English life and expression than those of Greece and Rome. Behind the Bible, finally, and furthering its acceptance by the popular mind in countless unperceived ways, was the influence of the medieval pulpit. We have recently been shown in abundant and painstaking detail how the English medieval preachers conducted their criticism of manners and morals, laws, customs and social conditions by the aid of an extensive vocabulary of devices fundamentally literary in nature, by trope and metaphor, allegory and symbol, dialogue, drama, fable, beast-tale, *exemplum* and *facetia*.[13] These things became and, there can be no doubt, remained far down into modern times an important familiar part of the apparatus of popular imaginative expression. Thus the common vernacular, the English Bible and the body of forms and images which had come down from the medieval pulpit supplied to the Puritan preachers an idiom by no means barbarous, unaccustomed or lacking in vitality. The Puritan reaction against the sophisticated stylistic fashion of the moment seemed to them and their people, naturally enough, not an innovation but a revival of the good old English way.

The calculated effort to appeal to the popular audience affected the structure as well as the style of the sermon. The preacher carried into the pulpit, as a rule, little more than the heads of the discourse he was to deliver. These represented the traditional scheme which he had learned in the schools.[14] 'The Order and Summe of the sacred and onely method of Preaching,' as prescribed by Perkins, required first that he read the text out of scripture and then explain or 'open' it in its context. He should then proceed 'to collect a fewe and profitable points of doctrine out of the naturall sense.' This was to 'divide' the text. Finally he must 'apply (if he have the gift) the doctrines rightly collected, to the life and manners of men in a simple and plaine speech.' These were called the 'uses.'[15] The temptation of the preacher as an intellectual and a technician was to spend most of his time dividing and subdividing his text and spinning doctrines out in hairbreadth distinction. If he were bent upon dazzling his audience or avoiding anything that might give personal offense, this was the safe course. On the other hand, the tendency of the preacher who sought to search hearts and stir emotions was to dwell upon the 'uses' of a few general doctrines and to drive these home in direct application to the experience of the audience. In this practice, John Dod, who would stand up to preach with nothing more in his hand than 'the Analisis of his Text, the proofs of Scripture for the Doctrines, with the Reasons and Uses,'[16] as usual set the example for younger men. His manner was to begin by 'opening a verse or two, or more at a time, first clearing the drift and connection, then giving the sense and interpretation briefly, but very plainly, not leaving the text untill he had made it plain to the meanest capacity.' Next he cleared and exemplified the doctrines by reference to scripture itself, the preacher 'opening his proofs, not multiplying particulars for oppressing memory, not dwelling so long as to make all truth run through a few texts.' Finally he spoke 'most largely and very home in application, mightily convincing and diving into mens hearts and consciences, leaving them little or nothing to object against it.'[17] Dod's admirer and imitator, Robert Harris, complained that some preachers spent too much time insisting upon doctrinal points and too little upon the applications, 'wherein . . . a Sermons excellency doth consist.' He for his part 'contrived the Uses first,' and 'did often handle the same Texts, and the same Points, and yet still would pen new Applications.'[18]

What all this meant in practical effect was that the spiritual preacher lavished his strength on turning the currents of emotion in his audience into the molds defined by the doctrine of predestination. He could not entirely avoid getting himself involved in a certain amount of abstract metaphysical and theological argument, but his real concern was to shape and direct feeling and conduct. His doctrine became in fact a theory of human behavior, a system of psychology. This being the case, it was inevitably subjected to the testing of observation and experience. Its acceptance, but not its practical validity, derived from scripture. Whether it would work could not really be deduced from a literary text no matter how sacred. The attempt to prove the theory out of scripture quickly resolved itself for all practical purposes into mere sophistry and sciolism, the unreality of which became more than half patent to the preachers themselves the moment they faced the task of carrying the popular audience with them. They found common men perhaps respectful toward abstract theory but for themselves fundamentally pragmatic, interested only in something that would produce results. Hence the emphasis placed by the Puritan pulpit on 'uses.' Doctrine and proof in moderation served to indicate that what the preacher said must be true whether his reasoning were wholly understood or not. 'Applications,' 'uses,' on the other hand, made truth seem apposite and real. They suggested most powerfully what to do and how in the light of results to judge the value—so why not the verity?— of the teaching received. A man did not need to become a scholar in order to attain certitude, but merely a 'professor,' an empiric of the spirit.

The sense of reality thus conceived, however, is the concomitant of sensation, and the illusion of reality is the product of sensation stirred by memory and imagination. Therefore it turned out that the preacher's surest method of winning his public was not dialectic but, however they might be masked by dialectic, rhetoric and poetry. When schoolboys were set to transcribe and study a sermon, they were made to rule off the margin of the page to take the notes and glosses they were expected to supply. When sermons came to be published, frequently from manuscripts which were the product not of the author's but of some disciple's hand, the ruled margin and its legend appeared upon the printed page. We are thus enabled to observe what the dutiful were trained to listen and look for as they sat in church or conned the sermon afterwards in a copy taken down by 'brachygraphie' and then transcribed or printed.[19] The extemporaneous sermons of Preston, recorded in this manner by the faithful and carefully prepared for the press by Sibbes, Davenport, Goodwin and Ball, are equipped with a particularly full apparatus of this sort. The devotee, one hardly needs to say, glossed countless scripture references. He noted in greater or less detail the structure of the discourse, the opening of the chosen text, the divisions and subdivisions, doctrines and proofs, objections and answers, all as a rule carefully numbered. But frequently he noted something more. When, for example, Thomas Draxe has cited and glossed several texts to prove that the elect have the very assurance of grace in their own breasts, he goes on to say that this doctrine will be the easier to understand if 'I . . . explaine and make it lightsome by some familiar comparisons and similitudes.' Whereupon he writes:

Can a man carry fire in his hand and not feele it? . . . Can a woman be wedded to an husband and not know it? . . . Can a man buy, and possesse a precious pearle, and a rich treasure, and yet bee ignorant of it? . . . Can a man doubt of the garments wherewith he is clothed? . . . Can the elect (the friends of God) know all things needfull for their salvation . . . and shall they erre and be ignorant in the knowledge and certaintie of their owne justification and salvation?[20]

At this point the copyist, probably not the author, writes in the margin 'Similitudes and Comparisons.' To gloss the similes as well as the 'firstlies' and the 'seventhlies' of doctrine was also a convention of the connoisseur of sermons. He need not be systematic or exhaustive in this, since the occasions in the text were generally too numerous, but when a particularly elaborate or striking image came, down might go 'simile' in the margin, and when the sermon came from a particularly imagistic preacher like John Preston, it must go down on nearly every page. The fame of the more noted preachers in this sort of thing was, as we should expect, recorded in the legendary accounts of their lives. Baynes 'had a good dexterity, furthered by his love to do good, in explaining dark points with lightsome Similitudes.'[21] The same praise in the same phrases was given to many another. One of the most noted, of course, was John Dod, whose discourses were 'intermixed with such variety of delightfull expressions and similitudes as would take with any man.'[22]

Many other preachers exemplifying the intensive and conscious exploitation of such devices for setting forth Puritan doctrine could be cited. Let us turn for a moment to but one of the most popular of them. Richard Bernard,[23] after graduating from Cambridge and veering dangerously close to separatism, became in 1613 the fortunate recipient of a good living in Somersetshire. He was the author of two books which were widely read in edition after edition. *The Faithfull Shepheard*, first issued in 1607 and extensively revised in 1627, was a popular treatise on the whole duty of preachers, describing the proper conduct of their lives, the learning they required, and—what is especially to the point here—the method and style they should observe in their sermons, not forgetting eloquent insistence upon the glorious function of the pulpit. *The Isle of Man* of 1626 was Bernard's account of the process of regeneration, set forth, however, in the terms of a sustained allegory, the use of which for such purposes the author felt constrained explicitly to defend when he came to publish a thirteenth edition. The pages of few preachers were more thickly sown with imagistic language.

'How can people call on him in whom they have not beleeved?' Bernard exclaims at the opening of *The Faithfull Shepheard*. 'How can they beleeve of whom they have not heard? and how can they heare without a Preacher?' Preaching should be upheld by princes if only out of policy, and—the words anticipate Milton's own—none, not even the sons of nobles, should disdain to take this calling upon themselves. The dispensers of the mysteries of the gospel, 'set a part to be Gods voice to the people, and againe, the peoples unto God,'[24] should,

of course, teach with their lives as well as with their voices. That is
but a painted star which gives no light, a counterfeit fire which gives
no heat, and he is 'only the emptie shadow and meere picture of a
Minister . . . who doth not enlighten others in the wayes of well-
doing by the beames of his good workes.' The sun bears away the glory
of the day and the moon of the night, 'yet there is never a little starre
in the firmament but doth in some measure and proportion contribute
to enlighten the Heavens,' and though some of us may be more eminent 'in grace and place,' yet there is some light and influence required
and expected from us all.[25] 'Common people respect more a Preachers
life than his learning, as Herod did John Baptist.' He must 'speak
soundly, and withall experimentally.' A gracious and zealous heart is
the best rhetorician, 'the sweetest tuner of the voyce, and the most
forcible perswader.' 'It speakes to another what first it feeleth in it
selfe; as it is affected, it endeavours to affect others.' It makes him
'speake to others as to himselfe, and from himselfe to them.'[26] All this
is not to say that, when he goes up into the pulpit, he does not need
learning too, in fact 'all manner of knowledge in humanity.' 'What Art
or Science is there, which a Divine shall not stand in need of,' if he is
to unfold exactly and judiciously every word in scripture? 'Grammar,
Rhetorick, Logicke, Physicks, Mathematicks, Metaphysicks, Ethicks,
Politicks, Oeconomicks, History, and Military Discipline' are all useful
to him.[27]

But not the least important art is the art of the sermon itself. The
preacher first shows his wisdom in teaching by his choice of a text. The
'men pleasers' choose texts to suit their well-placed hearers, pick their
words 'for waight and tuneable measure, for fine pronouncing to delight the eare, more for a *plaudite* than to convince conscience, or to
remove impietie; they glance at sin som times, but faire and farre off,
for feare of hitting.'[28] Not so the true servant of Christ. He, having
chosen a fit text and expounded its meaning and doctrine, proceeds to
persuade and exhort men to the use of it. He states it as a command-
ment, approved by God and good men, supported even 'by the sayings
of the heathen, touching morall duties.' He offers the promise of
divine favor and the assurance of 'profit to a mans selfe and others.' He
sets it forth by examples from scripture, from writers Christian and
profane, from 'the shaddowes of those in brute creatures: which be of

great force to perswade, and verie lawfull to be used,' by examples both of those who have practiced God's commands and of those who have 'received blessings from God and honor with man therefor.' He uses similitudes, 'to win the hearer by so plaine and evident demonstrations,' but similitudes like those in Scripture, drawn from 'things knowne, easie to be conceived, and apt.' Men consent to such and, consenting, are urged by conscience to obey. 'By which it is manifest, that similies are of excellent use even to teach, move, and delight the hearer, and their ministerie most powerful which must [most?] use them.'[29]

The aim of *The Isle of Man* was 'to discover to us our miserable and wretched estate through corruption of nature' and 'to shew how a man may come to a holy reformation and so happily recover himself.' The figurative device used by the author is indicated on the title-page: *The Legall Proceeding in Man-Shire against Sinne. Wherein, by way of a continued Allegorie, the chief Malefactors disturbing both Church and Commonwealth are detected, and attacked; with their Arraignment, and Immediate tryall, according to the Laws of England.* Man is, that is to say, an English county wherein a bawd, the heart, lives in the town of Soul. Warrant is sworn out for her arrest, and she and her companions are tried and convicted before judge and jury. Bunyan may very likely, of course, have known Bernard's book, though he need not have done so to have written the trial scenes of his *Pilgrim's Progress* and *Holy War*. To any reader of *The Isle of Man* who expects something closely resembling Bunyan's realism, the book will be disappointing. It is, however, though still too much a sermon to be a dramatic narrative, nevertheless a lively sermon, so lively that Bernard had to apologize for it. Fortified by scripture precedent and knowing human nature, 'I perswaded my selfe that the allegory would draw many to read, which might be as a bait to catch them, perhaps, at unawares, and to move them to fall into meditation . . . of the spiritual use thereof.' He admits that 'two or three passages carry not that gravity in shew, as some, perhaps, could wish they did.' But what of that? 'There is a kind of smiling and joyful laughter, for anything I know, which may stand with sober gravity, and with the best mans piety.' So he concludes with the injunction that the reader be 'Christianly merry' with his book.[30]

Before taking up the work of other noted practitioners of the art of the homely similitude, we must note that no inconsistency was felt by the preachers between the use of such tricks of style and on the one hand their professed devotion to plainness or on the other their strictures against the wit and rhetoric of their rivals. Their own use of wit and rhetoric, even in the act of decrying these things in others, was, as a matter of fact, quite unblushing. Consider for example the terms in which Valentine Marshall recommends that preachers keep close to the words of Jesus:

The Gold upon the Pill may please the eye; but it profits not the patient. The Paint upon the Glass may feed the fancy; but the room is the darker for it. The sword of God's Spirit can never wound so deep, as when it's plucked out of these gaudy Scabbards. Nakedness . . . is the best garnishing, and Ornament the truth can have.[31]

Sibbes, warning preachers not to hide their meaning in dark speeches, declares that 'Truth feareth nothing so much as concealment, and desireth nothing so much as clearly to be laid open to the view of all: When it is most naked, it is most lovely and powerful.'[32] Yet these sentiments did not prevent him from expressing himself on the same subject thus: 'the swelling words of vanity may tickle the ear, tip the tongue, and please in matters of discourse: But when it comes to push of Pike, they afford but little comfort.'[33] The point was that stylistic virtuosity must push the pike of the spirit. Whatever contributed to edification was but a means of preaching naked Christ. Whatever did not was vanity. The primary objection to metaphysical wit, learned allusions, tags of Greek and Latin, snatches from the heathen poets and philosophers, and all figures of speech depending upon recondite knowledge was that many members of the audience were sure to miss the point. The Puritan preacher was quite prepared to use anything he knew as means to his end, but the end was to make everybody feel the force and reality of what he was saying. Therefore he tried to avoid whatever smacked of esoteric and aristocratic culture while creating in his auditory the pride of possession in what was felt to be a truer culture, both universal and democratic. His sermons were sown thick with imagery, but his images were drawn from sources which people felt they knew, and they bore directly upon the theme of redemption.

They were drawn, that is, primarily from scripture and the human experience and emotion there depicted, so readily intelligible to the English folk. They were drawn also from nature and the common life of the field, the home, the shop and the roadside, and from the stores of fable, imagery and proverb left in the popular mind by generations of forgotten preachers.

To classify the forms and trace the antecedents of Puritan imagery is beyond the scope of the present study. We are less concerned in these pages with the links that connect Puritanism to the past than with the ways which Puritanism marked out for the future. 'Similitudes' of many types and from several sources were used by the preachers to drive home the lesson of faith. But all imaginative effort converged upon certain inclusive concepts which gave supreme reality to doctrine. The preachers sought to express the significance and purpose of life in images and fables drawn from a mythology and an epic cycle the truth of which their people were in no state to resist or deny. One way of defining the aim of these men is to say that they were trying to deal constructively with the psychological problems of a minority, a minority which was becoming conscious of itself and perplexed both by the realization of its position and by the sense of dissatisfaction and unfulfilment attending that realization. They were trying to inject moral purpose into men who felt lost in moral confusion. The preachers had, therefore, to drive home the application to the individual life of the theory of predestination, election and sanctification. It would be a mistake to suppose that they occupied themselves very much in direct attack on prevailing manners. The prohibitory phase of Puritan morality developed only as the dynamic phase made good its hold upon the popular will. It would also be a mistake to suppose that they spent much time describing the tortures that awaited the damned in hell hereafter. Puritan sermons before the revolution were chiefly concerned with charting in infinite detail and tireless reiteration the course of the godly soul out of hardness and indifference to the consciousness of its lost condition, and so out of despair and repentance to faith in God, to active perseverance and confident expectation of victory and glory. As we have seen, the preachers soon hit upon a way to exemplify the working of the formula by individualizing the soul to which it applied; that is, they transposed the theory into spiritual biography or a sort of spiritual case history. Thus every man is impersonated by the preacher himself or by Master John Dod or by Mistress Mary Gunter or by common seaman Vincent Jukes. But another device was to link the formula and the individual case with the sacred associations of biblical poetry and in general with moving experiences of ordinary life and knowledge. This allowed the pulpit to make use of trope, simile and metaphor, of myth, allegory, fable and parable, in short to approach if not to attain symbolic narrative. Out of such beginnings arose the Puritan saga of the spiritual life.

The Puritan imagination saw the life of the spirit as pilgrimage and battle. The images of wayfaring and warfaring which fill the Old Testament had been exploited by that fighting itinerant, Paul, and by generations upon generations of subsequent evangelists. Reaching the pulpits of the seventeenth century by a hundred channels, they there underwent new and peculiarly vigorous development. The occupants of many of those pulpits would undoubtedly have tried to enforce their ideals by law if they had had the power. Lacking the power, they had to dwell upon the responsibility of the individual for enforcing them upon himself. They told him that his soul was a traveler through a strange country and a soldier in battle. He was a traveler who, fleeing from destruction, must adhere through peril and hardship to the way that leads home. He was a soldier who, having been pressed to serve under the banners of the spirit, must enact faithfully his part in the unceasing war of the spiritual against the carnal man. Few sermons, it goes without saying, gave anything like a straightforward narrative of the pilgrim's progress or of the rebellion of Satan against God. The preacher generally assumed that people could piece the story together out of scripture for themselves. Or to state the matter another way, they were engaged in making their hearers aware of being actors in a universal drama which was going on all about them and the grand outlines of which they all knew. Having to counsel them how to conduct themselves in this or that crisis of the journey and struggle, the messenger in the pulpit brought news of the ordeals, ardors and triumphs of other participants. Few sermons lacked and many abounded in such allusions to spiritual wayfaring and warfaring. Sometimes the preacher would be so caught up by these images that his whole sermon would be composed of little else. All the preachers collaborated upon the saga. The number of extant sermons and of individual authors dealing with the theme is indeed so great that to discuss severally any considerable number would entail much repetition of details, significant chiefly in the mass. The penalty paid by spiritual warriors in pulpit and print is diffuseness and tautology. Until the great masters take up the tale, we are more interested in the saga itself, in its growth and spread and human significance, than in the work of successive individuals in communicating it to others. We shall do best at this point, therefore, to review the Puritan epic of wayfaring and warfaring as illustrated by representative preachers rather than to chronicle the preachers themselves. By so doing we shall at the same time gain the clearest view of the ideas and the way of life which the preachers, in recounting the epic, carried to the people.

Preachers and good Christians in general, according to Edward Topsell, 'are the starres [that] give light in the night; they are captaines that are foremost in service; they are the soules that shield others from danger. Nowe if there be no starres, and no captaines, and no shieldes, how shall we walke in the night of this worlde, or fight in the battle of Christ, or be saved from the fierie darts of sathan?'[34] The preacher was above all the leader of a crusade and holy war. The story of his life was the story of his adventures on the road to the heavenly city, of his feats in the battle of the spirit. Thus he was able out of his own experience to supply other pilgrims and warriors with a spiritual guidebook and manual of arms. But in his anatomizing of the soul, in his painstaking analysis and description of each step in the process of regeneration, what more natural than to resort to allegorical or semi-allegorical images of wayfaring and warfaring?

The case of Thomas Goodwin supplies an excellent example of the way in which the Puritan sermon commonly labored to escape from abstract to imagistic methods of presenting doctrine. The preacher saw, and generally recorded, his own life as an image of the truth. In his sermons too he was impelled to present truth in images, images which tended to fall into allegory, allegory which often shadowed forth his own experiences. We have already seen how the temptation to trust to natural reason for salvation and to an ornate pulpit style for success had troubled Goodwin's youth, how he had been brought by spiritual preaching to trust in God's power and grace and in a 'plain' and 'spiritual' style. These facts, which could, of course, have been no secret at any time to Goodwin's friends, were not committed to print until many years later in 1704. In 1636, however, he published a volume of sermons entitled *A Childe of Light Walking in Darknes: or a Treatise Showing the Causes by which, The Cases wherein, The Ends for which God leaves his children to distresse of conscience. Together with Directions how to walke, so as to come forth of such a Condition.* Eight years before, he says, he had preached certain sermons, probably at Cambridge or Ely, 'and some notes thereof were (to say no more) dispersed into the hands of many to my prejudice.' He now therefore publishes them himself 'with little alteration or addition in method, style, or matter.' They clearly transpose the spiritual trials the author had undergone in the course of his conversion at Cambridge into the more general terms of the pulpit—into the jargon, that is, of the theologian, but of a theologian who feels urged to make more and more frequent use of lightsome similitudes. He himself warns his 'weaker readers,' 'to whom more speculative, and doctrinall discourse, though about things practicall, prove usually tedious and unpleasing,' that they may find the opening chapter of the book too 'craggy' and advises them to begin at once on Chapter II, 'from whence to the end they shall finde what is more accomodate to their understandings and conditions and more practically speaking to their distresse.'[35] In plain language this meant that as the preacher went on he gave less and less time to systematic exposition of doctrine and more to the vivid description of what happened in the sinner's heart. He became, indeed, so carried away by this that he added to the sermons as originally delivered several additional ones which he describes as 'that whole discourse about Satan's part.'

Goodwin's purpose is to give encouragement to those who even after conversion are afflicted by rational doubts concerning predestination and, more important, by fears for their own election under that great law. The learned doctor's prime method of persuasion is the dialectic he has learned in the schools, and he never wholly abandons it. But his chosen text is Isa. 50:10, 11, and the poetry of that passage repeatedly leads him off into 'lightsome similitudes.' Thus the divinity lecture is in continual danger of breaking into a poetic allegory about a child trying to find its way out of the dark. The elect soul, the child of God, is not exempt from doubt and distress of conscience but may suffer a sense of 'desertion in the want of assurance of justification.'[36] He does not know that, though the sun may be eclipsed, the earth still feels its influence. Walking in darkness, the child of light meets many terrors. He fears that God does not love him after all. Carnal Reason, a desperate foe to faith, confirms his fears. The child of light knows that he is also a child of sin; he knows that he is guilty, and he grows incredulous of salvation. Satan comes on him in the night like an enemy bearing a dark lantern, seeing, but himself unseen. It is one of the devil's favorite modes of attack. He was unable to get within the soul of Adam in the garden before the fall or within the soul of Christ, the second Adam, in the wilderness, but into our souls he can creep, a subtle disputant plying us with false reasoning against the light, a bold accuser bearing down upon our own inward weakness. 'The wards of conscience are of themselves loose and naturally misplaced, but he with his false keyes wrings & perverts them much more.'[37] Nevertheless, though we may be thus momentarily lost in despair, lost in spiritual darkness, God, who alone knows our hearts, will surely save us. We are children of light even in the dark. God does not desert us. He merely lets us encounter Satan in order to strengthen us by great spiritual trials for great spiritual happiness, in order to make us wise 'experimentally to comfort others.'[38]

Goodwin's similitudes are not without color and vivacity. The elect, he says, are as prone to distrust as the damned are to hope, the needle of their souls veering as far toward hell as that of the others toward heaven. Overconfidence has its concomitant in despondency. 'Especially if they [the saints] were in the Sunshine before, but now sit in the valley of the shadow of death: if dandled in Gods lap afore and kist, now to be lasht with terrors and his sharpest rods, & on the tendrest place, the conscience.'[39] Passions such as these, which Satan rouses in us for his own ends, are 'like to heavy weights hung upon a clocke, which doe not only make the wheeles, the thoughts, move faster, but also perverts them and wrests them the wrong way.'[40] But for the child of light there is always an escape from danger, ready to his own hand. He is 'often cast into prison, into feares and bondage,' but 'after he hath layen long in them and begins to reade over the writ and Mittimus, he findes it to be false imprisonment, a meere trick of Satan his Jaylour.'[41] 'If a man be falsely imprisoned or cast in a suit at Law, what doth he to remedy it? He seeks to find the error in the writ: so do thou search out the ground of the trouble; go to some spirituall Lawyer skilled in Soul-work; keep not the devils counsell.'[42] Satan 'prevailes most in this sort of temptations with melancholy tempers; who dwelling in darke shops, he much deceives with false colours and glosses.'[43] Do you trust God no farther than you can see him? 'What a trouble is it to a wise man to have a fond and foolish wife, who if he be but abroad and about necessary businesse, haply for her maintenance, yet then she complains he regards her not, but leaves her; if he chides her for any fault, then she sayes hee hates her; and is much distempered by it, as a whole dayes kindnesse cannot quiet her againe.'[44]

Whether the author of *Comus* ever heard Goodwin at Cambridge instructing saints how to walk safely through the night of doubt and fear, we cannot tell. Sermons from some quarter depicting the journey of the saint guided by light within his own clear breast, he could hardly have avoided. *The Garden of Spirituall Flowers* concluded a brief plain statement of doctrine with 'Twelve Steps which a man may stride towards Heaven; and being in the first step, he may thinke himselfe a good Christian: yet except he stride the thirteenth, he shall misse Heaven-gate, and fall into the fire of Hell, for ever.'[45] The author in this instance does not pursue the figure further. But as Preston observed, 'there is a great similitude betweene a Christians life and walking from place to place,'[46] a similitude which many were ready to trace in more detail. The outlines of the image remain generally the same. 'We are ignorant and unskilfull,' Downame tells us, 'in travelling the strait path . . . and everie houre readie to take the bywaies of error which leade to destruction.' Our goal is the kingdom of heaven. Our guide, our cloud and pillar of fire, our line out of the labyrinth, our star of Bethlehem, is the word of God. With that in hand, 'let us constantly and boldlie travaile in our Christian pilgrimage . . . not staying where it biddeth goe, nor going when it staith.' It will lead us to our redeemer, a right Puritan redeemer, since he will be found 'not now lying in the armes of his mother, but sitting at the right hand of his father in all glorie, power and majestie.'[47]

At this point Downame introduced a variation of the figure which had interesting possibilities. The pilgrim soul, in his fancy, goes to sea. If the spiritual mariner does not take God's word for his card, 'Satan will raise against him such stormie tempests and contrary blasts of temptations' that he 'will suffer shipwracke upon the rockes of sinne and bee drowned in a sea of destruction.' This transference of the journey of the spirit from land to ocean, though not rare in the sermons of the earlier period, was not characteristic. Seafaring was probably not yet so common an experience as it was shortly to become. At any rate the people seemed readier at first to see themselves as travelers setting forth on foot from an inland town with the word to help them face the perils of the road than to picture themselves as seamen putting out from port to endure the dangers of the deep, peradventure to be shipwrecked and cast up, still not without a Bible, on an uninhabited island.

Downame's use of the image of seafaring remains generalized; the telltale word 'pilot' for mariner smacks more of Latin poetry than of the sea. The same conventionality in some instances hangs about the use of images of wayfaring. But in many others we receive the color and feeling of actuality. Doubt, says Sibbes, 'damps . . . the spirits of those that walk the same way with us, whenas we should, as good travellers, cheer up one another both by word and example.' Doubt affects us as though our spiritual wheels were taken off or wanted oil, 'whereby the soul passes on very heavily, and no good action comes off from it as it should, which breeds not only uncomfortableness, but unsettledness in good courses.'[48] Preston, speaking in the same vein, gives a more intimate glimpse into the homely affairs of barnyard and roadside. He is telling us that in every act, even the commonest in our daily existence, we are walking either toward God or away. 'Even those common actions are steppes that lead to the Iourney; Even as you see; take a servant that is set to worke or to goe a Iourney, that is to mowe or to drive a Cart; even the whetting of the Sithe is a part of his worke as well as his mowing of the grasse; the provendring of his horse is a dispatching of his Iourney, a going on in it, as well as when he rides, and so the oyling of the wheele is a drawing on, as well as every steppe he takes.'[49]

'Lightsome similitudes' such as these, frequent though they are in Sibbes and Preston and in many another, are used for the most part as incidental helps to illuminate teaching. The preacher, ready at any moment to allude to the common experiences of wayfaring, did not in many instances let imagination run at length upon the figure. But the temptation and tendency to do so grew strong. Illustrations of doctrine drawn from everyday life, especially when touched with something like the interest of narrative, plainly took with the people. The men of the pulpit consequently began to make a feature of such devices, exercising their ingenuity to make the little picture or fable familiar, vivid, appropriate, and in itself striking and amusing. The next step was to convert the whole sermon into a series of related apposite analogies. After that, it was only a question of time before some lively mind would turn the thing about and from illuminating the moral with a tale point the tale with a moral.

Most interesting evidence of such tendencies in the development of the similitude of wayfaring and of similitudes in general is to be found in Thomas Taylor, graduate of Cambridge, fellow of Christ's College, a famous preacher and the author of many published sermons. While at Reading he maintained 'a little nursery of young Preachers, who under his faithful Ministery flourished in knowledge and piety.' There, as at Cambridge and in London, 'he was a precious seeds-man' and 'did throw abroad many heavenly sparkles which did burn apace in the brests of his Auditors.' 'He was a guide to others, who did not wander out of the way himselfe: he was a walking Bible.'[50] He was, in fact, a kind of poet of the pulpit, his sermons exploiting the imagistic suggestions of such texts as the parable of the sower or the likening of the kingdom of heaven to a pearl of great price. The most interesting of his discourses is *The Pilgrims Profession*. The close relation between the spiritual biography and the allegory of the pilgrim, so clearly instanced in Thomas Goodwin, appears again in this work of Taylor's. *The Pilgrims Profession* was a funeral sermon which sought to use the example of Mary Gunter's passage through life for edification, and it was accompanied by the actual account of her experiences to which we have several times referred. It took its cue from the twelfth verse of the thirty-ninth Psalm: 'I am a stranger with thee, and a sojourner, as all my Fathers.' Taylor 'opens' his text, briefly states the 'doctrines,' and then takes up the more congenial task of explaining the 'uses.' If we are indeed of the elect, then we must strive to carry ourselves like saints. The carriage of the saint through this life is like the journey of a traveler going home through a strange country. So the preacher explores the experiences of the wayfarer for analogies to the spiritual experiences of the elect soul. The studied similitudes, animated though they are, never quite cross the line that separates the sermon from symbolic narrative. Taylor cannot quite transform his saint into a dramatic person, never quite say Christian rather than the Christian or that the Christian is a pilgrim rather than like one. Yet his power to perceive and suggest the familiar emotions of the traveler is so sensitive that he almost, if not quite, succeeds in putting us on the road with him.

The Christian, knowing that he is only a stranger and eager to be at home, takes no delight in his journey. He enjoys the world only like a passer-by, having other and better business of his own elsewhere: 'hee useth other mens goods for a night, but he setteth not his heart on them . . . because he knoweth he must leave them next morning, and may take none with him.'[51] Indeed, for the things he uses in this inn, he knows that he is 'countable' and will have a reckoning to pay. He turns not aside for the barking of dogs, for a shower of rain, or for the roughness and foulness of the way. 'Hee will through thicke and thin, through drops and drout and all because he is going home.'[52] He heartens himself by saying, 'It is never an ill day that hath a good night; and though many bitter pills of harsh and strange usages must be swallowed by . . . strangers, yet the consideration of home is as sugar in their pockets to sweeten them all.'[53] He carries, of course, a heavy burden, the threefold weight of sin, worldly care, and fear of death, and the preacher spares us few details suggested by this figure. But the Christian, daily winding up his heart towards God, delights in the expectation of arriving at his estate and his patrimony. This goal, if he be properly prepared and equipt, he cannot fail to reach. 'Now how happily shall this man compasse his journey and goe singing through the most tedious wayes of his Pilgrimage that hath . . . furnished himselfe with the understanding of the way, with a faithfull and unerring guide, with sufficient provision for his expence, with a serviceable weapon, and with a sweet and chearfull Companion.'[54]

That Bunyan may have been familiar with *The Pilgrims Profession* goes without saying but has not been proved.[55] The effort to find a specific original for the Bedfordshire 'mechanick's' allegory must in the nature of the circumstances be unavailing. Puritan preachers in general could have cited, as Bunyan did, the text from Hosea, 'I have used similitudes.' Similitudes took with the public and the more popular the audience the more freely they were used. Common though they are in the pages of men like Downame, Sibbes and Taylor, they abounded more and more as with time more and more of the populace came within the scope of the preachers' influence and made its own influence felt upon their preaching. The extant outpourings of lower-class religious demagogues, which were naturally slower and less likely to find their way into print, are perfect extravaganzas of imagism. True of the sermons which came into print, this could certainly be no less true of those preached but never printed, and we must bear in mind that for every sermon sent to press, especially after 1640, a hundred or more came from the pulpit or the tub. It is, then, necessary to assume that Bunyan, who undoubtedly read more than he would have us suppose, heard even more sermons than he read, and that the sermons he heard were even more full of 'similitudes.' His great allegories were but single items coming from a single practitioner—though a genius—in a vast literature, only a portion of which has been preserved and the forms and conditions of which have been almost completely overpast and forgotten. Hence it is that the resemblance between *The Pilgrims Progress* and *The Pilgrims Profession* is general and not specific. As a matter of fact, the two works reveal a significant difference of tone. Bunyan brings his pilgrim to glory but tells us chiefly of the perils of the way. Taylor on the other hand keeps constantly in view the Christian's joyful expectations of home.

We shall have to deal later with the happy ending of the Puritan saga. At the present point in our discussion we must note that the strait path was always bestraddled by Apollyon and that the main business of Christian wayfaring was war. The spiritual attitude which the preachers endeavored to inculcate was one of active struggle on the part of the individual against his own weakness. The supreme image which, for that purpose, they sought to impress upon the minds of the people was that of the soldier enlisted under the banners of Christ. They could not and did not seek to eliminate all vestige of the doctrine of the atonement, but they made the atonement signify the appointment of the elect soul to join with Christ in the war against

the eternal enemy. Thus the symbolism of the nativity and the passion
came to mean little to the Puritan saints, and Christmas and Easter
faded from their calendar. Their holy days were the days when they
fasted and humiliated themselves for defeats they themselves had
brought upon the spirit or the days when they gave thanks for the
victories which had been vouchsafed to them by divine providence.
 These observances merely evidenced the change which their imagination had effected in the sacred epic. The Puritan saga did not cherish
the memory of Christ in the manger or on the cross, that is, of the
lamb of God sacrificed in vicarious atonement for the sins of man. The
mystic birth was the birth of the new man in men. The mystic passion
was the crucifixion of the new man by the old, and the true propitia-
tion was the sacrifice of the old to the new. Hence the preachers lavished their powers upon describing all existence and every human life
as a phase of conflict between Christ and Satan. The first scene was the
encounter of the old man, Adam, with Satan in the garden, and
Adam's fall. The second scene was the encounter of Satan with the
new and greater man, Christ, the second Adam, in the wilderness, and
the tempter's rebuff. The final scene was the ultimate overthrow of
Satan by Christ and his saints, and their triumph upon earth as prelude
to triumph in heaven.
 'Manifold,' John Downame tells us, 'and most dangerous are the
temptations and assaults of our spirituall enemies, whereby they labour
to hinder the salvation of God's elect.'[56] 'This life,' says Thomas
Taylor, 'is the time of warfare, and the world is the great field of God,
in which Michael and his Angels fight against the dragon and his
angels.'[57] 'For the time of our life,' says William Gouge, 'being a time
of war, a time wherein our spirituall enemies (who are many, mighty,
sedulous, and subtile) put forth their strength, and bestirre themselves to the uttermost that possibly they can, Seeking whom to de-
voure, what can be more behoofull, then to discover their cunning
stratagems and wyles, to declare wherein their strength lieth, to fur-
nish Christs souldiers with compleat armour and sufficient defence,
and to shew how our enemies may bee disappointed of their hopes,
and we stand fast against all their assaults.'[58] The preachers did indeed
endeavor to serve as a kind of general staff to the hosts of the spirit in
a campaign against the evil one. In sermons and treatises they set

forth the lessons to be learned from the fall Adam got from Satan in the garden and from the defeat of Satan by Christ in the wilderness. Thus William Perkins prepared his spirited dialogues between Satan and a Christian and his sermons on the fourth chapter of Matthew, called *The Combate betweene Christ and the Devill*. John Downame's *The Christian Warfare Wherein is first generally shewed the malice, power, and politike stratagems of the spirituall enemies of our salvation, Satan and his assistants the world and the flesh*, first published in 1604, was another widely read work. The image from Paul (Eph. 6:11) which supplied Downame and many another with a text suggested the title of Gouge's *The Whole-Armor of God or the Spirituall Furniture which God hath provided to keepe safe every Christian Souldier from all the assaults of Satan*, 1616. Gouge's text came from Paul to the Corinthians, 'Watch ye, stand fast in the faith, quit ye like men, be strong.' Thomas Taylor in 1618 emulated Perkins' exposition of the temptation of Christ in *Christs Combate and Conquest: or, The Lyon of the Tribe of Judah, vanquishing the Roaring Lyon*. Thomas Goodwin's *Childe of Light Walking in Darknes*, preached, as we have seen, about 1628, depicted the encounter of the soul with Satan during its pilgrimage through this benighted world. Richard Sibbes appropriately dedicated his *The Bruised Reed and Smoaking Flax* to a military man with the statement, 'Soldiers that carry their lives in their hands had need, above all others, to carry grace in their hearts, that so having made peace with God, they may be fit to encounter with men.' The sermons themselves, published in 1630, like those published five years later and called *The Soules Conflict with itselfe, and Victory over itselfe by Faith*, were among the most brilliant and popular of all the utterances of the Puritan church militant. John Preston, finally, in sermon after sermon, printed after his death in 1628 by his friends under such titles as *The Breast-Plate of Faith and Love*, *The Doctrine of the Saints Infirmities* and *The New Covenant*, never wearied in setting forth the ways of the soul beset by the devil.

The works just mentioned were typical and widely read, though they come far short of exhausting the list of those that might be cited to illustrate the reiteration of the theme of the war of the two Adams embodied in the members of every man. This, indeed, interwoven with the theme of man's pilgrimage, was the great device for presenting the central experience of Puritan morality, namely temptation. God had revealed to Moses a law of righteousness, and the preachers supplied a code of righteousness based upon the law. But they knew right well that the weakness of the flesh was such that complete fulfilment of the law by any man was impossible. The liability to err, not knowledge and righteousness, was the absolute condition of all human life. Once and for all, men had broken the divine law and stood condemned. That was the universal depravity of the carnal or natural man, that man was Adam, and that Adam was present in each of his children. But the weakness of the flesh gave no necessary occasion to abandon hope. Rather it was cause for the encouragement of all. Since to be human was, notwithstanding anything one might do or be or know, to err, then the worst of sinners could not be so much worse than the least as to make any difference with God. The absolute levels all relatives; all men are born equal. This equality was the very basis of hope. Since no sinner, no matter how righteous, wise, learned, powerful or rich, could hope to satisfy the law, the least righteous and the humblest, weakest and poorest had as good a chance to be saved as any. For God saved whom he would, not whom sinners deemed he ought. The grace of God was free, and so all men were born free as well as equal—free, that is, to share as absolutely in his favor as they had in the depravity of the original Adam. There was another Adam, Christ, who had withstood the tempter as completely as the former had given in to him, and he too might be present in our members. The manifestation of the new Adam was unsleeping opposition to the old. Thus there might be help for any man, but this help came only from God and worked only through a man's own self. He must become a new man, must acknowledge the law of his nature, fight his own weakness, blame none but himself for his troubles and failures, endeavor to be strong, believe that providence was with him, persevere, and trust that all would be well in the end. If he suffered no sorrow for the unrighteousness which he partook with the old Adam, he should partake none of the joy that ensues upon the righteousness of the new; he was not of the elect. The ordeal of the flesh was the victory of the spirit. So long as sin vexed him, he might know that God was with him. All he had to do was to continue to be vexed, and he was sure to triumph, because all existence is the conflict of Christ against Satan, the foreordained outcome of which is the triumph of the elect.

Satan was not the hero of the Puritan epic, but he was the character in whom the hero was bound to be chiefly interested. The protagonist was the human soul which Christ had enlisted in his cause, and the rebellious angel was the antagonist. The endeavor of the preachers was to make the common man conscious of himself, to organize a minority in the expectation of power. They had, therefore, in the first place to arouse men out of indifference by warning them of the wrath to come. After that they were engrossed with two supreme dangers to morale, the failure of confidence and the excess of confidence. They must teach every man not to be afraid of what the world and carnal men might do to him if he embraced the new life, not ashamed of anything except his own failure to make the most of his own gifts and opportunities, and yet not too discouraged by his own lapses. He must struggle against hesitation to make his faith known by word and act. He must endeavor to believe that there was something in himself not to be defeated and that providence was his ally. In short, he must try to do his best, confident as to the outcome. But he must not let himself grow overconfident. The saint must not expect that once persuaded of his own godliness he could take his ease in Zion and enjoy the comforts of security. It was easy for the sinner promoted to sainthood to forget that no man is exempted from spiritual warfare until he rests in his grave. This danger, which occupied less of the preachers' attention in the early stages, naturally grew greater as the saints moved on to success. The only real hazards in life were those that sprang up in the soul itself, namely despair and pride, but they were the very devil incarnate, and that was the whole point and meaning of the saga of the fall of man and his redemption. Adam in the garden before the fall was natural man, innocent and happy but carnal and weak. This weakness was his undoing. Satan was the weakness of the spirit that betrays the spirit to the weakness of the flesh. Hardened in pride, lost in despair, he lives in hell and embodies death. He stole and still steals into the soul of the old Adam, persuading him to his fall. Christ was man recreated in spirit. His war upon Satan in heaven and in the wilderness was the image of the war he waged upon Satan in the human breast. Irresistible in strength, his life, which was all of life, was the subduing of the old Adam who by yielding to despair and pride enslaved himself to the devil.

Such are the themes of the countless expositions of the fourth chapter of Matthew, of the epistles of Paul, and of many other texts the images of which carried similar implications. There can be no question that the chief service of the preachers before 1640 was by such means to build up the courage and self-confidence of the people. The prime temptation of the devil was timidity, confusion and despair. Sinners had to be helped out of the slough of despond and up the hill difficulty before they could proceed upon the later stages of their pilgrimage toward the heavenly city and the Puritan commonwealth. Hence the reiterated praise bestowed upon the spiritual brethren for comforting perplexed consciences. The very titles of many of William Perkins' sermons yearn eloquently over the troubled soul, and we may take as typical the statement with which he prefaces one of them, namely, *A Case of Conscience, the Greatest that ever was: how a man may know whether he be the childe of God or no.* 'In Gods Church,' Perkins observes, 'commonly they who are touched by the Spirit, and begin to come on in Religion, are much troubled with feare, that they are not Gods children . . . and are not quiet until they finde some resolution.'[59] So he offers help to 'the simple and the unlearned, who desire to be informed concerning their estate.' Another treatise written for the same purpose he called *How to Live, and that well: in all estates and times. Specially, When helpes and comforts faile.* This is an explanation of the uses of faith. Men multiply their cares and worry about the future, but when they are at wit's end 'faith gives direction and staies the minde.'[60] The author of care is, of course, Satan, who makes that one of the means by which to quell our spirits if he can. This duel of the soul with the tempter is the subject of many of Perkins' sermons and dialogues as well as of his more extended *Combate betweene Christ and the Devill.*

John Downame tells us that his purpose in writing his *Christian Warfare* was to comfort the afflicted in conscience by assuring them beyond question that they were saved and to lead them 'unto the haven of eternall happinesse' past the temptations of pride and despair, that is, neither running 'upon the rockes of presumption' nor plunging 'into the gulfe of desperation.' He observes that it had been the custom of ministers to perform this service for their private friends, that indeed he did not at first intend that his work 'should come into the publike view,' but 'finding it grow to such a volume, that it was too great to passe in a written copie; and hoping that that which was profitable for one might bee beneficiall unto many,' he concluded by sending his labors to the press.[61] The book in its final form makes a large volume of over seven hundred pages. The first part is wholly devoted to the description of the new man aroused by Christ against the old man betrayed by the devil. The profit the reader was to get from the book was, first, instruction concerning the wiles of the devil in spiritual war and, second, assurance that, if, never yielding to discouragement or to the delusion that he was safe, he kept on fighting, he would win. Downame does not begin these lessons with doctrinal argument, which is reserved for the second part of his book, but with thronging images. The reader's soul is a pilgrim taking his life in his hands, a city besieged, a soldier going forth to battle. Let us remember, the preacher tells us, that they that listen to the siren music of the world or drink of its golden cup are lulled asleep in their souls, or if they awake, it is as Samson strengthless out of the lap of Dalila. But if we stop our ears and put aside the wine, 'then shall we constantly go forward on our pilgrimage towards our heavenly home: and though honours stand before us, riches on the one hand, pleasures on the other, alluring us to enter into the broad way which leadeth to destruction; yet shall wee not forsake the strait path which leadeth unto life everlasting.' It is death to grow weary 'in travelling thorow this desert and unpleasant wilderness,' death 'to returne back to the bondage of spirituall Pharaoh' and there sit by the fleshpots, glutting ourselves 'with cucumbers and pepons of carnall pleasure.'[62]

Sin, the old Adam, he says, is an intestine enemy: 'we cannot fight against it, unlesse we raise . . . civill warres in our owne bowels.' Beset by foes without, we harbor more traitors than true subjects within. 'We are besieged with forraine forces, the world and the divell, and we nourish in us secret traitors, even the flesh, with whole legions of the lusts thereof, which are continually readie to open the gates of our soules, even our senses of seeing, hearing, touching, tasting, smelling, whereby whole troupes of temptations enter and surprise us.'[63]

Thus we live in danger, our greatest danger being that we should feel no danger, and our safety lying in the very dread of feeling safe. When 'Satan (quietly) keepes the house, the things that he possesseth are in peace; but when a stronger than he cometh to dispossesse him, he will never lose his possession without a fight.'[64] Only the wicked are at peace; the elect are always at grips with the fiend in their bowels. The point, to turn aside from Downame for a moment, is succinctly put in the *Garden of Spirituall Flowers*. There we learn that the difference between the ungodly and the godly is not that the former sin and the latter do not, for both sin alike, but the ungodly sin and rejoice and the godly sin and abhor. A man may tell for himself into which class he falls by three tokens. If he never intends or desires to sin; if in the act of being surprised and overcome by sin, his heart nevertheless rises against it; if after he has sinned he is displeased with himself and repentant; then it is only the old Adam and not his true spiritual self that has offended. Downame also helps us to tell the difference between God's child and the others. The former may fall into sins even more heinous than those of the mere worldling, but after his fall, he is vexed and grieved and tries to forsake the odious thing which the reprobate commits again and again with greediness and delight. Thus we may sin and be saved. God 'respecteth not so much our actions as our affections; nor our workes as our desires and indevours; so that he who desires to be righteous, is righteous; he that would repent, doth repent . . . For the Lord accepteth the desire for the deede; and if there be a willing minde, it is accepted according to that a man hath, and not according to that a man hath not, as it is 2. Cor. 8. 12.'[65] One wonders what Samuel Pepys in his lapses of lust and peculation would have done without such knowledge.

Downame reserves some of his most striking images to illuminate the implications of this principle in its effect upon the moral attitude of the saints. 'If a man never enter the field to fight against Satan, or if at the first encounter, hee yeeld himself prisoner, . . . it is no marvaile that hee doth not rage in his conscience.' But if he resists, Satan will fight back, and he 'must needes feele the conflict.' 'While the prisoner lieth in the dungeon, loaded with bolts and tied in chaines, the keeper sleepeth securely, . . . but if, his bolts being filed off and his chaines loosed, he have escaped out of prison, then the Iaylor beginneth to bustle and pursueth him speedilie with Hue and cry.'[66] The saint is a soldier. Let us 'march forward, and shew a courageous heart and earnest desire to overcome,' and 'surely Christ our grand Captaine will acknowledge us for his souldiers, and will give us our pay, even a crown of victorie.' If we receive a foil in the fight, he will stand over us. Wounds and imprisonment argue that the invincible courage of the soldier's mind surpassed the weakness of his body. 'Rather thereby is a souldier disgraced, if either he dare not march into the field, or being entered the battell doth shamefullie flee away, or cowardly yeeld unto the enemie.'[67] The loyalty which Downame sought thus to instill in spiritual soldiers would presently be accorded to Captain Cromwell as well as to Captain Christ, and King Charles like Satan would discover that he had a fight on his hands.

Thomas Taylor's gift for concrete expression, which we saw in his treatment of spiritual pilgrimage, is also fully evident in his *Christs Combat*. The epic of the two Adams in his imagistic pages is held within the strait limits of the sermon, but the sermon is far more than half allegory and not far removed from narrative. The dramatic scenes of the saga in which he tries to make his hearers see themselves are vividly suggested and kept constantly in mind, while the temptations of Job, of Samson and of David are set before us in passing. With his biblical material he mingles intense flashes into actual life in his time. God so orders it, he says, that where he gives greater strength and grace, there must be greater exercise of these gifts. Let no one, however strong in faith, think that Satan has ceased troubling him. 'Alas poore soules; the more grace, the more trouble.'[68] Who can hope to be safer from the attack of that roaring lion than Adam and Christ? The whole compass of the earth is his circuit, and wherever we are, we must remember him. 'Seeme the place never so secret, . . . the greenest grass may harbor a serpent.'[69] He knows our estates, our tempers, our desires. 'By our outward behaviour and gesture, he can gather our speciall corruptions, as a Physitian by outward signes . . . can judge of the particular disease within . . . like a cunning angler, he can bait his hooke, so as he hath experience the fish will take; and though he see not the fish in the water, yet by his quill and corke he can tell when it is taken.'[70] Particularly in church or about our ordinary trades, we are most likely to meet him. He lures the learned to preach above the people's capacity, and the unlearned to think themselves too ignorant to understand or to be taught the doctrine of grace. He teaches the tradesman to say, 'Why I must live, I must not put forth my wife and children to begge . . . I must utter my wares, though I lie, and sweare, and exact, and deceive.'[71] Usury and oppression of the poor are signs of his conquest over us just as is our love of stage plays and strong drink. Safety lies only in fighting him, but we must remember that the harder we oppose him the harder he resists; 'Reach once at Satans head, and he will surely reach as high as he may at thine.'[72]

Taylor was one of the most accomplished masters of the edifying similitude. Having exploited brilliantly the images of wayfaring and warfaring, he takes up in another sermon still another image that had interesting possibilities for illuminating the spiritual life of common men. Matt. 13:45 suggested that the saint might also be 'like unto a Merchantman that seeketh good pearles. Who having found a pearle of great price, went and sold all he had, and bought it.' Taylor is far from insensitive to the poetic implications of this ancient figure so well worn in the pulpit and in religious literature. Pearls may make a man rich in this world, but the kingdom of heaven is the only pearl worth having. The poorest man that seeks after grace has a way to prosper that the worldling lacks. 'Men cast up their heads, and looke aloft, if they bee Lords of some small Manour, or possession: but to be a King or Prince of a peece of earth, lifteth them in their conceits above the tops of the clouds: But a poore Christian is better contented with poore and naked Christ.'[73] Men long for trifles, for shoestrings, for goods wanting goodness; they have chests full of silver and gold and hearts empty of God. 'Woe to so rich a beggar; and unhappy is that man that hath onely not purchased what was onely worth purchasing.'[74] As he goes on, the preacher's fancy warms to the parallel between spiritual and business enterprise. Getting to heaven is made to seem like a matter of thrifty sacrifice. The saint invests in a safe security sure to return a handsome profit in the long run. The market, moreover, is open to all. 'Let this consideration also comfort godly poore men despised in the worlde: thou that art a poore Christian, in a low estate in the world, labor busily for grace, and thou maist be as rich a Merchant, have as rich a stocke, and deale in as great and rich commodities . . . as the richest. Thou that hast no money, and but little credit in the world, maist here make as good a bargaine and as gainfull returne for thyselfe, as he that hath thousands of mony beyond thee.'[75]

The strategy and tactics of spiritual war were the principal themes of Richard Sibbes at Trinity Church in Cambridge and at Gray's Inn. *The Bruised Reed*, written in an English nervous though clear, touched but not muddied by imagination, is perhaps the most effective statement that any preacher accomplished of the dynamic element in Puritan morality. It describes the process of conversion. The elect soul distressed in conscience is the bruised reed upon which God blows. The smoking flax takes fire, and the soul finds itself involved in the duel of the two Adams, backed respectively by Satan and Christ. Satan finds something in us 'which holdeth correspondency and hath intelligence with him.' We have, that is, a 'mint' of sinful thoughts within us, 'all scandalous breakings out' being 'but thoughts at the first.'[76] The similitudes in Sibbes, for whose *Soules Conflict* Quarles wrote a commendatory poem, double and redouble upon the page. The preacher comes near to giving us the clue to his own character when he says that the soul of man was created 'as an instrument in tune, fit to be moved to any duty; as a clean, neat glass' representing 'God's image and holiness.'[77] So having likened sinful thoughts to betrayers and to a mint, he quickly adds that they are also 'little thieves, which creeping in at the window, open the door to greater,' and then, again, they 'are seeds of actions.'[78] But Christ sets up his chair in the hearts of his elect. It does not matter how dull the scholar when Christ takes it upon himself to be the teacher. He is not like other princes for he writes his laws in the breast, and the simplest man can understand them. The *Soules Conflict* enlarges upon the struggle that follows conversion. Satan assails the new man with doubt and despair. He is 'a cunning rhetorician' who 'enlargeth the fancy, to apprehend things bigger than they are.'[79] His method is that of the tyrant who enslaves men by promoting ignorance and false reasoning. 'Ignorance being darkness is full of false fears. In the night time men think every bush a thief.'[80] Thus our souls are kept in tumult. We are like debtors 'subject every minute to be arrested and carried prisoner' by the devil. Hell gapes for us; nay we carry hell about us in conscience. But 'Despair to such is the beginning of

comfort; and trouble the beginning of peace.' Hell is the way to
heaven, and 'not to be disquieted is but the devil's peace.'[81]

Sibbes, we must remember, preached to the lawyers of Gray's Inn,
to other solid citizens who came to the chapel of the Inn to hear
him—perhaps upon occasion to a certain wealthy scrivener of Bread
Street who may now and then have brought his boy to hear him—
and to members of the Puritan nobility and gentry. These were men
who had small reason to think meanly of themselves and more and
more occasion to think ill of those who set up to be their betters and
governors in church and state. What they heard from Sibbes was not
theological speculation and not railing against manners and morals
or persons and conditions. Rather, he counseled courage and action—
against the devil, of course, but the devil was to be met everywhere
and in many disguises. What the soul was to the body, Christ was to
the soul. A dead soul like a dead body was ugly, deformed, 'unfit for
anything,' unable to 'rule itself.' Christ made it beautiful and, even
more important, busy: 'where hee is, he workes, and stirres us to all
holy and heavenly duties.'[82] 'God is a pure act,' always working,
always doing; and the nearer one's soul comes to God, the more it is
in action and the freer from disquiet. 'A heart not exercised in some
honest labour works trouble out of itself.' The way for men to experience comfort is 'in doing that which belongs unto them, which before
they longed for and went without.'[83] The Christian is a nimble wres-
tler anointed by the spirit; 'he can doe more than the world.' For
his 'Religion is not a matter of word, nor stands upon words, as wood
consists of Trees . . . but . . . of Power, it makes a man able.' It
'is an Art, not of great men, nor of mighty men; but of holy men: it
is an Art, and Trade: a Trade is not learned by words, but by experience: and a man hath learned a Trade, not when he can talk of it,
but when he can work according to his Trade.' You would be known
for a Christian? 'What canst thou doe then?' Can you resist sin? Can
you enjoy riches and honor without pride? Can you be abased by the
world without being 'al amort'? 'Thus if thou be a Christian, answer
thy Name . . . For a Christian in some measure is able to doe all
things, through Christ that strengtheneth him.' He is still subject to
infirmities, of course, but he will be ashamed of them. He will never
plead them in excuse but get the better of them. When he falls he

will arise and be stronger than before. 'Well, you see, then,' the preacher concludes—he has been preaching on contentment—'this Point is cleare, that a Christian is an able man . . . There are many things required of a Christian: Christianitie is a busie Trade.'[84]

It was psychologically imperative, one need hardly say, that by all this doing there should be something done, that some profit should accrue to the trade of Christianity. Sibbes does not fail to urge as vigorously upon his hearers the coming rewards of faith as the present duties. This life here and now is only a beginning designed by Providence to fit us 'to live in the more open and spacious world, whither [we] must shortly be sent forth.'[85] There could be no doubt, thanks to predestination, that the saints would succeed. Were they not all made kings and priests by justification, lifted above the world and the devil? What could more effectually quicken them against presumption and discouragement than confident expectation of good fortune? No need for the saint to care for losses and disgraces in the world, when he knew the glory that awaited him. 'What, will a man care for ill usage in his pilgrimage, when he knowes he is a King at home? We are all strangers upon earth, now in the time of our absence from God: what if wee suffer indignities, considering that we have a better estate to come, when we shall be somebody?'[86] Wealth, applause, reputation, such things or the lack of them need not concern us. We can afford to do good in secret. 'Christians should be as minerals, rich in the depth of the earth,' ready for discovery at the fit time. Let us obey conscience, 'and God will be careful enough to get us applause . . . As much reputation as is fit for a man will follow him in being and doing what he should.' Let us spread our sails for the spirit, not for fame, and we shall 'be known enough to devils, to angels, and men ere long.'[87]

In thus warning the busy, able, self-respecting, conscientious Christians, his listeners, against the last infirmity of noble minds, Sibbes, it goes without saying, was nothing if not passionately sincere. Yet, however often he and they might tell themselves that fame is no plant that grows on mortal soil, nevertheless a lively expectation of becoming 'somebody' does not conduce to a willingness to remain nobody. Men who have assurance that they are to inherit heaven have a way of presently taking possession of the earth. The practice of the Puritan code, with its insistence upon active use of individual abilities in the pursuit of an honest calling, was, as a matter of fact, already putting a solid share of the fruits of the earth into the coffers of the elect. Sibbes did not indulge his hearers in dreams of the Fifth Monarchy, but the same ferment was at work in him as in the enthusiasts who did anticipate that King Jesus was momentarily to replace King Charles. The lawyers and citizens at Gray's Inn were not permitted to lose sight of the happy ending of the spiritual saga, and in the many reminders Sibbes gave them of the grand climax in the hereafter might be heard the approach in the more proximate future, if not of the millennium, certainly of the Puritan Revolution. 'The greatest enemies of a Church and State,' he said to men who were soon to be heard of in the Long Parliament, 'are those that provoke the highest Majesty of heaven, by obstinate courses against the light that shineth in their own hearts.'[88] To be sure he also said 'let us be content to be hidden men,' 'hidden to the world till the time of manifestation comes.' Yet he did not neglect to add that that time was certain to come, when 'we shall be discovered what we are.'[89] No one could say he did not mean a time in heaven, but the saints who heard him, when sufficiently provoked by obstinate courses, naturally ventured to set a more definite and prior hour for the manifestation of the spirit within them. Five years before the Long Parliament, their preacher was exclaiming, 'What can daunt that soul, which in the greatest troubles hath made God to be its own? Such a spirit dares bid defiance to all opposite power, setting the soul above the world, and seeing all but God beneath it, as being in heaven already in its head.'[90] The speaker of these words appears to have been a rather bland, sweet-natured, mild-mannered, charming, learned and highly respected middle-aged gentleman, but putting heaven into men's heads was to have consequences this side of heaven. In any one of four editions of the great Doctor Sibbes's *Soules Conflict* published between 1635 and 1639, men could have read that Moses and Micah had no regard for 'the angry countenances of those mighty princes that were in their times the terrors of the world.'[91] Why then, they might ask themselves, should they regard the anger of King Charles?

While Sibbes thus edified the Puritan spirit at Gray's Inn, his friend John Preston was drawing crowds hard by at Lincoln's Inn. 'He that lookes not for much from the creature,' he said, 'can never be deceived: he that lookes for much from God, shall be sure to have his desire answered and satisfied.'[92] Preston's sermons, most of them printed without revision from shorthand copies taken in church, have the faults of extemporaneous oratory, but though diffuse they are very much alive. None of the preachers was more eloquent and tireless in filling men's minds with the immediacy of God's interest in man or their imaginations with the picture of the elect fighting the good fight against Satan and the old Adam and pushing ever on toward Zion. None was more famous for illuminating similitudes drawn not only from the affairs of men but also from goings on among God's other creatures of earth, water, air and sky. Immediately after his death, Sibbes and Davenport published eighteen of Preston's sermons with the title *The New Covenant*. They dedicated the volume to Preston's friends, the Earl of Lincoln and Lord Saye and Sele, begging the reader not 'to catch at imperfections' but to consider that the text was presented with few alterations as it was 'taken . . . from him in speaking.'[93] Published in 1629, the book in the next ten years underwent on the average one new printing a year. The point of these sermons, reiterated again and again throughout six hundred pages and sustained by pervasive reference to the epic of the two Adams, was the all-sufficiency of God and of the saints he had covenanted to save. Human knowledge, human merit, human power are nothing in themselves. Trust in God and you will not need them or fear them, but you will certainly come to possess all you require of them. 'I say, there is no creature in heaven or earth, that is able to be the author of the least good, or the least hurt.'[94] This should free us from every fearful perplexity. All beings under God are but his creatures, the instruments of his grace toward his chosen ones. 'Are they not like servants in the great house of the world, and we as children? and the servants are all at the Maisters command . . . : there is not any creature in heaven or earth, that stirreth without a command, without a warrant from the master of the house: if he doe command them, they goe: they are ready and nimble to doe us any service.'[95] 'I say . . . they are all but as so many servants, which are in the Lords house, prepared to waite upon his children, to convey such comforts to them, as he hath appointed to them, so that there is not one creature in heaven or earth stirres itselfe to doe you the least good, but when the Lord commands it, and sayth, Goe, comfort such a man, goe, refresh him, doe him good.'[96]

To secure the services of these agents of the Lord, it is not necessary that our own obedience be perfect. That, indeed, is impossible. Something continues amiss in all human nature. Unless we still plow and manure and weed our hearts, they wax fallow and overgrown. The flesh gets upon the hill of temptation and has the wind to drive the smoke into the eyes of the spirit. But all this is the means and evidence of God's grace. The obstinacy of the old Adam is God's way of exercising and strengthening the new in faith and repentance. The very extent of our affliction by sin is the incontrovertible proof of grace. For, if the righteousness of Christ imputed to the elect were not sufficient to overcome all the evil in the soul, 'the plaister then should be narrower than the sore, and the remedy should be inferior to the disease.'[97] All we need do is to believe we can be saved, to take Christ's side of the battle within our breasts, and we shall be saved; the fiercer the fight, the more likely the victory, the harder we fall, the surer we are to rise. We become in effect perfect not because we have not sinned but because we do not consent to sin. When a man finds that his principal motive in all he does, 'that which sets him aworke upon all occasions,' is 'some Commandement from God and not selfe respects,'[98] when he finds that without the sense of divine command his heart stands still as a ship becalmed or 'as a Mill doth, when it hath no water nor no wind to drive it,'[99] then he has the assurance of grace and is as though he were perfect.

But how could the preacher assure earnest practical men that, if they ventured all upon this enterprise of the spirit, they would gain their ends, that the master of the household had indeed appointed all creatures, even the devil, to serve their wishes? The answer was found in the text drawn from the first two verses of the seventeenth chapter of Genesis: 'The Lord appeared to Abram, and said unto him, I am the Almighty God; walk before me, and be thou perfect. And I will make my covenant between me and thee, and will multiply thee exceedingly.' It was found earlier in holy writ when God promised that the heel of the seed of the woman should bruise the head of the serpent. It was found, in fact, throughout the whole story of God's dealings with Adam and Eve, with the chosen people, with Satan and the second Adam, all of which Preston now reviews. The meaning of it was that, under the conditions described, God agreed to save men. This was the covenant of grace, preached by God to Adam in the garden, preached by Christ, preached by all true preachers since, preached by John Preston. 'My beloved, it is the greatest point that ever we had yet opportunity to deliver to you, yea, it is the maine point that the ministers of the Gospell can deliver at any time, neither can they deliver a point of greater moment, nor can you hear any, then the description of this Covenant of Grace.'[100] The lawyers of Lincoln's Inn were left in no doubt as to their rights and interests under this solemn contract with God. First of all, spiritual warriors were to have inward happiness and peace. When they were afflicted by temptation and had to wrestle with Satan, they were privileged to cry out, 'Lord, hast thou not said thou wilt deliver me out of the hands of all mine enemies? Is it not part of thy Covenant?' But this was not all. They should also have outward peace, outward riches and all outward comforts. They were the heirs apparent to the lord of heaven and earth, for it is a part of his Covenant. The preacher reiterates: 'Beloved that is not all neither . . . wee shall overcome our outward enemies, . . . so farre as it is good for us . . . and therefore a man may goe and challenge this at Gods hands; Lord, if it be good, if it be fit, and meet for me to have it, thou hast promised it; I shall have victory over them also.'[101]

What was fit for the saints in the realm of England still remained undecided when Preston died in 1628. If, however, they never got what they thought should be theirs, it was not because he left them few exhortations to continue walking and fighting before the Lord. *The Breast-Plate of Faith and Love* offered them the same teaching, drawn this time from Paul. *The Saints Daily Exercise* directed them how to pray and how to get their prayers answered. The lesson is briefly conveyed in one of the preacher's most lightsome similitudes. 'If thou pray, and pray long and have not obtained,' then do 'as an angler doth when he hath thrown the bait into the river; if it stay long and catch nothing, he takes up the bait and amends it, and when he sees it is well, he then continues and waites.' So if you are sure your prayers are sincere and hearty, 'let the baite lye still . . . and the Lord will come in due time.'[102] *The Saints Qualification* was Preston's special treatment of the process of conversion. *The Doctrine of the Saints Infirmities* dealt with the spiritual benefits to be derived from keeping the field against the enemy, no matter what reverses might befall. It is appropriately dedicated to Henry Lawrence, the virtuous father of the virtuous son to whom Milton addressed a sonnet, a kinsman of Oliver Cromwell, later president of the Council of State, and author of *Of our Communion and Warre with Angels*, 1646, another treatment of the same theme under the image of the rebellion in heaven.

Preston, we have seen, became chaplain to the Prince of Wales as an incident to his intrigues in behalf of the spirit at the court of King James. Five of the sermons he preached before Charles were brought to light in 1630 by Goodwin and Ball. The editors said that they were 'composed of more exact materials, and closer put together' than those works in which the author 'did bow his more sublime and raised parts to lowest apprehensions.'[103] Perhaps the use of Plato's cave as an image in one of the sermons was a concession to the higher apprehensions of the Stuart court, but it does not appear in general that Preston changed his tune very much when he preached to a prince. Charles, too, had to hear of the covenant of grace and was not suffered to lack for similitudes to drive the meaning home. The future royal master of Archbishop Laud could thus have learned that the spiritual rebirth was 'not an emptie *forme of godlinesse*, but an effectuall prevalent power, that puts not upon us onely the washy colour of a good profession, but that dies the heart in graine, . . . changeth the whole frame of the heart, . . . turnes the rudder of life, and guides the course to a quite contrary point of the compasse.'[104] On another occasion he may have heard that men 'are apt to doe as that foole, that because he saw the river sliding away, standeth upon the shoare and hopeth at length that all will be past.' The moral offered for royal consideration was 'that God hath an army of sorrows; when he hath afflicted us seven times, yet he addeth seven times more, and yet if we continue obstinate, hee can do it seven times more; till at length his wrath swell and grow over the banks, and carry all away before it.'[105] Discussing the relation of church and state to divine providence, Preston uttered what might well have been taken as warning by his patron: 'It is apparent that God is about a great worke, yea to make a great change in the world, except we do as it were hold his hand by seeking and turning unto him, and by removing the things that provoke him: he doth not lay all these stones and move all these wheeles for nothing, & yet who knowes what it is he is about, till it be brought forth.'[106]

On his deathbed Preston left a large volume of sermons in manuscript to his friends Goodwin and Ball. This they published in 1631 with the title *Life Eternall.* Four later editions, the last in 1634, followed in quick succession. The editors told the reader that in these pages he would find 'those lofty speculations of the schools (which like emptie clouds flie often high, but drop no fatnesse) digested into useful applications, and distilled into Spirit-full and quickening cordialls to comfort and confirme the inward Man.'[107] What they meant was that Preston attempted to give for popular edification an account of the difference and the connections between faith and reason, between the law of revelation and the law of nature. The authority of the one in relation to the other was a question which troubled many minds. Preston's object was, maintaining the supreme authority of faith and revelation, to make reason and nature nevertheless support the doctrine of salvation by predestined grace. Great dogmas breed their own peculiar heresies. The historian should always note what implications the teachers of dogma take pains to deny or to interpret in the endeavor to keep their central tenets unimpaired. The Puritan preachers were at this time innocent of any intention of laying down a theory of natural rights as a basis for a democratic society. They were absorbed in their immediate object, which was to instill in the minds of country gentlemen, merchants, lawyers and their followers the idea that, over against the carnal aristocracy which ruled the world, there was an aristocracy of the spirit, chosen by God and destined to inherit heaven and earth. Their sympathetic hearers were quite capable of observing for themselves how the carnal men in control of government were ruining the country. Thus the preachers were in effect organizing a discontented minority into an opposition. An opposition must have something to oppose. At the moment, therefore, the restriction of salvation in the hereafter to a limited number of souls chosen out of all the rest by God alone, whatever one may choose to think of it as theology, was certainly sound political psychology. Practical men in considerable numbers can be persuaded to commit themselves to fight for a faith and a program when they can be induced to believe in the inevitability of a favorable outcome. If, however, some are predestined to win, some must be equally sure to lose. If any are elect, others must be damned. The certainty of election and reprobation was, then, an indispensable theme in the argument of the Puritan preachers prior to 1640.

But the leaders of Puritan opinion were thus drawn into propaganda in the course of which it would be increasingly difficult for them to maintain their intellectual position. For the success of the movement, they required the indefinite accession of numbers, and the numbers were to be found among the populace. Argue though they might that many were damned from all eternity, the preachers were to find it practically inadvisable as well as theoretically impossible to name the many who might not be saved. Rather, all their interest lay in exposing everybody—the great mass of the people—to the preaching of the covenant of grace. They spoke and acted, therefore, as though there were no conscience which could not be awakened, as though every common sinner might be converted into a saint. The inferences from all this, by which leaders of the mob were to plague the orthodox, were obviously that grace was vouchsafed to all who did not voluntarily reject it, that if not actually every man then the multitude of men were saved from the law by the atonement of our Lord, that all men were naturally born free and equal. This consequence of spiritual preaching was also unintentionally promoted by another essential element in Puritan doctrine and practice on the eve of the revolution. As university graduates and ordained clergymen, the preachers still insisted upon intellectual culture and academic learning as necessary for the preaching of the word. But for the understanding of the word, for conversion to the faith, they were equally insistent that nothing was required but the natural capacities of the lowliest, most ignorant and least gifted of men. The light of nature could not in itself save, but when aided by the light of faith as revealed in scripture, which everybody should therefore read, and in preaching, which everybody should therefore attend, it was all that any man needed. The limitations placed upon the light of nature were essentially important in the minds of the preachers. They grew rapidly less important to minds that could boast of little else. The common mind leapt to the conclusion that the common mind was enough, that indeed, because it was uncorrupted by vain human knowledge, it was more likely to apprehend truth. Learning, therefore, might be, should be, dispensed with, even learning in preachers, finally even preaching itself, since every man had common reason and the book. By such arguments the notion spread that it was the people who were the elect, that no man was predestined to damnation, and that, thanks to nature and the God of nature, the heart of every man was wise in its own right.

The direction in which the Puritan leaders were thus being led by the logic of their position and by the fire of their own imaginations is well indicated by Preston's *Life Eternall*. The more the preachers exalted God the more they tended to reduce all things human to one level. The more they succeeded in persuading each of their hearers that God took an immediate interest in him and his eternal welfare the more they exalted the individual in his own opinion above whatever in church or state displeased his conscience or thwarted his desires. Preston begins by exalting the author of creation. In the course of his discussion he advances the usual arguments for the necessity of faith added to reason and for the light of the word added to the light of nature. But the force of his eloquence is directed to proving that there is that in every man which cannot escape God as revealed in creation and in the book. The preachment starts from Paul's statement (Acts 17:27-28) that God, having made the world, has made all men to live and move and have their being in him and to feel after him and to find him. With these words is linked the statement (Rom. 1:20) that 'the invisible things of him from the creation of the world are clearly seen, being understood by the things that are made.' The existence of God, that is, is revealed first of all in nature and in the heart of man. 'All Nations doe acknowledge a God.' This, Preston says, we may take for granted. Even the American Indians support the observation of Paul concerning the Athenians: 'those Nations discovered lately by the Spaniards in the West Indies, and those that have been discovered since; all of them, with-

out exception, have it written in their hearts that there is a God.'
This is the law referred to by the apostle, and 'everymans soule is
but (as it were) the table or paper upon which the writing is.' This
is the law of nature and 'the workes of Nature are not in vaine.' He
turns, then, from the Bible to nature for confirmation of his faith as
many another worshiper of nature was to do: 'when you see the fire
to ascend above the aire, it argues that there is a place where it would
rest, though you never saw it; and as (in winter) when you see the
Swallowes flying to a place, though you never saw the place, yet you
must needs gather that there is one which Nature hath appointed
them . . . so when you see in every mans soule an instigation to
seek God, . . . this argues there is a Deitie which they intend.'[108]
'There is enough,' in fact, 'in the very creation of the world to
declare him unto us,' and 'there is a delight of the understanding or
reason put into us, whereby we are able to discerne those characters
of God stamped in the creatures,'[109] 'Arguments enough,' 'reason
enough,' 'for looke upon all the creatures, and we shall see that they
have an end,' 'and if they have an end, it is certaine, there is one did
ayme at it.' The purpose revealed in the creatures is, of course, that
they serve man. Sun and moon and stars quicken the earth to bring
forth plants to feed the beasts, and horses run, oxen plow, and dogs
hunt in our behalf so that we may consummate nature's work by
serving God.[110] What more we need to know—those mysteries that
leave 'no prints in creation'[111]—is revealed to faith in the Bible. But
even for understanding these profundities, our natural endowments,
the law of God written in the heart, are sufficient. How can any man
fail to be moved, the preacher exclaims, by the 'majestie and plainness' of the style which only the Holy Ghost has designed or could
have designed for common comprehension?[112] Therefore we may
read of the miracles, the prophecies, and the testimonies contained in
scripture and be convinced for and by ourselves of the existence of a
God whose intention is to save all who believe in him.

Thus Preston is led to argue, as Paul did to the Athenians, that
nature leaves us no excuse for unbelief. He is particularly eloquent
upon this theme, but he was not alone in entertaining such thoughts.
His friend Thomas Goodwin's early temptation to trust utterly to
nature continued to be reflected in assurances in his sermons that
nature led us at least part way to God, and similar assurances were

common in the sermons of others. Most of the more respectable would, of course, stop far short of any of the heresies, Arminian, antinomian, Arian or what not, which marked the way that led to deism, the religion of nature, democracy and all that followed thereafter. But their zeal for bringing souls to God made them lead the people no little distance on that way.

How far astray the people were soon to go from the strict path leading to the presbyterian Utopia, the preachers were soon to learn. The spiritual brotherhood from the beginning had been nursing two serpents in its bosom, the press and dissent. Many pages would be required to describe in detail how the preachers exhorted the people to supplement their attendance upon sermons and their conning of scripture by reading the books which preachers wrote for their instruction. It will suffice to cite William Gouge's pithy summation of the common attitude and procedure. He is dedicating his *Guide to Goe to God* to his parishioners. Wishing them 'all needfull Prosperity in this world and eternall Felicitie in the World to come,' he writes:

What privately I first digested in mine owne meditation and then publickely delivered by word of mouth, whereof in the open church you heard your children and servants examined, and for a blessing whereupon many prayers by us all joyntly and severally have been poured out before God, is now thorow Gods gracious providence so published as it may be reviewed so oft as you please. Well accept it: for it is A GUIDE TO GOE TO GOD.[113]

Thus the preachers went to press, the people became a reading people as well as a godly people, and the press waxed strong, bold and less and less godly. What had at first been regarded as the pulpit's humble handmaid became an engine of spiritual war which threatened not only prelacy and other carnal powers but the pulpit itself. The other homebred menace to the reform of the church and the dominance of the Puritan clergy was the individualism they had themselves fostered and which came to natural fruition in the sect. The preachers told the people that they must obey conscience, thinking that they could hold the conscience of the saints in their own keeping. But when they said one thing to the saints and conscience said another, the reformers were destined to find their authority as fragile as that of pope and prelate had been.

V

Reformation without Tarrying

THE object of the Puritan reformers was the reorganization of English society in the form of a church governed according to presbyterian principles. Until they were summoned by Parliament to the Westminster Assembly, they were granted no opportunity to put their ideas into effect, but they were allowed within limits to preach to the people and to publish books. They were very far from approving in principle the tolerance by which they profited. Their ideal was uniformity based upon the will of a godly people and maintained with the support of a godly civil state. They would have had the state set up presbyterianism first and trust the preachers to render the people godly afterwards. As it was, the condition actually imposed upon them by the policy of the government was that they begin by trying to convert the people and trust in God to bring about presbyterian reform in his own time. The immediate result was that, in the hope of establishing ultimately their cherished scheme of uniformity, they spent two generations preaching a doctrine and a way of life which promoted active individual religious experience and expression, promoted it much faster than means could be found to control or direct it. What the preachers as a whole believed was that heresy and schism should be firmly suppressed. But what they taught was that any man might be a saint and that the mark of the saint was that he obeyed his own conscience at any cost. They themselves practiced conscientious objection, in whatever degree they dared and in whatever direction they chose, to the form of religion established by law. The ultimate effect, as later the reformers learned to their sorrow, was to encourage in their followers the habit of going each his own way toward heaven and the notion that it was every man's native right to save himself or not in his own way without interference from anybody. From the very beginning of the movement, therefore, heresy and schism dogged the steps of the Puritan reformers, and in the very day of victory, when prelacy lay overthrown, brought their schemes for the godly Utopia to confusion.

The relation of the Puritan presbyterian reformers to the Puritan sectaries and independents, of Puritan orthodoxy overshooting its mark to Puritan individualism running wild, is of importance for the understanding of the Puritan movement.[1] Up to 1643, when the long-awaited opportunity to reorganize the church was finally realized, the spiritual leadership, the energizing ideas and the literature which in such large measure helped to bring on the revolution came mostly from the preachers already discussed in these pages. But their preaching had also engendered a left wing, a growing minority opposed to certain features of presbyterianism. In the days before the old regime collapsed, before the adoption of presbyterianism by the Westminster Assembly in 1644 became imminent, the independents and the separatists of all sorts remained relatively obscure and seemed unimportant. After that date, they suddenly came forward to oppose the majority in the Assembly, disrupt its plans, multiply sermons and pamphlets beyond number, fill Cromwell's army, push forward a revolution far more sweeping than any which the original Puritan reformers had conceived, and eventually to give the term Puritan the meaning it has to a large extent since retained. But, as the beginnings of Puritanism are to be traced to the activities of the Puritan reformers before 1643, so must the early signs of revolutionary Puritanism be looked for in the activities of the various minorities which the reformers, in spite of themselves, evoked by their preaching.

The original energy of Puritanism came from the independence of the individual preachers. As Puritanism developed, it attracted to the pulpit a larger and larger number of imaginative, idealistic, self-centered, histrionic, articulate, Quixotic dreamers and talkers—half-saints, half-poets—fired by passion for self-expression and equipped with an incomparable apparatus for self-justification. Consequently no revolutionary movement in all probability ever gave fuller utterance to the hopes and dreams that attended it, and none was ever more beset by the congenital schismatics and martyrs of its time. Given the popularization of the Bible and of the technique for extracting truth from the poetry with which that book is filled, given the belief in the supervening power of the individual mind to know God and of the

individual conscience to voice his will, given the opportunities afforded by the loosely controlled pulpit and press, and Puritanism,
though solidly respectable and firmly enough disciplined at its center,
was certain to deploy in most varied and fantastic extravagance at its
periphery. The members of the spiritual brotherhood by the very
vigor and success of their effort to convert the people inevitably
started some of them off upon the spiritual pilgrimage at a speed and
with a disregard of consequences which the preachers had not foreseen and could not approve. It was not merely that some of their
more reckless supporters, now a Martin Marprelate, now a William
Prynne, from time to time launched ill-considered attacks upon the
prelates. Belief in the eventual coming of the New Jerusalem and
triumphing of the saints, too confidently proclaimed from the pulpit,
led some men to grow impatient with the slow processes of reform
and to attempt the erection of the true church for themselves in their
own time. The doctrine, too convincingly set forth, of God's immediate concern in the individual soul and of the individual's apti-
tude for understanding what the Holy Spirit revealed through the
spoken and the printed word, encouraged some to the idea that they
need trust nothing so much as their own untutored notions even in
defiance of sense and sound learning. The call of the preachers to the
unconverted, too evangelically urged, suggested to many that every
man either could be saved if he chose or was saved already and must
reject grace of his own will if he were to be damned at all. Such were
the deviations from orthodox Puritanism which led to the rise of
the sects and were reflected, though in milder terms, in the emergence
of independents within the reform party itself. There was still another, more far-reaching, result. The clash of disputants, each equally
certain that he alone was in the right way and the others doomed to
destruction, prompted some minds to the conclusion that perhaps
nothing could be surely known except that God was revealed in
nature and in the Bible and that men were meant to believe in him
and for the rest to bear with one another's errors in mutual love
and tolerance.

It is probably safe to say that before the revolution the various
minority Puritan groups made no considerable contribution to the
spread of Puritan ideas or of the Puritan epic of the spiritual life,

none at any rate that can easily be traced. The sects and the independents, particularly the former, require consideration here chiefly because in one way or another they early betrayed those momentous implications in Puritanism which were not to be fully exposed until after 1640. The part they thus played in the whole revolutionary movement can best be presented not by attempting to disentangle the history of each dissenting group from the mass but by focusing attention upon certain significant figures which supply in their extant writings the most vivid and intelligible illustrations of some of the more important extreme developments of pre-revolutionary Puritan thought and expression.

Though the term anabaptist was quickly adopted in England as a term of opprobrium to be directed at any sort of religious radical, the influence of continental anabaptism was obscure and probably slight.[2] The seeds of historic English dissent are found among the Protestant congregations of Queen Mary's reign. They developed after the Elizabethan settlement of the church and the rise of the Puritan reform movement. Dissenters probably did not, to begin with, regard themselves as separated from the church but as devoted to a purer, more apostolic organization and worship from which the main body of the church had temporarily departed and to which they hoped it would soon return. The exigencies of their position, however, soon inclined them to the conviction that the Church of England had abandoned Christ for Antichrist and that all true believers must remove themselves from it. Once having seceded, the sect was faced by the problem of maintaining its solidarity, a problem not always successfully solved. First of all, it identified the true church not with society nor with the nation but with an exclusive congregation of saints, unanimous in belief and uniform in practice, admitting to its communion only those who could give satisfactory proof of their divine election. Admission to the congregation, that is, could only be by consent of the members, and every member must bind himself in some signal way to accept the will of the whole group as his own. It was, of course, not difficult in that age to prove that the separation of the saints from the Church of England and their voluntary association by agreement with one another were precisely commanded by scripture. Such were the essential characteristics of the

English sects as finally and fully developed. But not every minority group after 1570 proceeded promptly or directly to the extreme separatist position, and differences of doctrine and observance, accompanied by much internecine controversy, divided and subdivided the congregations again and again. Hence to attempt to distinguish one group or one sect from another and to determine exactly how far each had proceeded at any given time in its withdrawal from the church or in its cohesion with like-minded bodies would be for our purposes here an unnecessary as well as a difficult task. All were products of the same strange ferment, the growing intoxication of the people with the poetry of the Bible and with the hope for heaven on earth.

The sects were important historically on several counts, some of which were more significant than others in the general development of Puritanism. Out of the shifting, frequently broken and confused, dissenting and non-conformist minorities of the sixteenth and early seventeenth centuries have arisen two of the major English and American Protestant communions of modern times, the Congregationalist and the Baptist. The progenitors of the former, those who placed chief emphasis on the independence of the congregation or 'gathered' church at varying degrees of separation from the established church, played the major part in the settlement of New England, though the early baptists also had a share in that enterprise of the Puritan spirit. Both, perhaps more especially the baptists, were of importance in promulgating ideas of democracy and toleration. The importance of the sects at the time of their inception and of their contribution to the cause of liberty has, however, probably been exaggerated by their later apologists. The modern sectarian historian is concerned with running the lines of his peculiar people back as far as possible, and he is prone to define as special to the sect characteristics which are, at best, variations upon those common to the whole Puritan movement. His particular temptation is to claim for his own sect a priority in advocating ideas of democracy or toleration which is of little significance and an influence which is at best difficult to establish. A juster perspective shows the individual sect to have been less influential than the sects as a whole and the sects as a whole to have been chiefly noteworthy as exaggerated expressions of aspects of Puritanism which had the greatest significance for the future development of society at large. Relatively obscure in the early stages of the Puritan movement, they became more important as it gained momentum, and they played a decisive role when it reached its peak in the period of the civil wars and the Commonwealth. As revolutionary Puritanism declined, they too declined as factors in public life and became merely aspects of Protestantism in modern society which less and less concern the historian of thought and expression in general.

Eventually the sects of the revolutionary period produced in George Fox a great religious personality and in Bunyan the one Puritan preacher whose preaching flowered into a great literary classic transcending sectarianism of any sort. But before 1644, they contributed little in comparison to the preachers who continued to adhere to the Church of England in the hope of reforming it. They are important chiefly as symptoms of the democratization of English society and culture which was being steadily advanced by Puritan preaching in general, by the translation and publication of the Bible, and by the spread of literacy. The end toward which the whole movement was tending was the reorganization of society on the basis of a Bible-reading populace. Calvinism helped this movement forward by setting up a new criterion of aristocracy in opposition to the class distinctions of the existing system. But there was also a concept of equalitarianism implicit in Calvinism which transcended aristocracy and which the necessity the preachers were under of evangelizing the people brought steadily to the fore. They had to try to make everybody at any rate wish to be saved, wish to believe and to be of the elect. Wishing, however, is next to believing. It became difficult not to think that election and salvation by the grace of God were available to everyone who really desired them. Moreover, once the Calvinist preachers admitted that the only true aristocracy was spiritual and beyond any human criterion, they had gone a long way toward asserting that all men in society must be treated alike because only God knows who is superior. The main body of preachers, to be sure, professional intellectuals with their own positions and prestige at stake, held to the notion of a national church, reformed from within, and did their best to keep the disruptive implications of their doctrines from being pressed too far. But granted their premises, it was natural that there should start up among them as well as about them many impatient individualists unwilling to wait upon the slow processes of reform.

The cause of the steady development of the centrifugal tendencies of Puritanism was Puritan fostering of individualism in religion in the course of the accelerating democratization of English society. The force behind the sectarian offshoots of the spiritual brotherhood was the imaginative energy and force of character, the passion for self-expression, the zeal to refashion the world, of the individual preacher. Whatever quirk of doctrine or practice an excited uncritical attention to scripture suggested to his mind, this was but the mode offered to him for expressing himself. He gathered a sect about him in the name of the truth revealed to him, but the cohesive force of the sect was less the heresy than the heresiarch. Dissenting congregations waxed and waned, divided and redivided, largely as they found leaders to inspire them. Whenever in any given sect or congregation, two leaders of something like equal force arose, there would generally occur sooner or later a serious clash of opinion and then a split, some of the brothers adhering to one leader and the rest to the other. Hence the history of the dissenters is occupied almost as much with the strife of sects with one another as with the attacks of the sects upon the main body of the orthodox from which all had sprung. The groups which finally survived as important Protestant communions were those which found the more vigorous leaders, men possessed with gifts of statesmanship as well as of prophecy.

The sects and their leaders were from the start preoccupied with the problem of organization. They were in large measure a product of the preaching of the Puritan epic of individualism, but for a long time they could find few occasions and little time to contribute to its elaboration in the pulpit or in print. The dissenting preacher had something else to do. He had first to lead his followers out of the security of the church, then to keep them out, and always to hold them together. Separation in the period before the revolution put something of a check upon proselytizing. The sect was composed of people who were already converted; the unregenerate were abandoned to their fate. Consequently, the separatist preacher had to devote himself to the task of maintaining the solidarity of his little group, whether ostracized, persecuted or exiled. The inner organization of the sect was necessarily democratic. Its strength depended directly upon the number of those who freely consented to the authority of the group and its leader. The pastor must retain the loyalty of his flock. Two notable devices serving to this end, one of organization the other of ritual, were early resorted to. The first was the covenant, a solemn pledge, a contract, entered into by the members with one another and with God, to adhere to the congregation and never to depart. This became the normal feature in some form or other of all the separatist groups. Some, not content with the covenant alone, adopted in addition a special form of baptism as an initiatory rite. Such were the principal historic procedures of the sects for gathering in their people and keeping them together. The literature of dissent for half a century or more is chiefly concerned with such matters. It is largely abstract and controversial. It is devoted to arguing that the Church of England or, it may be, this or that rival sect, is no true church; to establishing scriptural authority for separation; and to technical defense of the peculiar practices of the sects. Since every preacher was potentially or actually a rival of every other preacher for the suffrages of the saints, the sectarians were forever being drawn into controversy with one another as well as with their orthodox competitors. Hence it is that we have to look long in the writings of the left-wing Puritans of the prerevolutionary period before we find any notable contributions to the Puritan literature of confession, pilgrimage and war. Only when one group of early separatists happened upon one of the great human adventures of all time did a separatist write something of more than sectarian interest.

The disputes with which so much of sectarian literature was occupied raged over differences regarded by the disputants as of the most profound significance. Actually, of course, in everything that seems significant to us, the Puritan sects were far more alike than they were different. All believed that every man could come to know God in his own heart and in the word, that the inner voice of conscience was the voice of God, and that nothing short of complete obedience to God's commands vouchsafed through conscience was exacted of the saints. There was nothing in this to mark the sectarians off from the other Puritans. What distinguished them was that in matters relating to the church they believed their obedience must be instant as well as perfect. They could wait upon no consideration of prudence or charity. They must tarry for none but flee the city of destruction, the church of Antichrist, at once. This course did not argue great political prudence on the part of the sectarians, nor promote it in them, but it did serve to intensify still more deeply their essential Puritan traits. Above all, it further invigorated the individual spirit and aggrandized the individual's sense of dignity and self-confidence. Hence we find the dissenters, and only to a less degree the independents who still managed to stay just inside the church, running far out upon various limbs of the tree of doctrine. Some remained orthodox upon the grand matter of predestination. It was perhaps easier to maintain the solidarity of the saints over against the multitude of the damned outside if one held to the belief that only a few were elected to salvation. But separatism was the extreme expression of the religious individualism of Puritan faith and doctrine, the individualism which most drastically leveled all men before God. The dissenting preachers, moreover, were happy to find converts wherever they could, and found them in greater and greater numbers among men who by any leveling process felt themselves likely to gain rather than lose. The adherence of the underdog is easy to enlist if he is told that all men have the same chance for heaven. Sectarian preachers were forever falling into that error which everywhere dogged Calvinistic orthodoxy, namely that the grace of God is free to all upon the same terms and that any man can help himself to enjoy it. Consequently the notions of universal grace and free will, which the main body of Puritan preachers opposed so bitterly in the church but which were the natural expression in theological terms of some of the most important implications of Calvinism on the moral and social plane, these flourished among the sects and served to intensify and accelerate the work of the Puritan epic in bringing the dream of a presbyterian Utopia to confusion.[3]

The career of Robert Browne,[4] whose name as the father of Brownism is notorious in the annals of Elizabeth's reign, clearly illustrates the origin and character of separatism. Up to a certain point, nothing distinguished him from the typical Puritan reformer and spiritual preacher. A kinsman of Lord Burghley, he came from a respectable country family. He was at Corpus Christi, Cambridge, during the Cartwright excitement, graduating B.A. in 1572. He says of himself that he was one of those 'which had lived & studied in Cambridge [and] were there knowne & counted forward in religion . . . more carefull & zelous, then their froward enimies would suffer.'[5] The grudging of his enemies and his own doubts sent him back in a few years to live at Cambridge in the household of Richard Greenham. There he enjoyed the word and did some preaching, but his intransigent temper prevented him from following the normal course of the spiritual brotherhood. He rejected ordination, spoke openly against bishops, abandoned any hope of reforming the church, went to Norwich and gathered a little band of disciples about him on separatist lines. The usual vicissitudes of persecution and exile followed. Dissension sprang up among his followers. He returned to England, presently recanted and accepted ordination and a country living in the church. His notoriety was chiefly due to his advocacy of such startling ideas as are expressed in his handful of controversial tracts. The title of one, the most famous, is in itself a classic statement of the point of view of reformers of all ages who will have nothing but complete reform in their own time. It is called *A Treatise of Reformation without tarying for anie, and of the wickedness of those Preachers which will not reforme till the Magistrate commande or compell them.*

Browne's writings betray the weakness that was for a long time to beset the outpourings of the sectaries. They are directed against their author's enemies; they are not directed to the reader for the inspiration and edification of the weak and as yet unawakened. *A True and Short Declaration,* for example, is an autobiographical apology for Browne's course of action, not a confession of his inward struggles. In this and other tracts, however, the man states clearly, even vigorously, the extreme Puritan position in respect to church government. The magistrate, all reformers agreed, should be under the spiritual oversight of the church. How then can he have any authority over the pastors of the church? How can the church do anything but reform itself at once without tarrying for his approval? What is reform but the casting out of every evil thing and every evil person completely and at once? The church which will not reform, as the English church under the rule of the bishops would not, is no church, and true believers must abandon it to its fate, gather together, and carry on at all costs by themselves, excluding the unregenerate and binding themselves by covenant with one another. Such ideas, carried to their logical extreme, pointed to nothing short of a democratic revolution envisaged as popular government in the church. Later proponents of such ideas went farther than Browne toward realizing them in the democracy of saints within the sect, and some, as we shall see, went on to seek their realization in society and government at large. Browne founded no sect and, losing the glory that might have come from such achievement, was traduced in legend—until modern research rescued him—as a radical and a crank who ended by quarreling with his wife and going insane.[6]

John Smyth[7] and John Robinson, both sprung from the yeomanry of the Trent valley and converted by the word at Cambridge somewhat later than Browne, took together the same path into separatism. Parting in the course of their careers, the one became the spiritual father of the English baptists, the other of Plymouth colony. Each was in his way a portent of what Puritanism held in store for English-speaking peoples. Smyth, the elder of the two by a few years, entered Cambridge as a sizar at Christ's College (1586) in the days of Sir Walter Mildmay, Chaderton, Perkins and Hildersam. Francis Johnson, until his expulsion in 1588, was Smyth's tutor. By some one of these, no doubt, he was converted to the Puritan faith and launched upon his spiritual pilgrimage. By 1594 he had been elected a fellow of Christ's and was shortly afterward ordained. Six years later he was appointed lecturer by the city of Lincoln at £40 a year with an allowance for house rent and permission to keep three cows on the common. Certain of his sermons of these years are still extant in print. He published them, he says, because 'seeing every bald tale, vaine enterlude, and pelting ballad, hath the priviledge of the Presse,' he thought it reasonable that 'the sermons and readings of ministers may challenge the same.' Why should the stationers' shops and some men's shelves contain nothing but 'Guy of Warwicke, William of Cloudeslee, Skeggins, and Wolners jests, and writings of like qualitie.' The sermons Smyth offers are undistinguished discourses of the Puritan type. He says that he has not varnished his writing with 'the superficiall learning of words and figures, tongues and testimonies of men,'[8] but has written a plain and homely style 'seeing that learned men can understand things plainly delivered, but the unlearned cannot conceive the easiest doctrines, except they be delivered also after an easie manner, with homely, familiar and easie speeches.'[9] This was, of course, but the commonplace of Puritan asseveration concerning style and was not as a matter of fact very fully or brilliantly exemplified in Smyth's own practice as represented in these sermons.

Up to his leaving Lincoln, indeed, Smyth appears no different from the scores of young men whom the leaders of the spiritual brotherhood were sending out to preach the word in the pulpits of the church. Something, however, went wrong at Lincoln, and he soon (1602) found himself dropped from his lectureship. The young man conferred with Arthur Hildersam, with his friend Richard Bernard, very probably with John Dod and others. The next thing we know for certain is that about 1606 he was at the head of a group of saints centered about Gainsborough who had abandoned or were in the act of abandoning all hope of purifying the English church and who now united under a covenant in a congregation devoted to the true faith. Another group, committed to the same course and closely identified with the first, drew together shortly at Scrooby under the leadership of William Brewster with John Robinson as preacher and pastor. The separatist ferment was at the moment working strong in the region, several of the local preachers being tempted to proceed without tarrying upon the work of reformation. Besides Smyth and Robinson, the most notable of these was Richard Bernard.[10] The latter had been at Christ's with Smyth a few years before and was now the incumbent of Worksop-St. Mary and St. Cuthbert, only a few miles away. He was, it would seem, almost persuaded to follow the dangerous example of his two bolder friends, but after being briefly suspended from his living, he recanted, retreated to a position similar to that of Hildersam, controverted his former friends in print,[11] and a few years later accepted at the hands of an admirer a comfortable living in Somersetshire, whence he issued those edifying and imagistic writings already discussed. From the congregationalist point of view, Bernard is a backslider and an enemy. Actually, he shows how closely

linked the early separatists were in their beginnings to the brotherhood of preachers which emanated, and continued to be guided, from
Cambridge. Bernard took the right turn, and Smyth, taking the left,
fled with his people in 1607 or early in 1608 from Gainsborough to
Holland. The Scrooby people under Robinson followed soon afterwards.

John Robinson[12] entered Cambridge, a sizar at Corpus Christi, in
1592 to become another of the growing band of young men inspired
by Chaderton and Perkins. He rose to a fellowship in 1597 and was
ordained. He soon withdrew from the university, married and found
a preaching post at St. Andrew's, Norwich. What happened thereupon we do not know except that Robinson soon left his pulpit and
cast in his lot with Smyth and the other separatists about Gainsborough, more particularly with those who gathered at the house of
William Brewster in Scrooby. He became their guide and prophet
and led them in the footsteps of Smyth and the Gainsborough group
to Amsterdam in 1608.

When they found themselves in Holland, each as the pastor of a
flock of exiles on foreign soil, Smyth and Robinson took different
paths. The former was obviously the more impractical and visionary
of the two and proceeded faster upon the road marked out for him
by the reasoning which had led him into separation from the church.
Having concluded that the Church of England was not the Church
of God, he first sought to bind his followers together by a covenant
which they subscribed at Gainsborough before their departure. But
that action, it would seem, set his mind running upon the mystery
of man's communion with the divine. If the English church was no
true church, its sacraments could effect no mystic union of the soul
with God. God was not in the established church, and Smyth concluded that, baptized in that church, he and his flock had never been
baptized at all, and that no church at that time visible to them in the
world could administer the baptism of the Holy Spirit. But Smyth
had found God in his own breast, and so he baptized himself, after
which he felt authorized to baptize any who would acknowledge God
on the same terms and enter upon the covenant of the saints. He
began by rebaptizing his followers and so instituted the peculiar and
historic rite of one branch of English dissent. It is of some impor-

tance, however, to note that Smyth's followers were separatists before
they were baptists, and that they were baptists before they hit upon
total immersion as the most signal and dramatic as well as the most
scriptural form of initiation into the true church. The development
of Smyth's doctrinal ideas kept pace with his conception of the church
and the sacrament.[13] The law which condemned all men to punishment for sin was abrogated for all by the atonement of Christ. The
grace which enabled the saint to believe and be saved was proffered
to all who would accept it. God lay in wait in every man's heart. None
need fear rejection, providing he would repent, believe, and by his
own free choice enter the communion of saints, enter, that is, the true
church which Smyth had set up in defiance of the church of Antichrist.

Smyth's career as the leader of a sect, like that of many another
devotee of the mystic brotherhood of man, was far from happy, prosperous or—at any rate until the end—gracious. His extreme individualism led him to conduct his congregation in Holland as a pure
democracy, each member communing with God directly in his own
breast and in scripture. Smyth's own ardent communing led him to
discover that there had in a congregation of Dutch Mennonites been
a true church all along and that therefore the baptism he had administered to himself and his followers had after all been of no
avail. But among his disciples was a country gentleman from Nottinghamshire who had followed him faithfully all the way to separatism
and exile, so faithfully that he could not find it in his heart to reject
the baptism he had received at Smyth's hands even after Smyth
repudiated it. So the little congregation fell apart. Some followed
their original leader into the fold of the Mennonites. Some went
with the new leader, Thomas Helwys, and presently (1612-1613)
conceived it their duty to return to England in order to attempt the
conversion of King James and his subjects. Smyth had then already
died in Amsterdam. Helwys was to suffer imprisonment and die a
few years later. His place as leader was taken by John Murton, a
man of humble origin, and the congregation becomes lost to view
among the lowly baptists who went on obscurely agitating and suffering until the revolution broke.

John Robinson, in sharp contrast to Smyth, proved to be signally successful in keeping his flock together and in helping its members to achieve a satisfactory existence. The congregation, when well-organized and firmly conducted, had something to offer its adherents besides spiritual excitement. It was an escape from confusion. On its way to the next world the compact brotherhood gave aid, comfort and some protection to its members in this one. This was strikingly demonstrated by Robinson in his leadership of the refugees from Scrooby. They seem for a time to have joined forces in Amsterdam with the congregation which had gathered in London about the unfortunate Barrow, Greenwood and Penry and had recently found sanctuary in Holland under Francis Johnson and Henry Ainsworth. Dissension, however, was already at work, and for that or some other reason Robinson in 1609 betook himself with his followers to Leyden. There they soon found means to set up their church, practice their trades and prosper. Their minister's gift for ruling his flock may be measured by the praises of William Bradford and by the memorable picture of the mother church of Plymouth colony which that worthy gives in his famous history. It may, indeed, be taken as something like the classic picture of the Puritan sect, justified by success.

Being thus setld [in Leyden] (after many difficulties) they continued many years, in a comfortable condition; injoying much sweete and delightfull societie and spirituall comforte together in the wayes of God. . . . So as they grew in knowledge and other gifts and graces of the spirite of God; and lived togeather in peace, and love, and holines; and many came unto them from diverse parts of England, so as they grew a great congregation. And [here we may note how easily insoluble or at any rate difficult problems could under firm leadership be thrust by the sect back upon society at large] if at any time, any differences arose, or offences broak out (as it cannot be, but some ther will, even among the best of men) they were ever so mete with, and nipt in the head betimes, or otherwise so well composed, as still love, peace and communion was continued; or els the church purged of those that were incurable and incorr[i]gible, when, after much patience used, no other means would serve, which seldom came to pass.[14]

What gifts Robinson may have had for imaginative expression in the pulpit we cannot tell. No doubt he kept the spirit of his people astir by reiteration of themes from the Puritan epic. But his audience was a congregation of saints requiring to be kept together rather than convinced. It was not a host of the unregenerate challenging the evangelist. At any rate, Robinson published no body of imagistic sermons on the spiritual life. His *Observations Divine and Moral*, sensible, pithy, didactic essays in the manner of John Dod, probably represent the lessons he gave his people on the Puritan code.[15] He wrote nothing besides, nothing which has survived, except polemics to champion the theory, the practice and the orthodoxy of the sect.[16] His entering the lists against Arminius was characteristic of so shrewd a man. The history of separatism seems to show that the sects which pressed Puritan individualism too far or too fast in the direction of antinomianism and pure democracy fell apart more promptly. Those which held or retreated to the belief that grace is limited to an elect few predestined to be saved were generally more successful in maintaining their solidarity, knowing that they themselves were the elect. Robinson would have nought of free will or universal grace. He kept democracy under control by upholding the authority of ruling elders. He was willing to discuss the idea of the independents that congregations within the established church might be found to be true churches in the separatist sense, and so he perhaps foreshadowed the ease with which the Plymouth congregation later fell in line with those of Massachusetts Bay. For himself, however, he never retraced the step he had taken into separation. Why should he? The Leyden congregation, as the loving industry of its historians has proved, was, notwithstanding dangers and difficulties, successful according to its lights, and Robinson was in a large measure the author of that success. Fate held in store for that people, moreover, a singular glory.

This is no place to tell again the legend of the Mayflower. Up to a point, there was little reason why the first settlement of New England should have fallen to Robinson's and not to some other Puritan preacher's flock. Puritanism supplied to all the saints the same spiritual preparation for such a venture. Their preachers were in many instances itinerants as well as mendicants. The separatist preachers with their flocks, goaded by fitful persecution, were forced to be always on the move or ready for it. More than one, doubtless, had thoughts of flitting to the New World. Many Puritans of all sorts would soon follow. Robinson's congregation succeeded first and so early in flinging a small detachment across the ocean, a feat of the greatest difficulty, because of the strength of its leadership and organization. But the voyage in the Mayflower was inspired by the ideals common not only to separatists but to Puritans in general. It was Puritan faith and character and the Puritan dream of a godly Utopia, transfigured by the Puritan epic, which were to bear fruit in Massachusetts.

Robinson began as a disciple of those patriarchs of the spiritual brotherhood, Chaderton, Hildersam, Dod and Perkins. The fact that Arminius had assailed Perkins may well have had some effect in bringing Robinson into the field against the Dutch heretic. A sermon[17] on Rom. 12:3-8, attributed to Chaderton, was reissued from William Brewster's press in Leyden in 1618 and was more than once referred to in Robinson's own writings. In the library whith Brewster, Robinson's deputy, assembled about him in Plymouth,[18] appeared all the early classics of Puritan literature, Greenham, Rogers, Hildersam, Perkins, Downame, Dod; many of the later writers followed as their books were published. On the soil of Plymouth itself, finally, was soon to be written a book which takes a novel and important place among the statements of Puritan, and we must now add, American experience. To one who has beaten his dusty way through the tomes in which the saga of spiritual wayfaring and warfaring found lodging before 1640, it is difficult to speak temperately of a book so loaded with past association and with augury for the American kind of future as Governor William Bradford's *History of Plymouth Plantation*. The author was a man of some education and could cite Pliny, Plato and Marcus Aurelius as he wished. But when he began his chronicle, he was still living in the mental world of the spiritual brotherhood, and he wrote, clear-eyed, unaffected, almost artless though he was, in the idiom of the Puritan saga. Life, when he first stepped ashore at Plymouth Rock, was still seen and expressed by him in terms of the war with Satan and of the journey from this world to the next. 'It is well knowne', he says, 'how ever since the first breaking out of the lighte of the gospell, in our Honourable Nation of England . . . what warrs, and oppossisions . . . Satan hath raised, maintained, and continued against the Saincts, from time, to time, in one sort, or another.'[19] The deaths, torments, imprisonments and banishments inflicted by persecutors, the errors, corruptions and dissensions of the church, these were but Satan's stratagems against that truth for which the saints gave unceasing battle. Lovingly he describes their peace and security at Leyden and then gives account of their debates before taking the determination to flee to the wilderness from the dangers of a threatened European war. The voyage to the new world was a terrifying prospect which, however, the Puritan teaching concerning God's calling the saints to strive and be of good courage, his direct interest in their welfare, and the success which he predestined to be theirs, all enabled them to face without flinching. To every objection

It was answered, that all great, and honorable actions, are accompanied with great difficulties; and must be, both enterprised, and overcome with answerable courages. It was granted the dangers were great, but not desperate; the difficulties were many, but not invincible. For though their were many of them likly, yet they were not cartaine; it might be sundrie of the things feared, might never befale; others by providente care and the use of good means, might in a great measure be prevented; and all of them (through the help of God) by fortitude and patience, might either be borne, or overcome. True it was, that shuch attempts were not to be made and undertaken without good ground, and reason; not rashly, or lightly, as many have done for curiositie, or hope of gaine, etc. But their condition was not ordinarie; their ends were good and honourable; their calling lawfull, and urgente; and therfore they might expecte the blessing of God in their proceding.[20]

Perkins or Sibbes or Preston in a sermon, Milton in a pamphlet or a poem, would have expressed the moral address of the Puritan soul with the accent of a different personality but not in a different spirit, nor, all things considered, more impressively.

The vocation of the elect was to go through this life as pilgrims. For describing the emotions of departure for the new world, that image was to Bradford the inevitable one. 'So they lefte the goodly and pleasante citie, which had been ther resting place near 12. years; but they knew they were pilgrimes, and looked not much on those things, but lift up their eyes to the heavens, their dearest cuntrie, and quieted their spirits.'[21] Thomas Taylor and John Bunyan would have understood the right Puritan sense in which this was said. One wonders how many of the pilgrim fathers' countrymen this side of heaven and the Atlantic still understand. They came looking for the New Jerusalem and found themselves to be at any rate in a new world. It was long since they had betaken themselves from the confusion of English society to the esoteric brotherhood of the sect. They came to New England seeking not only a refuge for the sect but a free field where it could grow in godliness, untroubled by the powers of the world. Their departure from the Old World and their arrival in the New are invested by Bradford with all the exaltation of the Puritan sermon and the Puritan epic. But once arrived in America, they must plant corn, build houses, treat with savages, govern the unruly, chaffer with the company in England. Bradford finds himself compelled to become a pioneer, a man of business, a lawmaker, a ruler, a realist. The energetic, executive, alert, practical, shrewd American, in a word the Yankee, begins to emerge out of the Puritan saint. From his book, the exaltation, the imagism, the mysticism fade. He becomes in time less and less occupied with the war on Satan, more and more with the practical problems of making a life for himself and his people, saints and sinners alike, in the new environment. He writes, as he goes on, less and less like a Puritan preacher and more and more like the author of *Robinson Crusoe*.

The majority of Puritans of the left, impatient though they were for the fruition of their ideals, underwent no such adventure as befell Bradford and wrote no such book. The Puritan imagination in them had still a long way to go before it could work free of partisan preoccupations. For one thing, books and pamphlets without number had first to be filled up by independents and separatists with arguments to prove that the church must be purified, that the elect and none besides were the church and that the church without pope or prelate or even presbyterian synod was perfect and complete only in the congregation, though in every congregation, of saints. After Browne and Smyth and Robinson, a steady succession of enthusiasts separated from the established church and then in pulpit and press engaged busily in the work of defending themselves and of controverting their opponents or, almost as often, one another. One group, more wary, followed the lead of William Bradshaw, author of the famous *English Puritanisme. Containeing the maine Opinions of the rigidest sort of those that are called Puritanes,* in taking the more politic course of arguing by the most intricate logic that the true church, as the separatists claimed, comprehended only the elect, yet at the same time that the English church was substantially pure enough for them to remain in it in the expectation of finally extruding from it all but the pure.[22] These latter, the independents, congregationalists in principle but not separatists, included such noteworthy figures as John Cotton and Thomas Goodwin. They were to take the leading part in founding Massachusetts and, by their stand in the Westminster Assembly in 1644, in frustrating the movement for making the English church presbyterian. The dialectic by which they justified their congregationalism has lost much of its human significance and need not concern us here. It was the Puritan spirit as set in motion by the Puritan epic and the Puritan code and not congregationalism, whether independent or separatist, which in the long run chiefly mattered both in the new England and the old.

The writings of the sectarians so far discussed in this chapter are chiefly the expression of more or less extreme and eccentric phases of the Puritan passion for church reform. That the doctrine of predestination should have acted as a powerful stimulant to the reforming temper need occasion no surprise. Any sort of determinism can, considered abstractly, be made by the individual an excuse for evading personal responsibility for assisting fate upon the course it is sure to take anyhow. The Puritan reformer's emotional need, however, was not for a reason that would justify him in evading responsibility but for one that would encourage him to embrace it, the more heartily the better. So with the world against him he did not resign himself to predestination but identified himself with God. His will was God's will, his plan God's plan, his enemies God's enemies, and his eventual success was certain because his work was God's work and could not fail. The fact that God's victory was predestined, whether he took part or not, was no reason for not fighting; on the contrary it heightened the exhilaration of the battle. Logically this may seem absurd, but psychologically it was most effective in steeling the Puritan reformer to his work of erecting the theocratic Utopia in the church or, if that proved too difficult or bade fair to take too long, in the sect.

Yet not every man who came in some fashion under the sway of Calvinistic dogma was at heart a reformer with an inner urge to act the part of God's vicegerent. Some were at heart mystics or philosophers and found themselves more concerned with the love of God than with making his will prevail, with the mystery of divine truth rather than with the manifestation of divine power. Such men were doubtless the more stirred to such thoughts by the very impact of Calvinist assertion upon their minds and spirits. The doctrine of universal depravity, of the arbitrary election of a few for salvation, of the special authority of the saints to declare and enforce the laws of God laid down in scripture, of the exclusion of all others from any freedom of thought or action in this world and from salvation in the next, did obvious gross violence to common sense and common charity, and this became the more clear and disturbing the more insistently such ideas were pressed. Orthodox Calvinism leveled all men under the law, made all equal in their title to grace, and then denied to most all prospect of realizing their hopes. It made the individual experience of God in the soul all-important, enormously stimulating individual spiritual experience, and then denied any freedom to the individual will. It declared scripture to contain the sum of all truth and the perfect rule of life, claimed too that human reason was capable of comprehending and obeying these, and then forcibly denied the right or possibility of finding there any truth or any law beyond that which the ministerial caste approved. The bars which Calvinism set up in the way of free development of the individual spirit could, however, never wholly suppress the positive energies which Calvinism itself did so much to evoke. Its own premises and its own dogmas, so sharply defined and trenchantly urged, provoked thought and activity which swept on, notwithstanding the iron limitations to freedom set up by the orthodox, to conclusions and practical consequences which were destined to render Protestant theocracy but a Utopian dream. From the beginning, wherever it penetrated, Calvin's version of the dogma of predestination encountered minds which came forward to insist that all men shared equally in the grace of atonement, that none were specifically predestined to reprobation, that every man must be free in some fashion to further his own redemption, that, since each must seek God for himself in his own heart by the light of scripture, none could deny the same duty to others even if the results of their quest in some degree differed, and finally that the union of men in this life rested not upon complete doctrinal agreement and religious uniformity but upon common faith in God and in the brotherhood of man.

Calvinism even at its fountainhead had early to confront such ideas. Its claims ran counter to two currents, humanism and mysticism, which singly or together proved no less powerful in their effect. It ran counter to the influence of Renaissance neo-Platonic idealism and to the rationalism promoted by knowledge of ancient philosophy, literature and history. It ran counter, too, to the type of religious feeling expressed in that *Theologia Germanica* which Luther had edited for publication early in his career.

The Platonic conception of the One reflected in the Many and the mystic notion of the immanence of Christ in the human soul were inherently difficult or impossible to reconcile with the Calvinistic dogma of predestination sorting out from all eternity the elect and the damned. Impossible too was it to reconcile rationalistic views of the relativity of all human knowledge with theocratic claims to infallibility in the understanding and interpretation of scripture.

Insistence upon a universal divine element in human nature, the sonship of men under the fatherhood of God, has frequently expressed itself in emphasis upon the humanity of Christ at the expense of his divinity and consequently in unorthodox views concerning the trinity. For heresy of that type Servetus was burned at the stake in Geneva in 1553. The French reformer, Castellio,[23] had recently published (1551) his edition of the Bible with a preface arguing for toleration, and the fate of Servetus provoked him to continue the argument in his *De hereticis* of 1554, his *Conseil à la France desolée* of 1562, and his *Contra libellum Calvini*, composed in 1562, published in 1612. He passionately defended the claims of individual conscience in matters of faith against those of any superior authority. There was, he claimed, room for the widest diversity of opinion within the limits set by the few essential tenets universally accepted by Christians, and there was no human power capable of determining which was absolutely true. God constrained men to believe what they believed, and the sword could do nothing to alter faith or make truth prevail. All that persecution could effect was to breed either hypocrisy or war. 'To kill a man is not to defend a doctrine, but to kill a man.'[24] The toleration of religious differences was the only condition that could lead to the progressive discovery of truth. Far from causing the ruin of the state, it alone led to civil peace and welfare.

Beza refuted Castellio with the classic argument of the persecutor namely, that the magistrate is bound by duty to God and man to take whatever measures may be necessary to protect the people against the contamination of error. Castellio himself died before the arm of the law could reach him. His ideas in the ensuing century spread far. They reached England indirectly through the influence of Castellio's anabaptist disciples in Holland and directly through the work of Acontius. About the same time as Servetus' execution and Castellio's protest, certain humanists and reformers, notably Ochino, the two Sozzini and Acontius, fled from Italy and betook themselves first to Geneva, then to Germany and elsewhere. Ochino and Acontius found their way to England. Under the influence of humanistic philosophy, they had reached an intellectual position similar to that of Castellio and the mystics and profoundly incompatible with the dogmatism either of Calvin or of the church. The name of Faustus Socinus soon became associated in England as elsewhere with that type of rationalistic simplification of Christian dogma which so generally led from the exaltation of conscience and reason to rejection of the doctrine of the trinity and denial of the infallibility of the church. Acontius, however, rather than Castellio or Socinus, was the principal intermediary for such notions in England. He arrived there in 1559, received the favor of Elizabeth, became a naturalized subject, and wrote his great work, *Satanae Stratagemata.* This was published in Latin and in French at Basle in 1565. It was not translated into English until 1648, and then only incompletely, but there can be little doubt that long before that date Englishmen were familiar with it and its ideas.[25] Acontius must certainly have been known to Anglican liberals like Chillingworth and to Puritan lay intellectuals like Lord Brooke. His book was finally translated by an anonymous friend of Samuel Hartlib and published under the sponsorship of two Puritan preachers prominent in the revolution, John Dury and John Goodwin. Under the influence of Acontius, seconded by his own considerable knowledge of ancient thought, the latter was after 1640 to become the most important exponent among Puritan divines of rationalistic reaction to the intransigent dogmatism of the presbyterian reformers.

The English translator of *Satanae Stratagemata* warns the reader that the book may seem 'in some places knotty,' but begs him to remember that 'the Author was an Italian, to which Nation subtilty in reasoning, seems natural, and let the goodness of the Kernel excuse the hardness of the Shell.'[26] Acontius, that is to say, wrote like a humanist philosopher, not like a pulpit dialectician or imaginative preacher. His book is a closely knit argument appealing for support less to biblical or other authority than to reason and common observation of human behavior. His fundamental principles are two. First of all he holds that nothing, neither learning, tradition, the church, nor any other authority or interest, should be permitted, unless we are ready to yield ourselves up to Satan, to take precedence over conscience, the voice of God in one's own soul. It is that, 'the spirit,' and only that which Satan fears and endeavors to overthrow. Acontius' other basic position is that no man is immune from error. 'No one person that is but a meer man ought to be so confident as to perswade himself he cannot err.'[27] 'And forasmuch as for the most part those that are judged to excel others in wisdom are at difference among themselves; it must be concluded that many also of those that are accounted wise doe err. And inasmuch as one man errs in one thing, another in another, and therefore those things in which every man errs must needs be many; and because none so excels in wisdom but he may be subject to humane frailty when he least suspects himself; Reason thus with thyself; all other men err, and that frequently . . . What therefore wilt thou judge of thy self?'

Consequently Satan has always one principal object in his assault upon the soul. It is to induce us to give our obedience not to the voice of conscience but to some claim of infallible authority in other men or conversely to the assertion of our own claim to authority over others. The temptation to fall into the latter is indeed the worst trial to which the evil one can subject our souls. Satan has many allies within the human breast. The most dangerous and powerful is, Acontius thinks, spiritual and intellectual pride. All other faults of human nature are 'loose and removeable' compared to arrogance. Commit any other crime, be it theft or murder, and you will presently learn of your wickedness and perhaps try to amend it. 'But in case thou shalt be possessed with too great a conceit of thine own wisdom, . . . it will be as hard a thing while thou errest to make thee understand that thou dost err as to make thee live and not to live at one and the same instant; for to err and to acknowledge thine Error were the same as to err and not to err.'[28] We begin by persuading ourselves that whatever doctrine we have drunk down is true and that we must oppose as false whatever differs. This up to a point is all very well, but Satan is always at hand to prompt us to lose our tempers and resort to violence of language or of action or of both. We begin by contending for what we take for truth. We grow angry with men who do not see the truth as we do, and our minds are soon so clouded by arrogance that we become the heretics and the thing we persecute is truth. We end by striving not for truth but for victory. 'Consider again and again the choyce thou art put unto. There is a double fight in which thou art ingaged, thou canst not in both be Conqueror. If thou art resolved to become victor on that side by the oppression of Truth, most sure it is, thou shalt be overcome in this other duel with Satan.'[29]

The notions that every man must be ruled by his own conscience and that no man is so free from error that he may dictate what others must believe obviously meant that no power existed in human form that could absolutely declare what is truth. This, as the critics of Acontius and men of similar opinions objected, calling them generally Socinians, was to come close to downright scepticism. The humanist reformers had, however, their own considered reply to such attack. They attempted to draw a clear line between the field of faith and that of reason. The things to be believed were few; they were revealed directly to the heart of man, and they alone were essential to salvation. The things to be discovered and determined by reason were well-nigh infinite in number, attainable only at the end of something like infinite inquiry and discourse, but inessential to salvation. Acontius pointed to the fact that the few indispensable tenets of faith were those known and acknowledged by all Christians and not those that men commonly disagreed about. Men persecuted one another over points on which revelation cast no light and which, therefore, reason was free to determine. Salvation was not secured, quite the reverse, by endless multiplication of needless distinctions of doctrine and of commentaries on every text and word of scripture, especially when attended by acri-

monious dispute. 'Those whose place it is either to teach the people or
to read divinity in the Schools, and those that apply themselves to
write, omitting curious questions and abandoning vain ostentation of
wit,' would do best, he says, to 'insist and urge only such points as tend
to the confirmation of faith, to the extirpation of vice, to instil the fear
of God, cherish piety, comfort the afflicted and keep them from desperation, to keep such as would be counted Christian brethren in
brotherly love with a sweet harmony of affections and the like.'[30]

If in the field of reason no man can hope to attain perfect knowledge
of truth, it does not follow that truth does not exist or cannot be
known. Truth is absolute, knowledge relative. Truth, in itself one and
entire, is reflected diversely in a myriad facets in the reasons of men.
Before it can be known, if ever, reason must discover and reassemble
all its countless particles into a whole, an infinite task which no man can
himself expect to fulfil, but one that must go on without end if truth is
ever to be known. Consequently, every man must be free to let whatever ray of light may be vouchsafed him shine forth and to search the
scriptures for more light. Preachers should not assume, because they
speak so much and without contradiction, that they alone are wise, that
they are in some fashion 'the authors of the Word of God.'[31] Tailors,
fishermen, butchers, cooks and silly women are also entitled to be
heard, even when they are scandalous and vexatious.[32] 'Who knows by
whom God will chuse to discover the truth?'[33] To be sure, some will
mistake darkness for light, but error is indispensable to the discovery
of truth. It puts us to the necessity of distinguishing the false from the
true, and the more we detect and reject of the one, the more we attain
of the other. Learning is an active, accelerating process. We must be
forever learning more and more in order not to be knowing less and
less. We must, then, not seek or expect to rid ourselves of error once
and for all but to grow more skillful in exposing it as the means of
discovering its opposite. The worst and most damning error, the prime
heresy into which Satan would betray us, is anger and persecution
directed at those who think differently from ourselves. Pride then
stops the process of search and discovery, of distinguishing the true
from the false, by which knowledge grows, while we go about extirpat-
ing not error, which is always with us, but our opponents, who may be
wiser than we. Truth requires no sword but only a free field for its

eternal argument against error. When men are free, truth goes on forever getting the better of the argument; when they are not, error always wins. The spirit of anger and persecution is evidence not that truth is victorious over its enemies but that the devil is victorious over us. 'And in case thou shalt wittingly oppose the Truth, and by so doing shalt make God thine Enemy, what wilt become of thee, wretched man that thou art?'[34]

The ideas of Acontius, fortified once more by the words of Gamaliel (Acts 5:38), were to be heard again when, in *Theomachia or The Grand Imprudence of men running the hazard of Fighting against God*, John Goodwin assailed the spirit of persecution evinced by the godly divines of the Westminster Assembly.[35] Born about 1594, he, like his namesake Thomas, had been at Cambridge in the days of John Preston. Admitted in 1612 as a sizar at Queens, he resigned his fellowship and left the university in 1627. It will be remembered that Thomas had been tormented by doubts concerning the doctrine of grace but had successfully resisted them. The same cannot be said of John. Though we have, unfortunately, no account of the latter's spiritual experiences in youth, we are able to piece together from his numerous tracts a fairly clear picture of the course his development took. He learned to be a preacher according to the pattern set by the spiritual brotherhood. In 1633 he was chosen by the parishioners as vicar of St. Stephen's in Coleman Street to succeed John Davenport, who had just departed for New England. He was a skillful dialectician, but more important still, his mind was deeply saturated with humanistic learning. The pages of his sermons and tracts in support of toleration and free will are strewn with references to the Greek and Latin philosophers, poets and historians he must have read in his Cambridge years. It is probable that he fell early under the influence of *Satanae Stratagemata*. It is not impossible that Goodwin was himself that friend of Samuel Hartlib who translated the first half of the book.[36] He did at any rate endorse its publication in 1648 by supplying an epistle to the reader which shows, what was already plain in his own published tracts, how thoroughly imbued he had become with Acontius' point of view.

One of the modes by which the humanist theologians expressed their scepticism concerning the Calvinistic dogma of predestination was by

advancing heterodox notions concerning the atonement through which
sinners become justified and by advocating some form of freedom of
the will. By 1638 Goodwin had begun preaching sermons alarming to
some of his fellow preachers. One of these, George Walker, had long
since (1611-1615) accused Anthony Wotton of Socinianism, heresy
and blasphemy because of his opinions on justification and had for some
reason recently resumed the attack. Goodwin took up the cudgels for
Wotton and for truth. Acquaintances, including Walker himself,
placed bets that he would not dare to go and have the matter out in
person with his opponent, but he did so, and got, so he said, nothing
but abuse for his pains.[37] The result was an exchange of written arguments which Goodwin published in 1641, Walker's as well as his own,
with the title, expressing an attitude he may have learned from
Acontius, *Impedit Ira Animum*. Walker at once renewed his attack in
Socinianisme . . . Discovered and Refuted, and Goodwin undertook
to clear up the whole issue the next year by a book which he called
Imputatio Fidei or a Treatise of Justification. The technical point for
which Goodwin contended was that the atonement did not impute or
transfer to sinners the righteousness of Christ but only the power to
believe that by that righteousness they might be justified and saved if
they would. Man was saved by faith, but faith saved him by setting
him to the task of seeking truth and obeying it when found. Justification or redemption from sin was manifested not by infallible knowledge or by absolute righteousness but by increasing endeavor to learn
more and more truth and to live more and more like the son of God.
These distinctions, the affinities of which to the ideas of Socinus and of
Arminius were properly recognized by Goodwin's critics, were of
significant import for their time. *Imputatio Fidei* was the most impressive statement that had yet come from a Puritan preacher of a theological formula for toleration, for intellectual freedom in the widest
sense. The truth that men should seek was, Goodwin believed, to be
found simple and entire in the Bible, but the finding of it called for
inquiry of almost endless duration. The method of that inquiry was
discourse and disputation. For the full use and enjoyment of his own
talent, Goodwin as a preacher and a dialectician required an audience
and an opponent. He liked, one suspects, nothing better than to par-
ticipate in one of those public debates upon points of doctrine in which

rival champions of the pulpit pitted themselves against one another for the edification of their supporters and the enhancement of their own reputations. In such controversies, Goodwin was eager to follow thought wherever it might lead, convinced that when each point had been disputed it would be settled and that as point after point was settled truth would become known. The elect were, so to speak, appointed to debate *sine die*. This was a conception which bore important implications for the future development of separatism and independency. In such minds as Goodwin's, the foreordained organ for all such debate, that is to say for all significant thought and expression, was the religious congregation. The practical impossibility of confining public discussion in future to that or any other single organ or channel was as yet beyond his comprehension.

The argument over justification and the special pleading for congregationalism which Goodwin developed at such length in later writings have lost much of their interest. Not so his plea for a rational approach to the whole problem of the quest for truth. The finespun dialectics of *Imputatio Fidei* are prefaced and throughout their course interspersed by eloquent and ingenious argument for the principles of intellectual freedom and tolerance. It is here especially that we perceive in Goodwin the influence of Acontius. The language of *Satanae Stratagemata* must have been in his mind when he wrote: 'The only art and method of raising an estate of honour and peace out of our errors is by sacrificing them upon the honour and service of the truth. This is a way to circumvent the Divell, and to turne his weapons upon himselfe. He sends errors out of Hell to curse the truth: but by this meanes you shall cause them to bless her altogether. Truth never gets up into her throne with that advantage as when her enemy (the opposite error) is made her foote-stoole.'[88]

In the epistle in which he dedicates his book to the London clergy, he begins by saying that he has tried to seize the opportunity which opposition has afforded him of gaining greater knowledge. 'I apprehend a marveilous bewtie, benefit, and blessing in such a frame of spirit, which makes a man able and willing and joyfull to cast away even long-endeered and professed opinions, when once the light hath shone upon them and discovered them to be but darknesse.' 'Therefore to me it is no more grievous to abandon any opinion whatsoever, being once cleerely detected and substantially evicted for an error, then it is to be delivered out of the hand of an enemy or to take hold of life and peace.' 'And if you will please to communicate of your light unto me when you meet me in the darke (which is a walke much frequented by mortalitie) I shall be as thankfull a Proselyte of yours as you can lightly wish or desire.'[39] Having thus admitted to his fellow clergy his own fallibility, he goes on in a second epistle addressed to the lay reader to point out that not even the Protestant reformers were any more infallible. It was as much a mistake to swallow their errors as the pope's. If America could remain so long unknown to the rest of the world, why may there not remain many truths yet undiscovered in scripture? Thousands of texts still wait to be understood and many are the interpretations which have been discarded by those whose own have in turn suffered the same fate. Hakewill's *Apology* helps him to a long list of opinions in divinity, history, natural history and philosophy which have in course of time been exploded. The way to truth, then, is plain. It is the way of peace and tolerance; through willingness to persuade and to be persuaded. Stop progressing in that way, and ignorance and error, fears, tumults and contention prevail. 'Truth is not to be drawne out of the pit where she lieth hid by a long line of calumnies, reproaches and personall aspersions upon him who is supposed to oppose her.' Men who grew fierce and fiery in disputes generally are lacking in knowledge. It is a ridiculous argument against any opinion merely to cry 'Heresie, Blasphemie, Socinianisme, Arminianisme, Popery and the like upon it.' 'Such passionate arguments may (haply) ravish the simplicity and weaknesse of women and children . . . but men of understanding are little affected with them, except it be as they are arguments of the weaknesse and insufficiencie of those that so use them.' What Goodwin asks of his own critic is that he neither quibble nor rail but 'bend the maine body and strength of his discourse against mine, and not brouze or nibble at some outward branches, but strike at the maine body of the tree.'[40]

Imputatio Fidei was one evidence, an important one, of the steady development within the Puritan fold of ideas and tendencies profoundly incompatible with Puritan orthodoxy, with the Puritan hope of reforming society by turning it into a godly Utopia dominated completely by a church in its turn dominated by the ministerial caste. By

1642 Goodwin had already gone far over to the independent or congregational wing of the reform party. After 1643 he was to become one of the doughtiest opponents of presbyterianism and for a time the ally, though an uncongenial one, of the Levellers. Eventually his position becomes impossible to distinguish from that of the extreme separatists.

Long before that time the current of Puritan religious excitement had swept the baptists in a direction that on its own plane paralleled that taken by such men as Goodwin. The individualistic, equalitarian reaction against predestination and uniformity marked a cleavage more profound than any schism within the church, one that was no respecter of boundaries between communions. The separatist John Robinson stuck fast to orthodoxy and predestination. The separatist John Smyth did not, and the latter's experience illustrates what happened to more than a few of the more enthusiastic disciples of the spiritual brotherhood, more at any rate than we can give any particular account of. Starting as doctrinaire reformers to make over the church without tarrying for the magistrate, they ended as mystagogues. Beginning as a self-conscious remnant of the saved out of the multitude of the damned, they wound up as lovers of all humankind. John Smyth, as we have seen, was at first so possessed by the doctrine of election that he set out to exclude from the church all who were also excluded from grace. The English church, since it admitted the unregenerate, he consigned to Antichrist; he then arrived at the conviction that only the elect could baptize the elect, even though, as in his own case, one were therefore compelled to baptize oneself. To such a point were men brought who obeyed only conscience and who linked conscience to the belief that outside the church of the elect there could be no hope. But, as the internecine controversies of Smyth and other sectarians showed, every sectary tended to draw the lines of tolerance about himself so close, to reject so vast a proportion of the human race as by definition reprobate, that the remnant of true believers still beside him bade fair to dwindle until he should be left utterly alone with his private God, whatever that God might be. The principle of the limitation of grace to a predestined few, of conscience as the determinant of election, of the exclusion from the church of all but the elect, could go no farther, and to go so far as that was, from most prevailing points of view, unthinkable. When circumstances permitted, some sects were prepared at some point to call in the arm of the law to stop the logical unfolding of their own principles in actual practice. If that were for any reason not permissible, then the only alternative, at any rate for sensitive and honest minds, was to abandon the dogma of the election of the few and the rejection of the many by God's predestination.

That is what Smyth and his followers came to. Smyth had separated himself from the communion of the church and from the sympathy of one diminished circle of friends after another. He found no time, at any rate after his early sermons, to write any statement of Puritan morality or any personal version of the Puritan saga. At successive steps of his departure into dissent, he wrote to defend and explain himself. He wrote with that acrimony which overenthusiastic idealists often feel for those who disagree with them. The moment came, however, when he seems to have undergone a great revulsion of feeling. *The Last Booke of Iohn Smith Called The Retractation of his Errours, and the Confirmation of the Truth* is one of the most remarkable confessions, one of the clearest, most intense, and least encumbered by cant or jargon, in the whole body of Puritan confessional writing. It is such a confession of the futility of intolerance, of the wisdom of charity and forbearance, as only a truly fine spirit at the close of such a career could have penned. On all the points of doctrine concerning which he has so bitterly contended with other men, he still thinks himself in the right. But it was sin to contend in the spirit of bitterness and not to recognize true saintliness wherever found regardless of the error and ignorance with which it might be mingled. 'I am not of the number of those men, which assume unto themselves such plenarie knowledge and assurance of their wayes, and of the perfection and sufficiencie therof, as that they peremptorily censure all men except those of their owne understanding and require that all men uppon pain of damnation become subject and captivate in their Judgement and walking to ther line and levell.'[41] His desire now is to end controversies rather than to make them; 'and it is the grief of my heart that I have so long cumbered myself and spent my time therin.'[42]

The doctrinal expression of Smyth's final thought is found in the early confessions of faith which emanated from his congregation and in the tracts of such successors of his among the English Baptists as Thomas Helwys, John Murton and Leonard Busher. 'Originall sin,' wrote Smyth, 'is an idle terme.' God created Adam able to choose for himself between good and evil. Adam chose evil and might with all his posterity have in consequence been utterly lost forever. But, through the atonement of Christ, 'effectuall before Caine and Abells birth,'[43] man kept his freedom and is still free to adhere to good or yield to evil as he will. 'God,' said John Murton, 'is no respecter of persons, he calleth all effectually, and in good earnest, and whosoever holdeth otherwise, he hath an evil conceit of God.'[44] This was to say that no man was naturally reprobate and damned, that God's favor was vouchsafed equally to all, and that every man until the day of his death must be presumed capable of becoming a saint if he was not one already. Thus did baptist antinomianism help to express and foster that popular equalitarian idealism which in the effort of such men as Lilburne and Walwyn was soon to turn the current of revolution in the direction of political democracy.

Meanwhile the same principle led the baptists, hard pressed by persecution as they were, to advance a claim for general religious toleration. They conceded the duty of obedience to the civil laws of the state, but since all men were spiritually equal all must be left free to understand the truth for themselves and to convert others as best they could. Enforce the laws against crime and treason, but leave sin and error to the sword of the spirit. The word of God alone can convert. The sword of the flesh can do nothing but compel men to hypocrisy, force heretics into the church and foment civil and religious strife. 'By fire and sword to constrain princes and peoples to receive that one true religion of the gospel is wholly against the mind and merciful law of Christ, dangerous both to king and state, a means to decrease the kingdom of Christ, and a means to increase the kingdom of Antichrist.'[45]

The baptists were, of course, far from being the originators of such ideas. A rather curious sect devoted to similar principles had won a footing in England as early as 1570. The writings of its founder, a Dutchman named Henry Nicholas, were translated and published in English about 1575 and were reprinted in 1649.[46] Nicholas, to judge from his rather finely poetic rhapsodic and allegorical tracts, was one who had learned that vain is all hope but love. He taught that the love of God, mystically experienced in the soul, is one with the love of man. Loving God and one another, men should live together as one great family. Nothing else can avail to free them from ignorance, error, strife and tyranny, from sin in this life and hell hereafter. He scorned those who cried 'We have it, we are the Congregation of Christ, we are Israel, lo here it is, lo there it is, this is truth, here Christ, there Christ.'[47] Nevertheless his universal brotherhood dwindled to a sect known as the Family of Love. Though little is known about its history in England, it is frequently mentioned and probably survived until the revolution. Familist became a term to be applied, deservedly or not, to any eccentric religious mystic.

Concerning the influence of anti-Calvinistic Protestants of the continent upon Puritan minorities in England, too little is known to warrant more than tentative general assertions. The spiritual brotherhood seems to have generated its own dissentients, such men as Browne, Smyth, Robinson and John Goodwin, precisely as Calvinists abroad had done, and these men in one fashion or another sooner or later came under the influence of or in contact with corresponding continental groups. Henry Nicholas' Family of Love was but one of the several mystical sects springing up in Holland at the time. It appears to be the only one which was definitely transplanted to England, but many Dutch and English enthusiasts of one sort or another must have passed back and forth between the two countries. The separatists who fled to Holland, especially the baptists, certainly came under the influence of the Dutch sects and through them, no doubt, of the earlier continental mystics and of Castellio and his disciples. John Goodwin owed something directly to these men as well as to Acontius. The sources of that idealism which based itself on belief in the mystic brotherhood of man, which expressed itself through the various Puritan minorities, and which emerged later as revolutionary effort for the establishment of political democracy, were several and more or less obscure and remote. One source for it was undoubtedly to be found in feelings among the people that reached far back into medieval popular Christian faith. However that may be, the fact is at any rate significant that, in addition to the sermons and polemics of preachers, both reformers and sectaries, there began to appear in England after 1600 vernacular versions of the writings of continental enthusiasts and mystics of an older time.

Most important of these, perhaps, was the famous *Theologia Ger-*

manica, the work of an anonymous fifteenth-century author, published
in German by Martin Luther in 1518, and frequently reissued by him.
Castellio put out a Latin translation in 1557,[48] in which form, at least,
the book must have been known to educated Englishmen by the end
of the sixteenth century. By 1628 an English translation by John
Everard was in circulation in manuscript.[49] 'The German Divinitie,'
we are told by Giles Randall in 1648, no doubt referring to Everard,
was 'some years since, through the desires and industries of some of
our own Countrimen, lovers of the Truth, . . . translated and made
to speak to thee in thine own Dialect and Language.' The 'late wise
and wary Hierarchie,' he adds, were then making it their affair to keep
truth from the people 'lest they should grow as wise, if not wiser then
their Teachers; and so the rude vulgar should become one of us.'
Consequently the *Theologia Germanica* had had to walk 'up and down
this City in Manuscripts at deer rates, from hand to hand . . . in
clandestine, and private manner . . . never daring to croud into the
Presse, fearing the ruffe usage of those then in authoritie.'[50] One of
these clandestine manuscripts is now preserved at Cambridge.[51] Giles
Randall finally issued the book in 1648, though in a translation which
differs somewhat from that preserved in the manuscript just referred
to and for which he may himself have been in some measure
responsible.

Theologia Germanica is a classic statement of the belief in the real
presence of God in the human soul. God is the universal essence of
good, acting in man and creation. Men are leveled in sin under the
law but freed by grace to receive God. He is apprehended only in the
soul, and to the end that men may receive God, the scriptures and the
sacraments are a useful but secondary and not necessary means. Man
receiving God abandons self, loves nothing but God, loves all men
because all men are of God. Since God loves only God, man deified
through Christ can but love man as a vessel of Christ. Men who love
God live in the contemplation of the divine and in the inner peace of
brotherhood with all humankind.

Everard translated for his fellow countrymen other continental
mystical writings as well as the *Theologia Germanica*, such as *The
Tree of Knowledge of Good and Evil* of Sebastian Franck, *The Vision
of God* of Nicholas of Cusa, and selections from Hermes Trismegistus,

Dionysius the Areopagite, Denck, Tauler and probably others. Some of these are preserved in the Cambridge manuscript along with the *Theologia Germanica,* and some were published later either with the collection of Everard's sermons of 1653 called *Some Gospel Treasures Opened*[52] or independently by Giles Randall. There can be little doubt that Everard, seconded by Randall and other disciples, was an important agent in putting into circulation in the decade before 1640 the type of mystical enthusiasm which was to flourish so abundantly and so much more extravagantly a little later. He was himself a writer of force and charm. Born about 1575, he proceeded through the usual course at Clare College, Cambridge, to the degrees of M.A. in 1607 and D.D. in 1619. He preached at St. Martin's in the Fields, served as chaplain to Lord Holland, and held forth in various pulpits in and around London. He seems to have kept himself perpetually in hot water. Even, it was said, while he was still 'but a bare, literal, University Preacher,' he ventured to oppose the Spanish marriage, choosing texts to show the great sin of matching with idolators. For this boldness and for his heresies, he was from time to time imprisoned, but 'then by the next Sabbath day one Lord or other would beg his liberty of the King, and presently, no sooner out, but he would go on and manage the same thing more fully, not withstanding all the power of the Bishops.' After this had happened six or seven times, King James is reported to have said 'What is this Dr. Ever-out? his name (saith he) shall be Dr. Never-out.' Everard prophesied, two years before the event, that a parliament would abolish prelacy. When the Scots rose against the prayer book, he said 'The work was begun; and I do observe by their countenances,' meaning the king and his supporters, 'their hearts fail; for I see very Lead in their eyes.'[53] The final outcome was that he was haled before High Commission in 1639 for familism, antinomianism and anabaptism and fined a thousand pounds. But he lived to see Strafford and Laud go to their ruin.

When the conservators of traditional ideas accused a man like Everard of familism, antinomianism and anabaptism, they did not necessarily know that he had actually identified himself with any particular followers of John Smyth or of Henry Nicholas. The accusation meant that the man had been swept by Puritan individualism into such exaltation of the individual soul as more than one enthusiastic idealist or mystic before him had expressed. Up to a point, Everard's career was similar to that of any other preacher; he does not appear even to have separated himself from the church. His admiring biographer, Rapha Harford, assures us that he was 'a very great Scholar, and as good a Philosopher, few or none exceeding him,' an assertion obviously supported by the man's academic attainments. True to tradition also was the statement that 'he was a man of presence and Princely behaviour and deportment' though at the same time 'familiar even with the meanest, and if any were willing to be taught, he was as willing to instruct and teach them; . . . he not thinking it any disparagement to accompany with the worst and lowest of men, so he might do them good.'[54] In his early days, the days of what he called his ignorance, he walked 'as other Gentiles, and as men living without God in the world, in the vanity of his mind, having his understanding darkened, being alienated from the life of God, because of the blindness of his heart.' If, however, he came at all under the influence of such men as Richard Sibbes and John Preston, with their growing insistence upon the immanence of God in nature and human life, upon the inwardness of all true experience of God, and upon the predestined happy ending of all striving after God, his imagination was well prepared to kindle to the mystical teachings of the *Theologia Germanica* and similar works. The illumination he received from those sources soon began to shine from him in the pulpit. The sermons preserved in *Some Gospel Treasures Opened* were not published until 1653, some time after Everard's death. Their editor, Rapha Harford, obviously a disciple, says that they had been preached 'in the dayes of the last Bishops,' who always did their utmost 'for the suppression of light, and men of light.' Everard had much ado to keep his written copies 'out of the Bishops fingers; the Pursevant, upon search for any thing of his, missed them very narrowly.'[55] They were printed, we are told, 'as they were Preached and Pressed . . . to the Capacity and Conscience of his Auditors, and taken from his mouth by a Notary; yet afterward owned and approved by himself, and compared with his own notes.'[56]

They are the utterances, diffuse at times as all such things tended to be, of a genuinely imaginative mind glowing at the thought of the divine presence in man and nature. God, infinite and incomprehensible though he be, has put forth the perfect image of himself in Christ and through Christ in all creation. Veiled from our sight by accidents and appearances, he is nevertheless there, the fire in the bush, the salt in creation, filling with his being every creature according to its capacity to receive, 'as the river Thames or the Sea, by its streams it flows in all the adjoyning Creeks & Arms.'[57] 'He fills even the lowest hell, and is as well in the damndest Lucifer in hell, as in the gloriousest Saint in heaven.'[58] 'He is the Motion and being of everything, great or little, glorious or mean.'[59] He is the workman who has made all things, but also the very substance whereof they are made. Could we but see him behind the garment of creation with which he clothes himself, then we should see him in the gold, in the light, in the sun, in the water, in the earth, in the trees, in the flowers, in every pile of grass. All these speak of him, speak aloud, and yet 'still cry *Plus ultra, plus ultra,* there is more behinde still, look beyond us, for we are nothing . . . to him that made us and gave us to be what we are.'[60]

Are the souls of all men and angels therefore saved, sinners and saints alike? This was a deduction frequently made by opponents and sometimes by irresponsible disciples, but one which mystics of Everard's calibre did not like to admit. 'Christ,' says Everard, 'lives in every man . . . and is as much in the one, as in the other: But, I say, here is all the difference, to the one Christ is manifested, to the other he is not; God lives in all, but all know it not: A good man hath God in him, and he seeth, knoweth and believeth it; the other do neither see, know, nor believe it, and so rejoyce not in the manifestations of God in them.'[61] We must know the gift that is given us and who it is that is speaking to us, if, as our Lord told the woman of Samaria, we would drink of the living water. There is a beam of the divine in every creature, but a man must lay his eye to that beam if he would see God. It is an angel, however small, which looks always toward the almighty, and we must beware how we despise one of these little ones. Worship God through the creature. 'A Gods name praise him in a tree, praise him in the wind, and in all Creatures; for the life of every Creature, of every tree, is Christ Jesus, the Son of God, and his first begotten of all his Creatures; the power of the wind is Christ Jesus, the life of a man is Christ Jesus.'[62] God loves only God; the saints, knowing that God is among them not less or less gloriously than he was in Sinai, 'will upon the sight of God in any Creature fall down before him, in

a holy extasie and amazement of spirit fall down and worship him.'[63]
Not so those who are reprobate; they might if they would but will not.
They turn away when God comes knocking at their hearts. They
worship not God in the creature but the creature merely, their own
comfort, their pride, riches, glory, honor, ambition. God is thus,
though still within them, removed from their sight and believing.
They are estranged from him. They crucify Christ anew in their own
hearts, and so they 'live in Hell, . . . in the very condition of Devils
and Reprobates.'[64] But the saint is an inhabitant of Zion. He has but
to look within to see there the City of God, the temple adorned with
the rich jewels of faith, repentance, love, joy and hope. 'Never look
nor never expect outwardly to find God, for God dwells within . . .
there he preacheth and there he teacheth: for outwardly are nothing
but obscurities, darkness, thick darkness, outward darkness . . .
where is nothing but weeping and gnashing of teeth.'[65]

What God preaches and teaches in the illuminated heart is, moreover, all that in this world one really needs to know. One of the most
brilliant of Everard's sermons describes Christ disputing with the
doctors in the temple. Doctors Pleasure, Profit, Honour, Arrogance
and Reason are learned men reared in the university of Satan. 'What
need,' says Doctor Honour, 'all this stir about Religion? canst not thou
be content to go the old way thy fore-fathers went? Canst not thou be
content to go that way the State goes, that way that Kings and Princes
and Great men go? then shalt thou walk safely and enjoy thine own,
and be honoured for a wise man, a prudent man . . . There is none
but a company of poor beggerly fellows, Tinkers and Coblers, and
schismatical and conceited fellows that are so hot, and they are every
where despised.'[66] Such arguments, such temptations, Christ in the
temple, like Christ in the heart of the saint, confounds with the wisdom
of the spirit alone. Disputation is of no worth and leads to no end. The
apostle wisely refused to debate with the great Rabbins. For every one
of them 'stuck so fast and unmoveable to his opinion, one to shew his
wit and eloquence; another to gain honour and riches; another because
he had declared what he held, and being once past the bars of his lips,
he must not recant and be a flincher, and discover his ignorance,
wherein he had declared so much confidence, but must then stand it
out to the death; so one for one end, and another for another.'[67] 'Well

beloved,' Everard concludes, 'our Apostle sleights all, away with all these things, I count them nothing, they are dross and dung: I desire to know nothing . . . but . . . Christ and him crucified.'[68]

Such reasoning naturally did not lead Everard to look upon either the academic learning of his day or the English Church and its clergy as at all essential to salvation. The most that men of his opinion could say for them was that they might aid in the awakening of the spirit but only as a means, useful in some cases but not necessary in all. What part scripture played was a more delicate question. Obviously the function of the book was to speak to the soul, but only of a God who could be encountered, if at all, not or not only in the book but in the breast. Everard was in this, of course, but following in the tradition of Puritan preaching, which for its emotive effect on the people wove together out of the scriptures a version of the sacred epic as an image of inner life. He, however, urged this conception of scripture with special and conscious emphasis, even took the trouble to translate Sebastian Franck's *Tree of Knowledge*, wherein it was definitely argued that the temptation of Adam and all that followed thereupon was a picture of what happened within the individual soul, that Christ and Satan, Paradise and Hell, were actually present in the breast of man.[69] Everard protested, since unimaginative minds were bound to misunderstand such a notion, that he did not at all deny the letter. Scripture was also a faithful record of fact. He was ready to stake his life 'that those things were Externally and Literally acted.' He was not making 'all the Scripture a Fable, and meerly Allegorical.' Nevertheless, when all was said and done, it was also a representation of facts that recurred in the inner life of man, and that recurrence was their proof and their significance. 'Friends, Bear·me Record,' he exclaims, those things 'were All, Actually and Really done in the flesh; but yet I also say, They were To Teach us That the same things are Alwayes In doing.'[70] The letter is true, but one must look within to verify it. There and nowhere else were to be found the very life and marrow of the word of God.

Concerning the implications of Everard's teaching which were particularly disturbing in the situation existing on the eve of the revolutionary crisis, it will be necessary to speak in a moment. First, however, we must note that he was probably further from being alone in his opinions than the extant documents would indicate. Not only familists and baptists were tainted with antinomianism. Thomas Goodwin in his youthful doubts on the subject of grace skirted close to danger, and though his friend John Cotton did not yield to that species of error, Cotton's disciple Ann Hutchinson certainly did, and his friend Roger Williams' position was at best equivocal. There would be many presently, when prelatical control of pulpit and press collapsed, to take the matter up in earnest. Besides Everard, however, the most important statement of early date now extant in print of the doctrine of the general redemption of man would appear to have been John Eaton's *Honey-Combe of Free Justification.* The substance of Eaton's teaching took form in an exposition of the doctrine of universal grace published after the author's death in 1642. Though substantially in agreement with Everard, this man was less of a visionary and a poet, certainly less gifted. Like the other, however, he refused to dispute with learned opponents for what he regarded as truth. His doctrine, he declares, is 'so strange . . . to carnall reason, so dark to the world, so many enimies it hath' that only the spirit can reveal or understand it. 'Learning cannot reach it, Wisdome is offended, Nature is astonied, Devils doe not know it, Men doe persecute it.'[71] It must be revealed, if it is to be known at all, and it may be revealed as easily to the ignorant and simple as to the learned and the wise. It is, briefly, that justification, remission of punishment for original sin, which by the orthodox was limited to the predestinated elect, is in Eaton's opinion free to all. 'Now all displeasure, all anger and enmity is utterly abolished from between God and you, and you are set in the compleat love, perfect peace, and full favour of God again.'[72] Believe this, and you will make truth manifest. Satan and the world will rise against you; the great, the learned, the rich and the mighty will condemn you, but your heart will 'laugh and leap for holy joy in God, being voyd of all care and trouble, and be made above measure confident.'[73] Jesus Christ has brought it about that men are born not guilty; he has made it that they may live happily in this world, good flowing from them, and that they may love one another as brothers.

The most brilliant of these early exponents of Puritan mysticism and of the doctrine of the brotherhood of man was John Saltmarsh. He was younger than Everard and Eaton, with whom he may or may not have had some connection. A Yorkshireman, educated at Magdalene College, Cambridge, a mystic, an enthusiast, a metaphysical poet caught up by the revolution and made a chaplain in Fairfax's army, he produced most of his writings in the years of turmoil between 1644 and 1647. As early as 1640, however, he produced a remarkable book called *Holy Discoveries and Flames*, dedicated to Charles I with the request that he 'suffer these Leafes, thus seeded with divine thoughts, to be a robe of holy Ermins to Your Soule.' The symbolic emblems, an eye and a burning heart, with which its pages are adorned, represent the two ideas which Saltmarsh ecstatically urged upon his generation, 'our faculty of discerning and affecting, of knowing and loving.' Knowledge, however, he is quick to say, is not in itself enough. 'He that is onely a seeing Christian hath his salvation meerely in perspective; and such is but Ethiopian holinesse, that hath a bright Eye in a darke body.' 'The single theorie and speculation of goodnesse lights us but to a brighter damnation, and serves onely to gild a little our darke condition.' We must also be on fire with the divine in Christ, in ourselves, and in our fellow men. The heart must be affected as well as the eye, 'and this must not be barely enlightened, but enflamed.'[74] There follows, then, in Saltmarsh's book a series of short lyrical discourses on texts from the gospels dealing with the life and teachings of Christ, with the theme of universal love leading to union and peace among men as brothers. That the author can be as ingenious as Quarles or Herbert may be seen in his exhortation to be made the Lord's bottle: 'Fill me, O Lord, thou that fillest all things living with plenteousnesse, till my Bottle, like Davids cup, overflow and run over . . . so that I may powre back myselfe to thee againe. . . .'[75] Within the quaintness and the ecstasy, however, of Saltmarsh's imagination, there is a keen perception of the human motives that prompted the dissensions of his time. How busy we are, he exclaims, plucking the mote from others' eyes, how sure we are that our religion is pure. 'Oh, my God, how ancient is this errour! how common! every religion, and heresie, and schisme, and professor hath a finger for the eye of his neighbour.'[76] He concludes, just at the moment of the King's campaign against the Scots, with a prophetic warning against war: 'is it not enough that wee have warre in our selves, and fight against principalities and powers, and spirituall wickednesse, but we must call new forces, and set up new standards, and above our Sheild of Faith, and

Helmet of Salvation, and Brestplate of Righteousnesse put on other armour; Must it be Nation against Nation, and Kingdome against Kingdome?"[77] It was the same cry for peace, for understanding, for tolerance that was also to be wrung from Falkland.

Well might cautious or unimaginative minds be disturbed at the notions coming from the enthusiasts of the Puritan left. The spiritual brotherhood had as much cause to be concerned as the prelates. Its members were reformers, but they were also churchmen bearing the prestige of learning and the privileges of their caste. They opposed the existing church government so far as they dared but only because they wished to reinvigorate the church, to make its authority and their own felt. They could conceive of no salvation outside the church, and of no society except within the frame of the church. This should be ruled by the elect, and the state should support the elect in making England a fit place in which to live the godly life. But as their means to gain power, the reformers had to preach to the multitude, to assure the multitude that God both could and would save any of them he might choose, that the call of God came directly to the heart, and that the outward sign of inward grace was struggle to obey the voice of conscience by word and deed. This, to the popular mind of the seventeenth century, was an inspiring message, but the more successful the preachers were in inspiring the multitude, the more difficult it became to reserve for less than a multitude the sanctification and glorification they taught the multitude to hope for. What could it avail to insist that the elect were not many when the many had been persuaded to hope that they might be elected? The greater the number of men who desired to be saved, the greater the number who believed that they were saved, who believed that only those were damned who wilfully chose to be so. Thus the populace, confusedly, haltingly, with many backslidings and false starts, began ominously to stir with the belief that they were the saints and that the saints were predestined to rule. If plutocracy may be said to have first reared its head among the orthodox Calvinists, democracy may equally as well be said to have stolen up behind the orthodox in the guise of the heretics, the mystics and enthusiasts of all sorts whom the preachers summoned to bear part under the banners of Christ in the war of the spirit on wickedness in high places.

The separatists, mystics and enthusiastic idealists stood to the left of the Calvinistic center of the Puritan reform movement. The immediate outlet of their activity was the religious congregation, the band of devoted disciples drawing inspiration from their leader and strength from one another in their struggle with the powers of this world. Though the world for a time worsted them, we can safely say that the sects, to use the term somewhat broadly, steadily grew in number and in the number of their adherents the nearer 1640 approached. Yet they were at the same time more generally repressed or at least more easily kept from making themselves widely heard than the more respectable reformers. They produced no such sermons as came from Sibbes and Preston and very few such spiritual biographies as are preserved in the pages of Clarke. Their literary revelation of the spirit within them was to come later. It is also important to note that at this early point their leaders staged no effective public attack upon the established regime and gave no direct expression of signal importance to the startling implications of their equalitarian religious ideas. What those notions might come to mean was expressed first not by a separatist or other heretical preacher but by a young man just out of his apprenticeship who, though full of notions derived from the sects, was probably at the time not yet actually identified with any particular dissenting congregation. This was John Lilburne, the most striking figure to appear on the left wing of Puritanism before the Long Parliament loosed the bonds that had been holding the separatists and enthusiasts in check. In 1638, fired by the conviction that the Church of England was the church of Antichrist and that poor fellows like himself were the first chosen of the Lord, he defied the Star Chamber in such fashion as presently to win for himself the attention of the mob and the favor of Cromwell. He also made plain that something much more was likely to come of the religious unrest bred by Puritanism than the mere substitution of presbyterian for prelatical church government.[78]

Yet the immediate occasion for Lilburne's revolt, though not for his ideas, was supplied not by separatists but by reformers who were to prove as fanatical in their opposition to the sects as they had been in attacking the prelates. The dangerous joys of martyrdom and the uses of the publicity which in the circumstances of the time martyrdom afforded were first displayed to Lilburne by William Prynne and John

Bastwick. The Puritan preachers as a whole after the repression of
Thomas Cartwright, still more after their failure at the Hampton
Court Conference, avoided direct attack upon the government of the
church and confined their efforts to setting forth Puritan ideals in
pulpit and press. They wisely refrained from meddling with the things
that were the prelates' as well as with those that were Caesar's. They
deprecated direct attacks upon rulers in church and state. It was, however, impossible for them to hold all their adherents to so moderate a
course. Not all the ardent spirits who refused to tarry for the magistrate to countenance reformation could find hope in the sects. To some,
rather, separation from the church seemed as bad as prelacy itself, and
they turned instead to shorter and more violent methods for the immediate overthrow of the bishops and reorganization of church government. The most reckless agitators for reform springing up before the
crisis of the revolution were not sectaries but fanatical presbyterians.
They were the men who, by flinging pamphlets full of imprecation
and ridicule in the faces of rulers and by defying the efforts of the
authorities to silence them, taught Lilburne and a host of other radicals
to do the same and so eventually to bring the whole movement for
church reform to irreparable confusion.

The most famous of the Elizabethan pamphleteers was Martin
Marprelate. In 1584 someone, probably William Fulke, Master of
Pembroke, Cambridge, had issued a small anonymous tract called *A
Briefe and plaine declaration, concerning the desires of all those faithfull Ministers, that have and do seeke for the Discipline and reformation of the Churche of Englande*. Commonly referred to as *A Learned
Discourse of Ecclesiastical Government*, it is a statement of the belief
in the responsibility of the ministers and governors of the church to the
people and in the transcendent importance of preaching. These were
the essentially revolutionary and Utopian elements in the presbyterian
program and therefore those most dangerous to the established regime.
The time was one of even more than usual political tension. Fulke's
pamphlet seems to have been widely read, widely enough at any rate
to alarm the ecclesiastical authorities. John Bridges, Dean of Sarum,
answered it in a sermon at Paul's Cross and followed up the attack with
a tremendous quarto called *A Defense of the Government Established
in the Church of Englande*. Counter-replies soon appeared, and then

in the midst of the excitement caused by the Armada, somebody, perhaps Job Throckmorton aided by John Penry and others, launched a
series of violent attacks on prelacy and the bishops over the pseudonym
Martin Marprelate.[79] Marprelate was a good Calvinist and no Arminian or antinomian, an earnest presbyterian and no separatist, skillful enough in the traditional dialectic and erudition. He was fundamentally a godly Utopian as yet unsuspicious of theocracy. He
provoked some rather heavy-handed replies in print; others, more
lively, came from the pens of Thomas Nash and John Lyly. His own
writing was vivacious, even at times vigorous, but hardly more so than
that of others on the Puritan side who failed to attract the particular attention of men like Nash and Lyly or to win a place for themselves in
formal literary history. What Marprelate chiefly accomplished in the
immediate situation was to frighten the government. His coadjutors, if
not himself, were tracked down, made to confess under torture and
some of them ruthlessly punished. Leaders of Puritan opinion like
Thomas Cartwright and Richard Greenham repudiated him. The time
was not ripe either for the use of ridicule or for root-and-branch reform.
His chief significance in the longer view was to demonstrate what
strength Puritanism was presently to command in the country and what
difficulty government would henceforth be put to in attempting to
withhold the weapon of the press from the hands of its enemies. Marprelate had more than one wealthy and high-placed supporter. He was
able to get possession of type and a press and to enlist printers in his
service. Some of his printing was actually done at Fawsley House in
Northamptonshire, the seat of Sir Richard Knightley, a wealthy squire,
an important man in the county and a member of Parliament. His wife
was a cousin of Edward VI and a daughter of the protector, Somerset.
Sir Richard suffered for his participation in the Marprelate affair, but
his heir was still to be found on the Puritan side as the patron and
protector of John Dod, John Preston and other spiritual preachers.

Puritan railing against the bishops, though necessarily sporadic, did
not cease with Marprelate. John Bastwick effectively reopened the vein
of satire in 1637, and a few years later Marprelate was both reprinted
and imitated. But until Milton entered the fray, the most savage pen
directed against prelacy was that of William Prynne.[80] This man had
gone from Oxford in 1621 not into the church but the law. Thereafter

he lived most of his long life, unmarried, in Lincoln's Inn. It cannot be said who indoctrinated him with the covenant of grace, but he can hardly have escaped the influence of Preston, who came to preach at Lincoln's Inn the year after Prynne's entrance there, and probably that of Sibbes, Gouge and other preachers about London. The steady rise of these men had not yet suffered the check that was to be administered to them by the elevation of Laud to the see of London in 1628. Neither can it be said what intimate cause set Prynne's character in its hard eccentricity. His egoism was nothing less than pathological in its excess; he espoused the dogma of election as a personal certification from on high of his own infallible rectitude. To such a self-assertive, contrary-minded, envious bigot the authority and prestige of the bishops, men who, as he must have known, came from no better beginnings than himself, seemed a personal affront as well as a moral wrong. He was, therefore, just the kind of person to turn the doctrines of the preachers into reckless assault upon the existing order. Those extreme applications of their teachings which they left unexpressed and might even have repudiated, he vociferated. The persecution they evaded, he courted. His instruments were the pamphlet and the publicity which punishment afforded. Both these he exploited with a temerity and an effect which surpassed anything of the sort which had so far occurred. Between 1627 and the assembling of the Long Parliament in 1640, for at least six years of which time he was in prison, he issued nearly a score of tracts, most of them unlicensed and some of prodigious length. Sympathizers and imitators sprang up about him. His avowed aim could be construed only as the overthrow of everything established in the church. He wrote for the utmost immediacy of provocative effect. If the authorities ignored him, he was outraged. If they noticed him, he grew more clamorous. If they proceeded publicly against him, he embraced the opportunity to make a louder outcry before a larger audience. Laud's forbearance in not proceeding against him before 1634 was fully as remarkable as the violence with which he thereafter pursued him.

Prynne's pamphlets seem now little more than historical curiosities if not grotesque horrors. We must consider, however, not what they are in themselves but what they signified in their time. Their very extravagance was their function. No one but such a reckless bigot would have dared to print the things which Prynne uttered so copiously and defiantly. Others might not dare or might not be willing to venture to such lengths, but whether they approved his course or not, he served their turn in expressing so unmistakably the direction their thought was taking. He pressed their quarrel and forced its issues, firing their courage by the violence of his example. How completely he covered their case may be seen in the series of tracts which, beginning in 1626, he continued to issue until he was dispatched a prisoner to the Isle of Jersey in 1637. Prynne began by applying himself to the expression of the dogma of predestination in *The Perpetuitie of a Regenerate Mans Estate*. He went on to more pointed criticism of Laudian policies in *The Church of Englands Old Antithesis to the New Arminianisme* and in *God, no Imposter nor Deluder*. We need not dwell upon Prynne's doctrinal asseverations. He urged the same views as the spiritual preachers, but in more violent terms and in more exaggerated form. He held that for the church to preach anything else was anathema. Nothing but faith could save a man, and faith was granted by God, granted once and for all and only to the elect. Who constituted the elect was no mystery to Prynne: 'He that now sticks fast and close unto the word of truth, and will not be withdrawne from it: he that shewes forth the power and efficacy of grace in the constant holiness of his life: he that is diligent and frequent in Gods service, and squares his life and actions according to his word: he that makes a conscience of all his waies and workes, and will not be so vitious and licentious, so riotous and deboist, so prophane dissolute and desperately wicked as other men,' such a man and such only is to be reckoned among 'the best, the dearest and holiest Saints of God,'[81] and the saints need fear no doubt as to the truth of this doctrine or as to the certainty of their own moral superiority. 'Come what will,' he assures them, 'you can never finally or totally fall from Grace, nor yet be severed or cut off from Christ, and this will comfort, strengthen, and rejoyce your souls in time of need, and beare them up in all extremities.'[82] To the saints' opponents he says, 'Goe on and perish; your blood shall light upon your owne heads, not on mine . . . there is a day of account, a day of death and judgment coming.'[83] This, of course, was substantially what was being uttered from the Puritan pulpits, but Prynne said it directly to the powerful in the land.

His immediately ensuing tracts foreshadowed the subsequent development of the Puritan attack. The preachers had adroitly confined themselves to doctrine in application to personal spiritual experience and in justification of the way of life embodied in the Puritan code. But the logic of their doctrine also demanded a complete reorganization of society, beginning with church government, and a thoroughgoing change in manners and morals. These demands Prynne uttered in no uncertain terms while reiterating his abomination of episcopacy and his detestation of individual bishops. The alternative he offered was presbyterianism, the transfer of ecclesiastical authority from the prelates to the preachers and their supporters. Actually, as time would tell, what he really desired was the transfer of ultimate control in the church from the crown and court to the hands of the respectable moneyed Puritans represented by Parliament. For the present he chiefly devoted his efforts to onslaught against prelatism combined with violent attack on the supposed vices and errors which evidenced the league of the prelates with the devil. Puritanism was a way of life with much of positive value to commend it, but every rule of conduct implies certain denials and prohibitions. Prynne made himself for all time the perfect exemplar of those things in Puritanism which have subsequently been called puritanical, the hammer of God against cakes and ale. He began in 1628 with *The Unlovelinesse of Love-lockes*, attacking the wickedness of prevailing fashions of dressing the hair. In the same year in *Healthes Sicknesse* he opened the long war of his kind upon drinking. A few years later came his notorious *Histrio-mastix: The Players Scourge or Actors Traegedie*, and finally an outpouring of wrath against violators of the sabbath in *Divine Tragedie lately acted, or a Collection of sundry memorable examples of Gods Judgements upon Sabbath-breakers*. Devoid as these things and others of the like seem now of anything but the most benighted prejudice, we must not forget that something was to be said for the zeal of the Puritans for moral reform. Much that appears to us innocent and joyous made a stench in Prynne's nostrils; much that the Puritans condemned would have made a stench in any decent nose. The swollen hordes that rendered the little overgrown town of London filthy and pestilent exhibited plainly enough the chaotic, reckless, dissolute behavior common to such conditions. The manners and morals of many of the great seemed but an aggravation of the evil. The glories of the Elizabethan theatre blind us to the fact that the theatre of Prynne's day was a scene where immorality could be made a public show. The extreme emphasis laid by Laud upon outward order in the service of religion, though itself in part a reaction against prevailing conditions, naturally enough seemed to the Puritans flagrant disregard of plain need for genuine reform. Opposing an ideal of order and discipline against a condition of riot and heartless irresponsibility, they could not, or at any rate did not, escape the extremes of an ignoble asceticism. But we should not ignore the fact that the extravagance of ill-balanced men like Prynne represented an impulse not uncalled for and served the needs even of more temperate minds for arresting expression.

Prynne's method, the same whether directed against the players or the bishops, was, though extreme, the method of his age. He did not, as a modern reformer might, investigate and report actual conditions. It was enough to settle his opinion of the theatre to attend four plays and to know two young men who had been ruined by the stage. To describe conditions objectively and in detail would have required a detachment, a technique and a kind of sentiment with which his time had little acquaintance and which for that reason would have been little to his purpose. It was more to the point to summon up authority by the aid of erudition. The Puritans professed in matters of faith and doctrine to appeal to the heart rather than to the past. But revolutionary movements, having to assail the past as embodied in existing institutions, must remold current conceptions of the past nearer to their own ideals. One reason why the preachers felt they must teach the people to scorn learning and trust their own hearts was that the people were still so little experienced in books as to be easily overawed by them. Prynne both shared and turned to account this proneness to superstitious reverence for the authority of print. What he did for the revolutionary cause was to heap up prodigious evidence of erudition to prove that players, bishops, the doctrine of free will, in fact all objects of Puritan abhorrence, were wicked innovations contrary to recorded precedent and authority. He ransacked libraries, looked for nothing that did not prove his case, and made notes upon everything no matter how superficially germane. The sweepings of his files he poured into his pamphlets. Whether anybody, even among his own sympathizers, was ever able to digest these mountains of print is doubtful and certainly unimportant. It was enough to excite and stiffen resolution merely to behold the spectacle of so much learning assembled in behalf of reform. There were many who were ready to think that God must be on the side that could marshal the most numerous citations.

But there was another feature of Prynne's pamphlets no less important. Prefixed to most such productions would be found one or more 'epistles' addressed to appropriate personages like the king, a bishop or bishops, parliament, or it might be any friend or enemy. Small tracts like Prynne's *Lame Giles his Haultings* consisted in many instances of nothing but such an address. Writings of this kind are not sustained arguments equipped with the panoply of learning, but diatribes against the author's opponents. They owed something to the minatory prophets of the Old Testament. They owed something no doubt to the tradition of railing against the great as practiced by medieval preachers. But they also owed much to the peculiar joy that Englishmen of that age took in abandoning themselves full-mouthed to expressive speech. The Puritans in opposing the theatre did not abate their love of ranting. Their flyting of the prelates was not so much a lapse from taste and manners as the exercising of a kind of convention, the out-Heroding Herod in a pamphlet. Thus Prynne in the vivid language of his day describes how the bishops climb 'by little and little from the miserable state of poverty, unto the highest seats of power' and there, 'greedie starvelings' hungrier than ever, 'suppress the poore, scratch and rake together all that comes to hand, . . . make lawes and keepe not the same, . . . justifie the wicked for reward, and take away the just mans desert from him.'[84] Warning Parliament that heretics such as Pelagius and Arminius, 'the Archest Traitors to our Church, our State, our soules, and saving Grace,' have lately risen from their graves, he urges that they be crucified again, entombed in stone and their sepulchres sealed and watched over during all succeeding ages.[85]

The immediate consequences of Prynne's pamphleteering in this vein were more significant than anything in the pamphlets themselves. Not by calculation but certainly in effect, the man served to exhibit the possibilities that lay in the press for making trouble for government. What he said mattered less than the dramatic violence with which he focused attention on the authority of the prelates over publication in print. This he did by challenging again and again Laud's right to impose and his power to exercise censorship, by forcing him to resort to repeated persecution, and by exposing in these ways both the existence of public opinion and the danger that always redounds on the head of those who oppose it by persecution. The rapid succession of Prynne's defiant pamphlets made plain Laud's practical inability to enforce the law. When by some trick or other, as in the case of *Histriomastix,* Prynne could get license to print, he did not fail to do so. But with or without permission, he got his views published, and the only way that could be found to prevent him was to ship him off to the Channel Islands. This is not to say that he had the slightest intention of seeking liberty of the press in the modern sense. On the contrary, he held with all the obstinacy of his nature to the position that only the truth should be permitted to be printed, that he himself published nothing but the truth, and that the prelates opposed nothing else. The height of their wickedness was to tolerate what Prynne would have suppressed. 'Christian reader,' he says in the epistle to his *Newes from Ipswich,* 'this is the deploreable News of our present age, that our Presses formerly open onely to Truth and Piety, are closed up against both of late, and patent for the most part to nought but error, superstition, and profanenesse. Witnesse those many profane erronious impious books printed within these 3 yeares by authority (point-blanke against the established doctrine of the Church of England, and his Majesties pious Declarations) in defence of Arminianisme, Popery, and Popish ceremonies.'[86] He minces no words. Hanging is too good for all such. Arminians should be crucified by act of parliament.

It was the irony of history that Prynne should have been the man to bring forward the question of censorship and to lead the way for champions of freedom of the press. His inveterate fanaticism without glimmer of charity made him an enemy of freedom in any guise. But it also made him a most dangerous enemy to Laud and all that Laud stood for. Anglicanism, ideally conceived, proposed a humane and rational view of religion and, within certain broad limits, a tolerant church. The difficulty was that, in order to make reason and charity prevail, the bishops could in practice hit upon no way but the use of their legal authority to prosecute those who intemperately attacked the church. They had had popular approval for action of that kind against

Rome. They could not conceive how deeply the case was altered when opposition came from men like Prynne, English to the core, with the people at their back. No Jesuit could have outdone Prynne in arrogance or zeal. Yet though the hope for freedom did not lie in him, he served for the moment the forces that were blindly making toward freedom. The silencing of Prynne did not silence his effect. On the contrary, it provoked still greater hostile activity in the press and prepared for throwing the press completely open to the prelates' worst enemies. Once the enemies of prelacy had got it open, however, not even Prynne could get it shut again. For the truth was that, in challenging prelacy on behalf of what would have proved a still worse tyranny, he was hastening the destruction of the only remaining restraint upon the many voices which were ready to cry out for a new heaven and a new earth. Thus the problem which was presented to Laud in the outbursts of Prynne and his immediate associates was not what to do with them or with any scheme of church government they might propose but how to deal with the rising storm of hostile public opinion which they portended.

VI

The Safe Way to Salvation

SO LONG as the people remained for the most part but a semi-literate rural populace, they remained the beast of many heads. With the changes that had come about in the modes of living, with the shifting of population, the growth of London, the spread of the Bible, and above all with the increasing activity of pulpit and press, the mob was put in the way of becoming an articulate public. The problem in church and state then became to determine what part must be conceded to that public in the direction of public affairs and what persons or institutions were henceforth to be its recognized exponents and organs of opinion. The ostensible purpose of the Puritan preachers was to let all men know of the immediate interest taken by divine providence in their welfare and of the bargains God struck with those who believed in his grace and felt called to enlist in his war against evil. The actual effect of the preachers' success in this was to make them the spiritual leaders of a part of the public which, though a minority, was rapidly growing in real power and, by their help, in self-assurance. The opinion of no other group was so highly organized for expression, expressed so vigorously, or potentially so disturbing to the existing disposition of authority. The preachers as a whole, notwithstanding what some of their followers might do, professed not to meddle with questions of government. But the things of Caesar are always difficult to distinguish from those of God. The keepers of men's consciences come close to keeping men's purses, and this becomes the more apparent to rulers the more crucial becomes their financial need. When Charles I asked parliament for money, he met not only the natural unwillingness of men to pay taxes but also the resistance of country gentlemen, city lawyers and men of business who had been taught that they must in all circumstances oppose wickedness in high places. Charles, therefore, as parliament proved intractable, undertook to reform religion on his own account. Whatever the professed object of that effort, the motive was the imperative need of the crown and court to regain the support of popular loyalty. If subjects grew unruly, it must be because the church had grown derelict in its duty.

A prime instigator and most active agent of this attempt to reform the people from above was William Laud.[1] There was much for him to do. Queen Elizabeth had not really set things to rights in the church, and they had not been substantially bettered since. Services throughout the country were conducted according to no consistent order. Edifices suffered from neglect, disrepair and decay. The properties and revenues of the church had been depleted. The ecclesiastical courts were the scene of grave abuses. The universities were torn by controversies that sometimes led to riots. Many of the parish clergy were ignorant, idle and vicious. The Jesuits proselytized covertly. The Puritans, what with their hold upon Cambridge, their chaplaincies and lectureships, and their impounding of impropriated tithes, preached openly and evaded regulations. Heresy and schism sprang up in their wake. The press, finally, had grown so prolific as to dare more and more boldly upon the ignoring or circumventing of censorship. No wonder the people were getting out of hand. Such being the case, the ruling party had either to strike out upon some policy of its own or surrender.

Laud was not one to surrender. Small, delicate, an only child, precocious, a prize scholar, at the age of sixteen he had been sent straight to Oxford. His triumphant progress from that point is laconically set down in his diary.

I was chosen Scholar of St. Johns . . . I was admitted Fellow of St. Johns . . . I proceeded Bachelor of Arts . . . I was made Deacon . . . I was made Priest . . . I was Proctor . . . I proceeded Doctor in Divinity . . . I was chosen President of St. Johns . . . I was sworn the King's Chaplain . . . The King gave me the Deanery of Gloucester . . . I was installed prebend of Westminster . . . His Majesty gave me the grant of the Bishopric of St. David's.[2]

The last event occurred in 1621. From then on his progress was even more assured. He checkmated the Lord Keeper Williams, Bishop of Lincoln, and the primate, Archbishop Abbot. He went from St. David's to Bath and Wells, to London, to Canterbury. He won over the Duke of Buckingham, was made a privy councillor, and after the great favorite's assassination became the first man in the kingdom.

Laud was a great man in the manner of his age. No Puritan surpassed him in resolute obedience to the will of God or in his concentrated passion for making the will of God prevail, not less over his own weaknesses than over those of other men. Heylyn quotes Dering's remark, 'he was always one and the same man: that beginning with him at Oxon, and so going on to Canterbury, he was unmoved and unchanged; that he never complyed with the times, but kept his own stand until the times came up to him, as they after did.'[3] He believed, as Clarendon observes, that 'innocence of heart and integrity of manners was a guard strong enough to secure any man in his voyage through this world, in what company soever he travelled and through what ways soever he was to pass.'[4] His strength as well as his ultimate undoing lay precisely in the clearness with which he conceived, made known and pursued his purpose throughout his career. He accepted the Anglican conception of society as it came to him by the way of Hooker and Andrewes. The church was one with the living whole which was the nation. Rulers were responsible to God for their subjects' welfare, a responsibility to be exercised vigorously and in the fear of the Lord. They should rule so as to secure and retain the reverence and loyalty of a united people, but there was no more notion in Laud's mind than there was to be in Cromwell's or Milton's that this meant that to rule righteously they must rule as the people or as the parliament of the day should prescribe. The church must make the way of righteousness plain to rulers and subjects; it must enforce spiritual unity; it must teach reverence and loyalty, respect for rank and authority, and decent manners; and it must maintain a beautiful and ordered worship of God. As power accrued to him, Laud made his own will felt wherever it would reach. He built and rebuilt churches. He recaptured property for the church. He prescribed decent and orderly procedure. He proscribed ignorant, lewd and contentious churchmen. He frowned upon needless polemic. He regulated both the gowns and the statutes of Oxford, enriched its library, helped promising youths to fellowships, created chairs and built a noble quadrangle for St. John's. He endowed a school and a hospital for the poor in his native town. He endeavored to repair the cathedral of St. Paul's.

Valiantly the little man did what a man could to impose decency, decorum, order and cleanliness, good manners and respect for law and authority, learning, beauty and good taste, all the things that England most needed short of the one thing that half of England most passionately desired, namely freedom for the individual to work out his own salvation in his own way.

The most revealing of Laud's writings is his diary. It begins with a summary of his accomplishments up to the time of his elevation to the see of St. David's and then chronicles in brief statements what he did during the next twenty-two years until in 1643 Prynne snatched the book from him, a prisoner in the Tower. Only in these pages is anything like the sense of human frailty betrayed within the prelate. Illness and accident shook him. He was troubled by dreams and omens. Once two redbreasts flew into his study. On another occasion his barge sank in the Thames. On another his picture fell from the wall. Such incidents he recorded but always with apprehension as presages of graver events. For the most part he had only events to record. He was elected to this. He preached then and there. He gave such orders. He saw the duke or the king and secured his purpose. Perhaps the most characteristic pages are those where he lists those 'things which I have projected to do, if God bless me in them.'

To build at St. John's in Oxford . . . Done . . . To overthrow the Feoffment, dangerous both to Church and State . . . Done . . . To collect and perfect the broken, crossing, and imperfect statutes of the University of Oxford . . . Done . . . To annex forever some settled commendams . . . to all the small bishoprics. Done for Bristol, Peterborough, S. Asaph, Chester, Oxford . . . To set up a Greek press in London and Oxford . . . Done for London . . . To settle an hospital of land in Reading of one hundred pounds a year . . . Done to the value of two hundred pounds . . . To erect an Arabic lecture in Oxford, at least for my lifetime . . . Done, I have now settled it forever.[5]

Even on the scaffold, with nothing left to do but lay his head on the block, he ordered the cracks between the boards to be stopped lest his blood fall on some of the rabble crouching beneath, and his last address to his maker commenced, 'Lord, I am coming as fast as I can.'[6]

The most convinced adherent to the doctrines of the Puritan pulpit could have given no clearer evidence by persistence in works of per-

severance in faith. Not the least of the works Laud set himself to perform was to reduce the preaching of religion to order, regulate opinion
and control the press. For a time his influence was somewhat checked
by the authority of the Calvinistic Abbot, the rather ineffective Archbishop of Canterbury, and by Puritan leanings in other members of the
higher clergy, but it grew strong at court as the troubles of Charles
increased. While the Parliament of 1628 by petition and remonstrance
was pressing its claims upon the king, Laud was promoted from Bath
to London. There, with authority over city pulpits and the press and
from the vantage ground of High Commission and Star Chamber, he
was in better position to make his will felt. In 1633, he succeeded
Abbot and had virtually the entire church under his command. The
history of these years is much occupied with the ensuing controversies
over the use of the prayer book, the wearing of surplices, kneeling and
bowing, and the placing of the communion table. Important as these
things were, the sharpest point of Laud's attack fell upon the Puritan
preachers and pamphleteers. His election as Chancellor of Oxford in
1630 enabled him to consummate his reform of that university. Before
disaster overtook him, he had established his authority over Cambridge. Naturally he frowned upon any preaching or writing which
smacked too strongly of Puritan doctrine, even upon polemic against
Puritans. Men so highly placed and regarded as Bishop Hall and John
Hales were not immune from being called to account. In 1629 he procured from the king a declaration severely restricting the activities of
lecturers, especially in towns, and the retention of private chaplains by
wealthy gentlemen. In 1633 he procured the dissolution of the Puritan
feoffees, that group of preachers, lawyers and rich citizens who had
been buying impropriations for the support of preaching. Decrees
quickly followed which were aimed to bring all lectureships to an early
end. Thus Laud endeavored to dissolve that fabric for the propagation
of the word which the unacknowledged Puritan brotherhood had
erected within the church. His effort came too late to preserve prelacy.
He could not now destroy Puritanism by expelling it in its less openly
dangerous form from the church. The only effect of his trying to do so
was to provoke the more determined preachers to a bolder stand and
extremists in general to more active agitation in the press and among
the sects.

The Puritan preachers, under pressure, found various recourses. Men like William Gouge and John Goodwin, who combined the cure of souls with spiritual preaching, conformed sufficiently to retain their posts. Richard Sibbes, protected perhaps by his eminence, continued to lecture at Gray's Inn but at the same time accepted the incumbency of Trinity Parish, Cambridge. Thomas Goodwin, on the other hand, rather than submit, abandoned that lectureship at Trinity which he and Preston and Sibbes before him had rendered so famous and influential. There were also others not a few who refused to yield to the regulations imposed upon them. The most immediate effect of Laud's policy was indeed to bring to light the more extreme notions for reform which had been spreading among Puritan churchmen themselves. Thomas Goodwin, John Cotton and many others now committed themselves to congregational independency, that leftward step which brought them just short of downright separation from the church. Some with Cotton fled to New England, some with Goodwin to Holland. This was the real beginning of independency as a positive influence in the unfolding of the revolutionary character of Puritanism. The harm which the independents suffered at this juncture can easily be exaggerated. Their exile was dictated at least as much by their own consciences and Utopian dreams as by actual danger. Laud's persecution of the Puritans was badly managed, far from thorough, and in the long run disastrously ineffective. It is noteworthy that the feoffees for buying up impropriated tithes, though dissolved and their enterprise declared illegal, were reimbursed, and criminal prosecution, though threatened, was never pressed. Even more significant was the fact that Puritan sermons and other writings, which had been accumulating for twenty years or more in printed form in the people's hands, continued to pour from the press in unchecked volume. The imprimatur of the Bishop of London's chaplain was not denied to such publications. The works of Dod, Downame, Sibbes, Preston, Thomas Goodwin, Thomas Taylor and the like could hardly have been palatable to the archbishop, but they were not directly hostile to his authority or on the surface anything but edifying. Their work of preparing the temper of the people for overthrowing prelacy was in fact by this time accomplished and past undoing. Laud could not have suppressed such books if he had wished, and he probably did not even think of trying to do so. All he could do was to turn upon the fanatics whose printed attacks were of such a character as the Puritan preachers themselves characteristically avoided.

The existing regulations for control of the press had grown up under Elizabeth. The Stationers' Company was intrusted with a monopoly over the publication and sale of printed matter. This protected the property of publishers and authors and enabled the authorities to exercise the censorship which was thought indispensable for the public interest. The stationers were held responsible for securing license to print from one of the two archbishops or from the Bishop of London. The company had the privilege and duty of proceeding against any who violated these regulations. Jurisdiction was vested in the Court of Star Chamber. The system was, of course, at no time wholly effective. Under the conditions of popular demand, the temptation to deal in the commodity of print was too great. The members of the Stationers' Company itself did not always respect one another's rights. If illicit books and pamphlets could not safely be printed at home, they could be put to press in Holland and smuggled into England. Censorship under the Calvinistically inclined Abbot was lax, freely ignored, and feebly enforced. Such was the situation which Laud, when elevated to the see of London and the tribunal of Star Chamber, set himself to put, like so much else, in order. Regulations were strengthened. The stationers were called to account. Censorship was more vigorously exercised; offenders were pursued and sometimes caught and punished. The case of Alexander Leighton was long remembered by Laud's enemies. The man was a disgruntled Scot who in 1628, during the excitement caused by the proroguing of parliament, put forth a pamphlet, called *An Appeal to the Parliament, or Sions Plea against the Prelacie*, in which he proposed that prelacy be at once abolished root and branch. He was upon the order of Star Chamber fined, imprisoned, whipped, his ears cropped, his nose slit and his forehead branded.[7] The purpose of this savagery was to deter others from committing similar outbursts, but the execution of it revealed not only a total disregard of the popular temper but a complete ignorance of the effect which human psychology may give to persecution. The real damage to the existing regime had been done by the men who, untouched by Star Chamber, had prepared the spiritual soil for such characters as Leighton to flourish in. The severity visited upon that single crank no doubt did intimidate some men, but it outraged still more and invited the emergence of others who were liable to that neurotic hankering for publicity which may be the chief animating motive for martyrdom. Such an ill-balanced nature was ready to make itself heard in the person of William Prynne. Probably no man ever lived in whom common caution weighed less in comparison to the intoxication of rushing into print. There is a vanity men of a certain kind enjoy in loudly expressing moral indignation and so figuring with self-approval in the public eye. They welcome the opportunity to mount the scaffold because they can use it for their stage. Such opportunity Laud offered to Prynne.

Concerning the intolerance of Laud, as indeed concerning the whole subject of toleration and freedom of speech, there has been much confusion of mind. The notion that the principles of spiritual and intellectual liberty in their pure entirety had to await discovery until the seventeenth century does not lead to a critical understanding of the past. A condition of relative toleration has probably always been present in stable societies. Absolute toleration has probably always been an illusion, more cherished, to be sure, at some times than at others. Men commonly seek the toleration or repression of this or that. They are concerned about particulars, endeavoring to establish or maintain the institutions with which they associate their own freedom. In our time we think of religious liberty not as a condition of religious life within the church but as a condition of life within society. Religious life at large is manifested in the flourishing of churches, mutually exclusive if not actively intolerant of one another. Religious liberty is maintained, if at all and then with difficulty, by the state, protecting each church from the possibility of persecution by other churches and each individual from persecution by any. For the maintenance and development of spiritual and intellectual life in general, we look to the churches, it is true, but even more to education apart from religion and above all to the press.

Laud was probably in his own mind as deeply devoted to the ideal of freedom as any man of his age, but that condition emergent in his time which has in its later stages become what we call freedom could only seem to him a chaos of irrational and tyrannical forces which it was his duty to keep under subjection. Every grown person in society in the seventeenth century was not presumed literate, but unless he were a Jew he was still presumed to be a baptized and communicating Christian. Education, literature, generalized thought, though rapidly escaping ecclesiastical bonds, were still regarded in all their institutionalized forms as aspects of the life of men as Christians. The press, as it arose, was therefore inevitably regarded as ancillary and subordinate to the church, a position from which it emerged only in response to technological advance in the manufacture of printed matter and to social changes promoting ease of communication. For the state to ignore the Christian condition of its subjects or to neglect or avoid responsibility for the support or welfare of the church was as impossible to conceive with equanimity as in modern times it would be to absolve the state from responsibility for the education of its citizens in reading and writing. Equally impossible was it to conceive of the church as free from obligation to the state for the Christian unity of the people or to the humblest individual for Christian communion with his fellows.

Such at any rate is the ideal which vibrates through those tense and earnest sermons which Laud preached from time to time before king or parliament. Like most sermons of the time, though more restrained in imagery and more rigidly clarified and controlled, they are devoted to the explication of scripture as a poetical analogy to the time at hand. The theme is always of the royal house and the temple, the king guarding and upholding the church and the people through the church, the church serving the people and the king through the people, in that living reciprocal union which was the goal also, no matter how differently to be attained, of the Puritan reformers.

Laud had no conception of, certainly no respectful attention to bestow upon, the seething activity of thought and expression which had sprung up among the populace with the dissemination of the Bible and the spread of literacy in the vernacular. He did not conceive the duty of the church to be to stimulate that activity by doctrinal preaching and theological polemic. He did not look to religious discussion to lead common men any nearer to salvation or the truth. The spiritual union of the people was to be quickened by the decent, beautiful, even splendid performance of the services and celebration of the sacraments, by the encouragement of humane learning and the arts, by the countenancing of innocent sports and pleasures. From his point of view Puritanism was one of the most intolerant of religious attitudes and the most divisive and destructive. It proposed to replace reason, charity and beauty by dissidence and asceticism. The strict Calvinist wing cried up a dogma which postulated at the very start an ineluctable division of men into elect and damned. The various separatist groups went even farther and denied, or so it seemed, the responsibility of Christians to the state and at the same time barred the generality of sinners from Christian communion altogether. When, therefore, the Puritans urged their cause without license in the press, Laud could not but proceed against them in the manner prescribed by law. It did not occur to him that the outpourings of Prynne and his fellows were but incidental currents, best ignored, in the running stream of the intellectual life of the time. Nor was he able to anticipate the finely drawn distinctions of nineteenth-century philosophers between speech which merely expressed ideas and speech which directly incited men to acts of violence. In that age a word, spoken or written, was an act which, if need were, should be punished as such.

Together with the policy which prompted Laud to Star Chamber prosecution of Puritan pamphleteers went, nevertheless, a high degree of intellectual tolerance. Puritan writers frequently expressed the fear of error as of something akin to physical contamination, a deadly spreading venom or contagion. The Anglicans, on the other hand, may be said to have had minds which enjoyed immunity to such poison. In the interest of social unity they insisted upon uniformity but not upon complete unanimity in all details of doctrine so long as the preaching of doctrine was not made a cloak for sedition and disruption. Already in the writing of these men before and during the civil wars there are patent anticipations of the manner in which the eighteenth century would relieve itself of theological dilemmas. They held that the truths necessary to be believed were few, that they were most evident to the reason of all men, that they were those concerning which there had been no controversy but rather universal agreement among good men in all communions. Let men believe in the atonement of Christ for the sins of man, revealed in scripture and administered through the sacraments, and then let them think and say what they like on other points so long as the church, the seamless garment of Christ within the nation, be not torn asunder. The polemics of faith and doctrine lead only to division, bitterness and no end to the mystery of iniquity.

This is the point of view unmistakably present in Laud's only considerable doctrinal work, the *Relation of the Conference* of 1622 between himself and Fisher, the Jesuit, in which the two contended for the soul of Buckingham's mother. This long, technical, point-by-point debate, characterized like Laud's other writings by a certain dignity, is mostly concerned with issues long since dead. But the author strikes out in a few pages an admirable statement of the central position of his party. The question which had given the lady pause had been, How can we know that we are in the way to salvation save by the one true church? Laud's reply was that of the liberal intellectual Anglican of his day. Actually it was in line with those ideas concerning nature and human reason which some Puritans also shared, though with far different practical import. There is no one true church, said Laud; there are true churches. Truth is revealed in the Bible, but the proof of that fact rests upon the book itself. This the church conveys to men, and the Holy Ghost inclines them to believe, natural reason to understand. Alone among books, this one book 'is or hath been received in almost all nations under heaven; and wheresoever it hath been received, it hath been approved for unchangeable good and believed for infallible verity.'[8] Surely this could not be but for the working of common reason in all men. Why should reason have been given to man but that thus and only thus he might discover God? The way of reason was open to all, whether in the English or Roman or other church. Let the lady take it, believe the Bible, and trouble her mind no longer.

The plea of the liberal humanist against the assertion of infallibility and of exclusive title to salvation vested in the Roman church was most cogently argued on behalf of the Anglican church not by Laud himself but by his godson, William Chillingworth.[9] *The Religion of Protestants a Safe Way to Salvation,* published in 1638, epitomized the best thought of the English church on the eve of revolution. The author's career and fate foreshadowed the tragic confusion by which Anglicanism was about to be overwhelmed. The book was directed against the aggressive dogmatism of the Catholic counter reformation. It could as justly have been directed against the bigotry of homebred revolutionaries. It appeared in the course of a controversy between an English Jesuit and an Oxford divine. The question at issue, as in Laud's *Conference*, was whether salvation was possible outside the Roman church. Born and bred at Oxford, fellow of Trinity College, Chillingworth was seasoned to such debates. Wood says that he used to walk in the college grove and, when he encountered a scholar there, would discourse and dispute with him 'purposely to facilitate and make the way of wrangling common with him.'[10] But in 1630 he was persuaded by Fisher, the same Jesuit with whom Laud had wrangled for the soul of Buckingham's mother, that 'perpetual visible profession' was lacking to Protestant churches, and so had betaken himself to Douai. There in a short time he learned also to doubt the profession of the Catholic church, and, prompted by letters from Laud, returned to Oxford. The convictions to which Chillingworth was led by his experience are expressed in his book.

The work was written in circumstances of peculiar charm. The passionate polemic spirit of the age relaxed for a moment into urbanity and set a scene suggesting the calm rather than the fierce strivings of thought. This came about through Chillingworth's friendship with Lucius Carey, Lord Falkland,[11] one of those fortunate and brilliant youths who have the gift of dazzling their teachers by their promise and who at the same time possess the means and the taste to surround themselves with scholars while surrounding scholars with the comfort and attention such men most desire. Falkland had been first an intimate of wits and poets in London, himself a writer of verses, and a patron of Ben Jonson. He wrote a stilted elegy on the dramatist, another on Donne. But the age of wits and poets was over. Falkland retired in his twenties to Great Tew in the Cotswolds in order to learn Greek and, as a greater poet was doing at Horton, to read the classics and the fathers and councils of the church. Perhaps better still, he opened his house to the learned men of Oxford, which lay near at hand. They were free to come and go without ceremony, constrained only to attend their host at dinner. The place became for them, it was said, like 'a college situated in a purer air,' 'a university bound in a lesser volume.'[12] There they could find the books and the discourse they most relished. When Falkland's London friends visited him, they found him still witty, good-humored and pleasant, but Clarendon does not omit to note that 'truly his whole conversation was one *convivium philosophicum* or *convivium theologicum*.'[13]

In such company Chillingworth matured his views and composed his *Religion of Protestants a Safe Way to Salvation*. The procedure taken was to search and try each stem and branch and twig of his opponent's argument, and then to destroy all by a logic no less scrupulously tested and by magisterial erudition. This was the manner of the age in such matters. The last consideration to trouble the author was the thought that he might exhaust his reader. Tireless and dignified as a river, but not without fine strokes of athletic wit, Chillingworth rolls on through four hundred and thirteen folio pages.

The result was the most impressive presentation of the Anglican approach to a rational theology. Much was foreshadowed in Chillingworth's prefatory statement that men should be governed in their religion as in other matters by 'right reason, grounded on Divine revelation and common notions, written by God in the hearts of all men: and deducing, according to the never failing rules of Logick, consequent deductions from them.'[14] Well did the author of these words deserve the praise of his eighteenth-century biographer for trying 'to free Religion from Enthusiasm and Fanaticism, and to establish it upon its true rational grounds and foundations.'[15] Archbishop Tillotson commended him for 'his worthy and successful attempts to make Christian Religion reasonable.'[16] The task which Chillingworth actually essayed was, without agreeing to Protestant assertion of the uniform literal infallibility and authority of the Bible in its every detail, to set up the scriptures, reasonably interpreted, against the claims put forth by the Catholics in behalf of the Roman church. As an Englishman he must give precedence to the book, and as a certain sort of Englishman he must place limits beyond which it was not safe to go in accepting the book. Chillingworth did not attack the idea of supernatural authority. He merely asserted the supernatural authority of the Bible and denied that of any particular church. The Bible was the word of God. But the deductions he drew from that premise were not such as would satisfy extremists, Puritan or Jesuit. The converse of the duty of believing the Bible was the duty of doubting everything else. Thus one could assert with new force the supremacy of natural reason upon every point except that of the divine character of the one book, and then one could proceed to explore the vast field in which reason was supreme. To believe the Bible men had to read it, and, reading it, they were bound to attempt to understand it for themselves. Once the role of the church as the appointed interpreter of the word was put in doubt, every man who could read at all became, potentially at any rate, a doctor to devise dogmas and a critic to call dogmas in doubt. Every bigot, every ignoramus, every fool or knave, or so it would soon seem, could quote scripture for his purpose. Yet this very condition compelled men like Chillingworth to conceive and define a more rational view of revealed authority. The impulse to understand aright that which one was required to believe called up the whole question of the nature of faith, of knowledge, and of human understanding. One could not in so momentous an affair afford to be mistaken or deceived. Yet the opportunities for error were manifold. The very canon determining which books of the Bible were inspired was matter for dispute. There were differing texts, some corrupt and even the best containing passages that were difficult, obscure and inconsistent. An authority that could be trusted to resolve all questions would admittedly be of great use. But where could such be found? Tradition, the fathers, the popes, doctors and councils had all erred and disagreed, and obviously one could not depend upon an infallibility which was infallible only sometimes. Chillingworth can fall back on only one cardinal truth, namely the truth revealed to reason in scripture, the light of God shining upon the eye of the soul. And this, he held, was sufficient. The points necessary to be believed are few, clear and universally accepted—the existence of God, the revelation of his word, the atonement and resurrection of his son, the indwelling of the Holy Ghost, the church universal. These points were to be found not in some manuscripts but in all, not in the hard places in scripture but in those easy to be understood and in the scriptures as a whole. They were to be found not only by the learned in the Hebrew and the Greek but by common men in their English. Therefore any man could have the comfort of knowing that he might be saved, whether he were of this church or of that and whether he adhered to this opinion or to that upon controverted points of doctrine. No church and no opinion could be wholly reprobate unless it denied the fundamental truths of scripture or man's ability to apprehend them.

Chillingworth thus laid the basis for what was to become the characteristic English attitude toward religion in its relation to other activities of life. Without foregoing the final and absolute assurance of
faith, he proposed to set his mind free from the tyranny of dogma.
The doctrine that there was no true church in Christendom but many
true churches, of which the English was one, made both certitude and
toleration possible. It pointed to the conclusion that in England too
there might safely be allowed more than one belief. It also prepared
men to think that in the world there might be many religions leading
to the same God. By limiting the field of dogmatic faith to super-
rational acceptance of the supernatural origin of the Bible, the way was
opened to indifference toward all other dogmas howsoever derived, to
the discrediting of many allegedly religious motives for public policy
and to the acceptance of toleration as the only possible basis for political
unity. An incidental feature of Chillingworth's argument, but of the
greatest importance, was to suggest the need for inquiring into the
workings of human understanding itself. He himself, he says, desired
as much as any 'to goe the right way to eternall happinesse,' but he
was completely indifferent 'whether this way lye on the right hand or
the left, or streight forward.' Men may go to heaven by divers ways;
they may all go the same way peaceably to hell. Whoever insists that
some single way is the only true way to heaven is probably moved by
his wish for 'ease or pleasure or profit or advancement or satisfaction
of friends or any human consideration,' and 'it is oddes but he will take
his desire that it should be so, for an assurance that it is so.' A man
believes his religion for any one of a number of reasons. His fore-
fathers believed it. He was brought up to believe it. No other is permitted in the country. The service is stately. He finds comfort in it.
And 'an infinite number [believe] by chance and they know not why,
but only because they are sure they are in the right.'[17]

Hence Chillingworth arrives at a ringing declaration of the principle
of toleration as a necessary part of public policy. The oft-cited texts of
St. Paul on the subject, followed by all the commonplaces of spiritual
freedom, are hurled at the Jesuit; 'the weapons of the Christian warfare are not carnal,' 'nothing is more against religion than to force
religion,' 'human violence may make men counterfeit, but cannot make
them believe, and is therefore fit for nothing but to breed form with-

out and atheism within.' Persecution is not the way to religious unity
or salvation but a perpetuation of disunion by worldly power for its
own ends. Chillingworth qualifies this doctrine in only one respect.
'There is no danger to any state from any man's opinion; unless it be
such an opinion by which disobedience to authority or impiety is taught
or licensed; which sort, I confess, may justly be punished as well as
other faults; or, unless this sanguinary doctrine be joined with it, that
it is lawful for him by human violence to enforce others to it.'[18] Violence in opposition is thus precluded; to die for one's religion is more
blessed than to fight for it. This, of course, affords to his mind no
defense of the Roman church, which, he believes, has sacrificed heca-
tombs of martyrs under the name of heretics and offered violence even
to the sacred persons of kings.

In this aspect of his thought Chillingworth was, of course, merely
rationalizing the position in which his countrymen found themselves
at the end of their long struggle against foreign power symbolized
by Rome. That struggle had eventuated for them in nationalism,
which he could think of only as organized under a monarchy which
held itself responsible to no power but God for the people's welfare
and under a church tolerant of differences for the sake of the people's
Christian and national unity. But in its larger aspects Chillingworth's
argument reached much further than defense of the English church
against Rome. Precisely similar reasoning had in all essentials already
been pursued by the humanist reformers against the claims of the
Protestant church at Geneva to be the sole judge of truth and the sole
way to salvation. With the writings of Socinus, Castellio and Acontius,
Chillingworth was undoubtedly familiar. Partly through their influence, the same way of reasoning, though with emotional coloring
foreign to Chillingworth, was also being taken up by Puritan minorities
whether against Anglican or presbyterian dogmatism and intolerance.
The followers of John Smyth, the baptist; mystics like Everard and
Saltmarsh; that tireless humanistic debater, John Goodwin; perhaps
in some degree Thomas Goodwin and others of independent leanings
among the Puritan clergy; idealistic, politically minded gentlemen like
Robert Greville, Lord Brooke, or merchants like William Walwyn;
these and others on the other side of the widening cleavage in English
life were at least getting ready to share with Chillingworth a sceptical

attitude toward the notion that any given church was infallible or gave its adherents an exclusive claim to heaven. There were men on the left as well as on the right who were beginning to perceive that toleration was the only possible basis for peace and unity among the English people.

Meanwhile the enemy to the ideal of a tolerant church as conceived by Anglicans like Chillingworth lay nearer home than Rome. That the Catholics deemed the English church no safe way to salvation was less important than that the Puritan reformers thought no better of it so long as it was governed by prelates. Not the Jesuit Fisher but the presbyterian Cheynell would live to triumph over Chillingworth in his grave. So far as the immediate practical situation was concerned, the latter had indeed come near to proving too much. He might justify himself against Rome by asserting that one must obey God and not man and that truth was to be found by 'right Reason, grounded on Divine Revelation and common Notions, written by God in the Hearts of all Men.' But in a few years, every revolutionary in England would be laying claim to the right to deduce by the unfailing principles of logic his own rules for church and state. Every rebel with a bishop or a king or even a parliament to overthrow would be appealing to scripture and the laws written by God on the tables of the breast, and every firebrand who might be forbidden to discourse against authority would indict his oppressor of the very sins Chillingworth had charged against the Roman church. The real question in other words was not what to think of the pope but what to think of Englishmen who seemed bent upon fighting one another ostensibly over dogmas perhaps no less inessential, faulty and incomplete, so far as religion was concerned, than that of papal infallibility itself.

Some such question may have been present in the mind of John Hales[19] when he penned the letter, later published as *A Tract concerning Schisme and Schismaticks*, which he addressed to Chillingworth while the latter was composing his book at Falkland's country house. Hales was no more able than his friend to deal with the question, but he did feel that the divisions of his time were at bottom irrelevant to religion, that the questions of doctrine which occupied Chillingworth had something about them futile and absurd. Heresy and schism, he perceives, are ridiculous terms, theological scarecrows, used to frighten men. The strength and ground of all society was communion. No man could be compelled to believe what he could not think true, and whatever any man thought true he necessarily believed. Breach of social communion, schism, was a sin not against truth but against charity. In any society it was as likely to break out in the form of persecution and oppression as in sedition and rebellion.

Hales was one of the rare spirits of his time. In 1618 he had attended the Synod of Dort as observer for the English ambassador.[20] He learned there, it was said, to bid John Calvin good night.[21] But he learned more than that. His reports on the doings and sayings of the theologians there locked in conflict over free will and predestination show him to have learned what to think of all dogma, of all pretensions of the human mind to encompass the mystery of God. The ferocity of those efforts to drive truth into a corner by dialectic and debate struck him as folly. Having faithfully described them with ironic detachment, he went back to his fellowship at Eton possessed by that scepticism at once Olympian and humane which marks a charitable and honest mind. Such a spirit was out of joint with the time. Hales refused to undertake the cure of souls and retired to his books and meditations, issuing now and then a witty letter or discourse or a sermon which was hardly a sermon, rather an essay with more in it of the spirit of Montaigne or Burton than of the seventeenth-century divine. He warned readers against *Abuses of Hard Places of Scripture*[22] and urged the utmost toleration in 'dealing with erring Christians.'[23] Perhaps most characteristic of all is his allocution on the text 'Be not deceived.' Here in gracefully managed sentences, with references to scripture and the classics, Saul linked with Oedipus and Solomon with Seneca, he expressed the one principle of which he was sure, namely that 'the chiefest sinew and strength of wisdom . . . is not easily to believe.' Knowledge of truth was so momentously important and so infinitely difficult to obtain that no man could afford to take the risk of delegating the task to any other. The only infallibility is or ought to be in oneself. Education and breeding give no ground for certainty; they are 'but the authority of our Teachers taken over our childhood.' What is antiquity 'but man's authority born some ages before?' The common voice of multitudes and majorities may 'excuse an error' but never 'warrant a truth.' Nothing will serve 'but to know things yourselves.' 'Unto you therefore, and to everyone, . . . from him that studies in his Library to him that sweats at the Ploughtail, belongs this precept of St. Paul, Be not deceived.'[24]

The implications of this attitude appear in the mellow essay on *The Method of Reading Profane History*[25] and in the pungent *Letter to an Honourable Person concerning the Weapon Salve*,[26] which might not unworthily have found place in Sir Thomas Browne's *Pseudodoxia*. But Hales's scepticism attracted most attention at the time in the *Tract concerning Schisme* which, circulating for some time in manuscript, found its way into print in three apparently unauthorized editions of 1642 and earned for its author a place in the list of execrated Socinians and atheists. Chillingworth had used all the weapons of learned dialectic to argue away the claim of the Roman church to infallibility. In a brief essay, humorous, epigrammatic, salty with common sense, Hales dismissed as absurd the claim of any dogma to an importance sufficient to affect men's peace and amity. The claim to infallibility in any quarter was a bar to charity and truth. The great historic disputes over doctrine dealt for the most part with trivialities and served chiefly to set men at variance over points on which anyone might err. Hales cannot deny that heretics lie and schismatics rebel against truth, but who is the heretic and who the true believer, which the conventicle and which the true church? And between any two who shall judge? Decision on most points, indeed, is unnecessary, since there is no reason why men of differing judgments cannot live in the same communion, and on the few necessary points agreement is not difficult to attain. It would not be difficult, that is—and here he plainly feels that he is treading dangerous ground—were it not that the very suggestion 'carries fire in the tail of it, for it bringeth with it a piece of Doctrine which is seldom pleasing to Superiors.'[27]

What doctrine Hales was here glancing at is made clear by the letter he felt constrained to write to Laud when word reached him that the primate was displeased with his opinions. This letter, the most finished and most brilliant of his writings, lets us see most clearly into the man's mind and temper. Craving pardon for the 'genius open and uncautelous' which had betrayed him, it might be, into too great 'gaiety of spirit,' he rests his defense on the integrity and humility of his disinterested search for truth. 'For this, I have forsaken all hopes all friends, all desires, which might biass me, and hinder me from driving right at what I aimed.' If after all this he has erred, then 'to err hath cost me more, than it has many to find the truth: and truth itself shall give me this testimony at last, that if I have missed of her, it is not my fault but my misfortune.' If he has been betrayed into seeming conflict with authority, it has been by love of truth itself, that and that 'uncautelous' gaiety of this. In such conflict, the lover of truth can, of course, never be concerned, because to dispute with rulers can never take him a jot nearer his goal. And yet, there is one doctrine which he can never let go. He will obey government, but though 'the exception of good conscience sound not well with many men,' since it may be merely a cover for pertinacity and wilfulness, nevertheless 'it concerns every man sincerely to know the truth of his own heart, and so accordingly to determine of his own way, whatsoever the judgment of his superiors be, or whatsoever event befal him. For since, in case of conscience, many times there is necessity to fall either into the hands of men, or into the hands of God; of these two, whether is the best, I leave every particular man to judge.'[28]

No defense of the right to intellectual freedom could have been at once more graceful and more firm. It met with characteristic response. Laud, after a long conference with Hales, offered him a canonry at Windsor, which he accepted rather from courtesy than from ambition. Like Chillingworth, he perceived that the religious quarrels of his time were of no avail for the furthering of knowledge and religion. He saw that the church need not and should not be the arena for quarrels which only served to trouble the religious life. But he did not therefore question the place and authority of the English church in society. That would have been to concede that social peace was to be sought in social rather than in religious union, and for that he was not prepared. He did not see that the passion for truth which moved men like himself and Chillingworth might have something in common with the passions of other men for other things—for reform, for economic freedom, for larger powers, richer life and ampler self-expression, for a new heaven and a new earth—even though those passions like his own were grounded upon the dogma of free conscience. So in the innocence of his heart, he could conclude his letter to Laud by expressing his satisfaction in the existing government of the church and his expectation that no religious disorder would ever occur 'so long as so good, so moderate, so gracious a royal hand shall hold the stern: which God grant may be either in him or his, till times shall be no more.'

Thus Hales and his friends expressed the fatal weakness of the Anglican outlook upon the England of 1637. Within very earshot of the bookstalls of Paul's Churchyard, Hales, preaching at Paul's Cross, urged his hearers to enlarge the phylacteries of their goodness, give all friendly countenance to the meaner sort but by no means admit them to the discussion of faith and religion.[29] Having achieved that true tolerance of mind which sets charity above dogma and the love of truth above the desire for power, having satisfied himself that in the interests of religion religious controversy ought to be avoided, he thought all occasion for controversy was removed. The only thing needed in the face of the unrest of the time was to discountenance religious discussion by the meaner sort. True, the populace would come no nearer to the truth than had the doctors of the Synod of Dort. But Hales and his party were blind to the fact that, if the weak, the poor and the ignorant thrust themselves upon the discussion of religion, it was chiefly because only so could they assert not alone their fantastic errors but also their desire no longer to be weak or poor or ignorant. They were seething with passion to know truth themselves, to attain the New Jerusalem in their time. Hales, broadminded, learned, wise, charming, tolerant and sceptical, knew only too well that all this was illusion, but who can persuade the tempest of its folly?

The high-minded Anglican rationalists went into the storm ill-prepared to stand the strain it put upon them. Deprived of his fellowship in 1649, Hales lived on obscurely until 1656 and died melancholy and despairing. Chillingworth, made a royal chaplain, was drawn off to construct siege engines for the king's army. He was captured by the Puritans in 1644 and died shortly after at Chichester. The presbyterian Cheynell attempted to argue him on his deathbed out of his Socinianism, so-called, and flung a copy of his book to rot with him in his grave.[30] Falkland went into the Long Parliament, expecting there to find practical realization of his dream of discovering truth at the conclusion of discourse and debate. Though he took part in the condemnation of Strafford and Laud, he was a man divided in heart, and when war commenced he went out with the king. In the course of the fighting, if we may trust Clarendon, he made himself so known for his longing after peace that in honor he sought the most dangerous posts in battle. On the morning of Newbury he put on clean linen, assumed the utmost gaiety of spirit, and rode at a gap in the hedge raked by the enemy's fire. 'He died,' says Clarendon, 'as much of the time as of the bullet.'[31]

The Anglican ideal as expressed by Chillingworth and Hales and attempted by Laud was the truly catholic ideal, not of the toleration of churches, but of a tolerant church. It was necessarily subject in practice to one important limitation. The one thing which could not be tolerated was active intolerance in any form, a limitation not peculiar to Anglicism. Toleration as a practical measure in any society imposes a certain restriction upon the members of that society. It presupposes that government should deny, by force if necessary, the freedom of any of its subjects to impose their will or their opinions upon their fellow subjects. What constitutes violence or a threat so menacing as to be tantamount to violence is a question which always rests with government itself to decide. The success of any government in maintaining toleration depends not upon the purity of its ideal but upon its success in wisely measuring and meeting the strength of the discordant elements under its authority. The failure of the Anglican and Stuart regime was the failure of rulers to foresee what few men of that time foresaw, that society could no longer be organized as an ecclesiastical polity however tolerant. The ruin of the church and the monarchy was, in other words, not due to their intolerance but to their inability to suppress revolution. If all man's hopes and dreams and thoughts concerning himself and his world, all that activity in expression which he calls his soul, could any longer have been comprised within the frame of an ecclesiastical polity, Laud's was at least as good as any. But the time for that had gone forever. Individualism could not be denied freedom to express itself and would not be content to put forth ideas only, leaving institutions untouched. It must attempt to reshape the church, to conceive the place of the church in society in quite another way, to develop a new kind of society in which the activity of expression would take many forms. In that society the church would eventually find its place but only beside not above education, literature, science and the press. Meanwhile Laud, the patron of Chillingworth and Hales, felt compelled to defend the church against men who for the moment had behind them an incalculable force, impregnable to charity and reason, it might be, but very much alive.

VII

Episkopomastix

WHEN Laud came to take charge of the resistance to Puritanism, he was quite right in thinking that the very maintenance of peace and unity in the church was at stake. The Puritan preachers themselves made no overt attack upon authority. They had, however, won a powerful hold upon the pulpit and the press. They had a large and influential following which promptly made its hostility felt whenever parliament was called together. They had Prynne, to whom war to the death on what he regarded as wickedness was the breath of life. He it was who personally undertook that smiting of bishops which Puritan pamphleteers were to continue, in spite of anything that could be done to stop them, until prelacy was finally overthrown. From Laud's point of view, Prynne fell precisely within the category of those who make a breach of the peace under color of religion. Though there could be no dealing gently with such a man, Laud withheld his hand until the publication of *Histrio-mastix* in 1632. That work supplied undeniable pretext for arraigning the author in Star Chamber on a charge of libel against the state, king and people. After a year in the Tower and an arraignment as well in the Court of High Commission, Prynne was condemned. He was fined and his academic degrees revoked; he was pilloried and had his ears cropped, but only partially; he was ordered to be imprisoned for life; and his book was called in and ordered to be burnt. Before we condemn the authorities of the day for the barbarity of this and of the still more violent punishment which ensued a few years later, we must make due allowance for seventeenth-century theory and practice in penology. The prevention of crime was thought to be accomplished by making a public spectacle of the condemned, a theory the more intelligible if we note the great inadequacy, especially under conditions as they obtained on the eve of the revolution, of prisons, prison discipline and police. The machinery for control of the press was especially ineffective. The licensing of books before publication was intrusted to a few chaplains, the prevention of unlicensed publication to the Stationers' Company, duties which in the circumstances such persons were quite unable to fulfil. As for the recall of such a book as *Histrio-mastix* when once published and given the notoriety which befell it, that proved impossible. Even when Prynne was presently immured in the Tower, it seemed beyond the compass of authority to deprive the man of books, writing materials and means of communication with his friends, even to prevent him from dispatching additional libels to the press.

Punishment administered under such conditions served as often as not merely to enhance the culprit's fame and appeal. The self-conceit which seems requisite for such a career as that of Prynne is generally accompanied by a large dose of the histrionic impulse to show oneself in dramatic postures. The Puritans in condemning the theatre did not lose the knack of showmanship. Prynne in prison merely went on writing pamphlets more virulent, if that were possible, than before. Presently too his example raised up imitators and coadjutors. John Bastwick, a physician, and Henry Burton, a preacher, joined in the war of pamphlets against prelates, and a poor but ambitious youth named Lilburne was ready to lend a hand. The outcome of the chain of circumstances that began with the publication of *Histrio-mastix* was the enactment of a scene at the pillory in the palace yard at Westminster such as England had seldom looked on, a scene in which the characteristic spectacle of ignominious punishment was turned by the victims into a curious and ominous kind of triumph. Prynne provoked Laud to arraign him once more by the publication in 1636 of an eight-page diatribe entitled *Newes from Ipswich*. This was directed against Bishop Wren and devoted chiefly to urging that the bishops, 'dunghill bred,' should be hanged for suppressing truth in the press and the pulpits. On this occasion, however, the writer had companions at the bar of Star Chamber in the persons of Burton and Bastwick, men who had also been exploiting in their own way the possibilities of public discourse and public opinion.[1]

Henry Burton occupied the pulpit of St. Matthew's in Friday Street. In 1643 he published one of the most detailed of Puritan autobiographies, a work in which he gives a vivid account not only of his sufferings of 1637 but of the spiritual experiences that led to that affair. 'As it is with a Mariner or traveller, who after a long Voyage comming within ken of his native Country begins to recount with himselfe the many hazzards he hath run, what by terrible stormes in the midst of Rocks and shelves, what by pirates and other perills,' safe at home at last, 'he sets him downe, and (to recreate him selfe and friends) begins to discourse of his travells, and of the most memorable passages therein.'[2] Possibly because Burton, unlike most of the spiritual preachers, took to such violent courses against the government during his pilgrimage, his life found no place in Clarke's collections. Burton's career was, however, in its beginnings typical of the spiritual brotherhood. He was a Yorkshireman, born about 1578. His mother encouraged him in his studies by showing him an English testament, 'which she kept lockt up (it having beene my Grandfathers in Queene Maries dayes)' and which was to be his when he had learned to read it. He went to St. John's, Cambridge, about 1595. There, he says, 'it was my happinesse to be a constant hearer of Mr. Chatterton and Mr. Perkins. . . . For from my first entrance in the Colledge, it pleased God to open mine eyes by their ministry, so as to put a difference betweene their sound teaching, and the University Sermons, which savoured more of humane wit, then of Gods word.'[3] In 1603 he left Cambridge, Master of Arts, to become tutor or chaplain in the household of Sir Robert Carey, a wealthy gentleman. His patron presently secured for him the post of clerk of the closet to Prince Henry and, after that prince's death, to Prince Charles. Upon the latter's accession to the throne, Burton failed of his expected promotion because of the successful rivalry of Bishop Neil. In his chagrin, he had the temerity to present a letter to the king protesting against the policies of the prelates, but this did not prevent him from being presented in 1621 to St. Matthew's. There he continued active against the bishops. For publishing a pamphlet called *The Baiting of the Popes Bull*, he was had up before the privy council in 1627, and for publishing another, *Babel No Bethel*, in 1629, he was imprisoned for a time in the Fleet. Not even this experience was enough to teach him moderation.

Burton incurred Laud's wrath by two sermons he preached at St. Matthew's in 1636 in commemoration of Guy Fawkes day. To the charge that they preached sedition under color of religion, the Puritans could always reply that the prelatical clergy 'creep into Courts and by their hypocrisy, false tales, and detractions of sincere teachers, and by a kind of collusion with Courtiers, . . . surprise the mindes of the great ones, and Magistrates.' Thus grave, constant and faithful ministers, who teach nothing but the truth, are traduced as troublemakers by court gnathoes, 'blind watchmen, dumbe dogs, plagues of soules, false Prophets, ravening wolves, theeves and robbers of soules.'[4] Couched in this tone, Burton's argument that Laud's policies in the church were papistical innovations could have had but one outcome for the preacher. At the end of the second sermon, a pursuivant summoned him to appear before High Commission. 'Therefore I shut myselfe up in my house, as in my prison, and there did compile my two said Sermons, with my Appeale, in one Book, to the end it might be published in print, as it was, sheet by sheet as I writ it; the while the Prelates Pursuivants, those barking Beagles, ceased not night nor day to watch and rap and ring at my doores to have surprised me in that my Castle, nor yet to search and hunt all the Printing houses about London.'[5] By God's providence, however, he got his book off his hands and printed before the sheriff of London himself arrived with swords, halberds and pickaxes to break in upon him. He was haled to prison to await arraignment and trial along with Prynne.

John Bastwick, a physician, pretended also to school learning. What first led him to join the attack on the bishops is not known. His version of the effort to identify prelacy with papacy was published in 1633 in the form of two Latin treatises bearing a Dutch imprint. They led to his being sent to the Gatehouse, there to remain until he should recant. What followed illustrates the difficulties which confronted the authorities in their effort to control the press. Bastwick was permitted to have his family about him in prison and freely to receive his friends. Among them was 'old Mr. Wharton,' 'a good, cheerfull, merry old man,' who urged Bastwick to write something against the bishops in English 'for the people (saith hee) understands not Latine, and therefore can reape no benefit by your labours, neither will you ever be knowne unto them.' Bastwick complied by writing a thing he called his 'Letany,' which made Wharton 'laugh as if he had bin tickled, so that I never saw a man more pleasant at a peece of grillery.' The old man promptly brought in some 'Citizens of good repute' also to hear what had been written. They bestowed ten pieces and a dinner upon the author, demanded copies, came again and brought others to share the fun.[6] Among these visitors was John Lilburne, an impecunious youth just at or near the end of his apprenticeship. With Bastwick's consent he presently secured a copy of the *Letany* from John Vicars and, probably with Wharton's connivance, carried it off to Holland to be printed. The result of the publication was that Bastwick took his way to Star Chamber and the pillory along with Prynne and Burton.

The three were arraigned for writing and publishing scandalous and libelous books against the state and the church. They were adjudged to have confessed their guilt by not filing proper answers to the charge within the allotted time. They claimed to have been prevented by the chicane of their persecutors. But they could not effectively deny what they had done. All they could do was to challenge the validity of the law and the authority of the court. This they did or endeavored to do, until silenced, in Star Chamber itself. Their behavior in the court, that is, was calculated to arouse the interest and sympathy of the public and thus at all risks to put their judges on trial before excited popular opinion. Prynne, who had indeed prepared an answer to the charge against him but an answer which was plainly but another pamphlet, took his cue to act the part of victim of unjust and illegal practice. 'If you condemn me for this, I hope all the world will acquit me,' was his last remark before they bade him hold his peace. Bastwick assumed the role of the poor subject unfairly repressed by princes and peers, and he appealed, supplying Biblical parallels, to 'the example of God, the law of God, and the law of nature.'[7] Would they cut off a Christian's, a Roman's, ears? 'What an age do we live in, that we must thus be exposed unto the merciless furie of every malignant spirit!'[8] Whereupon the Lord Keeper told him to cease, since he was angry and talking off the point. Burton posed as the conscientious minister of the word, craving leave to speak as such. What he chose to say was 'I pray God that this honorable court in the judgment of this cause doe nothing this day whereby they may sin against God.'[9] The Lord Keeper told him that his judges did not sit to hear him preach, but Burton was able to say, before he could be finally silenced, that he must willingly endure censure rather than disobey his conscience. At this 'a great humme was made in the roome by many of the hearers as an expression of their joy, being much affected with this his Christian resolution.'[10] The three were condemned to be fined, pilloried, shorn of their ears, and immured in separate remote prisons for life. Prynne, whose ears had been partially cropped once before, was also ordered to be branded on both cheeks as a seditious libeler. But as they had turned their trial into a dramatic condemnation of their judges, so they now made of their punishment a triumphant show of their wrongs and their righteousness.

The size of the audience amazed all who beheld it. The prisoners embraced at the foot of the scaffold. Prynne and Bastwick made speeches. Burton preached again, not neglecting the possibilities that lay in the potent analogy of the three pillories to the three crosses upon Calvary. Bastwick's wife kissed his ears. Prynne characteristically unrolled history and the law. Burton appeared upon the scene wearing new gloves and carrying a nosegay. He and his wife declared that this was their wedding day. We are asked to believe that a bee came and sucked honey from the flowers in his hand on the scaffold. The people watched every gesture the victims made, hung upon their words, shouted applause and comfort, and groaned as the axe fell upon their ears. When, a month later, they were transported to their respective prisons, multitudes followed in the highways to cheer them on their way.

The London mob had probably never beheld upon the boards of the Globe or the Swan a more moving drama than that which Prynne, Bastwick and Burton enacted in the Star Chamber and the old palace yard, enacted with full measure of that gift for histrionic gesture and utterance which was the common possession of the English populace. These men were the rivals as well as the enemies of the players, and of the playwrights too. As soon as time would allow, after Prynne and his fellows had been dragged off to prison, there appeared another illicit pamphlet in the streets of London. *A Briefe Relation of Certain speciall and most materiall passages, and Speeches in the Starre-Chamber, Occasioned and delivered June the 14th., 1637 at the Censure of those three worthy Gentlemen, Dr. Bastwicke, Mr. Burton and Mr. Prynne, as it hath beene truely and faithfully gathered from their owne mouthes by one present at the sayd Censure.* This gave no mean foretaste of the art of popular prose as it was to develop in the hands of the pamphleteers. It was in the first place excellent journalism, having about it the air of giving nothing but the news, that news which the three men had known so well how to make. It was couched as narrative, direct, lucid and dramatic, convincingly documented with copies of Star Chamber orders and the like. It had also all that interest of personality which is given by characteristic and convincing dialogue and action. Again, as so often in Puritan sermons and pamphlets, we are enabled to foresee the rise of a Bunyan and a Defoe. Thus Burton in the stocks is made to say:

Commend my love to my wife, and tell her, I am heartily cheerefull, and bidd her remember what I sayd to her in the morning, namely, That shee should not blemish the glory of this day with one teare, or so much as one sigh. She returned answer, that shee was glad to heare him so cheerefull; and that shee was more cheerefull of this day, then of her wedding day. This answer exceedingly rejoyced his heart, who thereupon blessed God for her, and sayd of her, Shee is but a young Souldier of Christs, but shee hath already endured many a sharpe brunt, but the Lord will strengthen her unto the end: And hee having a payre of new gloves, shewed them to his freinds there about him, saying, My wife yesterday of her owne accord bought me these wedding gloves, for this is my wedding day.[11]

Prynne is represented to have said to the executioner:

Come friend, Come, burne mee, cut mee, I feare it not. I have learnid to feare the fire of Hell, and not what man can doe unto mee: Come seare mee, seare mee, I shall beare in my body the markes of the Lord Jesus: Which the bloody Executioner performed with extraordinary cruelty, heating his Iron twice to burne one Cheeke: And cut one of his eares so close, that hee cut off a peice of his Cheeke [and cut him deep into the neck, neare jugular veine, to the great danger of his life. And then hacking the other Eare almost off, he left it hanging, and went down the Scaffold, till the Surgeon called him up againe, and made him cut it off quite.] At which exquisit torture hee never mooved with his body, or so much as changed his countenance, but still lookt up as well as he could towards heaven, with a smiling countenance, even to the astonishment of all the beholders.[12]

The *Briefe Relation*, with some added touches, was brought up to date by Prynne in 1641 as *A New Discovery of the Prelates Tyranny*. This exhibited again and with great force the literary power which the popular pamphleteers had at their command and of which Prynne had already given a foretaste in his short diatribes and the epistles to his longer tracts. When such men consciously attempted anything like intellectual prose, they were still hampered by an obsolescent intellectual method, by superstitious reverence for erudition and by a language that had not learned to move outside the strait jacket of scholastic Latin. When they laid aside intellectual pretensions and wrote merely to rouse and please the populace, the case was different. The native tongue, spoken without benefit of clergy but not without enrichment drawn from the pulpit, had not yet been diluted and enfeebled by academic education, by rationalism, or by the cultural aspirations of the middle class. It was still the marvellous instrument of expression it had shown itself to be on the Elizabethan stage. The strength of the Puritan pamphleteers did not lie in a purer or loftier ideal of liberty nor in a greater power of lucid and coherent thought but in their command of the art of suggestive, provocative, poetic speech, whether in rhapsodic diatribe or in racy journalistic description and narration.

This had been most signally demonstrated by the *Letany* which John Bastwick wrote at the suggestion of merry old Mr. Wharton for the benefit of people who could not read Latin. As discourse, this has well-nigh no recognizable shape or sequence, only the continuity of the protesting voice. It goes on and on like a man telling his wrongs at the street corner or in the tavern, ceasing only at the exigency of time and space. The writer uses the very language of street and tavern. His vivid, suggestive, homely, sometimes foul words come pouring forth with a sort of smack and leer. One can almost hear the feet of the standers-by shift and their lips guffaw as they take in and savor what is said, though the speaker may the next moment go on to some religious matter strange to us in such a context.

This too was part of that 'honest liberty of free speech' which more men than Milton were in the mood to claim as their right, and Bastwick like Milton justifies his speaking freely and vilely by the nobility of his cause. The cause nearest to his heart was the imposition of the Puritan code upon the reckless living of the time, that discipline which not without some justice he and his kind thought purer. The ideal picture of the Puritan family, which the preachers had conveyed by precept and example, reappears in Bastwick's pamphlet. He describes the saintly household with its daily reading of scripture, its morning and evening prayers, its instruction and catechizing of children and servants, all under the ministrations of a godly pastor and in association with other households governed by the same pattern. This religion and rule of life Bastwick opposed to the disorder of the age. What did the Anglican church offer instead but the base schemings of politicians and timeservers? It was a clear case of Christ and Antichrist. The prelates like the papists were content that men should kneel and mutter at the right points in the service book and go to the devil for the rest. Hence the extraordinary bitterness of the attack on the bishops whether of Bastwick's *Letany* or at so nearly the same moment of Milton's *Lycidas*.

The most striking pages of Bastwick's pamphlet are those in which he holds the mirror up to the ways of prelates as seen by the man in the street. The thing is done with quite extraordinary verve. He calls before us the pompous sumptuosity of Lambeth. Heads must uncover before my lord's meat as it comes up from the kitchen; yet a man may not piss in my lord's court yard. He describes Laud passing daily to and from the court and the Star Chamber. Gentlemen go shouting 'to the folke before them, to put off their hats and to give place, crying roome, roome, my Lords grace is comming, tumbling downe and thrusting aside the little children a-playing there: flinging and tossing the poore costermongers and souce-wives fruit and pluddings, baskets and all into the Thames.' Yet in spite of his indignation that a man who ought to comport himself as a meek, humble and grave priest should appear a Jehu in the streets, Bastwick 'can scarce keep from laughter to see the grollery of it . . . the noyse of the Gentlemen crying roome, & cursing all that meet them and that but seeme to hinder their passage, on the other side seeing the wayling, mourning and Lamentation the women make crying out, save my puddings, save my codlings for the Lords sake, the poor tripes and apples in the meane tyme swimming like frogs about the Thames making way for his Grace to goe home againe.'[13]

Garrulous, incoherent bigots though the Puritan pamphleteers often were, they nevertheless had in them the vital rage for utterance. Neither the gaol nor the scaffold could stop them from talking, writing and printing. Lilburne was ready in the wings the moment his elders left the boards. Laud might as well have tried to lock up the wind.

Bastwick, writing in 1645, said that the men who came to visit him at the Gatehouse to applaud his *Letany* were 'Godly Citizens,' 'old Puritans of England and now Presbiterians, not one of them independent.'[14] Some of the younger men they brought in their train, though Bastwick describes them as 'towardly and fearing God,' were destined to turn out worse even than independents. Lilburne, a youth in his early twenties, was emphatically not one of the 'old Puritans,' but he was nevertheless an unmistakable product of their influence. The preachers and their more important adherents approached 1640 confidently expecting the establishment of such a society in England as had arisen in Geneva and in Scotland and was at the moment taking form in Massachusetts, a Utopia founded on the word of God as interpreted and determined by Puritan churchmen. Their principal supporters were men of substance, gentlemen, prosperous merchants and lawyers, men accustomed to command respect and not without some practical justification for thinking they might before long put their hands on political power and effect reform in church and state. They had no thought of overturning society and looked for no such end to their efforts as Lilburne and his kind were presently to conceive. But the preaching of the doctrine of faith, of the pattern of redemption, of the epic of spiritual war and adventure, had not been confined to the educated and respectable, to country gentlemen, members of the Inns of Court and masters of established businesses. The humble and the vulgar too, beset by grievances peculiar to their lot, had souls to be saved, and the preachers welcomed all who would listen and be moved. There were many such in London, rough countrymen but recently uprooted and arrived in town, poor apprentices, artisans and petty tradesmen, needy, ill-mannered men with their hearts full of their wrongs and their heads full of the mystical populism of the Bible. They were not difficult to convert to a doctrine which taught or seemed to teach them to look into their own untutored breasts for evidence of the justification, sanctification and glorification of the poor.

Such a man was Lilburne, a cloth-merchant's apprentice, who was made into a saint and a demagogue by the Puritan epic of spiritual warfare.[15] He became imbued with Puritan religious ideas in their most enthusiastic form as a lad serving his time in London during the crucial decade that followed the dissolution of the Parliament of 1628 and witnessed the rise of Laud to power. The example of Prynne and Bastwick prompted him to stage an outbreak of his own and in behalf of his own kind against the prelates. The punishment he suffered for that act supplied him with occasion for emulating his betters too by turning pamphleteer. His pamphlets, composed in prison between 1638 and 1640, gave an account of their author's wrongs which outdid in journalistic vigor even the *Briefe Relation* of the experience of Prynne, Bastwick and Burton. They also presented Lilburne's spiritual autobiography and served as the prelude to his prolonged campaign for democracy and the rights of man. Nothing written at the time except Milton's *Lycidas* gives more intense expression of a personality or reveals a more striking personality totally devoted to essentially Puritan ideals. More vividly than anything else written at the moment they permit us to see into the mind and heart of the oncoming English mob. Lilburne's baptist associates repudiated him before he had run his course, and Baptist historians, notwithstanding their large claims for the service performed by their sect for liberty, have not cared to claim him. Cromwell at first aided and then made use of him but finally suppressed him. The historian Gardiner, following the example of his hero, Cromwell, is sympathetic to Lilburne in his early stages but concludes by disapproving of him as a dangerous demagogue. Other nineteenth-century historians, disliking demagogues, put him down as obstinate and quarrelsome. He undoubtedly was a danger and a nuisance to whosoever happened to be trying to govern the country. He asked too insistently to have rendered in a day what three hundred years have scarcely sufficed to bring forth. Yet for that very reason he is to the modern student one of the most significant figures of his time.

Lilburne turned out to be an agitator and a political journalist with a genius for dramatizing in his own person the most far-reaching implications of the Puritan Revolution. It has recently been shown that, with the astute, elusive Walwyn to clarify his ideas and act as party organizer in his and their support, he set forth in the decade of 1640 the doctrine and program which were to sweep through the world after 1776.[16] What has not been so clearly understood is the fact that Lilburne sprang directly out of the religious populism which had been seething under the surface of English life ever since the fourteenth century, which since 1570 had been, perhaps unwittingly, fomented by the Puritan preachers of the church, and which was now ready in the sects to break out in revolution. His mind and character were formed while he was an apprentice lad growing up in London among the common people who streamed into the city churches to hear such men as Sibbes, Gouge, Davenport, Norton, and John Goodwin, who read the books such men sent from the press and who, especially after 1632, flocked after the sectarian enthusiasts. We cannot, then, realize from what soil he—and in truth the democracy—sprang unless we can form some conception of the state of mind among the English populace which was suddenly to make the separatists of all sorts and the more radical independents the most important factor in the Puritan movement. Uprooted and swept this way and that by the confused forces of their age, plucked at on every side by contending interests cloaked in puzzling dialectic and cloudy image, common men in turning to the sects did not so much feel that they were abandoning the church as that the church had abandoned them to a doom from which, if they were to be saved at all, they must save themselves. What they had been hearing for more than a generation from the great learned preachers of the Puritan pulpits served only to strengthen such feelings and at the same time to quicken their sense of the wrongs they suffered, their impatience for reform and their anticipation of the triumph of the saints, whom naturally they identified with themselves. They were, of course, but following an ancient pattern. The failure of society to satisfy the needs and desires of common men upon the plane of this world had long been reflected in religious excitement and dissent. When the common lot grew more burdensome than patience would bear, customary modes of worship became emptied of meaning and people sought elsewhere for God. Whatever priests and rulers might do, he had not forgotten them. He would speak to them in their own hearts. None, indeed, to whom he did not speak or who would not listen could be counted as his children or claim to be of his church. No other church could in truth be except the church of Antichrist, and from that God's people were turned irresistibly away by the living word within them. They were the elect. God was no respecter of persons. He saved whom he chose or—a moot point, yet in the early stages of popular dissent a secondary one—any who chose to be saved. One thing was certain in either case. Every man had the same right to expect God's favor, and if any had the advantage, it was not the great, the rich or the learned but the multitudinous humble, poor and ignorant.

Laud could not stop the spread of such ideas by repressing Puritan lecturers and punishing a few of the more egregious Puritan pamphleteers. The danger, he well knew, was the recrudescence of something like Lollardry, but the wind of Lollardry was too strong by this time and had been blowing too long. The Puritan reformers had not, we must remember, planned to raise that wind. If they had succeeded in their reforming efforts in 1570, they certainly would have endeavored to keep it down. Permitted to preach and not to rule, they had, however, encouraged it to blow. That is, they supplied popular discontent on the religious plane with such leadership as had never been before. They were intellectuals devoted to circumventing the law and outwitting the constituted authorities. In language designed to be intelligible and exciting to everybody they set forth a religious doctrine which exalted the individual soul and urged it to expression and activity in all walks of life. The only check upon individualism which circumstances would permit them to acknowledge was, finally, nothing but the conscience of the individual himself. The result was a steady increase, under cover but breaking out every now and then, of Puritan populism.

There was always an infiltration of religious heresy from the continent into England just as there was always some homebred enthusiastic error among the lower classes. We first hear of Henry Nicholas and the Familists in Elizabeth's days. In 1627, Stephen Denison is inveighing at Paul's Cross against John Hetherington, a boxmaker, who had recently been punished by order of High Commission for keeping a conventicle and preaching familism.[17] In 1636, Thomas Heywood is assailing 'Two infamous upstart Prophets, Richard Farnham, Weaver of Whitechapell, and John Bull, Weaver of St. Butolphs Algate, now Prisoners, the one in *Newgate*, and the other in *Bridewell*' for following their own humors in religion.[18] If the liberty of button makers, cobblers and weavers is not curbed, will 'not all grow into confusion and disorder, and returne into that stupidity of ignorance which swayed in the World before the true Religion was first propagated?' The agitation of boxmakers, button makers, cobblers and weavers might, however, have remained as inconclusive as it had ever been but for the countenance and aid such men received after 1570 from the spiritual brotherhood. Most important were the renegades from the ranks of the Brahmins to those of the religious demagogues. They were the real leaders of the Puritan left wing, of the separatists and enthusiasts, in the early stages of the movement. We have seen that Brownism was the work of a disciple of Richard Greenham at Cambridge. John Robinson, leader of the Leyden, later the Plymouth, congregation, and his friend John Smyth, father of the English baptists, were also Cambridge men. Harrisson, Barrow, Greenwood, Johnson, Jacobs, Bradshaw, Ainsworth, Everard, Randall, Eaton, John Goodwin, Saltmarsh, and Knollys may be named as typical of the many Puritan academic intellectuals who in some marked degree went over to the popular, the independent or separatist, generally the enthusiastic, side, where presently they inspired a host of button makers and the like also to take up the preaching of the word.

One effect of the restrictions placed by Laud upon Puritan preaching in the pulpits of the church was to turn the excited rabble after 1630 more and more to the ministrations of such men. Puritan Brahmins yielded under pressure or fled to Holland or New England. Puritans of more reckless temper, educated and uneducated, whom it was more difficult for Laud to track down and still more difficult to quell, remained in England and redoubled their numbers, their activities and their influence. Now, in the decade of 1630, while Lilburne was growing up in London, was the time when the Puritanism of conventicle and tub, in a word populistic Puritanism, began to flourish and, under continuing pressure first from the prelates and then from the more moderate Puritans, rapidly became the decisive element in the whole revolutionary movement. Evidence in print for this rise of dissent on the eve of 1640 is naturally not to be looked for in abundance before that date. Directly the Long Parliament swept Laud from power, however, the press began to turn it out. The defenders of law and order seem to have been at first the most active in letting readers know what had been going on. The spate of pamphlets against 'mechanick' preachers begins; the mention of a few titles must suffice for our purpose: *The Brownists Conventicle: or an assemble of Brownists, Separatists, and Non-Conformists, as They met together at a private house to heere a Sermon of a brother of theirs neere Algate, being a learned Felt-maker; A Discoverie of Six women preachers, in Middlesex, Kent, Cambridgeshire, and Salisbury,* a work which mingles pious pornography with the baiting of heretics, as does also *The Brownists Haeresies Confuted Their Knavery Anatomized, and their fleshly spirits painted at full, in a true History of one Mistres Sarah Miller of Banbury in Oxfordshire, Wherein is contained the preaching of a Barber; A Nest of Serpents Discovered or, A Knot of old Heretiques revived, Called The Adamites,* with an indecent wood-cut; *Religions Enemies, With a brief and ingenious Relation, as by Anabaptists, Brownists, Papists, Familists, Atheists, and Foolists, sawcily presuming to tosse Religion up in a Blanquet.* John Taylor, the water-poet, was ready to begin the long series of verse satires against Puritans which was to culminate in *Hudibras.* He gives us *A Swarme of Sectaries, and Schismatiques: Wherein is discovered the strange preaching (or prating) of such as are by their trades Coblers, Tinkers, Pedlers, Weavers, Sow-gelders, and Chymney-Sweepers.*

> When Women preach, and Coblers Pray,
> The fiends in Hell, make holiday,

says Taylor or another versifier in *Lucifers Lacky, or The Devils New Creature, Being the true Character of a dissembling Brownist, whose life is hypocriticall, instructions Schismaticall, thoughts dangerous, Actions malicious, and opinions impious.* How, finally, the vulgar Puritan enthusiast of 1640 comported himself in the eyes of his betters is well set forth by Richard Carter in *The Schismatick Stigmatized*:

And in stead of Orthodoxe Divines, they set up all Kinde of Mechanicks, as Shooe-makers, Coblers, Taylers, and Botchers: Glovers, who preach of nothing but Mag-pies and Crows, Boxe-Makers, and Button-Makers, Coach-men, and Felt-makers, and Bottle-Ale-sellers, these predicant Mechanicks, and lawlesse lads do affect an odde kind of gesture in their Poopits, vapouring and throwing heads, hands and shoulders this way, and that way, puffing and blowing, grinning, and gerning,

shewing their teeth, and snuffling thorow their noses: hereby they as-
tonish and amaze the poor ignorant multitude, perswading them that
he is a fellow that looketh into deeper matters, than the common sort:
when indeed he hath lately rub'd over some old moth-eaten Schismaticall
Pamphlet: then he stampeth with his feet, and belaboureth the poore
Cushion, and maketh the dust thereof flye about both his eares, beating
the Pulpit with both his fists, in a passion of blinde zeale, able to drive
his unlucky Auditors out of their little wits, or seven sences.

Such is a small sample of the hostile evidence published in 1641 to
what had been going on under the surface just before. But there was
also evidence of another character. Most pertinent, perhaps, for its
personal bearing upon Lilburne, is what we learn of William Kiffin.
The original English sects, as we have seen, frequently sought refuge
in Holland. As events moved forward, many of them returned in
order to make their way actively if obscurely among the lower classes
in London. Especially noteworthy was the congregation of separatists
which Henry Jacob, a graduate of Oxford turned sectary, brought
back as early as 1616 to settle in Southwark, from now on a center for
heretics and radicals of various sorts. Under a succession of leaders
these people kept together through the vicissitudes of the ensuing
twenty years until in 1638 they divided after the fashion of such bodies,
one group drawing off to form a congregation of Particular Baptists.
Among the latter was numbered William Kiffin, a friend of Lilburne's,
of the same age and in similar circumstances.[19]

Kiffin's account of his youthful years, written after the Restoration,
though it discreetly avoids mention of what must have been the most
exciting external events in his early career, brings to light some of the
circumstances in which both the author and his friend Lilburne grew
up and illustrates as well how pervasive was the influence of the spiritual brotherhood among the lower classes. Kiffin was born in 1616,
orphaned by the plague in 1625, and then cheated out of his inheritance. In 1629, he says, he was apprenticed to a mean calling. Up to
the age of fifteen he had no sense of God's grace, but then, beginning
'to consider . . . [his] . . . outward estate,' he grew 'quite melancholy.'[20] He was soon aroused by the preaching of Thomas Foxley,
John Norton, John Davenport and Lewis du Moulin. Foxley, an
Emmanuel College man, lecturer at St. Martin's in the Fields, was

suppressed and imprisoned by Laud and later released by parliament. Norton, also hailing from Cambridge, preached in various pulpits about London until his departure for New England in 1634, where he eventually became John Cotton's successor and biographer. Davenport, later of New Haven, Connecticut, we have already encountered as John Goodwin's predecessor at St. Stephen's, Coleman Street, and as one of the feoffees for impropriated tithes. Du Moulin, 'who preached at the church by London stone,'[21] was the son of the French reformer and refugee, Pierre du Moulin, a professor at Cambridge. After hearing these men, 'being by this time arrived at the age of 17 years,' Kiffin read Thomas Goodwin's *Childe of Light* and Thomas Hooker's *The Souls Preparation for Christ* and came under the spell of John Goodwin. At about the same time, he and 'several young men who diligently attended on the means of grace,' all apprentices like himself, took to meeting for an hour on Sundays before morning lecture in order to pray, communicate their experiences, repeat a sermon and read scripture. The emigration of so many preachers after 1633 to New England set Kiffin to puzzling over the question of conformity and to searching the scriptures still more earnestly. The upshot was that, influenced in part by Jeremiah Burroughs, who was later one of the independents of the Westminster Assembly, he joined what he calls 'an Independent congregation.'[22] This was clearly the congregation of separatists in Southwark to which reference has already been made. Thus did Laud help to make a baptist out of Kiffin. Meanwhile Lilburne had got himself into trouble, and Kiffin was almost certainly one of those who gave him countenance and help. During his two years in the Fleet, Lilburne found means to convey out of prison and to the press the writings he composed in his own defense. Kiffin may well have been one who aided in this. It was this friend, at any rate, who in 1641 sponsored the triumphant republication of Lilburne's account of his defiance of the prelates and of his trial and punishment.[23]

Kiffin himself left no direct statement of the ideas which circulated among the people or occupied his own thoughts in these early years. There did not, however, lack other spokesmen for the sects directly after 1640. The two most notable were not themselves sectaries at all, though it is obvious that they were intimately familiar with sectarian notions. Of Lord Brooke's noble presentment of the ideas of the humble prophets of the conventicles, it will be necessary to speak a little later. William Walwyn, a man of very different origin but of very similar views, was a wealthy merchant who had for some time made it his business to inquire into the reasons why the sects were persecuted and therefore to observe their doings and to analyze what their preachers were saying.[24] He had read Puritan doctrine, but he had also read and learned to admire Montaigne in Florio's translation. He had come to believe, he said, that men were born free from sin and capable of living happily and prosperously together and that all their troubles arose from ignorance, deception, covetousness and intolerance. If they would learn, as they could, to act together like brothers for the common good in support of the commonwealth, particularly if they would refrain from using religion as an excuse for tyrannizing over one another, all would be well. Walwyn's ideas had obvious affinities to those of the baptist and other enthusiasts. He set them forth, indeed, in singularly lucid and ingratiating terms, as the very ideas which the sects were advocating. Walwyn's *Some Considerations* and *The Power of Love* were not published until 1642 and 1643 respectively. In 1641, however, appeared two curious little tracts, practically identical except for their titles, the one called *The Humble Petition of the Brownists*, the other *A New Petition of the Papists*.[25] If Walwyn was not the author of these, then someone else not a baptist and probably not a Catholic wrote them, but someone indoctrinated with the ideas concerning toleration which the baptists also held and equally gifted with the power of lucid, trenchant expression. Men differ in their religion, he says, and each man believes he has reason to believe his religion true. To force all men to the same faith will bring nothing but 'a mighty confusion.' To permit each to believe as he prefers will bring peace and the love of subjects to the king and state. As for 'Brownists, Puritants, Socinians, Arminians, Papists,' he reiterates in each case, 'let them alone.' 'Let everyone therefore follow his owne Religion so he be obedient to the State and temporall lawes certainely; that which is erroneous will in time appeare, and the professors of it will bee ashamed, it will perish and wither as a flower, vanish as smoake, and passe as a shadow.'

Lilburne was later to be associated with both Lord **Brooke** and Walwyn, and there can be little question that what these men **had to** say immediately after 1640 represented what some at least of the despised separatists had in mind before that date. The ideas are expressed, however, with a certain refinement and not with the fantastic exaggeration in which the enthusiasts of the conventicle set them forth and in terms of which Lilburne himself must first have heard them. For that we must turn to certain pamphlets which came from the preachers themselves, particularly to one by Samuel How, a leader of the congregation with which Kiffin himself was for a time associated; one by John Archer, a refugee in Holland; and one, sponsored by Kiffin, probably written by the famous baptist preacher, Hanserd Knollys. All three appeared between 1639 and 1641, later than those pamphlets in which Lilburne so boldly defied the bishops but representing beyond a doubt the kind of talk which must have been rife for several years before 1640 in the circles in which he moved. They are not exhortations from the pulpit to repentance. They are the expression, albeit fantastic and grotesque, of the insurgent democracy of common men who had hearkened to the pulpit, perhaps not wisely but certainly with enthusiasm.

The older and more respectable preachers, many of them silenced or banished after 1632, had repeatedly assured the people that common folk possessed all the wit and knowledge necessary to understand and believe the gospel. They had insisted that academic learning, though indispensable for the preacher, should never be obtruded in sermons. Everard in particular had eloquently described the confounding of the doctors in the temple by the youthful Jesus. If the spirit could directly teach the soul of a child or of any simple man, and if that teaching were all that was needed for the soul's good, what need any other, what need the teaching of the schools? Might not such teaching rather hinder than help salvation? Samuel How gave unequivocal answer to these questions in *The Sufficiencie of the Spirits Teaching without human learning: or a Treatise tending to prove humane Learning to be no help to the spirituall understanding of the Word of God*. This was published in 1639, frequently republished and in 1655 reissued with a postcript by Kiffin, by that time risen to be an important baptist leader. The author's method of argument, of course, was to wring scripture like a nose of wax to prove that learned men wring scripture in the same way to prove what they please but not what the Holy

Spirit intended men to believe. 'They do pervert all Scriptures to their own destruction, whenas the unlearned one, simple men and women having the Spirit of truth in them, shall rightly know them, and Gods mind in them for their great comfort.' Learning is a handicap to the soul. The Christ within the saint, like Christ in the temple, knows better than all the doctors of the universities. How was a cobbler and, dying in 1640 before the Long Parliament, was buried with some noise in Finsbury Fields.[26] He and his sermon, which was several times reprinted, became notorious. Lilburne in the Fleet, writing an indignant letter to the Wardens dated 4 October 1640, threatens to have it 'claimed up upon the Posts, and made as publique as the Coblers Sermon.'[27] He also says that he has left orders in his will to have his body, 'if the Priests will not suffer it to be buried in the Church-yard,' 'layd beside the Coblers in Finsbury Fields.'[28]

Another humble preacher who was at the moment advancing similar views was John Spencer, author of *A Short Treatise Concerning the lawfullnesse of every mans exercising his gift as God shall call him thereunto*. This man was reputed to have been Lord Brooke's coachman and was commonly vilified as a horse-rubber.[29] What he has to say is clearly indicated in the title of his brief and rather simply phrased discourse. He can cite Calvin, Ursinus, William Perkins and Robert Bolton, not to mention scripture, to prove that unlearned men as well as learned, sometimes better than the learned, 'may all prophesie one by one, that all may learne and all bee comforted.' The absurdities in the arguments of men like How and Spencer are easy enough to perceive. It is more to the point to note their significance than to sneer or shudder at them. The tinker Bunyan was one of them. The learned preachers had practiced the art of concealing art in the pulpit and had taught the doctrine of the gift or calling to such effect that many who were not learned but felt inspired knew exactly how the spirit within them might be expected to express itself. They were, of course, ranging themselves against the dogma of exclusive salvation vested in the church and against the special privilege of the clergy. What they meant to men like Lilburne was that men had equal rights to seek truth in scripture and, no matter how poor or ignorant, to think and speak for themselves upon any subject, such as the salvation of their souls, which closely concerned them. This was Puritan individualism carried to its logical extreme, an apologia for the oncoming host of lay preachers, for all the demagogues, religious and political, of the morrow.[30]

By 1640 the more extreme separatists were persuaded not only that the saints knew all they needed for salvation in the next world but also that they were by the authority of the spirit destined in the not distant future to assume sovereignty in this one. For this conviction they were, again, largely indebted to the Puritan preachers of the generation just passing. We have already seen how eloquently the great Richard Sibbes and how vividly Thomas Taylor, that master of the homely similitude, had set forth the inevitable happy ending of the spiritual saga, the certainty of the saints' title to inherit heaven and sit at the right hand of God. Everard, representing as he does in so many ways the intensification of Puritan ideas by mystical enthusiasm, had told them they had the heavenly city already in their souls. To be sure, he had also warned them of the danger of yielding too literally to that notion, but such warnings were of little avail. The more certain the saint became that he was already a citizen of Zion the more eagerly and the more certainly did he expect Zion to commence soon here on earth. When the Long Parliament began its work, this meant to the respectable Puritan reformer the early establishment of the presbyterian Utopia; to the saints of the separation, it meant the millennium. For the latter dream no less than for the former, scripture supplied all the proof that was needed. This was primarily to be found in the books of Daniel and Revelation. These books could, of course, be understood by the aid of no light but that of the spirit; yet if aid were desired, there were plenty of learned authors, presumably with minds not darkened by their erudition, to supply the need. Thomas Brightman's *Apocalypsis Apocalypseos*, published in 1609 and translated in 1616; Johann Heinrich Alsted's *Diatribe de mille annis* of 1627; William Mede's tremendous *Clavis Apocalyptica* of 1627; these were among the most noted works explicating in elaborate detail an image for the eventual triumph of the elect, which captivated the imaginations of men of all classes and opened a particularly thrilling prospect to the most discontented, enthusiastic and uncritical. The conception as commonly understood was briefly as follows. Daniel saw the vision of the Four Monarchies, Babylon, Persia, Greece and Rome. The first three had been, and the fourth in the person and power of the pope was soon to be, overthrown. There would be a time of great confusion—what more obvious than that now or at any rate the nearly approaching year of the mystical date 1666 was the time meant?—and then the Fifth Monarchy, the kingdom of God on earth, would arise. John in his vision saw the angel descend from the skies, lay hold of the dragon and cast him into the bottomless pit, saw Christ descend to reign over the world, with his saints beside him, for a thousand years, saw the holy city coming down from God, a new heaven and a new earth.

Such dreams were warmly cherished among the London populace on the eve of the revolution. The gathering of the Long Parliament was a signal for them to appear in popular versions from the press. One of the most noted and perhaps the earliest came from John Archer, not strictly a separatist but an independent preacher, a friend of Thomas Goodwin, who also had found refuge in Holland when turned out of his pulpit at Allhallows in Lombard Street. His pamphlet, *The Personall Raigne of Christ upon Earth*, first published in 1641 and several times reprinted, was a technical exposition of the mysteries set forth in Daniel, chapters 2 and 7, and Revelation, chapters 10, 12 and 17.[31] It illustrates what ingenious uncritical dialectic could make out of apocalyptical poetry but does not reveal the vital excitement which gave it meaning in its own day to men like Lilburne.

For that we shall do better to turn to another pamphlet which appeared anonymously at about the same time with the title *A Glimpse of Sions Glory*. This little work almost certainly came from the pen of Hanserd Knollys.[32] It was published in 1641 to be sold by William Larner, the bookseller who also handled Lilburne's reprinted tracts, with an epistle signed by one W.K., in all probability William Kiffin. Knollys,[33] at this time about forty, came originally from Lincolnshire in the time of that separatist ferment which had produced John Robinson and John Smyth. He was a student at Cambridge in the days of John Preston. Ordained in 1629, he first took a parish in his native county and was of course effectually called to the preaching of the word. He says that it was a godly old woman at Gainsborough who first told him of those who were called Brownists. However that may be, he abandoned his living, renounced his ordination, cast in his lot with the dissenters, and began to preach sermons which brought on prosecution by High Commission in 1636. He escaped like many another to New England, whence he returned in December 1641 to become one of the leaders of the baptist communion and to foster the dream of Christ's return to this earth. The sentiments and the style of the sermons he published in 1646, *Christ Exalted,* are the same as those of the *Glimpse of Sions Glory* of 1641. His faith in the millennium found final expression in his *Exposition on the Whole Book of the Revelation* of 1689, a discourse on 'The glorious State of the Church of God in the New Heaven and New Earth, in these Latter Days.' Kiffin writes shortly after the author's death in 1691 that he had known him for above fifty-four years, which would mean that the apprentice had had some sort of acquaintance with the preacher at about the time of the latter's prosecution in 1636.[34] It is probable that the two came more closely together soon after Knollys' return from America in 1641, and certain that a few years later and for many years afterwards they were intimately associated. Kiffin in 1641 was, with the help of William Larner, seeing to the republication of his friend Lilburne's account of his recent trial and imprisonment. Nothing is more likely than that he should have carried *A Glimpse of Sions Glory* to the same printer and the same bookseller at the same moment or that the author of that tract should have been his friend Knollys. The usefulness of the work, says W.K., the author of the epistle, with a modesty which clearly suits Kiffin, is 'beyond my reach or weake judgement to prescribe; and indeed my commendation of it doth but darken it, I being so far below the matter and the Author.'

A Glimpse of Sions Glory is a moving expression of the species of religious Utopianism to which the mysticism of the sects, especially their enthusiasm for the democracy of the saints, inevitably conduced in the circumstances of revolution and under the influence of the doctrine of the second coming of Christ and the dream of the Fifth Monarchy. Out of the desperation of the poor and humble arose hope of the millennium, and the writer of *A Glimpse of Sions Glory* has the gift of putting that hope into eloquent terms. It was a hope, moreover, to which the actualities of the moment seemed to offer some promise of fulfilment. In the turmoil of the Bishop's Wars and the summoning of parliament, what could seem more likely than that the latter days were at hand in which Christ was to come again and begin his thousand-year-long reign? As for the saints who were to rule in triumph beside him, who were they but the poor? Were not the poor singled out for possession by the spirit? 'The voice of Jesus Christ reigning in his Church comes first from the Multitude, the Common People, . . . God useth the common People and the Multitude to proclaime that the Lord God omnipotent reigneth: As when Christ came at first, the poore receive the Gospell, not many Wise, not many Noble, not many Rich, but the Poore.' 'You that are of meaner rank,' the author exclaims, 'common People, be not discouraged; for God intends to make use of the common People in the great Worke of preaching the Kingdome of his Sonne.' Let them pray, let them make their voices heard. Parliament will hearken to them and defend the saints against Antichrist. And once the yoke of Antichrist is cast off—the idealistic baptist touch—there will be 'liberty of Churches' and men will be free to search for truth that knowledge may be increased.[35]

Such were some of the ideas afloat among the London populace on the eve of the Long Parliament, and it was undoubtedly with some such notions in their heads that Lilburne and probably Kiffin too went to visit Bastwick in his prison in 1637. Kiffin's career, it turned out, was to fall into the normal pattern of the authentic dissenter. He grew to be a tall pillar of the conventicle and of the cloth trade. Withdrawing deeper and deeper into the bosom of his own congregation of Particular Baptists, he repudiated Lilburne, preached, made money, won the respect of Charles II and Clarendon, and lived to enter into the peace of the eighteenth century. Thus he exemplified the future course of much of the lower-class discontent of the Puritan age. As often as not the waves of popular revolutionary excitement were destined to run out upon the flats of sectarianism sunned by commercial prosperity. The poor would not attain the millennium, but fired by a glimpse of Zion's glory many a poor man would make his way to social and financial security while his early enthusiasm congealed into the fundamentalism and asceticism of indurated dissent.

It was not to be so with Lilburne. Before the Long Parliament met or the tracts of Knollys, Archer and How were printed, he gave by far the most signal expression that had yet been given to the aspirations which prompted separatism. He was called and converted after the fashion of his kind, and he recorded his experience in his own way. He became a saint and had the gift that might have led him to become a baptist preacher like Kiffin. But the same gift could go to the making of a tribune of the people. Baptist enthusiasm and mysticism pointed also toward democratic idealism; the sect carried also the seed of the popular political party. It was upon the attempt to develop these possibilities that Lilburne was to spend his strength before seeking and perhaps finally finding rest among the quakers.

His account of his early years and of his first experience as a sufferer in the cause of liberty permits us to piece together an unusually detailed and vivid picture of the conditions which the world offered to a poor youth of twenty-one at the eve of the Puritan Revolution. It also enables us to glimpse the mental life which Puritanism prepared for him. He was, as he boasted on more than one occasion, the son of a gentleman in the county of Durham, and his immediate forbears had held petty posts at court. Just at the time when he was being punished for unlicensed printing, his father Richard was attempting to persuade a court at Durham to allow a lawsuit in which he was involved to be settled by combat between hired champions.[36] The father was also involved in litigation which earned for him the enmity of Laud and which was not rendered more successful by his son's activities against the prelates. The son was born at Greenwich, probably in 1614, and sent north to be reared at the family's home. Upon certain occasions he claimed to have been educated in good schools, to have learned Latin and even to have been 'a little entred into the Greeke also.'[37] Upon other occasions, he made a virtue of knowing no tongue but English.[38] About 1630 his father brought him to London and apprenticed him to one Thomas Hewson, a cloth-merchant, 'neare London stone.'[39] Upon one occasion the youth had his master up before the Chamberlain of London over some grievance, but 'ever after lived at peace with him,' never wronged him of a groat, never was taxed by him with one base action, never quarreled, never gave or took a box on the ear or anything like it.[40] After five or six years of this, when Hewson talked of giving up his business, Lilburne begged and secured his release and began to look about him. He was a poor lad and it behooved him to hit upon some means of picking up a little capital with which to start out

by himself. He was led by his necessity and by some of his acquaintances and avocations into a dangerous course.

Lilburne's duties as a trusted servant were not so onerous but that
he found on several days in the week spare time which, he says, he
spent in reading. What he read we know from his own statement and
from the numerous references in the pamphlets which he wrote immediately afterwards. The first books he puts on his list are, as one would
expect, the Bible and Fox's *Book of Martyrs*. Next come the works of
Luther, Calvin and Beza, followed by Cartwright, Perkins, du Moulin
and Rogers. He also names Henry Burton, who preceded him by only
a little to the pillory, and concludes by claiming to have read while
still in Thomas Hewson's shop a 'multitude of other such like Books
with histories that I had bought with my own money.'[41] The picture
which he drew of himself in his early pamphlets was patterned upon
that image of the spiritual warrior enlisted under the banners of Christ
which had probably come to him in the sermons of a score of Puritan
preachers. The publications he chose to refer to most frequently in his
printed attacks on the bishops were naturally such as were especially
directed against prelacy. A little later the pages of his tracts are filled
with instances of popular right opposed by royal tyranny, drawn from
Speed, Holinshed, Martin, Daniel and Raleigh, the works of some of
whom at least were probably among the histories Lilburne bought
with his own money while still an apprentice. That he also began at
this early date his avid reading of law is probable but not so clear.
Popular reports of matters like the Petition of Right certainly reached
him. When he was himself presently arraigned, he showed that he was
familiar with the usual plea of the non-conformists against jeopardiz-
ing themselves by consenting to the ex officio oath, and he cites the
well-known argument against the oath published by Nicholas Fuller.[42]
Coke's *Institutes*, the source of those notions about Magna Charta with
which he was to plague later opponents, was not yet in print, but he
may already have come upon the English translation, called *The Doctor and Student*, of St. Germain's facile statement of the law of nature,
a book of which he made good use in 1645.[43]

The most important influence that came to Lilburne from books in
his prentice years was without a doubt that of the Puritan writers who
brought to him the doctrine of religious individualism clothed in its

well-known myths. It was this, further fortified by reading of history and law, which he soon attempted to transpose into political action. He would appear not to have been admitted to a congregation of saints until after his suffering at the hands of the bishops. He dated his actual conversion from the hour when he stood in the pillory with a shouting mob before him. 'I am but acquainted,' he wrote from prison in 1638, 'with very few of them,' the 'loving Brethren,' that is, 'which publiquely professe the same truth for which I suffer,' 'being never yet in any of their Congregations in England.' This statement, one suspects, had something in it of dramatic exaggeration. It suited Lilburne to make more of the direct influence of the Holy Spirit upon him at the moment of his suffering than of the prior influence of the saints. He quickly adds that, though the latter be 'but the contemptible ones of the world, yet my soule hath taken very much delight in their society, beyond the rest of my other friends, which though it be but little that I have enjoyed, and that but from a very few of them, yet it hath been very delightsome to me, because they have given declaration to my spirituall eyes and understanding, that their souls are enriched with the treasures of God.'[44] Chief among the friends to whom he is here referring were undoubtedly Edmond Rozer and William Kiffin. Little is known concerning the former except that he was a baptist preacher who together with Kiffin and others signed the manifesto in which the baptists repudiated Lilburne and the Levellers in 1649.[45] Lilburne in 1649 calls him 'teacher to the Congregation where I was a Member,' 'my pastor or teacher,' 'my familiar friend and neighbor, and fellow-professor of Religion, (conversant at my Masters house from the beginning of my coming to him).' The fact of Lilburne's early friendship with Kiffin is beyond dispute, but the circumstances of their relationship can only be guessed at. Lilburne might have been one of the group of apprentices with whom Kiffin met for prayer and religious conference, but we cannot tell. In 1649 he refers to the latter as 'once my servant.'[46] What this means, except perhaps that Lilburne employed Kiffin in the publication of his pamphlets while he was in prison, it is impossible to say. Kiffin, as we have seen, wrote an epistle for the republication of certain of these pamphlets in 1641, the bookseller being William Larner, who was probably another early friend and who functioned later as a publisher for the Levellers. The one inference which is perfectly clear from all this is that there was enough in Lilburne's personal associations with baptists prior to 1636 to account at least in part for the mystical religious enthusiasm with which he endured his persecution at the hands of Laud.

It was Rozer, he says, who 'brought me in *anno* 1636 acquainted with Dr. Bastwick then prisoner in the Gatehouse, whom after I visited constantly.'[47] From Bastwick he learned something besides enthusiasm. The doctor found him, though honest and religious, 'but a meere country courtier, and very rough hewen.'[48] He taught the youth how to put off his hat and make a leg like a gentleman, and he polished his rustic speech. He taught him something more. Lilburne was not well instructed at that time, Bastwick says, in the controversies of the church, and the older man repaired that lack. The youth was permitted to join the circle of those who enjoyed the latter's *Letany*, learned to look upon the author together with William Prynne as heroes in the struggle against prelatical tyranny, and conceived a hazardous plan to do something himself in the cause. Incidentally, it would appear, he may have seen a way to make some money which would help him to get started in the cloth trade. The business of publishing illicit attacks upon the bishops was attended by profits as well as risks. The merry old John Wharton, at whose instance Bastwick had written his *Letany*, was a hot-presser in Bow Lane over eighty years old who had, it would seem, traded on the side in contraband pamphlets for many years and had been in and out of gaol more than once.[49] Lilburne made his acquaintance and perhaps received from him suggestion for the plan he now proceeded to put into effect. He begged for a copy of the *Letany* in order that he might carry it off to Holland and get it printed and smuggled back into England for common circulation. Wharton or his aids, Edmund Chillington and John Chilliburne, were to receive the books when they arrived. They even had some sort of access to 'Sam Baker the Prelate of Londons Chaplaine';[50] this, however, probably proved to be Lilburne's undoing. Bastwick, after he had quarreled with his pupil, said that it was not so much zeal for the cause which put the latter upon this employment as an eye for his own honor and profit. The young man told him, he says, that his stock was very small, but fifty or sixty pounds, to begin business upon, but if he could have a copy of 'my Letany and my answer to the Bill of Information put up against me in the Star-chamber . . . he doubted not but hee should get money enough by them.'[51] Bastwick claims that Lilburne did indeed boast later of having made threescore pounds in a few days by the transaction. The doctor disapproved the scheme, when first proposed, and disliked the looks of the fellow Lilburne introduced as his lieutenant. Nevertheless, the older man consented, and the younger presently betook himself to Holland with a copy of the *Letany* in his pocket.

Lilburne when brought to trial roundly denied that he had had anything to do with printing Bastwick's pamphlet, but in doing so he either quibbled or told less than the truth. He was ready a few years later to claim credit for the great services he had at this time performed for Bastwick and Prynne. Certainly he went to Holland, banished, he said, because the prelates knew that he was intimate with the former, and he boasted that he spent his time there 'not like a drone, but for the welfare of England.' 'I both early and late without wearinesse, travelled without the assistance of any mans purse but my owne, and my industry; by boat, and shipping by water, and on my feet by land.'[52] Perhaps he did not actually see to the printing of the *Letany* and its despatching to England, but he learned enough about such matters to stand him in good stead a little later. The *Letany* was printed, and several thousand copies were sent to Chilliburne and Chillington. Those two were promptly caught by the authorities and as promptly put the blame on Lilburne. When the latter returned to London in person in December 1637, he was seized by the pursuivants of the prelate and sent to the Fleet by order of the privy council. On the thirteenth of February he and Wharton were arraigned in Star Chamber for the unlawful printing and publishing of libelous and seditious books.

Lilburne could not hope to escape punishment similar to that which had overtaken the men he had been emulating and assisting. But his attitude and behavior under persecution showed a significant difference. Prynne and Bastwick, especially, had defied authority chiefly on the ground that they held the truth and the prelates falsehood. Lilburne was just as certain that he was right and his opponents wrong, but he chose to argue not only for his opinion but even more for his native capacity and title to have an opinion and to express it. First of all, taking his cue from the non-conformists who had refused the ex officio oath before the High Commission, he too refused to put himself in peril by swearing to answer the questions of the court. He denied the accusation against him and defended his rights as an Englishman under the law of England to think and speak as his own conscience might direct. He was sentenced to be fined £500, to be whipped at the cart's tail from the Fleet to the old Palace Yard at Westminster, to stand there in the pillory, and thence to be sent back to prison. In the Fleet before the execution of his sentence, he found means to write a flaming account of his trial with a defense of the position he had taken. This he also contrived to have printed, in Holland it would appear, and circulated, contrary to regulations, about the streets of London. It was called *A Christian Mans Triall*.

The sentence was executed on 18 April 1638, and again the sufferer was able before long to get his story before the public in print, this time with the significant title *A Worke of the Beast*. What beast, that public, which thought it understood the true meaning of St. John's Apocalypse, would be sure to understand. There is probably no reason to doubt the substantial accuracy of Lilburne's account of the circumstances of his trial and punishment and of his own words and behavior. He seized the opportunity for making himself known to the mob and for setting before it those notions he had been learning from the Bible, the Puritan preachers, the enthusiastic sectaries and the English chronicles. On the morning of his punishment, 'attended,' he says, 'with many Staves and Halberts, as Christ was when he was apprehended by his Enemies,' he was stripped to the waist, led to Fleet Bridge and tied to the cart. 'I have whipt many a Rogue,' said the executioner, 'but now I shall whip an honest man.' The cart proceeded; the lash fell; Lilburne prayed. 'God hardened my back, and steeled my reynes, and tooke away the smart and payne of the stripes from mee.' By-standers, at Fleet Bridge, in the Strand, at Charing Cross, bade him be of good cheer. 'Soe I am,' he said, 'for I rest not in my owne strength, but I fight under the banner of my great and mightie Captaine the Lord Jesus Christ who hath conquered all his Enemies, and I doubt not but through his strength I shall conquer and overcome all my sufferings.' As he was passing Whitehall and entering the gate at Westminster, a multitude came out to look and to ask what was the matter. 'Against the Law of God, against the law of the Land, against the King or State,' Lilburne replied, 'I have not committed the least offence . . . but only I suffer as an object of the Prelates cruelty and malice.' One of the wardens told him to hold his tongue, but he bade the fellow to 'meddle with his own businesse, for I would speake come what would.' They let him rest in a tavern at the conclusion of the whipping and offered to let him off standing in the stocks if he would confess his fault. He refused and mounted the pillory. His judges were looking out at the Star Chamber window just above. Lilburne made obeisance to them and put his head in the hole.

It was not customary to deny to a man in such a position the privilege of speaking. Lilburne, finding himself on a platform with a crowd before him, took full advantage of the privilege. He began by telling his story and accusing the court of persecuting him contrary to the law, to the Petition of Right, and to the law of nature. He then went on to praise Prynne, Bastwick and Burton, who had only a few months before stood in the same spot, and to recommend in particular the arguments of Bastwick against the bishops. One had, he said, but to read the book of Revelations to learn that the pope was the Beast of the Apocalypse, the bishops were the creatures of the pope, their calling was by *iure diabolico*, and any, even the godly and gifted, who preached by their authority—the separatist touch—were rebels against Christ. Repent, he cries, study the book of Revelations, gird on your spiritual armor, 'quit your selves like good & faithful Souldiers, and fear no coulors; the victory and conquest is ours already.' 'God hath chosen the foolish things of the world to confound the things which are mighty.' He is himself a young man. He speaks, nevertheless, in the name of the Lord. 'And as I am a Souldier fighting under the banner of the great and mightie Captaine the Lord Jesus Christ . . . I dare not hold my peace, but speake unto you with boldnes in the might and strength of my God the things which the Lord in mercy hath made knowne unto my Soule, come life come death.'

At this point, Lilburne says, 'there came a fat Lawier, I do not know his name,' and ordered him to stop. 'Sir,' he replied, 'I will not hold my peace . . . though I be hanged at Tiburne for my paines.' The lawyer rushed off to the Lords in the Star Chamber. Lilburne talked on, put his hand in his pocket, pulled out three of Bastwick's pamphlets and scattered them to the crowd. 'There is part of the bookes for which I suffer, take them among you, and read them, and see if you finde anything in them against the Law of God, the Law of the Land, the glory of God, the honour of the King or state.' He was going on to recount the glory and inward happiness of the spiritual war against wickedness in high places when the fat lawyer returned with the warden of the Fleet and a fresh order from the Star Chamber. The three books were ordered to be brought in and the prisoner to be gagged. Lilburne stood out the rest of his time in the stocks, stamping with his feet because he could not speak. Blood issued from his mouth.[53]

The ruthlessness of Lilburne's punishment was the work of men exasperated by a situation they could no longer control. They had put Prynne and Bastwick in prison for writing pamphlets, only to have them from prison write even more offensive attacks and get them published. The authorities had redoubled punishment on the authors and seized their agents, only to have Lilburne from the very scaffold scatter some of the same libels to the mob. The wardens of the Fleet had orders, therefore, to give that reckless spiritual warrior short shrift upon his return to prison. They badgered him about those pamphlets he had somehow managed to carry about his person even to the pillory and which, it would appear, the authorities had not been able to recover from the crowd. The lords commanded that he be put in irons, kept in solitary confinement, denied the resort of friends, and particularly that he be not supplied with money from any friend, and that the warden 'take especiall notice of all letters, writings, & books brought unto him, and seize and deliver the same unto their lordships.'[54] Nothing, however, could completely avail to stop Lilburne from making his cause known. He had determined friends such as Kiffin and other separatists and the sympathy and aid of his fellow prisoners.

At least seven petitions and pamphlets now extant in print were written by Lilburne in prison between April 1638 and his release at the close of 1640. Of these, four were immediately published. This does not include other writings to which he refers but of which no trace has since been found. The pamphlets published before 1640 were in all probability printed in Holland. In one of them the author declares that he has published his griefs 'unto the view of England, Scotland, Ireland and Holland.'[55] In another he says that he has lately written more sheets than all his previously published books put together, 'which many moneths agoe I sent into Holland to my Printer.' 'Canterburies Catchpoles took from me last yeare at the Custome house, almost two thousand of my books as they came from Amsterdam.' And in threatening the wardens of the Fleet with exposure of their cruelty, he declares that 'if there be but a Printing-house in any of the Cities in the Provinces of Holland, I will cause this Letter to be Printed.'[56]

Lilburne was the dramatic embodiment of that eagerness for emotional experience and expression which Puritanism had inspired in the people. His first task, as we have seen, was to get the story of his punishment into print. This he did in *A Worke of the Beast or A Relation of a most unchristian Censure, Executed upon Iohn Lilburne . . . With the heavenly speech uttered by him at the time of his suffering. Very usefull for these times.* An epistle, initialled F.R. by some friend, recommended the tract in the language of separatist enthusiasm. In succeeding publications, Lilburne went on with his war against prelacy and at the same time registered the emotional crisis through which he was himself passing at the moment. *Come out of her my people* included 'A Iust Apologie for the way of Totall Separation' and 'A Challenge to Dispute with them [the bishops] publickly before King & Councell.' This was written sometime during the summer of 1638 and published in the following year with an anonymous epistle by some separatist friend. About the same time Lilburne wrote to a female admirer a rapturous account (published 1645) of the state of his soul and alluded in passing to something he had also written on the 'heavenly Jerusalem or spirituall Syon.' The latter has not come to light, but a long *Answer to Nine Arguments*, directed against the established church and describing 'the nature and properties of a true Church and Ministry' was composed in 1638 and finally published in 1645. As the months of Lilburne's imprisonment went by and his war with the keepers of the Fleet, who had, of course, the difficult task of trying to stop the flow of his pen, developed, he began issuing petitions and outcries for relief and release. He was not supposed to have the use of writing materials, but he was finally permitted in December 1638 the help of a scribe in drawing up 'An humble Petition to his Maiesties Honorable Privy Councill, for maintenance that I famish not.' Shortly afterwards, the petition appeared in print, 'Published by a backe friend of the English Popish Prelates,' accompanied by a full account, called *The Poore Mans Cry*, of the wrongs the author was suffering. The friend appears himself to have been in exile, probably in Holland, where no doubt the pamphlet was printed. In May 1639, Lilburne managed to submit his complaints to the lord mayor and aldermen, and he speaks of multitudes of other petitions sent 'both to the King and the Nobles, joyntly and severally.' He also dispatched supplications to friends at The Hague to be submitted to the Queen of Bohemia, pleading for her intercession with her brother, the King of England.[57] None of these various petitions has come to light, but at the same time that he sent his plea to the lord mayor, he addressed another, which is still extant, 'To all the brave, couragious, and valiant Apprentizes of the honourable City of London, but especially those that appertain to the worshipfull Company of Clothworkers.' This begged the author's former associates to go, but without tumult, before the mayor and aldermen and to plead that he be removed from the Fleet to some other prison where he would be in less danger of being murdered. It was printed on a single sheet, and Lilburne's maidservant was committed to gaol for throwing copies of it among the apprentices one day when they were at their recreations in Moorfields.[58] A savage letter, finally, which Lilburne wrote to the Wardens of the Fleet in October 1640, was circulated in print just as the Long Parliament came together in November. No sooner had that body assembled than a petition in Lilburne's behalf was presented by Oliver Cromwell to the House of Commons. The prisoner's release was at once ordered, and a few months later his sentence was revoked. The lord mayor was presently compelled by a committee of the Lords to pay £10 for imprisoning Lilburne's maid, whose cause was pleaded by Lord Brooke and Lord Roberts.[59] When Lilburne's claim for reparations on account of his sufferings reached the House of Lords in 1645, John Bradshaw and John Cook were his counsel. They had no difficulty in securing an award for him. Collecting it was another story.[60] Freed from prison, meanwhile, Lilburne, estranged from his father, who also had been made to feel Laud's wrath, thought first of going abroad, but encouraged by parliament's interest in his case, he remained in England, went into partnership with his uncle in managing a brewery, married and, according to his own account, began to prosper. When the civil war broke out, he gave up his business and went off to fight in Lord Brooke's regiment.[61]

The career of Lilburne as tribune of the people and agitator for the rights of man began as truly as that of any Puritan saint with religious conversion, and his pamphlets of the moment were, as truly as the spiritual biography of any saint in the pages of Samuel Clarke, a confession of being by the grace of God called, justified and sanctified. There was only this difference. God did not see fit to call John Lilburne until he had a mob before him to witness his agony, and both the experience and the attending dramatic circumstances were described by the newly awakened saint with a power that few saints ever attained. Lilburne won many admirers by the exhibition he gave of spiritual fortitude. Among them was a woman, unknown to him before the event, 'one,' he says, 'that may enjoy all outward things that heart can desire.'[62] She had come to see him before his close imprisonment, had written to him afterwards, prayed for him 'whole dayes together . . . having your cheeks bedewed with teares of Joy in remembrance of me.' Lilburne derived great comfort from her letter and desired that he might have one hour's discourse with her face to face. She had told him that her soul was 'beyond measure refreshed to see my boldnesse, comfortableness in the Lord, that it became as marrow to your bones . . . to behold the great goodness of God in giving me such meeknesse, patience and smiling merrinesse, in my tender yeares.'[63] Thus marveling at the works of wonder God had done through him, she had asked him to write to her, assuring him that he cannot spend his time better than in continuing to fill her ears with such wonders. So, addressing her as his 'dear and loving friend and fellow heire (I hope) of the same kingdom with me,' his 'beloved Christian friend and sister,' he poured out the story of what had been happening to his soul. The effect was to show what Puritan preaching and the Bible had done to raise up such a character, to touch his lips with fire and to teach him to play the role of a young David of the people smiting the Goliath of prelacy. The religious evangelicism of later generations never undertook to float Lilburne's spiritual autobiography into general esteem, but Bunyan's *Grace Abounding* scarcely deserves a higher place in the literature of personal religious confession.

Lilburne tells his friend that he has hitherto been acquainted with but few of the 'loving Brethren, which publiquely professe the same truth for which I suffer . . . being never yet in any of their Congregations in England.' Yet he says at the same time that, though these men be but 'the contemptible ones of the world,' his soul has taken great delight in their society, 'beyond the rest of my other friends, which though it be but little that I have enjoyed, and that but from a few of them, yet it hath been very delightsome to me, because they have given declaration to my spirituall eyes and understanding, that their souls are enriched with the treasures of God.' There was undoubtedly some understatement here. Lilburne found it more dramatic to owe his conversion directly to God and to date it from the moment when God strengthened him to defy the Beast. 'The day of my publique suffering was the first time of the manifestation of what the Lord had revealed to me.'[64] He had already recounted that experience in *A Worke of the Beast*. Before that, he says in another pamphlet, 'I was only a Novice, but a very Idiot in the right wayes of God, having muddy affections,' fiery zeal but no 'inward principles,' 'no grounded spirituall knowledge.'[65] He went back to his prison convinced by what he had been able to do that God was with him.

God had brought it about that 'his poore, weake and young servant' should have the glory of opposing his enemies, the bishops 'who have for a hundred yeares together . . . troden underfoot the holy Citie and the Church of God which Iohn in his Revelation long since largely prophesied of.' Lilburne confesses to being 'but a poore weake young worme,' but God has revealed to him 'that which he hath hid from the great, mighty and wise men of the world'; he 'hath drawne my soule unto him, and made me one with himselfe.' 'All the time of my outward miserie and punishment, I did not so much as shew one sad or heavie countenance, nor declare the least signe of a discontented heart, but by the strength of my God, . . . I did glory in them, and triumph over them all, and made his, and my enemies, the Prelates and Priests (many of which did behold me) to gnaw their tongues for paine, . . . that they could not endure to behold the power of

God, which shined in me, nor to heare the truth of God, which he caused to proceed from me.'[66] So, in prison, in irons, lying in his boots in summer, forced by the cold to wear three pairs of stockings in winter, he sings and rejoices. He could set his friend reading for days, for weeks, the matter his soul is filled with. No place like prison for enjoying God, no comfort like disgrace endured for truth, no delights so pleasant as those to be found in naked Christ. 'For'—the note upon which all the enthusiasm of these saints of the people always converged—'he doth not chuse many rich, nor many wise . . . but the fools, ideots, base and contemptible poore men and women in the esteeme of the world.'[67] They are the ones who 'receive the Gospel and entertain the glad tidings of life and salvation,' and Lilburne's soul is 'in the present possession of the assured hopes of living for ever in a better life, even the life of glory, with my God of glory, in the Kingdom of Glory, that never shall have end.'[68]

The ecstasy of Lilburne's conversion overflowed in his other writings from prison. He may not, as he professes, have been more than slightly acquainted with separatists before this, but he was now nothing if not thorough in his championship of their ideas and their cause. He wrote at length to prove that adherence to the Church of England was sinful and unlawful and 'the way of Totall Separation (Commonly but falsly called Brownisme)' was the way of truth.[69] His proof was found by the aid of his own untutored heart in scripture. Christ and his apostles needed nothing better, 'never made use neither of Logicke nor Philosophy,' which are the inventions of the devil.[70] The learning of the apostles was not human learning, 'for none of them had it but Paul, and he renounced it,' but 'spirituall knowledge, divine learning, and insight into the Scripture.'[71] This, of course, is the only knowledge Lilburne boasts. 'I am a yong man and noe Scoller,' he proclaimed from the pillory.[72] He was but 'a stripling, that never studied Philosophy, Logick, Rhetorick, nor ever was at any Vniversity, to learne any Lattin, Greeke, or Hebrew.'[73] Nevertheless, he has the advantage over the great learned doctors of the world. The pure truth of the gospel is too homely a thing for them to embrace, stoop and submit unto. Yet logic, though he despises it, is not beyond his reach. He knows how to make mock syllogisms to confound syllogistic reasoning with ridicule. His adversaries are 'learned in the Phariseicall, Philòsical

[sic], deceivable learning of the world.' They have 'studied and beat their braines, in their Vniversities and elsewhere, for many yeares together.'[74] Notwithstanding all this, Lilburne has in six months in prison, thanks to them, got more knowledge of the mysteries of Godliness than is to be found among all the bishops in England. For what does all their logic come to, what finally have they with which to maintain their tottering authority, but violence? The 'Episcopall Rabbies . . . had no other Argument to convince me with, then to put a Gagg in my mouth.'[75] 'Their surest pley and infallible Arguments to convince me, was Clubb-Law, that is to say, take him Iaylour, and lay him in Irons, in the obscurest and basest place in your prison, and let the stone Walls and iron grates convince him, for we dare not meet him in the plaine feild, in a publick dispute, though he be but an unlearned youth.'[76]

He told the warden of the Fleet to let the archbishop know that, if the latter disliked anything his prisoner had said in the pillory, he should send for him, and Lilburne would justify it to his face; 'if I be not able to make it good before any nobleman in the Kingdome, let me loose my life.'[77] He told the attorney general that he wanted nothing so much as the opportunity to debate with the bishops before the king. He was eager to argue his case out with the priests and deacons of the church at Paul's Cross, and if they proved him wrong out of scripture, he was willing to recant in every city in the kingdom.

The fact was, of course, that Lilburne was not so ignorant as he pretended. He was the master of a new kind of knowledge. He was what Bible reading, preaching and the printing of English books brought forth for government to deal with. The apprentice had found time to read Puritan sermons, the *Book of Martyrs* and the English chronicles. Before he arrived for the first time in prison, he had become deeply versed in the wide-spreading literature of the Puritan revolt in all its forms, edifying and controversial, licit and illicit. All this had made him, not more disciplined, critical and well-balanced, but confident, ready of mind and intensely articulate. The separatists had taught him, if indeed he needed teaching, an overweening faith in the sufficiency of the common man when armed with scripture and enlightened by the spirit. Bastwick, Prynne and the pedlers of prohibited print had initiated him into the dangerous game of fighting prelacy with pamphlets. They had moreover shown him how, if caught, he could win attention by defying authority. For the moment he seemed committed to the dream of the New Jerusalem, to the belief that all hope lay in the sect, and to the conviction that what stood in the way of that hope was prelacy. But he was not the typical religious enthusiast or sectarian. Time would show that the conventicle was no refuge for such as he, and that the Fifth Monarchy was not his goal. The whip, the pillory and the gag, by which the Star Chamber sought to silence him, set him before his public. Having found his public, he found his vocation. God called him at that moment, but called him to make a speech and then to print it, to enact before the mob the part of Jesus Christ in the person of a poor young man, lately balked of his hope of getting started in the cloth trade, laying low with arguments the great Beast of the Apocalypse. Freedom to exercise his gift for utterance and leadership, for demagoguery if one will, freedom to enjoy the right to an opinion and a voice in public life, these, whether he knew it or not, were Lilburne's real objectives. They were the same objectives which were at the moment hardening under fiery conviction in the mind of Milton, a man in one way a world removed from Lilburne but in another his spiritual next of kin.

VIII

Church-Outed by the Prelates

THE year 1638 witnessed the appearance in print of still another attack on prelacy.[1] *Lycidas* was published early in that year as part of a collection of academic elegies by various young Cambridge graduates on the death of one of their university comrades. The blazing distinction of its author's genius and character has made it difficult for later generations to understand clearly how intimately and completely he was related to his own time. Milton's poem, with its extraordinary denunciation of the prelatical church, has become one of the most admired poems in literature. Yet, it was an expression of the same spirit which had been long making itself heard in the Puritan pulpit and which was at the moment clamoring in the reckless pamphlets of Prynne and Lilburne. Edward King, the subject of Milton's lament, was a Christ's College man who at the time of his death had just entered the church. Milton, also of Christ's, had been bred for the same career but, disgusted by the conditions imposed by Laud, had recently determined to forgo the pulpit and to further reformation as a scholar, a writer, a poet. *Lycidas* was not regarded by him as in any sense the fruition of this plan but as something written for an occasion. It was nevertheless struck out of the heat of his resentment at the condition of the church, and it voiced his decision not to be defeated in his ambition to use his talent in the service of the word.

More than any other English poet Milton may be said to express the moral energy of his race. He presents the soul of his people in its most masculine phase, not as it has turned aside to love, nature or religion for escape, consolation or rapture, but as it has wreaked its energies on the ruling of men and the making of laws. For him to have stood apart from the struggle that convulsed his age would have been impossible, and equally impossible would it have been for him to have chosen any side in the struggle save the one he did. The result has been that it has proved impossible for most of his readers to judge him without personal feeling. The cardinal spiritual experience of too many of the descendants of the Puritans has been the struggle to forswear allegiance to Puritan ideals and the Puritan code, to refuse service to the God of their fathers in order to save their souls another way. Hence they have inclined to the belief that freedom, grace and beauty, gentle manners, good taste and high literary culture can never have associated, at any rate never happily or for long, with the Puritan temper and way of life. Hence too Milton has always seemed to many something of an enigma. What should he, the great artist and apostle of freedom, be doing among the Philistines? How could it be that he should be an exception to the rule stated by Matthew Arnold that great English poetry is written only by members of the established church? Over this paradox successive critics have boggled. Some have acknowledged Milton's genius while deploring his morals and his political opinions. Others have admired him but not entirely for the things he himself most esteemed. Some, of course, overborne by his power, have made a hero of him. Most have agreed, however, that he was, the more the pity, a man somehow at war with himself, the poet and the Puritan within him struggling for mastery and ruling him by turns.

Little remains to be said concerning this view of Milton. It may be true, but we do not know. What we can truthfully say is that, though he tells us much about himself in relation to his art, he never acknowledges the war between poetry and Puritanism, which may be after all nothing but the reflection of our own divided souls. Rather he reiterates his conviction that beauty should serve no cause but righteousness and righteousness hope for no stronger aid than poetry. His view of the part he must play was formed early, pursued vigorously, never relinquished, and frequently confidently asserted. His antagonist not his hero was Satan, and though he gave the devil his due, he never wavered in his allegiance to the Puritan God. He believed that men could through reason come to know the will of God sufficiently for their own good. The truth could be made known to men by the power of words. Whatsoever talent a man might find within himself—and it was his duty to know and esteem his own gifts—was, he held, a command to serve God thereby. Samson must quit himself like Samson upon peril of his soul. But the talent Milton discovered within himself was this same power to use words. This discovery and the shaping into act of the resolution to render back his talent enriched by great accomplishment was the decisive experience of his youth. In his own mind he was but another recruit in the warfare of the spirit, another adherent to the Puritan code, ranging his talent on the side of those lesser talents which in pulpit and press were training the artillery of words against the forces of evil and the prelatical church.

In the generation which saw Shakespeare come to seek his fortune in the theatre and Spenser to seek his at court, Milton's father came from Oxfordshire to apply himself in another quarter. His own father was a Roman Catholic who put him out of the house for turning Protestant and having an English Bible in his room. He became a scrivener with a house and shop in Bread Street just off Cheapside in the City of London. The trade of scrivener was that of engrossing legal documents and, it followed, of supplying a certain amount of legal and other advice. It was a good trade, and it offered opportunity to the thrifty for investing profitably the gains it provided.[2] The poet's father prospered, bought London property and a house in the country, educated one son ostensibly for the church, another for the law, and eventually left to the elder means sufficient to enable him to live as he chose. The family was, as we should expect, Puritan in its faith, its sympathies and its way of life.

The house in Bread Street was in the parish of Allhallows. The church of Allhallows stood only a short distance off on the other side of the way. The preacher receives no mention anywhere in Milton's references to his childhood, but he must have been a familiar figure, exercising at least the usual degree of influence which such men bore over such households. He was a Yorkshireman named Richard Stock, a graduate of Cambridge and an eminent member of the spiritual brotherhood.[3] He was at St. John's College in the days when William Perkins was in his prime. He was a favorite of William Whitaker, the master of St. John's. Having received his M.A., he left Cambridge about 1594 and lived for a time in Northamptonshire with Sir Anthony Cope, also a patron for a time of John Dod. He soon came to London, and preached in the neighborhood of Bread Street for over thirty years, dying soon after Milton's departure for Cambridge. He began preaching as a lecturer, first at St. Austin's in Watling Street, then at

St. Mildred's in Bread Street and finally for most of his time at Allhallows where he succeeded to the living upon the death of the former incumbent. He was probably somehow involved with the feoffees for impropriated tithes.[4] His sermon at the funeral of Lord Harington of Exton was published in 1614 and found its way into Samuel Clarke's *Marrow*.[5] The sermon for his own funeral, also duly enshrined by Clarke, was preached by his intimate friend Thomas Gataker. It depicts him as a perfect exemplar in pulpit and parish of all the familiar Puritan ministerial virtues. He was not, says Gataker, 'like the hand on the highway that pointeth others the way, but never walks therein itself.' 'He was none of those that say and do not; but as he taught so he wrought.' He delivered himself in the pulpit 'with clear method, sound proof, choice words, fit phrases, pregnant similitudes, plentiful illustrations, pithy perswasions, powerfull enforcements, allegations of antiquity, and variety of good literature, that both the learned might receive satisfaction from him, and the very meanest and dullest might also reap benefit by him.' He was, moreover, not 'like the sword-fish that hath a sword in his head but no heart in his body or like a cowardly companion that carries a weapon to ruffle with but dares not draw or make use of it.' He spoke freely in the faces of great ones whether they liked it or not. It was ill-taken when at Paul's Cross early in his career he attacked abuses in the tax rates 'whereby the meaner sort were overburdened.' He won finally the highest praise that could come to the preacher, namely, that he was not only a winner of souls but a winner of such as proved winners of others. 'Many famous lights in Gods Church and faithfull Ministers of the Word do profess to have lighted their candles at his Lampe.'[6]

The quality of Stock's preaching may still be sampled in the *Learned and Very Usefull Commentary upon the Whole Prophesie of Malachy*, which a disciple, Samuel Torshell, published in 1639 out of materials left him by the author, or in the treatise published in 1641 by James Cranford with a dedication to Lady Anne Yelverton and called *A Stock of Divine Knowledge, Being a lively description of the Divine Nature*. The latter is a plainly written exposition of such Protestant doctrine as Milton himself held in 1641. The former is the more interesting since it is really a collection of sermons in which doctrines are briefly and 'uses' much more fully and forcefully stated.

Stock writes rather in the manner of John Dod than in that of Sibbes or Preston, but his teaching would not have been lost on the young Milton and the elders of his family. The scrivener and his son may very well, for example, have heard Stock urge parents to dedicate their most gifted children, not those good for nothing else, to the ministry, pressing upon each of his hearers the duty 'to honour God with the best he hath, to thinke nothing too good for him, and to labour that nothing be deare to him in comparison of him, if he call for it.'[7] Such was the kind of preaching which Milton must have heard, week after week, all through his youth. Needless to say, he was probably also taken to hear other noted preachers within easy reach of Bread Street: Gouge at Blackfriars, Sibbes at Gray's Inn or Preston at Lincoln's Inn. From acquaintance with the sermons of such men as these, the author of *Lycidas* and the anti-prelatical tracts no doubt derived some part of that lofty conception of preaching which he defended so vehemently against the bishops. From such men too the author of *Paradise Lost* first heard the Puritan epic of man's fall and redemption.

Godly living, justified by the assurance of grace, was the rule in the household in which the poet grew up. This is not to say that men like his father, in whose case godliness was attended by so solid a measure of worldly prosperity, were persuaded of the sufficiency of the spirit's teaching alone. The obscurantist stage of Puritan asceticism was to be reached only later in the tension of the revolutionary crisis. The scrivener was no doubt a man of some learning, certainly one who respected learning. He was himself an accomplished musician and a composer of note.[8] He recognized the brilliance of his son's promise and earned the grandiloquent praise which the son presently bestowed upon him for the education he had provided. 'My father destined me from a child for the pursuits of polite learning.'[9] We are told that a housemaid was ordered to sit up for the lad when he studied until midnight. Having mastered Latin and Greek, he was urged by his father to go on and learn French, Italian and Hebrew. 'Afterwards,' he could say in the Latin poem addressed to his father, 'whatever the sky holds or mother earth under the sky, or the air of heaven between; whatever the wave hides, or the restless marble of the sea,—of all this through you I am enabled to learn, through you, if I care to learn.'[10]

A godly divine, according to the custom common in well-to-do

Puritan households, was early retained to be the boy's tutor. This was Thomas Young, an Anglicized Scot in his early thirties, concerning whose previous history little is known.[11] At eighteen Milton thanked him in a Latin poem[12] for having first led him to the knowledge of classical poetry and at the same time expressed his admiration for him as a preacher and pastor. Young went to Hamburg about 1620 to minister to a congregation of English merchants, and Milton protested against the harshness of England in driving such men from her shores. He also assured Young that he need fear no personal danger in the wars that then threatened on the continent because God would watch over him. When the preacher, after his return to England, joined several others in the pamphlet war against prelacy, he drew Milton after him into the fray. Eventually Young took his seat in the Westminster Assembly, became Master of Jesus College, Cambridge, and was mentioned no more by his former pupil.

Milton in his twelfth year entered St. Paul's School. In his seventeenth year he was sent to Christ's College, Cambridge. He arrived at the university supremely confident of himself, possessed by love of learning and the gift for poetry. His intention was to prepare for the pulpit. Literature, in the seventeenth century, was not yet regarded as a profession in itself sufficient for a man of Milton's social position. The English poets of the preceding age had been public men, courtiers and playwrights with now and then a country gentleman or parson. Milton's profession was to be the church, and his formal education was of the sort universally regarded as appropriate to that end. The outcome was that he abandoned the church and its pulpit in favor of literature and the press, but with no flagging of his youthful ambition to be a great teacher of religion and morality. His independence and vigor of mind and character showed themselves in no way more clearly than in that by which he came step by step to conceive of the profession of the scholar and the man of letters as a kind of evangelic priestly service to society. The development of this conception was what chiefly and most critically occupied him at Cambridge. .

Milton entered Christ's College in February 1625. He proceeded bachelor of arts in July 1632. At the close of his academic course of seven years, the fellows of the college signified, he says, 'how much better it would content them that I would stay.'[13] This probably means that, if he had chosen, he might have been elected a fellow of Christ's and so have had opened to him that door which had led so many before him to eminence in the spiritual brotherhood. He did not accept the opportunity. Whatever other causes may have affected his decision, the changes he had had occasion to observe in the university and in the church would have been enough to turn him aside. Charles I came to the throne at the moment when Milton was entering Cambridge. Laud had since that time been rising step by step, and he had made his power felt at Cambridge as he had done before at Oxford. Directly after Milton's departure from the university, Laud became archbishop. Consequently no such career as that of Chaderton or Perkins or Preston was longer possible. Indeed, the main strength of the spiritual brotherhood had already begun to ebb at Cambridge when Milton arrived there. By 1625 the influence of Perkins must surely have died away at last. Dod and Hildersam had long since removed to country parishes. Chaderton was nearly ninety, Sibbes was chiefly active in London, and Preston, though no doubt he continued to fly back from Lincoln's Inn periodically to preside at Emmanuel or preach at Trinity Church, was a dying man. John Cotton was occupied with his flock at Boston in Lincolnshire. There remained none of the famous Puritans except Thomas Goodwin, who preached frequently at Ely and who succeeded to the lectureship at Trinity upon Preston's death. The sermons he published a few years later under the title *A Childe of Light* may have been heard in church by Milton, who must certainly have heard and approved of the scruples which made Goodwin and Cotton presently resign their pulpits and flee, the one to Holland the other to America, rather than conform to Laud's will.

If the spiritual brethren had been permitted to continue unchecked after 1625, Milton in the normal course of events would have taken his place among them. As it was, he had while at Cambridge to watch the steadily increasing repression of that kind of preaching he had been brought up to follow and approve. He had not been long at the university when he wrote his poem to Thomas Young lamenting the fact that such men were being sent into exile. Addressing his native country, he says: 'Those whom God in his providence sent to thee, bearing good tidings from Heaven, to teach the way to the stars after the body is in ashes,—will you force these to seek their food in distant regions?"[14] Some years later we find him accusing the prelates of unpeopling the kingdom, of driving 'faithfull and freeborn English-men and good Christians . . . to forsake their dearest home, their friends and kindred, whom nothing but the wide Ocean and the savage deserts of America could hide from the fury of the Bishops.'[15] The resentment thus expressed was not merely on behalf of England and the church. Milton's temper was not one that brooked patiently the thwarting of any purpose he had himself once conceived. To deem himself debarred from preaching, to feel menaced by a compulsion that might cause him too to take flight, was a personal indignity as well as a public wrong. The prelates had 'church-outed' John Milton. This made a lesion on his pride which he never forgave. He had been destined for the church, he says, 'of a child and in mine own reso-lutions,' 'by the intentions of my parents and friends.' But when he had come 'to some maturity of yeers,' he discovered 'that he who would take Orders must subscribe slave and take an oath withall, which unlesse he took with a conscience that would retch, he must either perjure or split faith.' At the time, he 'thought it better to preserve a blameless silence before the sacred office of speaking,' that is to say, before accepting the office of the pulpit 'bought and begun with servitude and forswearing.' But he was not always to remain silent. His experience and the anger and disillusion it brought gave him, he asserted, the right at the appropriate time to speak concerning the church on even terms with any churchman.[16]

If there could be any doubt as to the sincerity of Milton's early ambition to enter the church, it would be removed by reading what he had to say concerning the ministry in 1641 and 1642 in his tracts against the bishops. Whether or not he could ever have been anything but a poet, the fact was that the prelates had in effect refused to let him become a preacher. He did not allow them to forget that fact. He was professing to argue for presbyterian church government, but what he had most passionately to say for presbyterianism was that it was designed to foster the kind of ministry prelacy had repressed. Again and again in the course of his polemic he returns to the picture of the ideal preacher and physician of souls, one content with spiritual re-wards alone, teaching out of scripture what all men can understand, practicing what he preaches.

The attack Milton directed against prelacy after revolution was actually under way will require discussion later. We are now concerned with the personal experience which did so much to make him an active revolutionary. His relinquishment of the profession of preaching resulted from his resentment of what he regarded as tyranny and corruption but also from the awakening and conversion of a kind peculiar to himself which he underwent at the same time. The record of it, Milton's spiritual autobiography, though singularly complete, has to be pieced together from various sources in his writings of different dates. We have first of all certain oratorical exercises or prolusions which he composed as a student for public delivery in the university. Except for a few English verses included in one of them, they are written in Latin. Also in Latin are a group of poems and several letters written during or soon after his academic residence and addressed either to friends or, in one instance, to his father. Most of his English poems prior to 1638 are intimately concerned with the same inner experience. Finally we have a number of explicitly autobiographical passages in his controversial tracts composed after 1640 and deeply colored by the passions of the revolution. The whole constitutes a remarkable record of the development of an extraordinary poetic mind. It is also, however, the record of the steps by which in a uniquely gifted individual Puritanism went beyond the expression of momentary interests in sermon and tract to the expression of its most far-reaching ideals in enduring eloquence and literary form.

It seems at first thought surprising that Milton has nothing to say concerning the preachers he may have heard at Cambridge and little concerning particular preachers at any time. The omission can, however, be explained. As we have seen, the heyday of Puritan preaching at Cambridge was over when he arrived, and the preachers were beginning to feel more sharply the hostility of the authorities. He could not have referred to preaching while a member of the university without complaining of the repression to which the pulpit was being subjected. He did privately express his admiration for Thomas Young as a teacher and as a spiritual adviser, and complained to him of what was being done in the church. A kind of pride as well as common prudence made him at other times maintain silence; he was waiting for an opportunity when he could speak to some effect. What he did as a student was to protest against the program and method of study which official authority as well as tradition still maintained at Cambridge. Directly after his departure, he made the death of his fellow collegian, Edward King, an occasion for unburdening his mind on the corruption of the clergy under prelacy. When he next found occasion to write about the church and university education, it was to assail what prelacy had made of them and to hold forth his own exalted notion of what preaching and teaching should be. But by that time his ideas, as events rapidly made manifest, had gone far beyond the intentions and desires of the Puritan divines, including his old friend Thomas Young. The preachers were just then about to attempt to subject the church to a rigid presbyterianism profoundly incompatible with the Utopian ideal which possessed Milton. No wonder after that that no preacher he had known came within the measure of his praise and that the Cambridge he knew seemed to deserve nothing but his scorn.

We are not told in Milton's spiritual autobiography the precise moment when he first felt the conviction of grace. The sense of personal election seems to have been his from the start. He arrived at Cambridge assured of his powers and intentions, determined to learn, expecting to be approved. The evidence indicates that he was at first disappointed and for a time disliked.[17] He quarreled with his tutor. Haughty, high-minded and looking like a girl, he was called in derision the lady of Christ's. The importance of these details, however, should not be exaggerated. He recovered from his disappointment sufficiently to make a success of his university career. He was soon transferred to another tutor. The students in the end chose him upon one occasion to give the customary mock oration called for at the close of the summer term. He left the place by his own acknowledgment with friendly feelings for the fellows of his college, whom he describes as 'curteous and learned men.' They wrote him letters 'full of kindnesse and loving respect,' and he could not suppose 'I had that regard from them for other cause then that I might be still encourag'd to proceed in the honest and laudable courses, of which they apprehended I had given proofs.'[18]

Yet his friendliness toward the fellows of his college did not prevent Milton at the time as well as later from venting his disapproval of university education and condemning its effects upon men destined for the church. If in 1642 he liked Cambridge less than he had done, it was not that in his earlier judgment he had liked it greatly. He came there versed in the Bible, in humane letters and in Puritan ideas of reform. He found there the course of study and system of education dictated by medieval tradition.[19] He was expected under the direction of his tutor to learn rhetoric, logic, metaphysics, Latin and some Greek before proceeding bachelor of arts. After that he might go on to the study of theology, the degree of master, perhaps a fellowship, and, if he entered the church, ordination. He received no formal instruction in history, literature, mathematics or science. Academic success depended upon the skill and address a youth could command in public disputations on such topics as those Milton had to deal with in his own academic exercises, namely, whether day is more excellent than night, the harmony of the spheres, whether there be resolution into first matter in the destruction of any substance, whether there are partial forms in an animal in addition to the whole, whether learning is more full of blessings than ignorance. John Preston's rise had begun some years earlier when he successfully defended before King James the thesis that dogs can reason. Needless to say such training helped to sharpen the wits and make fluent the tongues of the men who filled the pulpits and wrote the pamphlets of the revolution. Needless to say too the reading a young man might pursue at the university, given the impulse and the right tutor, was much wider in range and of far more vital interest than the topics assigned for formal dispute would indicate. Teachers like Chaderton, Perkins and Preston, like Mede at Christ's in Milton's time, were men of active minds, acquainted with humane letters. They could not, certainly, have confined themselves in their intercourse with students to the conventional round of scholastic topics. The main effort of the Puritan reformers at Cambridge for a generation before Milton came there had been to make students as well as other people read the Bible under the intense illumination of Puritan doctrine and the spiritual epic. The real object of the instruction such men gave their pupils was not to turn them into scholastic disputants but into preachers of the word. Long before the battle of moderns and ancients was heard of in its eighteenth-century terms, they were the natural opponents of traditional authority.[20] They held that sermons were more important than disputations and lectures in metaphysics and divinity. Sermons should be couched in plain English. The preacher should spend less time on the explication of doctrine than on the application of the teachings of scripture to human use in daily life. He should depend on no authority but the Bible, and he should teach his auditors to verify what he told them by referring to the Bible for themselves. He must at the same time teach nothing which he had not first tested in his own experience, and he must teach his people to subject all doctrine to the test of experience. Thus the preachers made experiment a familiar word on the plane of religion and morals long before it became supreme on that of natural science. Man was, to be sure, saved by faith alone, but the question whether or not he had faith could be determined only by himself through observation of the workings of the spirit in himself. Faith evinced itself in work, in any work performed as an adventure of the spirit, an experiment in godliness. In this fashion religion was made to justify devotion to practical and useful objects and to encourage confident expectation of success, progress and glory. The spiritual brotherhood was as deeply devoted as Bacon to the advancement of the kind of learning which, its members believed, would most directly express the glory of God and contribute to the relief of man.

The decline of Puritan influence at Cambridge in Milton's time could only have thrown into sharper relief the arid traditionalism of the formal curriculum. In spite of everything that had been happening for a hundred years in thought, letters, religion, exploration and science, Cambridge still adhered in the main to the medieval round of academic studies and procedures. But, though the influence of the Puritans momentarily abated, the influence of Bacon, also a reformer by temperament if ever there was one, was at the same moment about to make itself felt, intensifying in another way the contrast between what was taught at the university and what eager and active minds deemed most useful to learn. It should not seem at all surprising that Bacon presented Cambridge with a copy of his *Novum Organum* and of his *De Augmentis* or that he should have followed up these gifts by his prescient, if barren, bequest for a lectureship in natural philosophy. His attack on the old learning and his faith in the new were to receive no heartier support than that which presently came from the Puritan classes. Nor should it seem surprising that Milton, who was a boy at school in the year the *Advancement of Learning* was published and had been scarcely a year at Cambridge when Bacon died, should have chosen to assail scholasticism in the classrooms of the university and to raise his undergraduate voice in favor of studies which Bacon too had urged. Not long after 1626, Milton was called up to address the members of his college on the question 'Whether Day or Night is the more excellent.'[21] In discussing this subject, he conceded to custom the expected play with words and erudition, but he also betrayed the fact that he had already made himself conspicuous among his fellows by his independent attitude toward the usual ways of study. He said that he saw few friendly faces in his audience, though the approval of those few was more grateful to him than that of 'countless hosts of the ignorant, who lack all intelligence, reasoning power, and sound judgment, and who pride themselves on the ridiculous froth of their verbiage.' He was about the same time writing to his friend the younger Gill to say that he had found few congenial companions at college, few 'who do not take flight to theology before ever they are full fledged, almost untrained and uninitiated in literature and philosophy alike.'[22] He said no more in his first public appearance at Cambridge about his own intellectual pursuits except to note how 'provocative of animosity, even in the home of learning, is the rivalry of those who pursue different studies or whose opinions differ concerning the studies they pursue in common.' Not very long afterwards, however, he took occasion to speak his mind much more freely.

The third of his college orations was a direct attack on scholastic philosophy.[23] The attempt has sometimes been made to condone the violence of Milton's language in his controversial tracts on the ground that he was perhaps unfortunately carried away by the passions of the moment. Yet even as a nineteen-year-old boy, dealing at college with an academic subject, he was hardly less violent. The fervor for reforming the world was in him from the start, and he began where undergraduate reformers generally begin, with the curriculum. The works of the scholastic philosophers he was required to study reek, he says, 'of the monkish cells in which they were written,' and they produce in him nothing but boredom and disgust. Their subject matter is trivial, feeble and dull, their style dry and lifeless. The questions with which they occupy themselves are never decided, are not worth deciding, and are only the more confused the longer they are disputed. The net result of all the labor spent upon them is 'to make you a more finished fool and cleverer contriver of conceits, and to endow you with a more expert ignorance: No wonder, since all these problems at which you have been working in such torment and anxiety have no existence in reality at all, but like unreal ghosts and phantoms without substance obsess minds already disordered and empty of all true wisdom.' What effect if any Milton's strictures had on his teachers and critics, we do not know. He was not relieved of the obligation to take part in the disputations he condemned; yet on the other hand he was not prevented from expressing his distaste another time. Called up presently to discuss a metaphysical question, he made no concealment of his feelings. Truth, he begins by saying, has fled back to heaven and left error supreme in the schools. Hence philosophy merely disgusts those lovers of truth who seek to understand it. 'For it often happens that a student who turns the pages of the philosophers' books and is busied about them day and night departs more puzzled than he came.' One writer confutes another, but to determine which of them is on the side of truth is not worth the trouble it would take, since their most heated disputes are about matters of the least importance. After these remarks, Milton goes on to discuss, as he was required, the question concerning substance and matter which was his topic. But he does it with a wry face, and as soon as his time is up, he breaks off, saying, 'I might bring up other arguments on both sides, but will refrain, to spare you boredom.'

The echo of Bacon in all this is, of course, unmistakable. So also is the echo of Hakewill's *Apologie* in Milton's Latin verses, *Naturam non pati senium*, of the same date. We must, however, note that, though Bacon's attack on scholasticism fell in with Milton's mood, his mood continued to be that of the Puritan reformer rather than of the Baconian philosopher. The reformers and Bacon alike opposed tradition in the field of learning, sought as the ends of knowledge things they regarded as immediately and concretely useful, and exalted individual experience as the means of gaining and testing knowledge of the truth. But the Puritans' ends were first moral and then political; they were striving after power in the church, in society and the state. The knowledge they urged men to get was to be sought by observation of the operations of the Holy Spirit in their own breasts and in the lives of men about them, by the reading of useful books, above all by the reading of the Bible interpreted as an image of spiritual war and adventure and supplemented by other books conducive to the same effect. The intellectual leaders of Puritanism were interested in biography and history. They were not primarily interested in nature except as a revelation of divine providence secondary though parallel to scripture. Thus though they helped greatly in preparing the way for experimental science, that was not the business to the accomplishment of which they addressed themselves, and the same was true of Milton.

The objectives of the Puritan reformers and the results of their pursuit of them in the field of education were, we may note in passing, to be clearly exemplified in New England.[24] Harvard and the colleges which one after another were patterned upon it sprang up under the inspiration of Cambridge—of the Cambridge, that is, of the spiritual brotherhood, particularly of Emmanuel, the most Puritan of the Cambridge colleges. The colleges of New England, though founded in order to insure a supply of learned men for the ministry, developed as training schools for evangelical preachers, not on the one hand for disputants in theology and metaphysics nor on the other for scientists. Students were enveloped in an intensely religious atmosphere, they were instructed in rhetoric and oratory, in the Bible and the Greek and Latin classics, in moral and natural philosophy. In course of time, history, the modern languages and literatures, mathematics and experimental science, finally the social sciences, all found acceptance within this curriculum as the vestiges of scholasticism, followed by evangelicism, faded away.

The ideas concerning education advocated by Milton in his student days agreed substantially with those which governed the development of the new and Puritan Cambridge in America. His attack on scholasticism was accompanied by clear indication of the studies and methods with which he would have it replaced. His program did not, however, include experimental science. Milton assailed the prevailing system, both while he was a university student and, even more violently, as an active revolutionary after 1640, because he was convinced that it turned out nothing but ignoramuses unfit for the duties of the pulpit. The universities should be judged primarily by the quality of the preachers they produced. Yet in saying that this was the criterion which ruled Milton's conception of university education, we must note that from a very early date in his career he conceived the function of preaching in exalted terms colored by his own character and ambitions. The word preacher, indeed, falls considerably short of suggesting at the present day what Milton really had in mind. He invested the preacher's role with powers and responsibilities which no ministerial caste not composed of Miltonic archangels and which no religious pulpit not occupied by one could ever have encompassed. In his mind the preacher was transfigured by Hebrew prophet, ancient orator, classic and Renaissance poet and philosopher. He must be a master of moral wisdom and of all the arts and sciences that might be used to persuade men to their good. He must, in short, possess all the learning and the kind of skill of which Milton himself wished to be the master.

Two things there are, he says in the course of his attack on scholasticism, which most enrich and adorn England, 'eloquent speech and noble action.' Eloquence is his personal goal, the goal which he naturally enough thinks the university should teach its students to attain. The studies which lead to that end are those which Aristotle himself pursued, but not those pursued in the schools. Poetry is indued by heavenly grace with power to raise the soul aloft and set it in the heavens. Rhetoric is able to captivate the minds of men and move them to pity, to hatred, to valor beyond the fear of death. 'History, skilfully narrated, now calms and soothes the restless and troubled mind, now fills it with delight, and now brings tears to the eyes.' Abandon this contentious dueling with words, he exhorts his hearers; 'let your eyes wander . . . over all the lands depicted on the map, . . . behold the places trodden by heroes of old, . . . range over the regions made famous by wars, by triumphs, and even by the tales of poets, . . . spy out the customs of mankind and those states which are well-ordered; . . . seek out and explore the nature of all living creatures, . . . turn your attention to the secret virtues of stones and herbs.' The clouds, the lightning and the stars should not escape us. 'Ask account of time itself and demand the reckoning of its eternal passage.'[25]

The most remarkable of Milton's academic exercises was the seventh and last, an oration delivered in the college chapel near the end of his

course. Its object was to demonstrate that 'learning brings more blessing to men than ignorance.'[26] He voices again, though with slightly
less asperity, his disapproval of established academic procedures. He
admits to feeling no incapacity for making such speeches, but he seldom
undertakes them of his own free will. Mediocrity in an orator as in
a poet is intolerable. He would prefer to spend his time acquiring the
knowledge requisite for the highest accomplishment of his calling. The
subjects he would learn for this purpose, in contrast to those taught in
the university, are again glowingly set forth. 'What a thing it is to
grasp the nature of the whole firmament and its stars,' 'the movements
and changes of the atmosphere,' 'the hidden virtues of plants and
metals,' 'the nature and the feelings . . . of every living creature,'
'the delicate structure of the human body,' 'the divine might and
power of the soul.' 'What delight it affords to the mind to take its
flight through the history and geography of every nation and to observe the changes in the conditions of kingdoms, races, cities, and peoples, . . . to live in every period of the world's history, and to be as
it were coeval with time itself.' Grammar and rhetoric can help in all
this, but not the despicable quibbles which the teachers of them talk,
'sometimes like savages and sometimes like babies.' Logic, again, is
admittedly the queen of arts, 'if taught as it should be,' not as it is by
teachers who more resemble finches feeding on thorns than men.
Metaphysics he will have none of; 'it is, I say, not an Art at all,
but a sinister rock, a quagmire of fallacies, devised to cause shipwreck
and pestilence.'

The main purpose of Milton's speaking on this occasion is not, however, once more to assail the scholastic curriculum. He is like Bacon in
that he clearly perceives the diseases that afflict learning. He is like
Bacon too in taking all knowledge for his province and in believing
that knowledge is power. But the power he is hoping to gain through
knowledge is not that of the scientist but that of the orator, the
preacher, the poet in public life, in a word the seer and prophet. He
is clearly one of that sort of men who feel assured that they possess a
body of truth which, given the necessary devotion and effort on the
part of its adherents, will by a single stroke and in a day bring in
Utopia. He imagines truth to be always gloriously at war with error
in the minds of men, and himself a warrior for truth.[27] He has but to

make himself perfect in knowledge, perfect in persuasion, and truth will triumph through his utterance. We have, any of us, but to sacrifice ordinary animal pleasure and luxury, even, if need be, health; we have but to live modestly and temperately, 'keeping the divine vigour of our minds unstained and uncontaminated,' in order to discover that life is not too short or art too long for us to traverse seas and master continents of learning. 'If from our childhood onward we never allow a day to pass by without its lesson and diligent study, if we are wise enough to rule out of every art what is irrelevant, superfluous, or unprofitable, we shall assuredly, before we have attained the age of Alexander the Great, have made ourselves masters of something greater and more glorious than that world of his. And so far from complaining of the shortness of life and the slowness of Art, I think we shall be more likely to weep and wail, as Alexander did, because there are no more worlds for us to conquer.' The final glory is as certain as the process of attaining it is easy. When learning is wedded to virtue then wisdom takes her seat 'on high beside the king and governor, Intellect, gazes upon the doings of the Will below' and 'claims as her right all excellence and splendour and a majesty next to that of God Himself.' The learned virtuous man has the pleasure 'to be the oracle of many nations, to find [his] home regarded as a kind of temple, to be a man whom kings and states invite to come to them, whom men from near and far flock to visit, while to others it is a matter for pride if they have but set eyes on him once.'

Milton concludes his speech with a kind of valedictory injunction to Cambridge. 'I have sounded the attack,' he tells the members of Christ's College; 'do you rush into battle; put this enemy to flight, drive her from your porticos and walks. If you allow her to exist, you yourselves will be that which you know to be the most wretched thing in the world. This cause is the personal concern of you all.' When in a few years it appeared that these words of his were not heeded, he made it his own personal concern to wage open war on the universities themselves.

By 1632, when he left Cambridge, Milton in his own mind had dedicated himself to the career foreshadowed in his academic exercises. It is hard for us to believe that he ever could have confined his energies to a pulpit, but, be that as it may, the repression of the preachers by the prelates was enough to make him abandon his intention of entering the church. Forsaking the church did not, however, mean that he wished to serve God less. It meant that by enlisting the muses in God's service he expected to serve him more effectively. Milton's ideal aims did not alter; they did not differ from those of the spiritual brotherhood. He merely conceived them with greater imagination and pursued them with the force of a greater personality. The very rise of Puritan preaching in the generation before him testified to the intoxication of the age with words, with the dream of power to be attained through the arts of discourse. He too was dazzled by visions of what might be accomplished if truth were freely spoken, and therefore he would not, any more than Prynne or Lilburne, be stopped from speaking it. Moreover, since discourse was able to make truth prevail, nothing could satisfy his conscience but that he must make the utmost effort to attain the utmost eloquence, the utmost mastery of all knowledge and skill that might contribute to make utterance engaging and convincing. If the prelates chose to church-out him, so much the worse for them. He could be a poet.

The preacher's career ordinarily proceeded, as we have seen, from his effectual calling by God to his discovery of his special gift and calling to proclaim the word. He then dedicated all his energies to the cultivation and exercise of his gift in the service of the word. He endeavored to make his life one long uninterrupted sermon. Milton undertook his career in the same spirit and according to the same pattern, though neither his gift nor his calling were of the ordinary kind. Neither did he have the ordinary kind of personal confession to make. His rebirth in the spirit started with the discovery of the spiritual function of poetry. It turned upon his discovery in himself of the power of poetic utterance, and it led to his decision to make poetry rather than the pulpit his weapon in the war of the spirit. Poems were to be his sermons, and his life was to be a poem.

It may well be that this was a mistaken view both of poetry and of life and that Milton became a great poet in spite of a great error of judgment. But however that may be, the fact remains that the development of his talent took place under the dominance of Puritan didacticism. The essence of his *biographia literaria* is that, when in the cultivation of his gifts he found his way to the poetry of the ancient world and the Renaissance, he found not distraction and escape from the Puritan urge to salvation and service but the strongest possible confirmation. The man who, he says, first showed him the way to Parnassus, who taught him to drink of the Pierian fountain and sprinkle his lips with Castalian wine, was Thomas Young, a man well trained, he also tells us, to feed the sheep that follow Christ.[28] The schooling of the young Puritan, even though university education still centered in scholastic dialectic, was far from excluding humane letters. Milton as a boy was required to read the ancient orators and historians. He thought he loved them, he says, but he adds that he understood their matter 'as my age then was.' 'The smooth Elegiack poets,' meaning particularly Ovid, whom he was also set to read, were more agreeable to 'natures part' in him, and he found them 'in imitation . . . most easie.'[29] Like other lads he wrote Latin verses patterned upon Ovid. Some of them dealt, of course, with love. When he was sent home for quarreling with his tutor, he fancied himself like Ovid in exile, and, the season being spring, went walking out-of-doors and admired girls, English maidens more beautiful by far than any celebrated in the books he had been reading.[30] Ovid helped him both to enjoy the spring[31] and to fall in love,[32] helped even more perhaps to the intoxicating joy of writing about these experiences. We must not read too much into the literary imitations of a gifted precocious boy. There were luscious and licentious pages in Ovid, and Milton was not a milksop. Whether by reading Ovid or in some other way, he discovered elements in his nature which it was his nature to deal with but not to deny. He learned quickly to love beauty and to shun unchastity. In this spirit he soon discovered even greater pleasure in those poets who revealed in the beauty and the love of women the express image of the soul's progressive participation in the transcending universal good. He went from Ovid to Petrarch and Dante, to chivalric romance, to Ariosto, Montemayor, Sidney, above all to Spenser and finally to Plato himself. His conclusion was that every free and gentle spirit should be born a knight without need of spur or laying on of sword. Thus nature's part, which made him enjoy Ovid's love stories to begin with, led him on to that idealization of love which was the great theme of Renaissance poetry. The books, he said, which incited others to wantonness, by divine indulgence incited him to the love of virtue.[33]

The Puritan spirit was by no means necessarily at war with the poetic idealism of the Renaissance. The Puritan idealist, of whom Milton was a supreme but by no means unique example, was shown by Platonism, as how many of us have not been, a way to select and arrange whatever aspects of the flux of things would fall into harmony with his own aspirations. The idealist puts himself at the pole of a universe, and in so doing marks off a surrounding chaos which is both a trial and a challenge. The more he endeavors to set his world to rights, the more aware he becomes of the abutting disorder which he must make it the more his business to subdue. All his thinking and asserting only force upon him the necessity for further thought and bolder assertion. Preoccupied as he thus more and more becomes with the struggle of his mind upon a task no less infinite than momentous, he grows the more sensitive, the more concerned, in respect to those motions of human nature, of his own nature, which seem to have less or no part in this life of the mind, which seem perhaps even to interrupt and impede. Love and beauty, sexual passion and the desire for pleasure are for such a man of an aching exigency. They must be either wholly banished from his cosmos or wholly incorporated within it. Beauty is for him either a snare of the evil one or a ladder reaching to God. Hence in all idealists the love and the hate of beauty, the poet and the iconoclast, lie close together. Or perhaps we should say that in a Puritan like Prynne we have merely an idealist who has lost nerve and in an idealist like Milton a Puritan who has had the courage to embrace what otherwise he must have abhorred.

At any rate Milton did embrace beauty. He felt the mysterious excitement which woman causes, but learned from Plato and the poets how to resist Cupid,[34] learned that 'the office of love begins and ends in the soul.'[35] To such a nature as his, nice, haughty, self-centered and self-esteeming, the idealism of Plato, of Dante, Petrarch, Tasso and Spenser made a final and effective appeal. It enabled him to find God, even the Puritan God, at the other pole of his universe. Engrossed in ideas, he was persuaded that the ideal was the one reality, that his thoughts had something of that supervening reality in them, that the very movement of his thought was a progressive approach to that reality. He had convictions which he took for truth, and he felt assured that what he took for truth was the will of God. He was moved by beauty, and it told him that beauty was the fair face of the good. He loved, and it told him that he might use love to reach heaven. He was a poet, and it told him that poetry was a voice to inspire love of truth in the minds of men. He was a young Puritan with an ambition to serve his country as a Christian preacher, and it informed Christianity itself with a new meaning by making Christ the symbol, not of weakness which human nature could never by itself overcome, but of the presence of the divine in man himself. Then, though it kept him from entering the church, it fired him the more to be an evangelist by enabling him to see himself in a larger vista of self-discipline and service.

Such a poet, above all other Englishmen, had Spenser been. Of Shakespeare Milton speaks with some reserve. He could not escape the marvel of Shakespeare's verse, but his inexhaustible mirroring of life's variety made the Puritan poet feel less sure of himself, less firmly centered in his own universe, more aware of chaos:

> Then thou, our fancy of itself bereaving,
> Dost make us Marble with too much conceaving.

Milton did not wish to be made marble, and took Spenser to be his master, 'our sage and serious Spenser,' whom he dares to think a better teacher, that is, a more effective teacher, than Scotus or Aquinas.[36] Much of what a patriotic, Protestant, idealistic Englishman most desired should be true had somehow been turned into poetry in *The Faerie Queene*. There in English, imbued with English spirit, was such a tissue of tales as Ariosto might have made, though Ariosto could not have made it more engaging or richer with beauty drawn from the poets the young Milton so much enjoyed. Spenser gave these delightful forms ideal significance. He used them to depict the war of the spirit. He showed England, the land, its kings and heroes, transfigured by a visionary, ideal England, which the reformer in Milton told him ought to be realized in fact. Spenser translated ideal truth into terms of public policy and private morality. He came, Sidney's poet, with a tale to draw children from their play and old men from the chimney-corner, and endeavored to win the mind from wickedness to virtue, 'to fashion a gentleman or noble person in vertuous and gentle discipline.' What then could he mean to Milton, born in a generation when practical energy was combined with religious enthu-

siasm and revolutionary passion for reforming the world, except that
poetry was a kind of revelation and the poet God's evangel.

Such, it seems, was the course which spiritual awakening took in the
case of John Milton. The stages by which it proceeded were recorded
in the self-revealing, self-justifying outbursts of the tracts written by
the poet a few years later against the bishops. The gifts that made him
fit for the church made him fit to serve God as a poet. He was certain
that he possessed the gifts.

After I had from my first yeeres by the ceaselesse diligence of my
father, whom God recompence, bin exercis'd to the tongues, and some
sciences, as my age would suffer, by sundry masters and teachers both
at home and at the schools, it was found that whether ought was im-
pos'd me by them that had the overlooking, or betak'n to of mine own
choise in English, or other tongue, prosing or versing, but chiefly this
latter, the stile by certain signes it had, was likely to live.[37]

He was equally certain of the use that should be made of such talents.
The abilities of a poet

wheresoever they be found, are the inspired guift of God rarely bestow'd,
but yet to some (though most abuse) in every Nation: and are of power
beside the office of a pulpit, to inbreed and cherish in a great people the
seeds of Vertu, and publick civility, to allay the perturbations of the
mind, and set the affections in right tune, to celebrate in glorious and
lofty Hymns the throne and equipage of Gods Almightinesse, and what
he works, and what he suffers to be wrought with high providence in
his Church, to sing the victorious agonies of Martyrs and Saints, the
deeds and triumphs of just and pious Nations doing valiantly through
faith against the enemies of Christ, to deplore the general relapses of
Kingdoms and States from justice and Gods true worship.[38]

These words were written, as has been indicated, at the time when
the rejected candidate for the church, having turned poet, turned also
pamphleteer in order to help in church-outing them who had church-
outed him. The poems he had written up to that time have never
failed to fascinate students of poetry. Many a man has written far
more verses by his thirtieth year than Milton did. Few beginners at
the art of verse have known so clearly what they were about or have
advanced by such sure and calculated steps to mastery of the medium
they set themselves to learn. Each of Milton's early poems in English

and Latin is of the nature of an experiment; some of the experiments were less happy and successful than others, but no mistake was repeated or wasted. By the time he comes to *Lycidas*, Milton is in full command of his powers. It is not, however, the development of his command over the technique of poetic expression which engages our attention here, but the development of his attitude as a Puritan reformer toward his art and toward himself as artist. The ardor of his discovery of his gift and of its possibilities for promoting reform is what, as he goes from one experiment to another, gives his early poems more and more of that intense vitality which is their peculiar quality. Their subjects and occasions are now one thing, now another. The theme upon which they all converge is poetry, the discipline it imposes upon the poet, the power and reward it offers him, the service it can perform for men.

In 1628, when he was nineteen, Milton was elected to deliver a mock oration before the students of Cambridge.[39] This was composed in Latin, but part of the entertainment consisted of English verses dealing sportively with some of the metaphysical abstractions Milton so much disliked. He did his duty with deft touches of the Spenserian manner in the English verses, but he could not forbear letting his audience have a taste of the loftier kind of poetry he also had it in him to write in English. 'The Latin speeches ended,' he addressed a greeting to his native language. He has to put it to the task of presenting his notions about father Ens and the ten Predicaments, his sons.

> Yet I had rather, if I were to chuse,
> Thy service in some graver subject use,
> Such as may make thee search thy coffers round,
> Before thou cloath my fancy in fit sound:
> Such where the deep transported mind may soare
> Above the wheeling poles, and at Heav'ns dore
> Look in, and see each blissful Deitie
> How he before the thunderous throne doth lie,
> Listening to what unshorn *Apollo* sings
> To th'touch of golden wires.

A little over a year later he ventured to supply a more generous sample of what he could do. During the Christmas holiday of 1629, he was writing a Latin elegy to his friend Diodati. The latter was away making merry in the country. Milton assures him that the gods who love feasting and wine love poetry too, though poetry of the lighter kind. 'But the poet who will tell of wars, and of Heaven under adult Jove, and of pious heroes, and leaders half-divine, singing now the holy counsels of the gods above, and now the realms profound where Cerberus howls,' he must live a different sort of life, simple and frugal. 'His youth must be chaste and void of offense.' He must lead a priest-like existence, like Tiresias, Orpheus and Homer. 'For the bard is sacred to the gods, he is their priest, mysteriously from his lips and breast he breathes Jove.' After this prelude, the writer does not hesitate to tell his friend that he himself is writing a poem, more than one in fact. He is 'singing the King of Heaven, bringer of peace, and the fortunate days promised by the holy book.' He is also meditating other strains, 'piped musingly on my native reed.'[40]

Milton is probably referring in the last statement to that poem on British legendary history which, paralleling the sacred epic, was to hover for a long time in his plans but never to be written. The hymn he refers to is of course that *On the Morning of Christ's Nativity.* This was his first attempt at the Puritan saga, and the result for all its brilliance illustrates the difficulties into which he fell when he too unwarily undertook to treat those episodes of the Biblical story which Puritan imagination found least congenial and expressive. The nativity and the passion have always been associated with the idea of atonement by the son of God for man's sin. But the young Puritan, full of the sense of his own power, felt in reality no need of a redeemer outside his own breast. As his party, when it had the power, permitted little to be made of Christmas or Easter, he would later relegate the Christ child and the crucifixion to a subordinate place in his version of the epic. Even in his youthful attempt, though he begins with clear enough announcement of the traditional theme, he fails to adhere to it or carry it consistently forward. The child is there in the manger, the Virgin Mary with him, the Magi hastening to give him homage, the shepherds in rustic row upon the lawn, but the poet, his verse up to this point encumbered by conceit, does not take fire until the angels begin to sing. 'Ring out ye crystal spheres,' he then cries, and the world in another moment is about to be redeemed by song. To such music time will surely run back and fetch the age of gold, sin die, hell pass away, truth, justice and mercy dwell among men. The Puritan poet, having in this manner overshot the theologian, interrupts himself long enough to say in two comparatively lifeless stanzas that to be sure all this must wait for the child to mount the cross. Then, leaving the mystery of that sacrifice unexpressed, he pours forth a marvel of words to say that after Christ's passion the oracles will be dumb, error retreating before truth. For Milton the atonement does not itself directly redeem; it merely starts a truth which redeems as it moves from mind to mind by the aid of prophets and poets. Attempting again a little later to go on with the theme of the lamb of God in two other poems, one on the circumcision and one on the passion, he found himself puzzled and without wings. The latter poem breaks off suddenly with the note, 'This Subject the Author finding to be above the yeers he had, when he wrote it, and nothing satisfi'd with what was begun, left it unfinisht.' He had learned to believe in himself, in poetry, in the power of truth. This was enough to make a great poem out of *The Nativity*. When he came to treat of any other kind of redemption, he had nothing to say.

Milton's abandonment of the career in the church for which he had been so carefully educated was definitely signified by his declining the invitation which, he says, was offered him by the fellows to remain at Christ's. This naturally called for some explanation to his family and friends. There is not the slightest evidence that he had up to this time received anything but encouragement from his father in the course he had taken. The scrivener possessed the means to enable his son to continue a life of studious leisure. Shortly after leaving Cambridge, the latter made the formal tender of a poet instead of a preacher for son in the poem, *Ad Patrem*. The defensive tone of the poem may suggest that there had been some demur on the father's part, but if so it must have been quickly withdrawn. The likelier explanation is that Milton, writing to his father, was in his own mind vindicating his choice of poetry as his weapon of spiritual war against all those persons and conditions which opposed the purposes of the young Puritan idealist. Let not poetry be disesteemed, he says. The gods love it. It can chain up hell. It can reveal the future. In the days before it was corrupted by luxury and greed, the bard used to sing of the achievements of heroes, the foundation of the world and the exploits of the gods. Milton's father is himself a musician favored by Apollo, and he has reared his son to love the muses. He might have put him to a trade or to the law, but he has preferred instead that he should get learning, a greater gift than the treasures of Austria and Peru. The poem ends on the note of spiritual arrogance so characteristic of the author, of self-assurance in the love of God and in the hate of his enemies, of confident expectation of success and fame. 'Therefore since I am a part, though the humblest, of the gifted throng, I shall sit amid the victor's ivy and laurel. I shall not mix obscurely with the dull rabble; my footsteps shall be far from profane eyes.'[41] So much he owes to his father's generosity, and he is not without hope that his verses will render his father known as an example for fathers in future ages. A few years later he expressed the expectation that, given a church reformed according to his ideas, rich fathers would feel no hesitation about meeting the expense of educating their most gifted sons for its ministry.

The result of all this was that Milton at the age of twenty-three went from Cambridge to spend six years at his father's house at Horton. His life there was conducted according to plan. Cambridge, if it taught him anything, taught him that he must take time to learn much more than could be learned there. To the heaven-sent gift of poetry must be added 'industrious and select reading, steady observation, insight into all seemly and generous arts and affairs.'[42] The mood in which he went from Cambridge to Horton is explicitly voiced in the last of the exercises he composed for delivery at the university and in the letter and the sonnet he wrote directly afterwards on his twenty-third birthday.[43] Cambridge, he says in the oration, would almost persuade a man that a life of ignorance was the more desirable, but for him happiness without great learning is impossible. He cannot tolerate the common and the mean. When ignorance lords it in the universities and the pulpits, piety goes into mourning and religion sickens and dies. 'Without Art the mind is fruitless, joyless, and altogether null and void. For who can worthily gaze upon and contemplate the Ideas of things human or divine, unless he possesses a mind trained and ennobled by Art and Learning . . . God would indeed seem to have endowed us to no purpose, or even to our distress, with this soul which is capable of the highest wisdom, if he had not intended us to strive with all our might toward the lofty understanding of those things, for which he had at our creation instilled so great a longing into the human mind.'

Thus he exulted in his decision, confident that life was not too short to encompass art. Yet a friend whom he does not name—we naturally wonder whether this was Thomas Young once more—was about the same time writing to him, apparently to express surprise that he was not taking his expected place in the pulpit. Was he dreaming his life away, abandoned to too great love of study? Milton admits in his reply that he remains as yet 'obscure and unserviceable to mankind,' but he denies that he has put aside duty, ambition, pride and the love of gain merely in order to study for his amusement and curiosity. Far from it, since that would be to cut himself off from all action, 'the most help-lesse, pusilanimous & unweapon'd creature in the world, the most unfit & unable to doe that which all mortals most aspire to—either to defend & be usefull to his friends, or to offend his enemies.' No, he would like to have a house and family of his own, he has the desire for fame and honor which is seated in the breast of every true scholar, and he fears the 'seasing'[44] that befell him that hid the talent. But he is taking thought to be not early but fit, since the greater talent must be returned with the greater increment. He could, he says, go on to say more upon this theme, but he is not yet ready. He will merely give earnest of the work he expects finally to accomplish by sending along a sonnet to which his reflections upon the passage of time have prompted him. This is the sonnet in which he gave assurance that, although at twenty-three he had as yet done little, still, 'be it less, or more, or soon, or slow,' he would in the end measure up to that lot 'toward which Time leads me, and the will of Heaven.'

> All is, if I have grace to use it so,
> As ever in my great task Masters eye.

The particular task he set himself at Horton was to read the ancient writers and to go through history 'in the method of time.'[45] Beginning with Greece and Rome, he came down through Constantine to the Christian centuries, to the fathers and councils, the Italian cities, and finally the Reformation and England. By 1637 he was asking Diodati to send him 'Justiniani, the historian of the Venetians.'[46] Precisely when he completed this program there is no telling. Ten years later he confessed that he had done no more than read here and there in the councils of the church, but he claimed to have read into them all and boasted that if provoked he would make himself an 'expert councelist' in three months.[47] Certainly he did not by that time hesitate to cope on even terms with erudite churchmen, interlarding his polemic against the bishops with references to the most respectable authorities as well as to philosophers such as Machiavelli, Bacon and Selden and to poets such as Homer, Euripides, Virgil, Dante, Petrarch, Chaucer, Gower, Langland, Spenser and Sidney. Near the close of this period he wrote that 'Ceres never sought her daughter Proserpine . . . with greater ardour than I do this Idea of Beauty . . . ever pursuing it by day and night, in every shape and form.'[48] He was looking in his study of history for 'things both nobly done, and worthily spoken.'[49] When he found such things outside of scripture and the classics—these were constantly open beside him—when he found, that is, some notable statement of principle he wished to remember, he copied it out in his commonplace book.[50] This has been preserved, and in the handwriting he employed at the time one may read the pregnant utterances he chose to enter under such headings as Rex, Matrimonium, De Liberis Educandis and the like. If, would be his cry at the outbreak of the revolution, we would but do what we ought and not be careless of knowing what were well done, the nation would come nearer to true peace. But he had long before concluded that men must be free to learn and to say and do what they thought would be well said and done. The tenor of the entries in the commonplace book is plain. Milton was already thinking of the limitations that must be put on the interference of custom and government with the freedom of thought, utterance and action of men like himself. When in later years he looked back over his career, it would seem to him that for such freedom he had been contending all his life. 'I have determined to lay up as the best treasure and solace of a good old age . . . the honest liberty of free speech from my youth.'[51] From his boyhood, he claimed, he had endeavored 'not to be ignorant what was law, whether divine or human.'[52] He had tired out his whole youth in 'wearisome labours and studious watchings,'[53] and even after eight years of study, he had not, he felt, 'completed the full circle' of preparation for the great poem which, in more than one aside in the revolutionary pamphlets, he continued to promise should be yet forthcoming.

The great poem which was to be Milton's justification for abandoning the pulpit was not to be achieved for many years to come. Meanwhile, however, the spirit in which the poet dedicated himself to the writing of it flowered in *Comus* and *Lycidas*. These poems were written at the very time when Laud, having done his best to repress the Puritan preachers, was turning his wrath upon the Puritan pamphleteers. There can be no question that Milton knew and felt a deep personal resentment at these circumstances. It is, therefore, tempting to infer some personal connection at this time between the poet, so thoroughly imbued with the revolutionary spirit, and other revolutionaries active at the moment. We must resist that temptation at this as at later points in his career. He was capable of taking a most passionate interest in immediate persons and events. Characteristically, however, he held himself in service to the ideal of freedom and in opposition to the principle of evil. He engaged in personal contest only when drawn by special circumstance and then only momentarily, returning always to the ideal plane upon which he was more at home. But on that plane *Comus* and *Lycidas* are as authentic expressions of the Puritan spirit on the eve of the revolution as anything that came from the hand of Prynne. No one has written English of surer beauty or made more surpassing music out of words. No one has made us thrill more deeply to the loveliness of the English countryside, to the mystery of the sea, to the majesty of rich names. No one, commanding such resources of genius, has held them more purely to his design and to his theme. Yet no one has made beauty come to heel of a more resolute morality. Protestant evangelicism, humanistic faith in literary art—the two became completely one in this poet who was no less a Puritan for being a poet.

The pastoral convention lent itself traditionally to criticism of the court and clergy, but in *Comus* and *Lycidas* a young trumpeter of the Lord is blowing upon the silver reeds. Milton took his cue for form in the masque from Jonson and Fletcher, the Circe myth from Homer by way of *The Faerie Queene*. For his allegory he makes his own the quintessence of that poetic idealism which Puritanism made militant in him. Spenser's Britomart went through evil unscathed, secure in the integrity of her purpose to find the lover she had seen in the mirror of her soul; Amoret sat spellbound but immune to sin because her heart was pure; Arthur without a struggle overcame the wicked and succored the good by flashing a shield which bore the image of ideal beauty impressed upon his mind. Such are the principal elements derived from literary sources to be found in *Comus*, these and the inspiration of Shakespearean verse. But for the startling intensity with which Milton utilizes his material there is another source. Puritanism may have narrowed but certainly it also sharpened and heightened the poetic force in him; and his expression of the Puritan spirit owed much, though much that must not be too definitely specified, to the Puritan preachers. They too cast the lessons of their inner experience into the image of the pilgrim, seemingly lost, but not abandoned by God, encountering temptation and danger but journeying steadfastly toward heaven, led by the light within. Whose sermons Milton may have heard or read, one cannot say. He could no more have escaped hearing a great many in which spiritual wayfaring was depicted than he could have escaped reading the Bible itself. Surely those describing the elect soul as a child of light walking in darkness, which Thomas Goodwin delivered about 1628 probably at Cambridge or Ely and which he dedicated to the kinsman and heir of Fulke Greville, would not have been beneath the notice of the scrivener's son, the creator of that Lady who also

> could see to do what vertue would
> By her own radiant light, though Sun and Moon
> Were in the flat Sea sunk.

At any rate, no one who has read many of the sermons which in the days of Milton's youth were sweeping young men into the Puritan movement can fail to be struck by their resemblance at a hundred points in thought and image to Milton's poems of the decade of 1630. *Comus*, with all its lovely reminiscence of the high poetry of the Renaissance, is the poet's version of that sermon of spiritual wayfaring which it would have been his part to preach if he had ever in fact mounted the pulpit.

The theme of Milton's sermon, like that of many another Puritan sermon, is temptation, or rather the sense of freedom from moral danger which is enjoyed by the good who know their own minds and are assured of their own election. 'Virtue could see to do what virtue would.' 'Love virtue, she alone is free.' 'Or if Virtue feeble were, Heaven itself would stoop to her.' To the young and high-hearted as well as to the saints of God, evil has no terrors, and Milton was both a young man and a Puritan saint when he wrote this poem. To his Lady, temptation is nothing but impotent vexation. She knows what is right for her to do. She knows no weakness, nothing but the fierce joy of moral self-sufficiency and self-assertion. The poet gives us, not wisdom concerning the problem of moral choice, but the exultation of a most extraordinary and very vital young person upon having chosen. It is the same mood which was heard in the last of his academic exercises, in the poem *Ad Patrem*, in his letters to Diodati, and in the letter and sonnet prompted by his twenty-third birthday.

Yet how engagingly the thing is done! The Attendant Spirit tells us that there dwells in this wild wood Comus, son of Circe, who urges a potent wine upon passing wayfarers. Those who drink become beasts. When any come whom God favors, the Spirit shoots from heaven to give them safe convoy. Such a one, a Lady, has lost her way at nightfall in the wood. Though slightly apprehensive, she is reassured by the thought that the virtuous walk attended by their own strength and that at need God will send a glistering guardian to protect them. At this point Comus finds her and leads her off with the promise of safe shelter. Her two brothers come looking for her, the younger expressing a reasonable fear lest his sister suffer discomfort and alarm. The elder assures him that the virtuous have nothing to fear, that the wicked are always, the good never benighted. Yet may there not, the younger asks, be danger for one who is a maid and beautiful? True, but the elder draws encouragement from poets and philosophers, who have told him that the pure mind not only bears power within itself but is lackeyed by liveried angels from on high. Their sister may commune in her solitude with these bright beings. They will help to make her virtuous, and virtue passing outward from her mind will keep her beautiful and safe in body. The bad grow beastly. 'How charming is divine philosophy,' the younger brother charmingly exclaims. Whereupon the Attendant Spirit comes to them, confirming the philosophy but bearing news of their sister's plight. Comus has lured her by deception to his hall and is offering her his wine. Not for a moment can he persuade her to drink. She roundly calls him fool for trying. 'Why are you vexed, Lady?' he asks but is spurned the more heartily. Only the good can give good gifts and to a wise appetite that which is not good is not delicious. 'O foolishness of men,' is his reply, of men who will not buy pleasure with beauty; 'be advised; you are young yet.' The Lady had not meant to have unlocked her lips in that unhallowed air—she has, of course, been far from silent—but like her author she hates

> when vice can bolt her arguments
> And vertue has no tongue to check her pride.

Milton can either be silent or give full cry. So the Lady lets Comus have not the last or least glorious tirade on virtue that vice was to hear from the Puritan idealist. The invective of *Lycidas* and of the anti-prelatical tracts against the blind mouths of the church are both anticipated when the Lady says that nature's blessings are meant to be dispensed in even proportion to just men, not crammed by swinish gluttons. 'Shall I go on?' she cries, 'Or have I said enow?' Comus is too base to understand, but if she were to try—had not the angels in the hymn on the nativity almost brought back the age of gold by their singing, and was not Milton himself expecting to try?—then the worth

> Of this pure cause would kindle my rap't spirits
> To such a flame of sacred vehemence,
> That dumb things would be mov'd to sympathize,
> And the brute Earth would lend her nerves, and shake,
> Till all thy magick structures, rear'd so high,
> Were shatter'd into heaps o're thy false head.

'Mere moral babble,' mutters Comus, but he knows in his heart what his author has come to believe, that eloquence, that poetry are irresistible by evil. Unable to enthrall the Lady's mind, he can do no more than place a momentary spell upon her body. But that is nothing. The brothers rush in with the Attendant Spirit, summon a goddess by song, by a song Sabrina frees the Lady, and the Spirit, Shakespeare's Ariel turned Puritan, flies off singing

Mortals that would follow me,
Love vertue, she alone is free;
She can teach ye how to clime
Higher then the Spheary chime.

Love virtue! The virtue Milton loved was perhaps that of those who hunger and thirst after righteousness, are pure in heart, and rejoice to be reviled and persecuted, but hardly that of the poor in spirit, the meek, the mournful and the merciful. *Comus* registers the exultation he felt in the realization of his powers and the choice of his career. He wrote to Diodati that God had made him love the beautiful vehemently, but he scorns what the vulgar and depraved think of beauty. He dares to feel and speak and be what the wisest men in all ages have deemed best. He will honor the wise, even though, prevented by fate and nature, he fail to make a place for himself among them. He is still at his studies, but he is also pluming his wings for another poem.[54] Something had happened to make him reflect once more on the course he had chosen, to count the risks in which his ambitions involved him, to take stock of himself and his purposes as he had done several years before on his twenty-third birthday. The result was *Lycidas*, Milton's most perfect expression of faith in his own conception of priesthood and his most memorable polemic against those who had kept him from exercising that priesthood in the English church.

Edward King had been a student with Milton at Cambridge, had written verses, and had accepted the lot which Milton had rejected. He was about to enter the church when he was drowned by shipwreck in the Irish Sea. His college friends went about preparing a volume of poems in his memory. It does not appear that the personal bond between him and Milton was anything but slight and casual, but he and his sudden death now assumed symbolic meaning for the poet who had been church-outed by the prelates. A little more or less and he might himself have been Edward King. As it was, he was asked to write an elegy for him. It was like writing an elegy on himself, on the churchman he had decided not to be, still more on the man the English church had lost by his decision. These were the suggestions which he chose to invest with poetry. He has to say: I was at Cambridge with this man; I might have been Lycidas; we studied together; he is dead;

such men are ill-spared; he cannot have died; he has but gone to live a larger life. The commonplaces of mourning, lifted above commonplace by Milton's art and personal convictions. The convention of pastoral elegy is cast over the timeworn theme but not permitted to embarrass or obscure. Arcady sets off Cambridge. English scenes are enriched by delicately poised association with the land of shepherds. But all this artistry is not employed for the exhibition of the writer's virtuosity or for the enhancement of Cambridge or of King. The poem is Milton's personal confession of his effectual calling from God to be a poet, as truly such as the testimony of any of the spiritual preachers, the confession of his calling and of his answering to the call by the dedication of his talents to service prompted by faith. The image carved in a few lines in *Lycidas* is the same picture that appears in sonnet, in letter, in Latin verse and in revolutionary pamphlet, the picture of Milton making a Miltonic poem or a sermon, whichever one chooses to call it, out of his own life. After the idyllic picture of college friendship with pastoral lament for the departed comes the question, why be a poet, why meditate the thankless muse?

> Were it not better don as others use,
> To sport with Amaryllis in the shade,
> Or with the tangles of Neaera's hair?

The right Puritan answer follows. He must be a poet because that best pleases God, not for sake of fame on earth, though that is but the last infirmity of noble minds, but fame in heaven.

Then the poet proceeds to do God and his church an immediate service. He may be called to meditate the muse, but nevertheless that church is to be condemned which will not take such men as he to be its ministers. St. Peter himself is brought on to condemn the prelates for church-outing Milton for sake of those blind mouths that creep and intrude and climb into the fold for their bellies' sake, shove away the bidden guest, and let the people go untaught or mistaught, 'swoln with wind and the rank mist they draw.' In two cryptic lines the dread voice speaks of smiting, and then ceases. We shall hear it again a little later, neither so cryptic nor so soon silent. Meanwhile the poet strews English flowers on Lycid's bier, invokes the vision of the fabled shores where his body lies, and again hears the angels singing.

There entertain him all the Saints above,
In solemn troops and sweet Societies,
That sing, and singing in their glory move,
And wipe the tears forever from his eyes.

Thus Milton in 1637 immortalized the zeal of the saints here below. Laud probably never heard of *Lycidas*, and the preachers had no real notion what manner of person they had in its author won to their cause. Yet there could hardly have been given more extraordinary evidence than that poem gave of the depth and sweep to which their influence had attained. The Puritan pulpit might temporarily be stilled, but it had done its work, done it thoroughly and well. By popularizing the Bible and the Puritan epic of the spiritual life, it had popularized an incomparable vocabulary for the expression of the people's discontent with the present and their hope for the future. In extending the range of its own popular appeal, it had fostered the press, and in giving such characters as Prynne a cause for playing the martyr, it had made the uses of publicity known to all. It had raised up such men as the two Goodwins and the other independents who were to prove the undoing of the dream of presbyterian reform. It had opened the way to the irretrievable disruption of the church, to dissent and to the incipient democracy voiced by Lilburne. In Milton, finally, the cause of the Puritan preachers had enlisted a great literary genius, one who brought the idealism bred by the poetry and philosophy of Renaissance humanism to the support of Puritan revolutionary zeal in church and state. The performances of Prynne, Bastwick and Burton and of Lilburne, the dialectics of John Goodwin, and the appearance of *Lycidas* showed that revolution was ready to burst forth and that repressing preachers, cropping the ears of pamphleteers and church-outing idealistic poets could not stop it. Laud had but to give the occasion, and the upheaval would begin.

Root and Branch

BY 1639 Charles and Laud had momentarily succeeded in repressing the more obvious expressions of Puritanism. The pulpits were quiet if not completely silent. Prynne, Bastwick and Burton had been sent far away to prison without their ears. The most intransigent non-conformists had left the country. The separatists who had not fled had taken to cover. Lilburne, though still protesting as best he could in clandestine print, fed off the poor box in the Fleet. Milton, still occupied in confirming his estimate of his talent and in preparing for his great poem, was traveling in Italy. The Puritan gentry were having to pay ship money or suffer the consequences. Yet all this would not yet suffice to meet the needs of the state if ruin were to be prevented. Something more must be attempted if the crown was to overcome the resistance of that public which the Puritans had done so much to make conscious of its interests and articulate in its opinions.

The next blow was struck at the Scottish kirk because in Scotland the preachers still had the upper hand. The Elizabethan settlement had kept the church in England under the control of the crown, but reformation in Scotland had reached a different outcome. The Scottish nobility had been content to take the lands of the church and leave the church itself to the clergy. Consequently the ministers had promptly succeeded, where their English colleagues had failed, in making themselves the undisputed leaders of the people. Knox and his fellow reformers brought in the English Bible, presbyterian church government, and the doctrine of predestination. The Bible helped the people to an expressive medium of communication and prepared them to enter upon the common stage with their English kinsmen. Presbyterianism, adapted from the Genevan model, gave them an ecclesiastical organization at once popular, representative and national. Dogmatic preaching of salvation by faith disciplined them for dispute and conflict and fired them to assert their rights against all claims of privilege bestowed by lesser hands than God's. The system was well suited to a people of such peculiar energy, situated in such a country. It supplied a means of ready intercourse and of making the popular voice heard in public affairs. It left the clergy unbridled, free to devote themselves to the direction and regimentation of public opinion. From every pulpit of the land not only the covenant of grace but the call to battle against wickedness in high places could be sounded with a promptitude, a unanimity and an effect that Laud might well have envied and had good reason to fear.

The example of the Scottish kirk, needless to say, had not been lost upon the English Puritans. Differences, the significance of which no one at the time could fully understand, were to keep England from ever falling into the presbyterian mold, but that such would be the event could not at the time have been foreseen. Committed to resistance against Puritanism, Charles logically concluded that, if he was to reunite Englishmen within the church under the crown, he must first bring the Scots to heel. The attempt led to immediate rejection of prelatism and the prayer book by the General Assembly of the kirk and to riots in Edinburgh. Twice Charles marched to the border, and twice his half-hearted army of courtiers, gentlemen and their retainers quailed before embattled saints.

The first so-called Bishops' War, ending in swift defeat, opened a new chapter in the literature of the Puritan Revolution. In his discomfiture, Laud was persuaded to sanction resort in self-defense to the weapon he had been attempting to debar. He had tried to prevent the use of the press in controversy even by his own adherents. Now he gave way and consented to try whether a pamphlet could succeed where surplice and prayer book, Star Chamber and High Commission had failed. The proceedings of the General Assembly of the kirk moved him to put upon Joseph Hall, Bishop of Norwich, the task of preparing for publication a general defense of prelacy. It was submitted to him page by page for correction and approval and issued from the press early in 1640 with the title *Episcopacy by Divine Right Asserted*.[1] It elicited a salvo of replies from the Puritan side and achieved a kind of immortality by deflecting Milton from his poem in order to resume more directly and aggressively the war he had already declared against prelatism in *Lycidas*.

Hall's pamphlet did not prevent defeat for his masters in the second Bishops' War, a defeat even more ignominious and disastrous than the first. Charles was left with an army of Scots encamped upon English soil. Since they refused to go home until they were paid off, there was nothing he could do but call the Long Parliament into being. Parliament assembled in November 1640. Among its very earliest acts was the issuance of orders for the recall of Prynne, Bastwick and Burton and the release of Lilburne. Prynne and his fellows were welcomed home in triumph by the populace. Lilburne's plea was presented in the House of Commons by Cromwell. At the same time exiled preachers came flying back from Holland and America. Milton had returned from his Italian journey the year before upon hearing of the commotion caused by the first Bishops' War. Laud and Strafford took their way to the Tower and to the block. Star Chamber and High Commission were swept away, and clamor began for the abolition of prelacy root and branch.

Yet though it seemed that the prelatical Babylon was falling, it did not follow that the presbyterian Zion was to rise immediately upon its ruins. The members of the spiritual brotherhood resumed their pulpits, but separatists and enthusiasts of all sorts at the same time mounted their tubs. What was even more important, the press, suddenly freed from all restraint, began to pour forth a flood of print. The educated ordained preacher of the church would now have to compete with the 'mechanick' who enjoyed the gifts and the instruction only of the spirit, and both would have to compete not only in the pulpit and not only with one another but in the press and with all who might choose to utilize no pulpit but the press. This, though few understood its true meaning, was certainly not the least far-reaching consequence of the demolition of the old regime. One man, fortunately, does seem to have been alive to the historical significance of what had happened. This was the bookseller, George Thomason. Directly upon the opening of the Long Parliament, he began trying to collect at least one copy of everything that appeared from the teeming press in London. He even took to noting upon each item the date on which he entered it in his collection. He did not succeed in laying his hands upon everything, but by the end of 1641 he had gathered in over a thousand books, pamphlets and single sheets, and before he desisted twenty years later he had collected over twenty thousand.[2]

One of the earliest publications to take its place on Thomason's shelves was another effort by Bishop Hall to make the pamphlet do for episcopacy what other means had so signally failed to accomplish. Nothing now could save the most sacred things from the ordeal of public discussion, and in consternation at what was going on Hall addressed to Parliament what he called *An Humble Remonstrance*. He was a cleric of a perennial type, a manly man fit to be a bishop.[3] He warmed easily to a choleric righteousness which quickly boiled over in a rush of words, well-chosen and neatly phrased. Though generally muddled in his ideas, he thought himself open-minded. Yet he was tenacious in the extreme of habits and possessions which he chose to regard as rights. His qualities had helped him from one good post to another. In his very first parish his path was impeded by one Lyly, whom he describes as a witty atheist and who may have been the poet and playwright. In answer to Hall's prayers the man was soon removed by the plague. Then Hall took to writing works of pious edification and of special pleading, the latter directed to all the dispossessed, Brownists as well as Catholics, of the English church. He was moved as by pained surprise at the wicked folly of men who could deem their own ideas more important than the peace of the establishment, but he was quite honestly prepared to tolerate ideas for the sake of peace. He was rewarded presently by a royal chaplaincy, by calls to preach in high places, by a prebend, encumbered by a lawsuit which he prosecuted with vigor, and finally by a bishopric. Bent always upon the safety of the church, he attempted as King James's representative at the Synod of Dort to moderate between Calvinists and Arminians. As Bishop of Exeter he got into trouble by hanging back in the matter of extreme uniformity, but made it up by going on his knees to the king. His theology smacked strongly of deism and common sense. Predestination meant for him divine authority for things as they were. Steeped in Seneca's smooth and engaging moralizings, he shows how easily a prosperous man could compound Calvinism and stoicism into the theory that all was for the best in the best of all possible worlds. He showed too how Anglican intellectual liberalism, so urbanely exemplified by Chillingworth and Hales, could be transposed into stand-

pattism in practical affairs. Whether in his *Heaven upon Earth* of 1606
or his *Remedy of Discontentment* of 1645, Hall's specific for the
divisions of the seventeenth century was something most nearly approaching the doctrines of *The Essay on Man.* To question nothing,
to trust providence, to be in all things content, this was to have a good
conscience. Discontent was sin. So he demonstrated the neat equilibrium of goods by which the poor are blessed with the better chance
for heaven and the rich run the greater risk of hell. Life is a game of
chess where some are appointed to play pawn, some king, and some, it
would seem, bishop. Righteousness is resignation to what may befall in
the game; religion, reverence for the hand that plays. Consequently in
the controversies of the church, Hall insists that differences of opinion
should never be permitted to rend the seamless garment of Christ.
'Never treatise could be more necessary in this curious and quarrelous
age than *De Paucitate Credendorum.*'[4]

Hall was notwithstanding a vigorous and ready writer. Far back in
Elizabeth's time he had written a kind of satirical romance, *Mundus
Alter et Idem*, and had distinguished himself in *Virgidemiarum* as one
of the earliest practitioners of satire in the heroic couplet. His assertive
temper and active, if not very profound, wit gave a kind of coarse vigor
to these works. For his prose style he owed something to Seneca's
epistles. Nothing could be in more striking contrast to the style of men
like Milton and the more imagistic of the Puritan preachers. Hall's
diction is crisp and clear; his sentences, cleverly balanced and pointed,
are neither heaped up syntactically nor clogged with figurative language. When, dropping the tone of hectoring self-righteousness, he
writes most purely for rhetorical effect, the result, as in his *Characters
of Vertues and Vices*, is not without charm. Yet *Episcopacy by Divine
Right* and *An Humble Remonstrance*, suave and lucid though they
are, nevertheless betray the failure of the Anglican intellectuals to take
the measure of the forces with which they had to contend. Hall's logic
proceeds in the conventional pattern. He has no intelligent attention to
give to the motives and desires behind the attack on episcopacy. He
never considers whether episcopacy would or would not accomplish
any of the things its opponents wanted done. Traveling the hard-worn
track of debate concerning the precise functions of apostles, bishops
and presbyters in the primitive church, he refers everything to author-

ity, bases every claim on divine right. The sum of the matter was that he had never heard of a church in England without bishops, could not without dismay think of one shorn of bishops. The best he could do was to concede that, if some bishops were delinquent, they should be personally punished but their sacred office left untouched. Though their estate was lordly, their minds were required to be humble, and was it not grievous that a certain bishop, whom he does not name, should out of twenty-seven rich manors be reduced to seven and those the meanest of the lot? After a few months of the Long Parliament, he was ready to concede almost anything so long as at least the form of prelacy were retained. True, God permitted certain churches to be without bishops, but he intended all to have them if they could. Those that lacked them were to be more pitied than disapproved; those possessing them would be mad to give them up. Thus the elderly dignitary caught in a revolution goes round and round in panic, defending his possessions.

Nothing that Hall could say was able to stop the movement which by 1641 was sweeping forward to the uprooting of prelacy and the calling of a national assembly of Puritan divines for the reorganization of the church. To abolish prelacy would, as a matter of fact, prove to be easier than to reconstruct the church, and this fact became immediately apparent in the divergence of ideas and interests among the attacking forces in the press. The principal argument which Hall advanced for the old order was that prelacy, as scripture and the fathers proved, had been divinely established in the primitive church. The pundits of presbyterianism at once joined issue on this point. The spokesmen for the Scots were Alexander Henderson with *The Unlawfulness and Danger of Limited Prelacie* and Robert Baillie with *The Unlawfulness and Danger of Limited Episcopacie*. In behalf of the English, five preachers, calling themselves Smectymnuus and numbering among them Thomas Young, Milton's friend and former tutor, jointly challenged Hall with an *Answer* to his *Humble Remonstrance.*[5] The arid prolixities of these polemics might lead one to suppose that the future of England hung upon the question whether the church as instituted by Christ and the apostles had been episcopalian or presbyterian and that this question was to be settled once and for all by theological technicians. The Puritans, if anything even more than the

Anglicans, relied implicitly upon the infallibility of their authorities and their intellectual methods. Syllogisms and citations, interspersed with accusations of popery and Arminianism, were what Henderson, Baillie and the Smectymnuans had to offer as reason and persuasion.

The Puritan Revolution could not, of course, have come to pass without the marching and countermarching of learned doctors on the printed page. But the decisive strokes which sent Strafford to the block, Laud to the Tower, and Charles to his tents, were delivered by the Puritan political leaders in Parliament. These were among the very men who had taken the spiritual preachers to be their guides and the objects of their protection and patronage. The names of not a few of them appeared in the dedicatory epistles to the preachers' published sermons before they did on the roster of the Long Parliament. But, though thoroughly imbued with Puritan principles, they were also most of them strongly moved by the influence of Renaissance humanism, especially by the political idealism which had descended to them from the great nationalist and Protestant courtiers of Elizabeth. There had been in Elizabethan days not only a Puritan element in the church but also something like a Puritan party at court. This was made up of the great peers and their adherents, conspicuously anti-Catholic, potentially when not openly anti-clerical, intellectually liberal, and strongly individualistic and nationalistic in temper and policy. Under the conditions of Elizabethan court politics they had found leaders of a kind in the Earl of Leicester and the unfortunate Earl of Essex, but they are best remembered in such shining figures as Sidney and Raleigh and in the literary expression given to their ideals by Spenser in *The Faerie Queene*. Bacon may fairly be counted as intellectually, at least, of the same kindred. All shared in the humane aspirations and high intellectual culture of their age. All hoped for the development of a powerful English state under the leadership of an enlightened patriotic aristocracy. No Puritans in any narrow sense, they and their successors were nevertheless fervid individualists in religion, and their imaginations kindled to the Puritan saga of spiritual wayfaring and warfaring. Consequently they gave their adherence to the preachers of that image of life and threw their weight against the baseborn clerics and upstart favorites whom they had, with increasing disgust, seen climb at the Stuart court into positions of wealth and authority.

Thus, as the troubles of the regime multiplied, the descendants of the Elizabethan idealistic, patriotic, Protestant peers and gentlemen came forward, *mutatis mutandis,* to take the leadership of the Puritan party at the revolution.

To this party belonged Robert Greville, Lord Brooke. His personal connections illustrate how close were the ties of neighborhood, interest and family which at the opening of the Long Parliament bound the Puritan leaders together and linked them to their predecessors. Brooke was the cousin, adopted son and heir of Fulke Greville, the first Lord Brooke, poet and friend of Sidney as well as an important man at court under Elizabeth and James. The second Lord Brooke was a personal adherent of the Earl of Warwick; and his man of business was Sir Nathaniel Rich, the neighbor and close friend of Sir Francis Barrington. The latter's lady was the aunt of Hampden and Cromwell. Other lines connected these men with such people as the Earl of Lincoln, the Fiennes family, John Pym and Sir Henry Vane. The members of this group did not in every instance find place and favor at court, but they did advance more and more as leaders of the opposition to Stuart policies in the nation. They sympathized with the Puritan preachers if for no other reason than that they resented the steady intrusion into politics of churchmen like Laud. Actually, as the event showed, they were little inclined to theocracy of any kind, Puritan or Anglican. It was the Puritan way of life as expressed in the Puritan saga which appealed to them, not the godly Utopia whether of the Scottish or the Massachusetts model. Their object was a strong nation, led not by preachers but by energetic, God-fearing gentlemen. As opposition leaders, they were naturally inclined to extend their protection to all dissenting elements, not only to the more moderate Puritan reformers within the church but also to the independents and the sects. They had sound political, patriotic and intellectual reasons for enlisting the support of all Englishmen, regardless of religion. No group in the course of the revolution did more to promote religious confusion or to bring forward the political necessity for toleration.

The attitude of the Puritan peers and gentlemen is clearly brought out in their relation to the beginnings of New England. They were, in the first place, prime figures in aiding emigration. John Cotton, Thomas Hooker and Roger Williams, each in some fashion enjoyed the friendship and support of members of the party, and well-known tradition has it that Cromwell and Hampden themselves thought seriously of removing to America. Lord Brooke and Lord Saye and Sele actually took steps toward the establishment in the wilderness of a new England that should accord with their ideals. In 1635 they applied to Massachusetts with a view to settling in that colony.[6] They stipulated that the state should recognize the rank of gentleman above that of freeholder and accord to it special political privilege and authority. This the theocrats of the godly commonwealth were willing to grant, but they insisted upon church membership as the qualification for citizenship. The two noble lords would stomach nothing of the kind. With several associates, including Hampden and Pym, they proposed instead to make use of the Earl of Warwick's patent to the valley of the Connecticut. The settlement of Saybrook ensued, but for some reason its two chief patrons dropped out of personal participation in that project, and when they resumed their intention of quitting England, turned their thoughts toward the Caribbean. Before anything could come of that scheme, the Bishops' Wars began and revolution was afoot. The only concrete result of the impulse of the aristocratic liberal Puritans to try the American experiment was Sir Henry Vane's brief sojourn in the New World and his unsuccessful attempt to defend Anne Hutchinson. To this might be added the establishment by Roger Williams of a kind of Utopia in Rhode Island, countenanced by Vane and his associates when they had attained power at home and based upon principles contrary to those which prevailed in Massachusetts.

These circumstances suggest the background of personal conviction and experience which animated the attack on the bishops by the great parliamentary leaders during the first half of 1641. The progress of their root-and-branch bill for the abolition of prelacy was interrupted by the recess forced upon parliament in the late summer of that year by Charles's ill-advised visit to Scotland. With Bishop Hall's pamphlets before him and in anticipation of the renewal of the parliamentary struggle, Lord Brooke occupied the interval by preparing for the press some of the arguments which he and his associates had been urging on the floor. The thought of *A Discourse Opening the Nature of That Episcopacie, Which Is Exercised in England*[7] secured the magniloquent adherence of Milton. They provided much of the basis of thought, from which Cromwell started in his endeavor to hew order out of chaos that was soon to come. Brooke writes the grave, elaborate style of a seventeenth-century grandee, sowing his pages thick with quotations from the classics, obligingly translated by his publisher in the second edition for the benefit of the unlearned. When moved to eloquence he is not always able to keep firm hold upon his sentence. But there is nothing archaic or confused in his thought. 'State Policy,' he says, 'is the Daughter of Converse, Observation, Industry, Experience, Practice.' Theologians 'spend their time in Criticall, Cabalisticall, Scepticall, Scholasticall Learning: which fills the head with empty aeriall notions; but gives no sound food to the Reasonable part of man.'[8] He, for his part, is unwilling to fight with shadows and proposes to deal not with words but with things. His quarrel is with the nature, not the look or the name of bishops. In a manner that would have become a Montaigne or a Bacon, he brushes aside the question so labored by clerical pens whether bishops were from the beginning. The real problem is whether they are such men as are fit to govern England now. The high-minded aristocrat concludes that for the most part they are men of low birth, bred in colleges on books, on terms and names of things. When, spurred by poverty and ambition, they rise to lordly power, they suffer a vertigo of pride. Vain, inexperienced, grasping, self-assertive, they ruin all by overreaching.

Brooke then argues from his own point of view that question of the relation of authority to truth which had so much concerned the Anglican apologists a few years before. Their position had been that the essential tenets of Christian faith were few, clear, and universally agreed upon by the churches of Christendom. All other matters were 'indifferent,' left, that is, to human decision. But it was upon these 'indifferent' points, inessential, as Hales and Chillingworth observed, to salvation, that controversy in the state chiefly revolved, and these the bishops claimed authority to decide in the interest of peace, order and safety. In the interest rather, says Brooke, of their own, but not of the nation's, security. He proceeds then to demolish the basis of the plea that prelacy was indispensable to the state, that with no bishops there could be no king. Granted that some matters are necessary to be

believed and some not, what but reason can decide which are the one
and which the other?

The basis for this attitude toward the question of authority had been
prepared by Brooke the year before in a little tract called *The Nature
of Truth, its Union and Unity with the Soule, which is One in its
Essence, Faculties, Acts; One with Truth*. This is an expression of the
idealism of the Renaissance which had been voiced in English poetry
by Spenser and by the poets of the Spenserian tradition, such as William Drummond, John Davies and the two Fletchers, and which was
to be revived with extraordinary vigor by Milton. It no doubt also
owed much to the rationalism of the humanistic reformers whose
influence must have reached Brooke through Acontius' *Satanae·Strata-
gemata*. Probably, too, he was familiar with the sermons of John
Preston, whose patron both he and his adoptive father had been, and
of John Goodwin. His tract, *The Nature of Truth*, is the attempt of
a thoughtful and idealistic mind to harmonize in a single formula his
Christian faith and his humanistic rationalism. The Platonic conception of the soul with its inborn reminiscence of the ideal and its
unceasing quest for the reflections of the one in the many had its
obvious affinities to the Puritan image of the soul called by God and
seeking to return to him by spiritual effort. The one doctrine served
to rationalize and transfigure the other. God, says Brooke, is the one,
the single reality and comprehensive being. Soul and body, spirit and
matter, in all their multitudinous variety, are therefore but one in
essence, and that essence divine. Metaphysical distinctions between
form and matter, substance and accident, are without meaning. Truth
is one both with God and with the knowledge of truth in man. The
light reflected is the light bestowed. Reason is the soul's response to
the divinity in all existence. Hence everything, every reasoning soul,
considered absolutely as an aspect of universal being, is good, and
nothing that really is is evil. The opposite of good is nonessence.
Considered relatively in time and place, the good is merely that which
reason deems better than something else at the moment, and evil is
that which appears to be not so good as something known to be better.
To keep choosing the better is to come nearer and nearer to immortal
life. To choose the worse is to go toward death. Knowledge and
understanding are the perception of particular aspects of the good in

infinite series up to God. The love of truth is the love of God prompting the soul to action. The life of the spirit is to go seeking, gathering,
sorting, testing, choosing and reassembling the dispersed particles and
reflections of truth. To live thus in the love of God is better than to
be learned or to look beyond one's ken into the mystery of the absolute
and the first cause.

And therefore that learned wit, Sir Francis Bacon, in his naturall Philosophy, bringeth only experiments, leaving the search of causes to those,
who are content, with Icarus, to burn their wings at a fire too hot for
them. . . . If now our humble spirits could be content to see all things
as they are, but one, onely bearing different shapes, we should according
to that rule, *Noli altum sapere,* improve in what we know, and there
sit down. But our spirits are mighty Nimrods, hunting after knowledge,
venturing all, to eate of the tree of knowledge of good and evill.[9]

These ideas provided Brooke with intellectual justification for religious toleration as the basis for political unity and more immediately
for his attack on prelacy. The purport of Bishop Hall's argument had
been that the religious forms prescribed by the church were essential
not to salvation but to the preservation of church and state. Since they
were inessential to salvation, he held that no conscientious objection or
disobedience might properly be raised against them, and if it were
raised, it might be punished by the magistrate as sedition and rebellion. Brooke's position was that no man and no church could fairly
decide what another man's conscience might or might not approve.
What was good or evil or indifferent to one might not be so to another,
and anyone who sought to impose his decision upon other men presumed to know the mystery of God, to know the entire mystery of
good and evil. Up to a point, Brooke's intellectual position was in this
not far removed from that of his opponents. The distinction came in
the practical application of these ideas to the problem of government.
Brooke, in arguing for freedom of individual conscience, stipulated for
the authority of rulers to suppress acts hostile to the state even though
conscience were alleged in their support. The difference between him
and the bishops, profoundly colored as it was by the suspicion and
contempt of the hereditary aristocrat for the risen churchman, was that
the bishops could conceive society only as an inclusive united church,
whereas Brooke and others like him had as their objective the organiza-

tion of a nation within which religious differences, so long as they did not disturb political authority, were to be treated as matters without public significance. The Anglicans had urged that in Christendom there were many true churches, among which the English was one. Puritans of Brooke's type merely went on to insist that there might also be more than one true church in England. In the interest of truth and of the nation, Englishmen must be permitted to choose among these true churches. 'I would gladly be shewed by Reason, what there is in Church government, why it may not derive itselfe into severall Corporations; . . . still subscribing to those things which are left by Christ to the Civill government, or Monarchicall power.' He even goes so far as to say, 'I am by no means of their judgements who say, None that are without the pale of the Church have the right to anything here below.' Only when anabaptists seek to overthrow government, Adamites, 'if there be any such,' attack property by setting up 'Communion of Wives,' or papists make it 'lawful to kill kings,' then the sword must intervene on grounds not of divinity but of policy.[10]

Brooke is thus led at the conclusion of his *Discourse* to an eloquent and chivalrous defense of the sects, the humble men of the conventicles, even tub-preachers. He and his friends were, of course, in no sense sectarians. They opposed prelatism, gave their support to non-conformists, and were presently to be classified as independents. But they were inclined to protect and to welcome the support of all elements in the populace, separatists included. The aristocratic liberals had, in consequence, more than once to defend themselves even in parliament against the charge of separatism. Now, therefore, in his *Discourse* against the bishops, Brooke, as a cultivated gentleman and peer of the realm, denies any personal connection or even full sympathy and agreement with the sects, but as a chivalrous Englishman and disinterested lover of truth, he launches into what purports to be a statement not of his own ideas but of the ideas of these people so much slandered and abused. 'I would not be mistaken by my Reader. All this time I am speaking *Their words*, not *my own*; All that I desire is, that they may have a fair Hearing, before they be severely censured.'[11] 'I dare not condemn them till I heare them.'[12]

Brooke was not quite ingenuous in these statements; at any rate the words he professes to take from the lips of tub-preachers are unmis-

takably his own. Which of the sectarian preachers or mystical enthusiasts of the moment he knew, there is no telling. Lilburne seems to have
had his protection and a little later enlisted in his regiment. What
Brooke had to say on behalf of the humble prophets so generally
despised by men of his education and position may well have been
inspired by the fiery tracts Lilburne had written from his cell in the
Fleet. It might also have been inspired by such men as Everard, Saltmarsh, Randall and Knollys, who have been discussed earlier in these
pages. Brooke's words are additional evidence that separatists of all
sorts were more active on the eve of the revolution than the extant
printed documents would indicate. At all events, the idealistic aristocrat recognized in the aspirations of the sects and of the mystical enthusiasts in general, in that dream of universal love which they too had
in fact derived in part from the humanist reformers, the lineaments of
his own ideals. The apology he puts into their mouths is an expression
of the same notions which he had put into his *Nature of Truth*. It is a
plea for liberty of thought, more specifically for the liberty of unlicensed preaching. Both in thought and in poetic eloquence it is no
unworthy predecessor to that defense of the liberty of unlicensed
printing in the course of which Milton was presently to give it praise.
Truth, though one, Brooke believed, was diversely reflected in divers
minds, and must be permitted to shine where and as it would. What
were called heresy and schism were in the main not the just occasion
for, but the effect of, persecution and of the suppression of that which
men, it might be mistakenly, took for truth. No man had complete
possession of truth; 'the wayes of Gods Spirit are free, and not tied to
a University man,'[13] or for that matter to any man, to any bishop or
magistrate or church. The light shines where it will among men, no
matter how humble or ignorant, moves them to utterance, to inquiry
and discussion, to ceaseless search for more light, until truth in its
entirety shall become known to all, and men have once more become
one with God. The tub-preachers, harmless, well-meaning men, more
to be pitied than persecuted, have, he says,

heard that God promised to poure out his Spirit upon all Flesh, all
Beleevers (as well Lay as Clergy) so that Young men should see
Visions, and Old men dreame Dreames, and though this were begun to
be accomplished even in our Saviours time, yet they (perhaps through

ignorance) Expect it should be yet still more and more accomplished every day, till Knowledge cover the Earth, as Waters fill the Sea; even till there be no more need that any man should teach his neighbor, for all men shall know the Lord; and they poore men expect a new Heaven, and a new Earth, wherein there shall neede [be] no more Temples of stone, but all good men shall be Prophets, Priests, and Kings. In the meane time they say Waters must flow out of the bellies of all that believe, till at length the great Waters of the Sanctuary flow forth without measure.[14]

The practical relation of this defense of the sects to the course of events in 1641 was of the greatest importance for the future unfolding of the revolutionary effort. The party of the Puritan peers and gentlemen was making its bid for power against that of the favorites and prelates, but also, as the event would show, against the church-state, against theocracy in any form, Anglican or presbyterian. Aiming at a strong secular state, Brooke perceived and expressed the need for allaying fear of the popular sects and for toleration of religious differences. He foreshadows the future alignment of sectaries and independents in the support of his party, lets us hear the oncoming tread of Cromwell's army. Upon the reassembling of parliament after the summer of 1641, during which the *Discourse* was written, events moved rapidly to the outbreak of civil war. Pym died and Hampden and Brooke were killed in battle. The defense of toleration and the political leadership of the Puritan left wing fell to Cromwell, perhaps a stronger spirit though certainly a man of narrower culture and more limited mind and imagination. Brooke defined a method of dealing with the problem of popular religious dissent in a manner consistent with political stability and the interest of his party. He did not envisage the problem, that would soon be presented, of controlling economic discontent and political opposition under an ordered government. Nor was Cromwell destined to solve that problem when champions of the people came forward to defend the natural rights of citizens not only against bishops and ministers but also against magistrates and governors. Cromwell, tolerant of the sects, would be able when the time came to think of no way to handle Lilburne and his friends save to prosecute them for treason.

Meanwhile the author of *Lycidas* joined the attack on prelacy as championed by Bishop Hall. It may seem surprising that he aligned himself at the start not with Lord Brooke, whom later he praised, but with the presbyterian divines, whom later he so bitterly opposed as enemies of liberty. The fact was, however, that the course he chose was the one to which in the circumstances of the moment he was naturally led by his previous history. The time had come to uproot prelacy and proclaim the New Jerusalem. It had not yet come for Milton at all costs to demand liberty. The preaching of spiritual war in the Puritan pulpit had been the animating force behind the movement for sweeping the bishops out of the church. The object of the vast majority of the preachers was to reorganize the church and restore it to its former place in society. Separatists with baptist leanings like Lilburne, perhaps an independent or two like John Goodwin, mystical enthusiasts for the brotherhood of man like Everard and Saltmarsh, a secular humanist like Lord Brooke, these men might be thinking in some fashion about liberty and toleration, but not so the great body of preachers. Their thoughts were centered on the completion of that reform which they had so long awaited in vain. Only after the Puritan peers and gentlemen had finally struck prelacy down was the problem of setting up a new order and at the same time of satisfying in some degree the demand for a new liberty forced upon the reformers' attention. Then the individualism the preachers had themselves done so much to foster arose to confound the uniformity they had all along hoped to establish. But in 1641 neither they nor their adherent Milton as yet faced that situation.

Milton entered the controversy full of the dream of that godly Utopia which in one shape or another possessed the members of the spiritual brotherhood. He was not himself actually one of them, but to begin with he completely identified himself in his own way with them. He had intended to become a preacher, he had made the necessary preparations, he had desisted from his plans because he felt himself rejected by the bishops, and he had turned to poetry as both a nobler, more effective means of accomplishing the same purposes and at the same time as a means of circumventing prelatical repression. He was far from forgetting all this when the crisis suddenly came in 1641, and he was far from forgiving the bishops for the indignity they had put upon him. He knew himself to be as competent as any churchman to deal with questions concerning the church. He had determined to lay up as the treasure and solace of his old age 'the honest liberty of free speech from my youth, where I shall think it available in so dear a concernment as the Churches good.' He had been granted 'ease and leasure . . . out of the sweat of other men.' He could not bear that God should fail to hear his voice 'when the cause of God and his Church was to be pleaded.'[15] Milton went, therefore, to the support of his old tutor, Thomas Young, and the other Smectymnuans in their attack upon Hall. We must again, however, resist the temptation to argue for a more intimate and concerted association on his part with other advocates of reform, with party movements within the church, or with sectarian organizations, than the facts will warrant. He was a very Puritan, but after a fashion solely his own. On his own plane of the highest idealism, he now paralleled the thought and effort of the presbyterians as later he was to parallel those of other revolutionary parties and religious groups. But he remained throughout on his own plane, loftily removed, never sinking his own personally conceived purposes in any party or sect, not even when he put himself to the service of the Cromwellian state. He was always, if one will, an impractical self-centered idealist. Or one may prefer to say that he never abandoned the character of poet-prophet of the godly Utopia as he himself imagined it. Smectymnuus dealt with Hall's *Remonstrance* by ploughing once more the arid sands of controversy concerning the type of church government which might be supposed on the authority of scripture and the fathers to have prevailed in apostolic times. Milton, defending Smectymnuus, chose a line of attack peculiar to himself. *Of Reformation Touching Church Discipline; Of Prelatical Episcopacy; Animadversions upon The Remonstrants Defence against Smectymnuus; The Reason of Church Government Urg'd against Prelaty; An Apology Against a Pamphlet call'd A Modest Confutation of the Animadversions upon the Remonstrant against Smectymnuus;* these writings do indeed urge presbyterianism as the unquestioned alternative to prelacy, but in a spirit and on grounds which the Smectymnuans and the godly divines who presently devised the Westminster Directory of Worship could not have conceived and were certain to repudiate. Their advocate of 1641 was already prepared to be their Abdiel of 1644.

In 1638, after the composition of *Lycidas*, Milton, still absorbed in the discipline and study which he regarded as the necessary preparation for his work as a poet, went to Italy. His aim seems to have been to complete his preparation and to have his gifts and attainments approved at the very center of learning and letters. He returned a little more than a year later, just at the time of the second Bishops' War, exulting in the commendation and encouragement he had received. He had met Grotius and Galileo. He had been cordially received in the literary circles of Florence. Members of the Academy of Florence had written verses in his praise. He had been honored by the attention of Manso, Tasso's friend. Thus he had been confirmed in his conviction, already supported by friends at home, that he 'might perhaps leave something so written to after times, as they should not willingly let it die.'[16] But he still regarded his chief purpose as a poet to be the liberation of man. When news reached him, just as he was about to go on in his travels to Sicily and Greece, of Charles' attack upon the Scots, he turned back toward home, 'for I thought it base, that I should be at my ease, even for the improvement of my mind abroad, while my fellow-citizens were fighting for their liberty at home.'[17]

During his travels and upon his return, the evidence is clear, he was maturing his plans for actually beginning the composition of the great poem for which he had been preparing. Perhaps there was some slight hesitation in his mind whether to essay universal fame by writing Latin or to be content with English, but if he wavered on this point, he must have done so only momentarily. It was in his native tongue that, as a student at Cambridge, he had proposed to write of the gods. He assured Manso, and reassured himself, that the muse could also flourish under the stormy skies of England. He would be satisfied to have his verses remembered beside English rivers. Manso was permitted to hear of the very poem he wished to write; it should deal with 'the kings of my native land,' Arthur, the knights of the round table.[18] He named this theme again in the Latin lament for Diodati, written directly after his homecoming. It was patriotism and, no doubt, the example of other literary epics which suggested at first that he should write his poem about the legendary history of his country. The fact was, however, that this meant little to his countrymen and, he soon discovered, little really to him. There was an epic which was actually filling the minds of Englishmen, his own included, but it was the Puritan epic of the two Adams, of the fall and regeneration of man. This was the saga which the preachers had made the chief vehicle of popular religious imagination, and this would have been Milton's principal theme if he had followed them into the pulpit. It was the theme which, given his conception of the role he must play, he inevitably chose for his poem. By 1642, along with notes for poems about 'British Troy,' he had set down plans for poems and for plays in Greek form on 'Adam unparadiz'd' and other biblical subjects.[19] By that time too, according to his nephew, he had already composed the lines addressed by Satan to the sun which eventually found their place in *Paradise Lost*.[20]

It was with such matters, along with study and teaching, that Milton was occupied when the storm broke about the heads of the bishops. He was little concerned with the details of the controversy over church government or of revolutionary politics in general. He was fairly launched upon the career he had chosen for himself, a career he could not but regard as of the utmost public importance. But, if poetry had power beside the office of the pulpit in teaching the nation, the poet must concede that the pulpit still had power beside the office of poetry. One of the very reasons for his turning to poetry was that the bishops barred the preachers from performing the duty which they shared with poets. Consequently when the opportunity suddenly offered itself for helping to remove that bar, Milton suspended his poetic activities and went to the support of the preachers. The presbyterian scheme of church government promised to set them free from the repression under which both they and he had suffered, and this scheme as he understood it he rushed to champion with all the high-minded vehemence of his nature. He could not, as a matter of fact, have known much about presbyterianism in its practical workings. He had no way of knowing and in his enthusiasm did not foresee that the effect of it was to give such prestige and authority to the ministerial caste as he of all men would be the last to stomach. Men of wider or at least different experience and more acute observation, men like Brooke among the aristocrats, Selden among the lawyers, and Walwyn among the merchants, perceived this from the start. Milton himself would not be slow to learn that new presbyter was but old priest writ large. But at

the moment when he assailed Bishop Hall, he had nothing but scorn
for those who feared lest reform should put a pope in every parish. He
knew the preachers as the men who had presided over his youth,
directing him in his studies, encouraging his ambitions and approving
his gifts. He knew little or nothing as yet of the stubborn churchmen
who were to dominate the Westminster Assembly and seek to suppress
his divorce tracts, of fanatics like Edwards or the Scotch what d'ye
calls, 'Gordon, Colkitto, or Macdonnel, or Galasp,' whom later he
objurgated. Geneva, where he had been the guest of the scholar and
theologian, John Diodati, stood in his mind as in that of others as the
ideal state, combining true religion with antique republican virtue.
Unworldly and inexperienced of men, he expected presbyterianism to
usher in not theocracy but Utopia.

The Utopian fervor which Milton and many others momentarily
felt for presbyterianism in the opening years of the revolution is not,
of course, to be found expressed in the pages of Smectymnuus, Baillie,
Henderson or the other Puritan polemics. There were, however, also
in circulation at the time idealized statements of the presbyterian
scheme, offering the enticements which paper constitutions generally
present to the imagination. One pamphlet, for instance, such as Milton
may have read, was published in 1641 with the title *The Beauty of
Godly Government in a Church Reformed.* The picture presented
offered an engaging contrast to prelatism and, of course, gave no hint
of the asperities which presbyterianism invariably developed in practice. It showed the people, pure in their love and obedience to God,
meeting freely to share in the miraculous word. Their ministers and
teachers are men whose calling is manifested by their gifts and confirmed by the laying on of hands by the people's chosen elders. By
baptism and by the bread and wine the communion of believers with
one another and with Christ is signalized and honored. Redemption is
accomplished by the word, through preaching, through fellowship,
through admonition and encouragement by friends. Only as a last
resort and even then with hope for repentance are the recalcitrant cast
out, an abandonment, however, only to Satan for punishment of the
spirit, not to the secular arm for punishment of life and limb. The
synodal linking of parish to parish serves, finally, as but the natural
means of Christian union in the nation. Such was the beauty of godly

government, and so much of presbyterianism, whether he read of it in one place or another, Milton made his own and urged against prelacy. He filled it, needless to say, with his own Utopian poetic spirit. Like other schemes of his, it would have been practicable enough for a race of archangels. He himself soon discovered that it would not do if it fell into the hands of the godly divines of the Westminster Assembly.

It is necessary to keep in mind this background of Utopian idealism to the presbyterianism Milton espoused if we are to understand his antiprelatical tracts for what they tell us concerning their author and the Puritan movement at large. Within the lines of Puritan approach to the great crisis, though in a way and with a force of character peculiar to himself, he brought his own personal experience, convictions and ambitions to bear in defense of the program of reform and in attack upon prelacy. His tracts are in the first instance the polemics of a man reared for the Puritan pulpit, but he is a reformer caught up by the Utopian vision which the Puritan program suggested and he is for the moment completely oblivious to the motives of self-interest which prompted a large section if not the great body of the ministerial caste to seek not only the overthrow of prelacy but the possession of comparable power by themselves. The arguments of his first two tracts, *Of Reformation* and *Of Prelatical Episcopacy*, keep pointing to Utopia, and this Miltonic Utopia becomes the main theme of the longest and most considerable of the five, *The Reason of Church Government*. But the entrance of Milton into the controversy, a layman almost, if not quite, unknown, provoked his opponent to challenge his claims to take any part in disputes concerning such matters, and this spurred him in *Animadversions* and *An Apology* not only to attack the personal motives and intellectual qualifications of Hall and other episcopal churchmen but also to defend his own character and attainments. Thus he was led to give an account of himself, of his education for the service of God in the church, of what he chose to regard as his rejection by the prelates, of his turning to poetry in place of the pulpit, and finally of his gifts, his studies, his plans for composing a poem which should do for the nation and the church the kind of service which the ministry in its own way should, he felt, also perform.

Milton opens with a sketch of the Reformation in England, its early and promising beginning followed by long delay in its fulfilment, a fulfilment now at last to be attained. He attacks the question, debated with equal and utter seriousness on both sides, whether the pattern of Rome and Canterbury or that of Geneva and Scotland was the one which obtained in the primitive church. But he is frankly disgusted by having to beat through the fathers on the track of Hall, Ussher and other apologists for episcopacy. If episcopacy be of divine origin, that fact ought to be plain from scripture to common intelligence. If it is not divinely ordained, then Englishmen have the same privilege which all men have had in all human affairs since Adam of consulting their own occasions and conveniences. But some men, he says, seem to think no doubt can be resolved nor doctrine confirmed 'unlesse they run to that indigested heap, and frie of Authors, which they call Antiquity.'[21] To be sure, most of them know little enough about it; many who pretend to be very profound in the fathers 'have scarce saluted them from the strings, and the titlepage, or to give 'em more, have bin but the Ferrets and Moushunts of an Index.'[22] They merely stuff their pages with the names of Ignatius and Polycarp and with fragments out of martyrologies and legends. He has read the fathers himself—his anti-prelatical tracts show that he had included them along with similar matter in the studies he had deemed necessary for his preparation as a poet—and found them, what? 'Whatsoever time, or the heedlesse hand of blind chance, hath drawne down from of old to this present, in her huge dragnet, whether Fish, or Sea-weed, Shells, or Shrubbs, unpickt, unchosen, those are the Fathers.'[23] Judicious men will agree that the learned should be acquainted with such authors, but chiefly in order to note how corruption and apostasy have crept in. They will read them to stop the mouths of the adversaries of truth, to bridle them with their own curb.[24] This is the purpose to which Milton now puts his own knowledge of the antiquity of the church. Prelatical pamphleteers have been attempting to stagger the credulous multitude with rubbish. He for his part, disdaining to be overawed, deems that he can do religion and his country no better service at the moment than by endeavoring his utmost to 'recall the people of God from this vaine forraging after straw.'[25]

Thus Milton seized the opportunity to resume in circumstances more satisfying to himself the zestful girding at slavish respect for tradition which he had begun at college. He also found satisfaction, no doubt, in turning thus upon the men whom he blamed for closing the pulpit to him and whom he never forgave. He had no hesitation in letting personal animus mingle with his zeal for public good; they were but the two handles of a single sword. Yet he had no taste for matching citations with his adversaries and more on his mind than to bandy epithets with prelatists and to stand up for presbyterians. He stands up for presbyterianism, but he spends his talent for vehement eloquence most lavishly on the Utopian dream it has awakened in him. Again and again in these pages the poet-prophet takes the floor from the partisan, and the epic for the Jerusalem which he believes is about to arise breaks again and again through the diatribes of the pamphleteer. He had been, or was just now, setting down in another place notes of the form and of the fable he might adopt for the poem. Into the tracts he was actually writing, he poured ideas which the poem was to express and which, developed but substantially unchanged, he finally did put into the great poems of his later years.

Milton was certain that there were such things as truth and a right way to live. Though granting that these in their absolute finality always remained to be found out, he was equally certain that by inquiry he could do something toward finding them out and that by discourse, whether as poet, preacher or pamphleteer, he could make them known. He believed that they needed but to be known by men in general in order to be desired and but to be desired in order to be attained. To this end he had consciously endeavored to fashion his own mind and character. A man's life should be his poem, expressive, it might be, of Puritan godliness but conceived and executed in the spirit of the purest classic art. To this end also he thought he saw presbyterian discipline dedicated. Thus he projected his personal ideal into a general ideal for English society, into a law, in fact, for the entire universe. The beginning and the end of all creation, the very reason for all being below God, the final explanation of the ways of God, were to be found in individual subjective experience, in a spiritual obedience self-sustained in a hostile, ever-changing world. The prime function of every polity is, therefore, to teach men to rule themselves or at least to maintain conditions under which they can most readily learn to do so. 'To govern well is to train up a Nation in true wisdom and vertue, and that which springs from thence magnanimity, (take heed of that) and that which is our beginning, regeneration, and happiest end, likenes to God, . . . this is the true flourishing of a Land, other things follow as the shadow does the substance.' And since it was axiomatic that the state should be 'but as one huge Christian personage, one mighty growth, and stature of an honest man, as big, and compact in vertue as in body,'[26] there must consequently be in the state an absolute division of function to accord with the twofold need and responsibility of the individual. The individual must be free to discover the truth and to obey and make known its laws as he discovers them. He must be always endeavoring to learn whom, what and why to obey. Anything else was superstition and slavery. The essential purpose of Milton's ideal commonwealth was to provide rulers who would so govern that such obedience should prevail and teachers who would so instruct the people that it should be learned. These are the two functions, parallel and equal in their separate spheres, to the performance of which the ablest and noblest spirits in the state dedicate themselves. 'To govern a Nation piously, and justly, which only is to say happily, is for a spirit of the greatest size, and divinest mettle. And certainly of no lesse a mind, nor of lesse excellence in another way, were they who by writing lay'd the solid, and true foundations of this Science.'[27]

No civil government, Milton avers, was ever 'more divinely and harmoniously tun'd, more equally balanc'd as it were by the hand and scale of Justice, then is the Common-wealth of England.'[28] The people are free to appoint their noblest, worthiest and most prudent men to determine state affairs under a monarch who is left free to follow the best counsel afforded him and is bound to seek and take no other. The magistrate is then free in England to perform his function, which is to maintain 'the outward peace and wel-fare of the Commonwealth, and civil happines in this life.'[29] That is to say, government and law should address themselves solely to the acts to which the outward man is prompted, not at all to the inward man which does the prompting. More particularly, the state is properly occupied with repressing acts which disturb the peace, with enforcing civil order and punishing transgressors. It is true that punishment may sometimes prove a medicine to the spirit of those that do evil but always it is applicable only to the sore not to the disease, to the effect not the cause, to the act not the motive, to the body not the mind. The state can keep the peace. It cannot make men good or wise. 'Temporall Lawes rather punish men when they have transgress't, then form them to be such as should transgresse seldomest.' To form men 'straight and blamelesse, that the Civill Magistrate may with farre lesse toyle and difficulty, and far more ease and delight steare the tall and goodly Vessell of the Common-wealth through all the gusts and tides of the Worlds mutability,'[30] this, properly, is the business of the church. For crime, which alone concerns the state, is the manifestation in act of sin, which alone concerns the church. Sin is double-headed, consisting of ignorance and malice. Not all the laws in the world, nor all the power of magistrates, Milton declares, suffice to make one man more wise or less malicious. The ills of the spirit are ineradicable save by the methods of the spirit. The only punishments or remedies that can reach them are 'a reprobate conscience in this life and hell in the other world.'[31] The methods of the spirit, which the church should administer, are teaching and discipline, or, as we should now say, education and organized public opinion. Virtue, true obedience, springs from the free love of God, hardly less from the 'pious and just honoring of ourselves.' We may attain it by the help of sound instruction and by the pressing about us of pastors, teachers, friends and neighbors with counsel and warning. We may submit or not under these ministrations as we will. If we refuse, there is nothing more to be done for us. We cannot with any success be compelled to be other than we choose to be.

Of first importance to the virtuous life is the increase of knowledge and the repulse of error. Milton asserts the unity of truth and the relativity of knowledge in terms of the intellectual experience which he shared with such men as Brooke. He drew his conceptions from Renaissance Platonism, and from the Christian idealism of humanistic poets but also from humanistic reformers and preachers. These sources supplied him and many another with a metaphysic for religious liberty and toleration. Truth, he says, probably recollecting one of Bacon's images, 'being to pass through many little wards and limits of the severall Affections and Desires, she cannot shift it, but must put on such colours and attire, as those Pathetick handmaids of the soul please.'[32] Paul himself bore unperceived scales upon his eyes. Consequently errors must always be expected to occur, even while we are reforming the church. But they are merely the rubbish and sweepings from the carving of a fine statue. They are suffered by God to be, but only for his own and our greater glory. They give our fortitude and constancy in the pursuit of truth the better occasion to grow strong and shine forth; 'the actions of just and pious men do not darken in their middle course.'[33] Except by such testing through error how could virtue ever be distinguished from 'mere vice revolted from itself and after a while returning?'[34] It is not error which damns, that were to damn all, but struggle which saves, and from the necessity for struggle, if we would serve God, there is no escape this side of the grave. The observance of no law, the practice of no rite, can shift from the soul 'the labour of high soaring.'[35] We get no help from shrines and relics. Even martyrdom, or what passes for it, may signify nothing. The martyr is 'not therfore above all possibility of erring, because he burnes for some Points of Truth.'

For Milton the one certain source of the knowledge of truth is scripture, but if we expect to find him a narrow literalist, we shall find ourselves far out of the way. In exalting scripture, he was, of course, but following the lead of Protestant reformers in general and of the Puritan preachers in particular. Already, however, we find him following that lead in a direction and with a vigor which were to carry him far beyond the limits of orthodox Puritanism. The exaltation of scripture meant in his case, to a much greater degree than the Puritan clergy as a whole would ever countenance, the exaltation of individual reason and private judgment. He freely conceded that the scriptures remained in some places difficult and obscure, but he believed that common reason was entirely sufficient to understand as much as was needed. 'The wisdome of God created understanding, fit and proportionable to Truth the object, and end of it, as the eye to the thing visible.'[36] This was as much as to say that the Bible is infallible to the extent that it is intelligible to human understanding. The essence of truth is plainness and brightness. Whatever is necessary to be known can be understood. Whatever seems difficult to understand, 'so farre expounds it selfe' as to manifest its unimportance. Scripture is the plain field, the transparent stream, antiquity the dark forest, the muddy waters, where the enemies of truth embosk or plunge. Milton would have the preachers urge nothing but the gospel upon all such, 'hold it ever in their faces like a mirror of Diamond, till it dazle, and pierce their misty ey balls.'[37] The very fathers of the church, after whom the votaries of tradition go a-gadding, confess that what they know they learned from scripture by the aid of nothing but human wit no better than our own and often as foolish and corrupt.

At this point Milton's zeal in pressing his opinions against opposition showed signs of carrying him farther than a more intimate and practical knowledge of men would perhaps have permitted him to go. He was probably little aware of the existence of those enthusiasts of lesser calibre who were already asserting the sole sufficiency of the spirit's teaching and the vanity of human learning. Yet on his own plane of passionate idealism, he was moving toward a position similar to theirs. To the charge that he was too young a man to engage in disputes concerning the church, he replies, 'for my yeares, be they few or many, what imports it?' He brings reason to the task, and to reason God makes truth plain in scripture, plain even 'to the grosse distorted apprehension of decay'd mankinde.'[38] He is as confident as Lilburne that with no weapon but the scriptures he can batter down the Nebuchadnezzar's image of prelacy.[39] Men who find it difficult to understand 'the knotty Africanisms, the pamper'd metafors, the intricate and involv'd sentences of the Fathers,' can easily understand the scriptures. The latter protest their own plainness, calling all men to be instructed, 'not only the wise, and learned, but the simple, the poor, the babes, foretelling an extraordinary effusion of Gods Spirit upon every age, and sexe, attributing to all men, and requiring from them the ability of searching, trying, examining all things, and by the Spirit discerning that which is good.'[40] The truth was, of course, that if the poet-prophet of the Miltonic Utopia was to function effectually, it was necessary for him to believe that the people he was to instruct had the capacity to understand his instruction.

Milton in 1641, putting aside all authority but scripture and all guidance but reason, thought that the type of church government plainly delineated in holy writ was presbyterianism. He accepted and defended the scheme in all its main outlines. But he did so because he momentarily saw in it the hope of effecting his own Utopia and did not see the rigid theocracy to which in fact it pointed. The very arguments he marshaled in support of Smectymnuus must, if they had thought about them, have made Thomas Young and the other godly divines included in that anagram more than a little uneasy. That the role which he assigned to the ministry was in some degree consistent with scripture and with the theory of presbyterianism was at least arguable, but it was not at all the role to which the Puritan churchmen expected in practice to be confined. The function of the state was, Milton thought, to repress crime and maintain peace so that the church should be free to carry on its war against sin by instructing the people in the truth. Not only should the state leave spiritual instruction and discipline entirely to the church; the church should look to the secular arm for no enforcement of its teachings or censures, not even for material support for itself as an institution. The church needed nothing but a free hand to employ the weapons of the spirit. It required no authority over the body. It required no collateral prestige or wealth, no tithes, no livings or endowments, no civil power to enforce any law. Its ministers should not seek to sit as magistrates, to hold office, to be lords of lands or counsellors of state, to go clad in rich vestments or fine linen or to wrap up the worship of God in pomp and ritual and to set up distinctions between sacred and profane. To Milton all such things seemed without exception devices for repressing the freedom of the church in the exercise of its appointed function.

He fears no lack of fit men eager to undertake the ministry of a church stripped of all but spiritual powers and rewards. It is, in the first place, 'the inward calling of God that makes a Minister, and his own painfull study and diligence that manures and improves his ministeriall gifts.'[41] No bishop is needed to tell whether a man is worthy. The people can choose their pastors precisely as they choose their representatives in parliament, and such election is the only basis for ordination. Any minister, himself 'inabl'd with gifts from God, and the lawfull and Primitive choyce of the Church assembl'd in convenient number,' has ample authority 'to ordaine Ministers and Deacons by publique Prayer, and Vote of Christs Congregation in like sort as he himselfe was ordained.'[42] God, of course, ordains who shall be the leaders of his flock. He replenishes them with knowledge and with abilities in the languages and the arts. He can stir up rich fathers to educate their sons for this work. Pastors, truly called, will not seek great revenues and high rank. Scorning money, they will ask for no more than 'a very common and reasonable supply of humane necessaries.'[43] Their calling itself is ennoblement beyond any in the gift of kings, 'for certainely there is no imployment more honourable, more worthy to take up a great spirit, more requiring a generous and free nurture, then to be the messenger, and Herald of heavenly truth from God to man.' Who would 'tugge for a Barony,' for a vote in parliament, for a seat on the judge's bench where he may shrive only men's purses? Who would do so, that is, that had 'the gift of wisdom and sound doctrine which leaves him free, though not to be a member, yet a teacher, and perswader of the Parliament.' To this lofty peerage Milton sees even the scions of best families moved by God to seek election. 'He can make the sons of Nobles his Ministers, and Princes to be his Nazarites.' For thus they may taste the unspeakable glory of preaching. At this point the poet-prophet makes ready to leave the ground. The singing of the herald angels is again in his ears. To preach, to be a messenger of truth is glorious work for a great spirit. To win the souls of men by moving speech is to make 'a kind of creation like to Gods, by infusing his spirit and likenesse into them to their salvation, as God did into him.'[44]

Ten years or so earlier the rejection of such ministry in the church had been the occasion for Milton's turning from the pulpit to poetry. Now the lively expectation of a Utopia in which eloquence was to be set free to do its work of teaching rulers and people to be wise and just was what made him momentarily turn from poetry to pamphleteering. It also gave him occasion to take vengeance on the prelates who had church-outed him. The disillusion and disgust he had suffered at Cambridge, his indignation at being balked in his ambition to preach and his scorn for the common run of graduates who took the permitted road to preferment, these he vented in a fresh attack, not now veiled as before in Latin or in poetic language, on university education and on the qualities of mind and character of the conforming clergy. What would become of learning, the partisans of the established system were demanding, if the endowments of the church were taken away? The clear spirit, Milton replied, enlarged by art and knowledge, 'thought it ever foule disdain to make pelf or ambition the reward of his studies, it being the greatest honor, the greatest fruit and proficiency of learned studies to despise these things.'[45] Under the present system, he says, simoniacal fathers, and such as would like to dispose of withered daughters by putting them into nunneries, send their superfluous sons, the simplest of them, to universities in anticipation of snug berths in the church. There they spend their youth in 'loitering, bezzling, and harlotting, their studies in unprofitable questions, and barbarous sophistry.'[46] Milton has seen and hissed them at Cambridge, acting in stage plays, 'writhing and unboning their Clergie limmes to all the antick and dishonest gestures of Trinculo's, Buffons, and Bawds.'[47] And this passes for education, the cost of which, it is pretended, could never be met were it not for the fat prebendaries, deaneries and bishoprics held forth as prizes for graduates. Hence the men who enter the church under prelacy are for the most part lazy haunters of taverns, neglectful of good literature, ignorant, almost illiterate. They know a little barbarous Latin; in Greek they are most of them unlettered; in Hebrew their lips are quite uncircumcised; in philosophy they have done no more than pester their heads with 'the saplesse dotages of old Paris and Salamanca.'[48] The best of them are but a sort of intellectual bastards, learned fools or learned hypocrites, 'putrid creatures that receive a crawling life from two most unlike procreants the Sun, and mudde.'[49] Once launched, they rise by sycophantic, time-serving arts. They are permitted to wield judicial power in the ecclesiastical courts. They are made lords of rich estates. They make themselves useful to courtiers and favorites and so get themselves elevated into bishoprics and the House of Lords. But in religion, like pots set to cool, their zeal evaporates, their gifts congeal, their queasy lukewarmness gives 'a vomit to God himself.'[50] At the same time they work their way into positions of political authority and endeavor to persuade even those who gave them their power that without them the state could not go on; no bishop no king, no wen no head.[51] The result, says Milton, is popular tumult, rebellion in Ireland, the danger of democracy, the flight of freeborn Englishmen to the savage deserts of America.

Such was the onslaught which the prelates unwittingly brought on themselves by church-outing John Milton. The ideal England with which in the name of presbyterianism he opposed prelatism really revolved about his conception of the poet-prophet and was based upon the divine right of the poet-prophet to speak freely whatever he took to be the truth. Milton's personal ambition of course lent added fire to his zeal for the public good. He himself wanted to speak. He knew he had the talent for speaking. He had used the leisure granted him out of the sweat of other men in order to cultivate his talent. It might be pleasanter, he says, not to be a troubler of other men's peace, but 'when God commands to take the trumpet and blow a dolorous or a jarring blast, it lies not in mans will what he shall say or what he shall conceal.'[52] Thus he justified his attack on the prelates, justified to himself as well his momentary abandonment of poetry but at the same time made plain with what assurance and with what purpose he meant to return to it. He chose to say that he wrote in the cool element of prose only with his left hand; he had not, however, forgotten or forgone the use and function of his right. Beyond the venal clergy of the prelatical church, beyond even the preachers of the spiritual brotherhood, he saw a still higher, all-embracing clergy at the very apex of which stood the poet, stood himself such as in a kind of anticipation of this very crisis he had been fashioning himself to be. In his ideal England all noble sciences that tended to the teaching of true Christian doctrine were to flourish and every art was to be provided for.[53] The call of wisdom and virtue was to be heard everywhere, 'not only in Pulpits, but after another persuasive method, at set and solemn Paneguries, in Theaters, porches, or what other place or way may win most upon the people to receiv at once both recreation, & instruction.'[54] And that he himself was to be a kind of primate among the poets of the new commonwealth which awaited the overthrow of prelacy he could have had but little doubt. It was in large measure for that reason that he felt he need mince no words with bishops. He may say the things he says against them because, in effect, he was reared for the church, because he has spent his youth in study, because he has dedicated himself to poetry as to a religious rule, because poetry has power beside the pulpit to breed in the nation the seeds of virtue and civility, because he himself expects to produce a great poem, because Dante, Petrarch, Ariosto, Chaucer, Langland, Spenser, better authorities than the fathers, have said such things about churchmen as he has said.

Nothing he wrote revealed more vividly what hopes the revolutionary crisis put into Milton's mind than the extraordinary prayer and curse with which he brought his *Of Reformation in England* to a close.[55] He accepted the plan for presbyterian church government, but what he anticipated would come of it was what the author of *Comus* and *Lycidas*, not what Smectymnuus, imagined. His mind was full of plans and ideas for a great poem to be written for the moral benefit of his fellow citizens in the mother dialect, and of this he was straining to give at least earnest and foretaste. His language grows too uplifted to be completely transparent, but it is intelligible enough to any reader who has followed Milton's aspiring thoughts up to this point. God has brought England through foreign invasions and civil wars, freed her 'from Antichristian Thraldome' of the Roman church, built up 'this *Brittanick Empire* to a glorious and enviable height with all her Daughter Ilands about her.' Now 'stay us in this felicitie, let not the obstinacy of our halfe obedience and will-Worship bring forth that *Viper* of *Sedition*, that for these Fourscore Yeares hath been breeding to eat through the entrals of our *Peace*.' He has been arguing that the reformation of the English church has remained since the beginning of Elizabeth's reign, 'these Fourscore Yeares,' but half-complete, that the treason of the prelates to the cause of the reformation was still at work. 'Hitherto thou hast but freed us, and that not fully, from the unjust and Tyrannous Claime of thy Foes, now unite us entirely, and appropriate us to thy selfe, tie us everlastingly in willing Homage to the *Prerogative* of thy eternall *Throne*.' This was Milton's way of praying for the final consummation of presbyterian reform.

But he proceeds at once to indicate in the same exalted language the effect that he, the poet-prophet of the Puritan Zion, expects from that reform. Let God but bring the prelates to battle, let them be broken, let, that is, the way be cleared for the reformation he had been outlining in his pamphlet, then someone, he had no doubt who, would set a great poem to work on God's Englishmen. 'Then amidst the *Hymns*, the *Halleluiahs* of *Saints* some one may perhaps bee heard offering at high *strains* in new and lofty Measures to sing and celebrate thy *divine Mercies*, and *marvelous Judgements* in this land throughout all AGES.' At this point Milton's sentence is, perhaps, not wholly clear. 'Whereby,' he says—by which he can best be taken to mean by such singing—'instructed and inur'd to the fervent and continuall practice of *Truth* and *Righteousness*, and hence casting farre from her the *rags* of her old *vices*,' England, 'this great and Warlike Nation,' may presse on hard to that *high* and *happy* emulation to be found the *soberest, wisest,* and *most Christian People* at that day when thou the Eternall and shortly-expected King shalt open the Clouds to judge the severall Kingdomes of the World, and distributing *Nationall Honours* and *Rewards* to Religious and just *Commonwealths,* shall put an end to all Earthly *Tyrannies,* proclaiming thy universal and milde *Monarchy* through Heaven and Earth.

Milton is not the naïve Chiliast, obfuscating his mind with the rig-marole of the Fifth Monarchy, but one cannot fail to observe that in his own terms and on his own plane he expected Christ's kingdom on earth with a confidence not exceeded even by John Archer whose *Personall Raigne* and Hanserd Knollys whose *Glimpse of Sions Glory* were on their way to press at about the same moment as Milton's *Of Reformation.* Prelatism once overthrown and presbyterianism estab-lished, poets were to be set free to prepare the English people for the reward that would surely be theirs when 'the Eternall and shortly-expected King' should come. And in the final distribution of awards, poets would receive that meed of fame in heaven by the 'perfect wit-ness of all-judging *Jove*' which Milton had set as his goal in *Lycidas;*

Where they undoubtedly that by their *Labours, Counsels,* and *Prayers* [by which he meant the wise teachers as well as the wise rulers] have been earnest for the *Common good* of *Religion* and their *Countrey,* shall receive, above the inferiour *Orders* of the *Blessed,* the *Regall* addition of *Principalities, Legions,* and *Thrones* into their glorious Titles, and in supereminence of *beatifick* Vision progressing the *datelesse* and *irre-voluble* Circle of *Eternity* shall clasp inseparable Hands with *joy,* and *blisse* in over measure for ever.

But, if Milton sees himself and his friends transfigured into the blessed angels who were to people the heaven of his own imagination in *Paradise Lost,* he sees his enemies, the bishops, consigned to a hell which, surely, was furnished him for this occasion by Dante. 'After a shamefull end in this life,' he says, 'which *God* grant them,' they shall be thrown downe eternally into the *darkest* and *deepest Gulfe* of Hell, where under the *despightfull controule,* the trample and spurne of all the other *Damned,* that in the anguish of their *Torture* shall have no other ease then to exercise a *Raving* and *Bestiall Tyranny* over them as their *Slaves* and *Negro's,* they shall remaine in that plight for ever, the *basest*, the *lowermost*, the *most dejected*, most *underfoot* and *downe-trodden Vassals* of *Perdition*.

In *Animadversions* Milton interrupts his diatribes against Bishop Hall to return to this theme.[56] God, because he 'hath yet ever had this Iland under the speciall indulgent eye of his providence' began the reformation of his church by first sending 'that glimmering light which *Wicklef*, and his followers disperst.' He blew 'a second warning trumpet in our Grandsires days.' Now 'if we freeze at noone after their earely thaw, let us feare lest the Sunne for ever hide himselfe.' The time has come to settle peace in the church and righteous judgment in the state by completing the reformation so long delayed.

Then shall all thy Saints addresse their voyces of joy, and triumph to thee, standing on the shoare of that red Sea into which our enemies had almost driven us. And he that now for haste snatches up a plain ungarnish't present as a thanke-offering to thee, which could not be deferr'd in regard of thy so many late deliverances wrought for us one upon another, may then perhaps take up a Harp, and sing thee an elaborate Song to Generations.

Which was Milton's way of indicating that his anti-prelatical pamphlets were less an interruption to his great poem than an impromptu anticipation. And again we hear of the approaching kingdom of Christ on earth.

Thy Kingdome is now at hand, and thou standing at the dore. Come forth out of thy Royall Chambers, O prince of all the Kings of the earth, put on the visible roabes of thy imperial Majesty, take up that unlimited Sceptor which thy Almighty Father hath bequeath'd thee; for now the voice of thy Bride calls thee, and all creatures sigh to bee renew'd.

In his two final tracts against the bishops, thinking of himself more than ever, if that were possible, as the poet of the imminent godly Utopia and thinking more and more of the poet's godly function, Milton drops whatever reserves he may have felt up to this point. It is in *The Reason of Church Government* especially that we hear of the peculiar obligation of those who are blessed with talent and leisure for the instruction of their fellows. We are told that poetic ability is the inspired gift of God, that poets have power to instill virtue, attune the mind, celebrate the Almighty and deplore the lapses of nations. Now too we hear of Milton's discovery, confirmed by friends at home and by good judges in Italy, that he himself had the power to write what men would not willingly let die and of his determination 'to be an interpreter & relater of the best and sagest things among mine own Citizens throughout this Iland in the mother dialect.'[57] Putting aside all wish to be named abroad and any fear lest the climate of England or the age he lived in should prove adverse, he had resolved to do for his language and country what the choicest wits of Athens, Rome and modern Italy, what the ancient Hebrews had done for theirs. He would write an epic after the model of Homer, Virgil and Tasso or of the Book of Job. Or he might write a dramatic poem like those of Sophocles and Euripides, should it seem 'more doctrinal and exemplary,' or like the Song of Solomon or the Apocalypse of St. John. He might also attempt 'magnifick Odes and Hymns' such as Pindar and Callimachus wrote and such as are found scattered through the law and the prophets.[58] He is not yet ready to begin this work, not having yet completed the full circle of his studies or encompassed the necessary 'industrious and select reading, steddy observation, insight into all seemly and generous arts and affaires.' But if the reader will trust him some few years, he covenants to write a poem not 'like that which flows at wast from the pen of some vulgar Amorist, or the trencher fury of a riming parasite, nor to be obtain'd by the invocation of Dame Memory and her Siren daughters, but [a poem obtained] by devout prayer to that eternall Spirit who can enrich with all utterance and knowledge, and sends out his Seraphim with the hallow'd fire of his Altar to touch and purify the lips of whom he pleases.'[59]

Finally in his *Apology* for Smectymnuus, stung by his adversary's clumsy attack on his personal conduct, he launches forth upon that famous picture of himself, the fair studious youth dedicated to learning and virtue, bred in poetry to the love of the beautiful, to the pursuit of an ever more comprehensive ideal beauty which should comprise every act of every individual in church and state. He describes how he has endeavored to follow that ideal, fashioning his own life as a poem according to it, and he promises that there shall be more in this vein presently. 'With such abstracted sublimities as these, it might be worth your listning, Readers, as I may one day hope to have ye in a still time, when there shall be no more chiding.'[60]

Before prelacy could be overthrown, however, and the poet could be given the victory and the Utopia which were to be his opportunity and his theme, there remained much chiding to be accomplished, and no one was doing more of it than he. One feature of these polemics which has caused amazement and even something like embarrassment and pain to the admirers of the poet has been the personal virulence of his attack on Bishop Hall, the butt of his antagonism to prelacy. Hall in his *Defence of the Humble Remonstrance* had indulged in expressions of contempt for the learning of Smectymnuus. In *Animadversions* Milton took up the cudgels for his friends. His announced purpose was 'to send home his haughtinesse well bespurted with his owne holy-water.'[61] There was little, in fact, that he was not willing to say if, in the heat of the moment, he could bring discredit upon his reverend antagonist. He descends to personal nastiness and to mere shouting Ha, Ha, Ha at his arguments. Hall was responsible for a return in kind called *A Modest Confutation.* This purports to give a circumstantial account of the poet's alleged shameless way of life, but depends for its information on dubious inferences drawn from the vocabulary of Milton's previous tracts. It reveals incidentally how little, at least how little that could be turned to malicious use, was known about the poet by one who surely had means to learn whatever was to be known. Milton returned to the charge with *An Apology against . . . a Modest Confutation.*

He was well aware that the tone he adopted toward Hall called for some explanation. His defense is that of a satirist, justifying himself by the nobility of his cause. He does not pretend to say why 'those two most rationall faculties of humane intellect anger and laughter were first seated in the brest of man.' He merely knows that laughter 'hath oft-times a strong and sinewy force in teaching and confuting' and that there can be no more proper object of anger than 'a false Prophet taken in the greatest dearest and most dangerous cheat, the cheat of soules.'[62] Moral indignation has license 'to utter such words and phrases as in common talke were not so mannerly to use.'[63] 'There may be a sanctifi'd bitternesse against the enemies of truth.' The utmost billingsgate as well as the highest eloquence was, therefore, at Milton's disposal; certainly it was at his command. 'I beseech ye friends, ere the brick-bats flye, resolve me and your selves, is it blasphemy, or any whit disagreeing from Christian meeknesse, when as Christ himselfe speaking of unsavory traditions, scruples not to name the Dunghill and the Jakes, for me to answer a slovenly wincer of a confutation, that, if he would needs put his foot to such a sweaty service, the odour of his Sock was like to be neither musk, nor benjamin?'[64]

By those who have thought it necessary to condone Milton's use of such methods, it has, of course, been said that he was but falling in, unfortunately, with a custom common among controversialists of his time. In a sense, this was true, but the custom was best observed by men with whom Milton had otherwise least in common and deplored by some of those with whom he had most. For precedent to Milton's virtuosity in flyting, we have to turn to Prynne and Bastwick; his most gifted successors were such fellows as Edwards, Vicars and the malignant presbyterians. The humanist reformers, on the other hand, had condemned intemperate abuse in religious controversy as itself a kind of persecution. Acontius had perceived that there was nothing like anger in defense of supposed truth for seducing a man into error and intolerance. Not only Anglican liberals like Chillingworth and Hales but Puritans like John Goodwin and Lord Brooke felt the force of this argument, whether they derived it from Acontius or not, and Goodwin and Brooke were advancing it again almost at the moment that Milton was letting fly at Hall. The explanation for the poet's intemperance is to be seen at least as much in his own character and state of mind as in the habit of the age. He was the kind of man who can brook anything with greater patience than opposition to his ideals. He lacked, moreover, the experience among men that might have bred more charity as well as greater finesse in debate. He is simply, in respect to Hall at this time as in respect to Salmasius and Morus later on, the idealist on the rampage. What makes his onslaught seem so virulent is, too, not necessarily his greater animosity but his greater expressiveness. He could say anything he chose to say with ten times the force of ordinary men and did, hitting harder than perhaps he knew. This power to express his thoughts was attended by fierce joy in the exercise of it, which strengthened his conviction that he was licensed by his cause to say whatever he might choose and need not scruple to name the dunghill and the jakes. One result is that flyting is raised in his pages to something like a high pitch of art, illustrating with peculiar emphasis one of the most striking features of Milton's style. He retains and transforms into something English the sonority and weight of Latin. His thoughts, however, are continually leaping to the figurative and poetic modes of the English vernacular. This is attended by the brilliant intermingling of Latin with native words, racy, vigorous, homely and suggestive in the extreme. So redolent was Milton's language that Bishop Hall made the perhaps natural mistake of supposing that the poet could have acquired such a vocabulary only by direct experience with the things for which he knew such plain English names. But Milton was revealing nothing more than an amazing virtuousity in verbal expression, a virtuousity which exemplified in heightened, even exaggerated, degree that organic intermingling of Latin and native elements in our speech which was becoming, not without the help of his example and influence, one of the most distinctive features of English style.

It would be difficult to state with any confidence what was the effect of Milton's antiprelatical tracts upon the immediate situation. Obviously, though written ostensibly in support of presbyterianism, they went to swell the increasing stream of religious and political individualism which was soon to overwhelm reformers as well as defenders of the old regime. In 1641 the energy of the revolution was supplied by the Puritan peers and gentlemen in parliament. Their point of view was well stated by Lord Brooke, whose pamphlet went promptly into a second edition. Milton's pamphlets, aside from the replies issued by, or on behalf of, Hall, made far less stir in the press, and his immediately ensuing activity took a direction peculiar to himself. Nothing in the accusations that came from Hall stung him more than the charge of immorality and the suggestion that he was about to marry a rich widow. This it was which roused him in his *Apology* to describe the manner in which his ideas of love had been molded by his reading of Renaissance poetry and to announce that when he married he would choose 'a virgin of mean fortunes honestly bred.'[65] Soon after writing these words, he took such a woman to wife, the daughter, strangely enough, of a royalist squire in Oxfordshire. His convictions on the subject of love coupled with the disillusion which this marriage brought swiftly upon him set him at once to writing on the nature of marriage and its proper place in the ideal commonwealth of his enraptured anticipation. Nothing could have signalized more clearly how far he was from sharing the expectations which preoccupied the hopeful theocrats whose cause he had been championing. They fell as violently upon his pamphlet concerning marriage and divorce as though they had never heard of the support he had given Smectymnuus. He for his part ceased to look to presbyterianism for the realization of his Utopian ideals.

Milton had come a long way with the spiritual brotherhood but could not stop at the point where they wished to halt reform. He had been won by the moral idealism of the preachers. With them he exalted preaching, embraced the doctrine of calling and the talent, and eagerly awaited the coming of reform in the church. But he went on from that point to conceive a society ruled by public opinion enlightened not only by preachers but by intellectual and moral leaders of all sorts, lay or cleric, above all by poet-prophets like himself. His Puritanism was a Puritanism transfigured by the idealism which had come to him from the humanist poets and philosophers. He never wavered in his devotion to the revolutionary cause, but the service he performed for it at this stage was not so much to supply parliament with advice its members could comprehend and apply as it was to express for later generations the most vital thing in the whole Puritan movement, the belief, namely, in the transcending importance of spiritual values and responsibilities and the sanctity of individual spiritual life. In doing this, he did not remove himself from the struggle which engrossed his generation, but he did address himself to the struggle on a level where he was almost alone. The most that can be said is that from time to time, but always for a time only, he saw now this party and now that moving on its own level in what seemed the same direction as himself. He was, however, never one of those who give up to party what they think is meant for mankind.

To write for mankind in 1641 was not the way to win immediate attention and support. Parliament did presently abolish prelacy root and branch, but beyond that went no farther than the Puritan churchmen desired. Its next step was to commit itself to the attempt at some form of presbyterianism, and with certain reservations, the importance of which appeared only later, referred to the preachers the question what form English presbyterianism should take. Milton was no doubt for the moment satisfied, but the larger issues which he and Lord Brooke had raised remained without recognition or provision for settlement. The fact was that under the conditions which had been developing now for over fifty years the activity of Englishmen in all directions had grown so intense and varied that belief, thought and expression could never, except at the cost of peace and security, be subjected by any church to any type of uniformity. A wide margin of tolerance had become indispensable for the maintenance of the state itself. Brooke's great distinction was that he clearly perceived and stated that necessity in the crisis over prelacy in 1641. Milton's was that, though his enthusiasm led him momentarily to accept presbyterianism, he lavished his marvellous gift of poetic eloquence on the freedom which he mistakenly supposed presbyterianism would ensure to all poets and prophets and sages as well as to all preachers in the new commonwealth. But the question what to do with the dissenters whom Brooke had so chivalrously championed and with poet-prophets like Milton had to wait until the Puritan churchmen had time to show their hand in the Westminster Assembly. Meanwhile civil war was beginning, and the focus of discussion shifted to another, though a related, question.

X

The Law of Nature

THE long effort of the Puritan reformers was to be rewarded at last by the opportunity to frame a form of church government for the expected godly Utopia. The very overthrow of prelacy, however, began at once to reveal how many and how complex were the difficulties which stood between them and the fulfilment of their hopes. While they and their supporters were doing battle with prelatists in the press, the king and the parliament engaged in a struggle which by the spring of 1642 had shifted from Westminster to the field of civil war. Englishmen were thus confronted with what seemed the unprecedented spectacle of their ruler taking up arms against his subjects and of subjects preparing violence against their sovereign. In the confusion of judgments and loyalties caused by this situation and in the lapse of all control over tongues and pens, the question which suddenly absorbed attention concerned not the rival pretensions of prelates and presbyters but the conflicting claims of crown and parliament. If either side had been able at the moment to command effective military force, the question might have been quickly settled. Lacking this but with the press at hand, each party appealed instead to reason and conscience in the people, that is to say to public opinion. Few men, whatever side they took, were, to be sure, prepared to admit that public questions were rightly or necessarily to be decided in any such fashion. The relation of throne and legislature, it was commonly thought, was one which could, and should, be properly settled for all time by some absolute rule of God and nature. Yet even though adherents of all sorts of opinions printed pamphlets in the effort to persuade the public of the validity of this or that absolute, many deplored the state of affairs which had brought such a condition about. Pamphlets were published protesting against the publication of pamphlets. ' 'Tis a bitter controversy,' wrote certain preachers, 'that our poore sinfull Nation is fallen upon, wherein not onely Armes are ingaged against Armes, but

Bookes written against Bookes, and Conscience pretended against Conscience."[1] Henry Peacham published a broadside with an engraving by Wenceslas Hollar under the satirical title *The World is Ruled & Governed by Opinion*.[2] Opinion, a blindfolded goddess with the world in her lap and a chameleon on her wrist, sits in the branches of a tree, the ripe fruit of which is falling to the ground in the form of pamphlets. A fool in motley waters the roots and a gentleman in cavalier costume engages the goddess in a dialogue, the point of which is that

> Opinions found in everie house and streete,
> And going ever, never in her waie.

One writer who seems to have had some inkling of the realities involved in the situation was Philip Hunton. To be sure, in his *Treatise of Monarchie* he labors like the rest to unriddle an absolute basis for government, but falling into the dilemma presented when king and parliament are found hopelessly at odds, he candidly concludes that 'in this case, which is beyond the Government, the Appeal must be to the Community, as if there were no Government: and as by evidence mens Consciences are convinced, they are bound to give their utmost assistance.'[3] This was an admission which, however faithful to the facts of the moment, worked havoc to all accustomed political reasoning. Here was good stuff, exclaimed Henry Ferne in another pamphlet, pointing out that such an appeal to the community had never been given as a rule before.

Nevertheless, in view of the indecisiveness of the opening engagements of the war and of the attendant negotiations for peace, the appeal to the community had to be made. The messages and addresses of the king and the speeches and pamphlets of his supporters and opponents were promptly sent to the press. The case against royalism was most strikingly presented by Henry Parker, an Oxford man, a lawyer and something of a wit. He had participated the year before in the attack on prelacy by publishing a *Discourse concerning Puritans*. His attitude on that question was similar to Lord Brooke's. Signing himself Philus Adelphus and writing in the self-consciously literary manner of the preceding age, he concluded with the statement,

I have said enough to make myself condemned for a Puritan, . . . but verily, if thou art not an antipuritan of the worst kinde, I am not a

Puritan. In my opinion, I am not scrupulous or precise, in my life I am not strict, or austere, the more is my blame; if thou art a downright Protestant and no more, I am the same and no more. If thou thinkest some men religious which affect not the name of Puritan, I thinke so too: if thou thinkest most men irreligious which hate the name of Puritan, I thinke so too: if thou art not to me a violent Antipuritan, I have no quarrel with thee; nor am I a Puritan to thee: if thou art, hate me as a profest Puritan and I will thank thee for the honour of it. Farewell. Thine to feare thee more than hate thee and to feare thy malice more than justice.[4]

The defenders of the crown had the initial advantage of being able to invoke the sentiment of loyalty. The advocates of revolt must find some no less moving principle to which to appeal. They turned logically enough to the law of nature which, Paul said, was written in the heart. The possibility of appealing from Caesar without to conscience within had been present in Christianity from the beginning, and the Puritan preachers had been steadily preparing men to take practical advantage of it whenever occasion should require. The majority of them had not themselves directly disobeyed the law or urged disobedience. They had contented themselves with merely exalting conscience, even while deploring the actions of those whose conscience would permit them to tarry no longer for the magistrate in reforming the church. It was the latter, the enthusiasts and separatists of various sorts, who had the courage long before 1642 to put instant obedience to conscience above obedience to the magistrate and so, whether they deserved it or not, had incurred the epithet anabaptist, an ill name vaguely remembered from stories about continental religious disturbances of the preceding century and loosely applied to any sect supposed to be hostile on principle to civil government. The most recent proponents of the doctrine of free conscience had, as we have seen, been mystics like Everard and sectarian enthusiasts like Lilburne and Knollys. These were not the kind of people nor were their pleas the kind of arguments to have as yet much weight.

At the moment the most effective appeal to conscience or the higher law of nature on behalf of parliament against the crown came from Henry Parker. As a lawyer he was doubtless familiar with the classic statements of the theory of natural law. He makes use of citations from

Fortescue and Cotton, and he must also have read Hooker and, like Lilburne, St. Germain. He was not innocent of quoting Machiavelli. As early as 1640 in his *The Case of Shipmony*, he had asserted that 'the supreme of all humane lawes is *salus populi*' and that 'that iron law which wee call necessity itselfe is but subservient to this law; for rather than a Nation shall perish, anything shall be held necessary, and legal by necessity.'[5] He had applied the same principle in 1641 to the argument against prelacy, and now in 1642 turned it against the king in *Observations upon some of his Majesties Late Answers and Expresses.*[6]

This tract showed how impossible it was to keep spiritual warfare within spiritual bounds. The preachers exalted only conscience and attacked only Satan. But conscience had compelled their proselyte Prynne to assail opinions, morals, laws and governors. Conscience had instructed separatists like Smyth and Busher to withdraw from the church and demand liberty of faith. Lilburne's conscience had told him that he had the right to publish unlicensed pamphlets. Lord Brooke found revealed in the heart a law that dictated the privilege of unlicensed preaching and the exclusion of churchmen from political power. Thus at whatever point the existing laws of the state interfered with prosecution of the war against the evil one, the Puritan spirit in its wider manifestations knew a higher law. That law now justified for Parker the claim of parliament to act independently of the crown, even to oppose the crown's commands. Parliamentary freedom seemed to him as much a matter of conscience and natural right as belief in the covenant of grace. The law written on the tables of the breast was ultimate and universal. Even if the conscience of the king, for Parker had to acknowledge that Charles Stuart, being a man, could not be without one, failed to approve the acts of parliament, parliament was still free, and the reason was still conscience and natural right.

Thus he arrives at a striking restatement of the ancient theory, which he asserts to be the cardinal principle of English government, that the fundamental law of man's nature is the necessity of self-preservation. This necessity speaks with the voice of conscience. Men cannot act or speak or swear contrary to its dictates without incurring a kind of suicide or slavery. The safety of the people is the sole end of the state. The people are the best judges of their own safety, and they are the 'essense' of parliament. The will, the conscience of the people, expressed in parliament, is the supreme law of the state, which it is the natural duty of each individual, monarch, private person or member of parliament, to obey as a matter of self-interest even in contravention of his own opinion. This, he says, is 'the ἀκμή of all Politiques,' the law of *salus populi suprema lex*.

The Law of [royal] Prerogative itselfe, it is subservient to this law, and were it not conducing thereunto, it were not necessary nor expedient. Neither can the right of conquest be pleaded to acquit Princes of that which is due to the people as the Authors or ends of all power, for meere force cannot alter the course of nature, or frustrate the tenour of Law, and if it could there were more reason why the people might justifie force to regain due libertie, then the Prince might subject the same.[7]

Parker supports his application of the law of nature to the contemporary situation by what may be best described as a free rendering of the myth of the social contract expressed in terms of the Puritan myth of the fall of man and his eternal struggle with Satan. Adam before the fall needed no governor but conscience, the law of nature written in his own heart. After the fall, man 'grew so untame and uncivill a creature that the Law of God written in his brest was not sufficient to restrayne him from mischiefe, or to make him sociable, and therefore without some magistracy to provide new orders, and to judge of old, and to execute according to justice, no society could be upheld.' Hence, still in pursuance of their natural end of self-preservation, the children of Adam were moved by God to agree with one another to obey a chosen ruler. This was the social contract. But men were not even yet done with the evil consequences of the fall, and 'when it after appeared that man was yet subject to unnatural destruction by the tyranny of intrusted magistrates, a mischiefe almost as fatall as to be without all magistracie,' then the law of nature came once more into operation and provided a remedy.[8] In England that remedy was parliament, the collective conscience of the people perpetually on guard against the tyranny of rulers who would disobey the law, *salus populi suprema lex*.

Parker's *Observations*, clear and plausible, was a singularly effective pamphlet and takes a striking place in the literature of revolution. It announced the law of nature as one of the chief shibboleths of revolution for a long time to come. A measure of the author's skill may be had if we compare his work to Prynne's seven tremendous tracts of the same moment. The latter asserted with customary ferocity the dogma of parliamentary supremacy and then stuffed his hundreds of pages with the precedents and citations which his persistent and infertile mind had raked together. The task of providing full formal statement of the ideas Parker so facilely advanced was executed in 1644 with all the accoutrement of erudition by Samuel Rutherford in his *Lex, Rex: The Law and the Prince*. The royalists gave their attention to Parker. Hardly a week went by during the year that followed the publication of *Observations* without the appearance in print of something dealing with that pamphlet or with the later ones in which Parker continued to argue his case. Other revolutionary pamphleteers all in some fashion followed his lead. No book, Sir John Spelman testified, did so much to entangle and intoxicate the vulgar. Londoners, reading such licentious things, went mad, he says, and like the citizens of Abdera took to acting the same seditious tragedy in the streets.[9]

The king's supporters, though none was Parker's equal in skill, were quick and numerous in reply. Like most of the parliamentary writers, they remained enclosed in their dialectic, writing not as he did for the public but at their opponents. There were two of them, however, who gave some forecast of the lines which royalist propaganda would finally follow, namely Henry Ferne and Sir Dudley Digges. They endeavored to turn conscience and natural law to the support of monarchy. Ferne, the unctuous churchman, royal chaplain and future bishop, protested more in sorrow than in anger that disobedience to the natural ruler could never square with any Christian conscience.[10] This vein of sentiment would be more successfully exploited when another cleric also destined for a bishopric should devise the *Eikon Basilike*. Digges, a man of the world, took the more rationalistic stand that to rebel against the sovereign was to dissolve, not to maintain, the social contract, to destroy, not to protect, the safety of the people. We hear the premonition of Hobbes in his assertion that 'when every man exercises his natural freedom, no man is free.'[11]

During the debate provoked by Parker, events gave practical force to his pleading. After the indecisive engagement at Edgehill in October, Charles and his cavaliers moved toward London. In mid-November they sacked the town of Brentford and the next day confronted the city trainbands at Turnham Green. London tasted danger and craved bolder words. Parker had been content to make a show of reasoned argument against the crown, but the crown could no longer remain immune from attack by religious passion such as had so far been directed against the bishops. The time had come for the rights of subjects to be not only argued as natural but preached as holy.

Who in 1642, as the civil war got under way, would undertake to incite the populace against the king by the potent stimulation of religion? The great body of more moderate Puritan churchmen, including those who were now returning from abroad, hung back. They were, it would seem, too busy bandying texts and syllogisms with prelatist and royalist clergymen. Milton—and the fact is additional evidence of his intense absorption in his own ideas—was occupied in getting married and in reflecting upon marriage.[12] The danger of the city evoked from him nothing more heroic than a sonnet adjuring Charles's troopers to spare his house for sake of the fame which as a poet he had it in his power to bestow. The spokesmen for the sects were not yet ready or were occupied with their dreams of the millennium. Lilburne was off at the war in Lord Brooke's regiment. Walwyn, as yet unheard of, was still quietly extending his personal acquaintance and influence among the lower classes. In these circumstances the man who undertook to inflame that spirit which, as Cromwell said, common men needed if they were to stand up to gentlemen was John Goodwin.

Goodwin's part in the oncoming struggle was to give timely, learned and provocative expression to ideas which men more daring even than he were to press to greater practical extremes and which led finally to the destruction of monarchy and the disruption of presbyterian reform. In his *Imputatio Fidei*, we have seen, he had taken the position that the sacrifice performed by Christ imputed to man not righteousness but power to further his own redemption by active faith. This provided Goodwin with the intellectual basis for the doctrine of liberty as he preached it from now on. He had also argued in that work against intemperance in controversy on the ground that it prevented freedom for rational inquiry and discussion. This, however, did not stop him from now flinging himself headlong from the pulpit at the cavaliers. Parker, Prynne and others were contending for the right of parliament to resist the crown. Goodwin set out to rouse the people to resistance as a duty. He threw the whole weight of his eloquence and learning into the work of fixing popular emotion in an attitude of aggressive defense and so of stabilizing public faith in parliament. Londoners had recently been horrified by reports of atrocities committed by Catholic rebels on Protestants in Ireland. Goodwin preached to them the duty of straining every resource to aid the victims; 'Ireland must be look'd after and provided for, as if we had neither Wives, nor Children, nor charge, nor were poore, nor wanted Moneys, nor knew what to doe with our Money otherwise.'[13] Now he told them that the same outrages were threatened against the citizens of London itself. One sermon on this theme bore the title *Anti-Cavalierisme or Truth Pleading As well the Necessity, as the Lawfulness of this present War, for the suppressing of that Butcherly brood of Cavaliering Incendiaries, who are now hammering England, to make an Ireland of it.*[14] The other was called *The Butchers Blessing*. If life, liberty and property be at all dear, Goodwin argued, Londoners must under the law of nature and the command of conscience make no scruple and spare no effort to defend themselves. 'Oh let it be as an abomination unto us, as the very shadow of death, to every man, woman and child of us, not to be active, not to lie out and straine ourselves to the utmost of our strength and power in every kinde, as far as the law of God and nature will suffer us, to resist that high hand of iniquity and blood that is stretched out against us; to make our lives, and our liberties, and our Religion good against that accursed Generation that now magnifieth themselves, to make a prey and spoyle of them, to make havock and desolation of them all at once, if the Lord shall yet deliver them out of their hands.' None is so young or weak or poor as not to have something to do for the cause. Let those who have physical strength be off to the war. Let the rich turn their money into soldiers and swords. Let those that have heads use them. 'Head-worke is every whit as necessary in such a time and exigent as hand-worke is.' Let those who can find nought else to do 'pray the enemies downe, and the Armies of the Lord up: Let them finde tongues to whet up the courage and resolution of others.'[15]

Thus, in the words of his title-page, Goodwin endeavors to exhort 'all men that either love God, Themselves, or Good men' to resist

King Charles. But he feels constrained also to 'clear and answer' all objections to such a course. Here we may see how the principles of *Imputatio Fidei* were to be applied in the political struggle. What in the last analysis weighs most with him is the force of his own interests and convictions, the vigorous shooting forth of that faith he thinks imputed to him by Jesus Christ. He concedes the divine institution of government whether monarchical or other but denies to the king and his party any advantage on that account either in the debate or in the strife of interests. The exercise of authority must be based upon discussion and agreement. The commands of authority must be obeyed only in the light and with the approval of individual judgment and conscience. Truth and justice can be determined only by inquiry proceeding to agreement by means of debate. Neither king nor subject is exempt from this condition. The king has no power to overrule, the subject none to delegate conscience. The subject had better defer when conscience is not clear, but when in the universal opinion of men the king or his servants command injustice, then only at the peril of their souls may men obey or, indeed, refrain from the most violent resistance. This conviction was wholly consonant with Goodwin's notion of justification. If salvation depends upon faith vouchsafed to men through the gospel of Christ progressively unfolded through preaching and discussion, then the gospel must be preached and discussed. But if government assails the lives of men seeking their salvation through faith and consequently through the process by which faith lives and grows strong, then government must be controlled in the interest of men, their souls, their lives and fortunes. The method of this control is plain. Justice in the acts of government like truth in religion prevails only but surely when conscience and reason have had full liberty to express themselves.

Goodwin is nothing if not outspoken and bold in pushing this argument to its extreme consequences. 'Is it fit to give way or allow, that every private man should scan, examine, judge, and determine either the righteousnesse or unrighteousnesse of the Kings commands?'[16] The answer is an unequivocal affirmative. The only alternative, he insists, is to hold kings to be the equal of God, and that is blasphemy. The king is no more infallible than the pope or the bishops. He goes farther and delivers a warning which Charles Stuart might have done well to heed. 'If this liberty, or duty rather, of examining the Commands of Superiours, had been preached and pressed upon the consciences of men with that authority and power, which the truth and high concernment of it will beare, or rather indeed required, those crownes might have flourished upon the heads of Kings, which now begin to droop and languish.'[17] The convictions of Milton's *Tenure of Kings and Magistrates* and of Goodwin's own *Right and Might Well Met*, not to mention the footfalls of Cromwell's troopers, are to be heard in these words.

Goodwin appears in 1642 as the apostle of the principle of government responsibility to public opinion and therefore as a supporter of parliament against the crown. Later he was to defend the army against parliament on precisely the same principle. Goodwin was not a statesman or a political philosopher. He was a preacher, sprung from the spiritual brotherhood. His immediate object in 1642 was to marshal public opinion against the power which, if it were victorious at the moment, might restore prelacy, Star Chamber and High Commission and renew the repression of preaching. His real object was to hold all governors under constant fire from the pulpit. His own preaching is a brilliant exhibition of the manner in which the sermon, as it had developed in the hands of the Puritans, could be turned to the uses of political polemic. The conventions of the pulpit compelled him to join battle on religious and theological grounds, and the conventions of the sermon held him to a dialectic that must proceed from scriptural texts to point-by-point rebuttal of all objections. This took time, and one wearies of Goodwin's exhaustive, though acute, analysis and denial of the claim that the propensity of primitive Christians to martyrdom argued the duty of passive obedience to King Charles. Yet debate as Goodwin conducts it is not mere logomachy. He does not merely wrest, divide and subdivide his texts, multiplying words. He interprets them with feeling and imagination and with the knowledge of human character he has learned from experience and humane letters as well as from scripture. Flaming convictions arising out of the needs and hopes of men in his time were what Goodwin set forth, and he did not so much prove them by syllogisms as express them by images drawn from the sacred text. Men like him were in temperament and thought more imaginative and poetic than rational and critical, even when they presumed to appeal to nothing but reason. They had learned to look for the truth in the metaphors and tropes of biblical poetry. What could be more natural than for them to suppose that whatever was said in trope and metaphor, especially if drawn from scripture, must be true? Revering reason better than they understood its canons, they enjoyed all the exhilaration of mystic faith under the illusion of rationality. In this peculiar art, Goodwin, to the raging discomfiture of an increasing host of opponents, was one of the most skillful masters of his time. Was there, for instance, any hesitation to be felt about submitting every law of the state to the conscience of every private individual? He could resolve it at once. The lawfulness or unlawfulness of the king's commands was 'written in their foreheads . . . with such Capitall letters, that he that runs may read.'[18] Daniel 3: 16, Shadrach, Meshach and Abednego passing judgment on the command of Nebuchadnezzar, clinches the argument. Religion and poetry are potent medicines, not less so when they are offered as logic.

The images, if not the syllogisms, of Goodwin's sermons probably helped to embolden the trainbands at Turnham Green. Charles drew back to Oxford for a winter of indecision and confusion. His rebellious subjects at Westminster, meanwhile, were compelled to face the problem of dealing with the two institutions which had had so much to do with bringing about the ruin of the old regime. By overthrowing prelacy parliament had struck a mortal blow at Stuart absolutism but had not determined what to do with the church and the press. That problem, toward the solution of which in the spring of 1643 it was compelled to make some definite attempt, was of quite incalculable complexity. Control of the church, unless everything that men recognized as social order were to disappear, involved control not only over religion, the training and appointment of ministers, and the property and income of the establishment, but control as well over public morals, the relief of the poor, marriage and the family, education and the press. The question how and in whose interest the church was to be governed involved also the question how and in whose interests the loyalties and beliefs, the intellectual and spiritual life, in a word the public opinion of the nation, were to be directed. It involved too, as immediately became apparent, the alternative question whether the minds and morals of the people as a whole could ever again be controlled at all, by the church or by any other single agency.

Yet, however that might be, parliament in 1643 could not avoid responsibility for at least attempting to reorganize church government. The Puritan leaders had gone too far to hope for peace without seeking a victory and had not yet made victory sure. Early in June they induced the two houses to pass a resolution intended to commit them definitely to continued resistance to the king. This was quickly followed by an ordinance for calling together an assembly of godly divines to advise parliament in reforming the church. When this body convened a month later in Westminster Abbey, the Puritan churchmen at last obtained the opportunity they had been hoping for ever since the opening years of Elizabeth. What seemed a willing parliament looked to them to draft a confession of faith consistent with Puritan doctrine and a form of church government based upon the presbyterian principle. They undertook their task, however, in circumstances profoundly different from those in which the Puritan movement had been launched. The churchmen summoned to the Westminster Assembly had never aspired to set the religious life of the people free from control. They had labored to revitalize it, looking forward to the time when they should wrest from the prelates the power to reduce it to uniformity and order. Yet for three generations, until Charles made the mistake, so disastrous to himself, of reversing his predecessors' politic semitolerance, the people had been permitted within the limits of expediency to differ in religion and to express their differences in one way or another. The Puritan preachers as a body did not approve such freedom. They had, however, taken advantage of it in order to preach sermons and produce a literature which enormously stimulated individual activity in thought and expression and in other forms of enterprise as well. Moreover, by their own activities and by their use and patronage, they had promoted the new outlet for individualism of all sorts offered to the Bible-reading public by the vernacular press. This, though they did not realize it at the time, was to prove the undoing of the scheme they now embarked upon for subjecting the new society arising in England to a presbyterian type of theocracy.

The need for reducing the press to order seemed to parliament, at the very moment when the decision was taken to summon the assembly of divines, hardly less important than the need for reorganizing the church. The overthrow of Laud had set the printers to work unchecked by fear of Star Chamber or the Stationers' Company, and they worked in behalf of any who would pay them for their services. The war of pamphlets initiated by Parker over the question of sovereignty and natural law was an immediate result, but publications of all sorts poured forth without license or regulation. Resolutions might issue from Westminster directing the stationers to be more vigilant or condemning this book or that, but without avail. The stream of print continued to overflow to such a degree that the stationers were moved to present a *Remonstrance* begging parliament for a new and stronger law upholding their authority.[19] Their complaints indicate the extent which the activity and power of the press had now attained. They also show that men little realized that the difficulty of regulating the press had become practically insuperable. 'The main care,' they advise, 'is to appoint Examiners for licensing of things profitable, and suppressing of things harmful: and the next care is that the endeavors of those Examiners may not be frustrated.' This, they failed to realize, was easier said than done. During the past four years the affairs of the press have grown, they say, 'very scandalous and enormious,' and this condition, they sapiently suggest, arises from the fact that there are too many printers and too many presses. Such is the case among members of the company itself, not to mention the outsiders, drapers, carmen, and the like, who have embarked upon the business in divers obscure corners of the city and suburbs. Consequently great numbers of opprobrious, incendiary pamphlets are being vented, many of them penned at the universities—a glance at the Oxford royalists—printed in despicable letters on base paper and hawked about the streets by 'sempsters' and 'Emissaries of such base condition.' This is bad for the book trade as well as offensive to the public good. 'The Printing of Pamphlets is now the utmost ambition of Stationers in England. And even in Pamphlets too there is great hazard, for scarce one book of three sells well, or proves gainfull to the publisher.' As for authors, they often get 'but the benefit of their Copies.' The *Remonstrance* concludes with a petition which shows that its authors were better at summing up the difficulty than at prescribing the remedy.

Now therefore all these premises considered, and foreasmuch as irregular Printing hath of late been the fewell in some measure of this miserable Civill-Warre by deceiving the multitude, and hath brought into both Church and State sundry other mischiefs and miseries as well as poverty and desolation upon the Corporation of Stationers, It is most humbly prayed, that some speedy course be taken for such a perfect regulation of the Presse, as may procure the publike good of the State by the private prosperity of the Stationers Company.

Parliament had good reason for attempting to satisfy this request. Thomason's attribution of the Stationers' *Remonstrance* to the pen of Henry Parker is significant. Since the preceding midsummer Parker had been defending parliament in the press against royalist pamphlets, which continued to come up from Oxford in undiminishing number. He was now supporting a proposal which would bring the law to his aid against the propaganda of the court and the prelatical clergy. The outcome was the famous ordinance for printing of 14 June 1643, re-asserting the right and the responsibility of the Stationers' Company to search for, seize and prosecute illegal publications and requiring that nothing be printed unless entered in the Stationers' Register and approved by one of the special licensers appointed by parliament.

With the summoning of the Westminster Assembly and the adoption of the printing ordinance, the Puritan movement as it affected ideas and expression reached a kind of period. The first condition for really establishing the godly Utopia would be the victory of the Puritan party over the king in war. Even that victory would prove fruitless unless the proponents of presbyterian uniformity could maintain their ascendancy in the Puritan party. But the presbyterian churchmen were now surrounded by a cloud of dissenters of many kinds, habituated to a certain degree of freedom and supplied now with an active press by which to make dissent vocal. The result was destined to be, not the triumph of Puritan reform, but a new struggle for liberty and a literature dealing with the issues which the struggle for liberty provoked.

Notes

CHAPTER I

1. It is, of course, well known to be made up of borrowings from actual thirteenth-century sermons. See Kate O. Petersen, *The Sources of the Parson's Tale, Radcliffe College Monographs*, Number 12, 1901.

2. G. R. Owst, *Preaching in Medieval England*, 1926, and *Literature and Pulpit in Medieval England*, 1933, have done much to suggest and confirm the view here taken of the continuity of Puritan preaching with the past.

3. Fuller, *Church History*, Bk. IX, under date 1563, §§ 66-67; Heylyn, *Ecclesia Restaurata*, II, 172; and Strype, *Annals*, II, Pt. i, Ch. 1, testify that the word was applied to Cartwright and his party at this time at Cambridge. Stowe, *Memoranda*, p. 143, says it was applied as early as 1567 to sectaries in London whom he calls Anabaptists and Browings [Brownists?]. See *New English Dictionary*.

4. A. F. Scott Pearson, *Thomas Cartwright and Elizabethan Puritanism*, 1925, is the indispensable source of information concerning Cartwright. I am deeply indebted to the same author's *Church and State, Political Aspects of Sixteenth Century Puritanism*, 1928, for the interpretation of presbyterianism, and to W. K. Jordan, *Development of Religious Toleration in England from the Beginning of the English Reformation to the Death of Elizabeth*, 1932, for the interpretation of Elizabethan policy. R. G. Usher, *Reconstruction of the English Church*, 1910, has also been useful. J. B. Mullinger, *The University of Cambridge from the Royal Injunctions of 1535 to the Accession of Charles the First*, 1884, is still the fullest account of conditions at Cambridge in the period, but S. E. Morison, *The Founding of Harvard College*, 1935, throws important light on the connection between the Puritan movement and university education in England, particularly at Cambridge. The same author, in his *The Puritan Pronaos*, 1936, and T. G. Wright, *Literary Culture in Early New England*, 1920, give important information concerning the intellectual background of early New England preachers which applies as well to Puritans in general.

5. 'Lives,' p. 17, in Clarke, *General Martyrologie*, 1677.

6. Scott Pearson, *Thomas Cartwright*, pp. 28, 29*note*.

7. For the Latin text see Scott Pearson, *Der Älteste Englische Presbyterianismus*, 1912, pp. 77-95, and Francis Paget, *Introduction to the Fifth Book of Hooker's . . . Ecclesiastical Polity*, 1899, pp. 88-89. Scott Pearson, *Thomas Cartwright*, pp. 258-259, says that the book was never printed in the reign of Elizabeth and that there is no evidence that the English version circulated among

Elizabethan Puritans. The translation was published with the title, *A Directory of Church Government*, 1644. The original was attacked by Bancroft in *A Survay of the Pretended Holy Discipline*, 1593, and *Daungerous Positions*, 1593.

8. 'M. Derings words, spoken on his death-bed,' in Dering, *Workes*; Fuller, *Abel Redevivus*; Clarke, *Marrow*.

9. *Sermon preached before the Queenes Maiestie*, in Dering, *Workes*, p. 12.

10. *Ibidem*, pp. 27-38; Epistle prefixed to *A briefe and Necessarie Catechisme* in Dering, *Workes*.

11. For a general account of the English sects, see Robert Barclay, *Inner Life of the Religious Societies*, 1876. For the distinctions among the sects and between the sects and non-conforming groups within the church, see Champlin Burrage, *Early English Dissenters*, 1912, and Perry Miller, *Orthodoxy in Massachusetts*, 1933.

12. Fuller, *History of the University of Cambridge*, p. 147, in *The Church History of Britain*.

13. This attitude is reflected in the otherwise useful survey by W. F. Mitchell, *English Pulpit Oratory from Andrewes to Tillotson*, 1932.

14. 'Lives,' pp. 218-219, in Clarke, *General Martyrologie*, 1677.

15. Information on popular taste in reading is furnished by L. B. Wright, *Middle-Class Culture in Elizabethan England*, 1935, and by H. C. White, *English Devotional Literature*, 1931.

16. See also William Crowe, *Exact Collection*, 1663, and William London, *Catalogue of the most vendible Books*, 1658.

17. Baxter, *A Christian Directory*, 1673, pp. 922-928.

18. Henry Martyn Dexter, 'Elder Brewster's Library,' in *Proceedings of the Massachusetts Historical Society*, 1889-1890, Second series, V, 37-85.

19. A. C. Potter, 'Catalogue of John Harvard's Library,' in *Publications of the Colonial Society of Massachusetts*, XXI (1920), 190-230. Interesting information concerning other colonial libraries is to be found in L. B. Wright, 'The Purposeful Reading of our Colonial Ancestors,' in *ELH, A Journal of Literary History*, IV (1937), 85-111, and 'The Gentleman's Library in Early Virginia,' in *Huntington Library Quarterly*, I, No. 1 (October 1937), 3-61.

20. Scott Pearson, *Thomas Cartwright*, pp. 422-427.

21. Preface by Henry Holland to Greenham, *Workes*. See also Clarke, *Martyrologie*, 1652, and Fuller, *Church History*.

22. Holland, Preface to Greenham, *Workes*. *The Short-Title Catalogue* lists several separate publications before 1600 of sermons attributed to Greenham; these were probably among the unauthorized publications to which Greenham's editor refers.

23. Greenham, *Workes*, p. 26.

24. *Ibidem*, p. 20.

25. Whately, *Oyle of Gladnesse*, Epistle.

26. Holland, Preface to Greenham, *Workes*.

27. Greenham, *Workes*, pp. 1-43.

28. Holland, Preface to Greenham, *Workes*.

29. The principal source of information concerning Browne is his *True and Short Declaration* and other tracts. The best account of him is Champlin Burrage, *True Story of Robert Browne*, 1906.

30. Browne, *True and Short Declaration*. For a fuller discussion of Browne, see above pp. 181-183.

31. Smith's sermons were issued and reissued in numerous editions. Fuller edited them with an account of the author's life as *Sermons*, 1657.

32. Quoted in *Life*, in Smith, *Works*, I, xviii-xix.

33. Smith, *Micro-cosmo-graphia*, translated by Joshua Sylvester, in Joshua Sylvester, *Complete Works*, ed. by A. B. Grosart, 1880, II, 95-101.

34. Strype, *Aylmer*, pp. 101-102.

35. Fuller, 'Life,' in Smith, *Sermons*.

36. In addition to Fuller, see Quarles, *On Chamber Christians*, quoted in Smith, *Works*, 1867, I, xx.

37. Smith, *Sermons*, p. 143.

38. Topsell, *Times Lamentation*, p. 25.

39. Smith, *Sermons*, p. 396.

40. M. M. Knappen, *Two Elizabethan Puritan Diaries*, 1933, prints an abridged text of Rogers' diary and supplies a biographical sketch.

41. Stephen Egerton, Preface to Rogers, *Seven Treatises*.

42. Rogers, *Seven Treatises*, To the Christian Reader.

43. Knappen, *Two Elizabethan Puritan Diaries*.

44. *Ibidem*, p. 61.

45. Evidence showing how largely students and preachers depended upon members of the nobility and gentry and upon rich lawyers and merchants is abundant in the dedicatory prefaces and epistles to the preachers' own works and in the numerous funeral sermons and spiritual lives.

46. Knappen, *Two Elizabethan Puritan Diaries*, p. 65.

47. *Ibidem*, p. 94.

48. *Ibidem*, p. 95.

49. *Ibidem*, p. 65.

50. *Ibidem*, p. 67.

51. *Ibidem*, p. 57.

52. *Ibidem*, pp. 73-74.

53. *Ibidem*, p. 77.

54. *Ibidem*, p. 54.

55. *Ibidem*, pp. 91-92.

56. *Ibidem*, pp. 78-80.

57. *Ibidem*, p. 69.

CHAPTER II

1. The extent and severity of the repression of the Puritan clergy at this time has been a matter of some dispute. Gardiner, *History of England*, I, 197, accepts the traditional figure of three hundred for the number of non-conform-

ists deprived of their posts, but this is probably an exaggeration. Usher, *Reconstruction of the English Church*, II, 3-19, is more nearly right in taking the position that many more Puritans were caused to fear lest they be ejected than were actually ejected or at any rate stripped of all means of support. The relatively small number who were turned out were, moreover, the less moderate, influential and learned of the party. Certainly persecution did not go to such lengths as to deter the Puritan preachers, who in most instances conformed, from increased activity in pulpit and press. Jordan, *Development of Religious Toleration in England, 1603-1640*, pp. 17-38, gives a good account of the difficulties of James in the situation, showing that the king, much as he disliked the presbyterians, was disinclined by conviction and temperament to persecution and was compelled by political exigencies to continue the policy of compromise.

2. Clarke, *Martyrologie*, 1652; Dillingham, *Vita L. Chadertoni*, translated by E. S. Shuckburgh; Fuller, *Worthies*.

3. Fuller, *Worthies*, p. 117.

4. *Ibidem*.

5. *Ibidem*.

6. A sermon attributed to Chaderton on the twelfth chapter of Romans, published in 1584, was reprinted by William Brewster at Leyden in 1618.

7. Clarke, *General Martyrologie*, 1651; Fuller, *Church History*.

8. 'Lives,' p. 122, in Clarke, *General Martyrologie*, 1677.

9. *Ibidem*, p. 121.

10. Clarke, *General Martyrologie*, 1651; Fuller, *Church History* and *Worthies*.

11. Fuller, *Church History*, Bk. XI, under date 1645.

12. 'Lives,' pp. 168-169, in Clarke, *General Martyrologie*, 1677.

13. Sibbes, *Bowels Opened*.

14. 'The Stationer to the Reader,' signed by W. Lee, in Dod and Cleaver, *Ten Sermons*, 1661.

15. Fuller, *Church History*, Bk. XI, under date 1645, §§ 86-92.

16. Durham, *Life . . . of . . . Harris*.

17. *Ibidem*.

18. *Ibidem*.

19. 'Lives,' p. 177, in Clarke, *General Martyrologie*, 1677.

20. Fuller, *Worthies*, Cheshire, p. 181.

21. John Taylor, editor, *Memorials of the Rev. John Dod*.

22. James Granger, *Biographical History of England*, 1769; 5th edition, II, 74.

23. 'Lives,' pp. 172-173, in Clarke, *General Martyrologie*, 1677.

24. John Taylor, editor, *Memorials of the Rev. John Dod*.

25. The sermon is reprinted in R. P. Tristram Coffin and A. M. Witherspoon, *A Book of Seventeenth Century Prose*, 1929, pp. 456-457, from a letter, attributed by the editors to Sir John Suckling, found 'on the back of fol. 102 of Ashm. MS. 826, Bodleian Library.' The writer of the letter gives a brief ac-

count of the circumstances in which the sermon was supposed to have been delivered but does not identify the preacher. Coffin and Witherspoon are, of course, mistaken in saying that they are the first to print it. Whether Dod was actually the author is doubtful and unimportant.

26. Whiting, 'Life of John Cotton,' in Young, *Chronicles*, pp. 419-431.

27. Norton, *Abel Being Dead*.

28. Clarke, *Collection of the Lives*.

29. Young, *Chronicles*, pp. 419-431.

30. Mather, *Magnalia Christi Americana*, 1820, I, 241.

31. 'Lives,' p. 135, in Clarke, *General Martyrologie*, 1677.

32. *Ibidem*, pp. 205-206.

33. *Ibidem*, p. 161.

34. Clarke, *Lives of Sundry*, pp. 4-22.

35. Fuller, *Holy State* and *Abel Redevivus*; Clarke, *Marrow*.

36. Cooper, *Athenae Cantabrigiensis*.

37. Fuller, *Holy State*, p. 90.

38. Norton, *Abel Being Dead*, p. 12.

39. Fuller, *Abel Redevivus*, p. 434.

40. *Ibidem*, p. 436.

41. Knappen, *Two Elizabethan Puritan Diaries*, p. 27note.

42. Baynes, *The Diocesans Tryall*, 1621.

43. 'Lives,' pp. 23-24, in Clarke, *General Martyrologie*, 1677.

44. 'Lives,' in Clarke, *General Martyrologie*, 1677. Catlin, 'Life' and Grosart, 'Memoir' in Sibbes, *Works*.

45. Baxter, *Reliquiae*, pp. 3-4.

46. Grosart, 'Memoir,' in Sibbes, *Works*, I, xx.

47. *Ibidem*.

48. Thomas Gouge, *Narrative of the Life*; Jenkyn, *Shock of Corn*; 'Lives,' in Clarke, *General Martyrologie*, 1677.

49. Thomas Gouge, *Narrative*.

50. 'Lives,' p. 238, in Clarke, *General Martyrologie*, 1677.

51. Jenkyn, *Shock of Corn*, p. 35.

52. 'Lives,' p. 239, in Clarke, *General Martyrologie*, 1677.

53. Jenkyn, *Shock of Corn*, p. 34.

54. *Ibidem*, p. 42.

55. *Ibidem*, p. 40.

56. Thomas Gouge, *Narrative*.

57. Norton, *Abel Being Dead*; Clarke, *Collection of the Lives*; Cotton Mather, *Magnalia*.

58. Norton, *Abel Being Dead*, pp. 13-14.

59. Ball, *Life*; 'Lives,' in Clarke, *General Martyrologie*, 1677; Fuller, *Church History* and *Worthies*.

60. Quotations relating to Preston, unless indication is given to the contrary,

are from Ball's *Life* as it appears in 'Lives,' pp. 76-81, in Clarke, *General Martyrologie*, 1677.

61. Prynne, *Newes from Ipswich*, 1636.

62. Fuller, *Church History*, Bk. XI, under date 1625.

63. *Worthies*, Northamptonshire, p. 291.

64. Goodwin and Ball, Epistle, in Preston, *Life Eternall*; Sibbes and Davenport, Epistle, in Preston, *The New Covenant*; epistles, *passim*, prefixed to other sermons by Preston, edited by the same hands.

65. Sibbes and Davenport, Epistle in Preston, *Saints Qualification*.

66. 'Life,' in Thomas Goodwin, *Works*, V, v-xix, from which quotations in the text are taken unless indication is given to the contrary.

67. Senhouse, *Foure Sermons*.

68. Partly occupied with the publication of Sibbes's sermons in collaboration with Philip Nye, namely: *Two Sermons*, 1637; *The Christians Portion*, 1637; *A Fountain Sealed*, 1637; *The Spirituall-Mans Aime*, 1637; *The Excellencie of the Gospell*, 1639; *Bowels Opened*, 1639.

69. Fuller, *Church History*, Bk. XI, under date 1629, §§ 5, 6.

70. *Ibidem*, under dates 1629, 1632; Thomas Gouge, *Narrative*; Prynne, *Canterburies Doome*; Heylyn, *Cyprianus Anglicus* and *Examen Historicum*; Barnard, *Theologo-Historicus*; Rushworth, *Historical Collections*, II, 150-152.

71. Fuller, *Church History*, Bk. XI, under date 1629, §§ 5, 6.

72. Thomas Gouge, *Narrative*.

73. Fuller, *Appeal of Iniured Innocence*.

74. Prynne, *Canterburies Doome*, p. 537.

CHAPTER III

1. Max Weber, *Die protestantische Ethik und der Geist des Kapitalismus*, 1904-5, translated by Talcott Parsons, *The Protestant Ethic and the Spirit of Capitalism*, 1930, argues that Calvinism, particularly in its conception of the calling, provided the indispensable religious motive for individual enterprise in the field of economic activity and so for the development of modern capitalistic society. I am indebted to this stimulating book, though I have concluded that it much oversimplifies the problem. I am also indebted to R. H. Tawney's presentation of the same thesis in somewhat modified form, *Religion and the Rise of Capitalism*, 1926. L. B. Wright supplies an interesting discussion of the doctrine of calling particularly as related to the middle-class virtues of diligence and thrift, *Middle-Class Culture in Elizabethan England*, pp. 170-200.

Several of the Puritan biographies which I have discussed in this chapter are listed in D. A. Stauffer, *English Biography before 1700*, 1930, but useful though this survey of biographical writing is, it supplies no critical account of the Puritan spiritual biography as such. References to confessional diaries mentioned in these pages are to be found in Arthur Ponsonby's *English Diaries*, 1923, and *More English Diaries*, 1927, but again we are given no critical discussion of the form itself. W. Y. Tindall, *John Bunyan, Mechanick Preacher,* 1934, discusses illuminatingly the spiritual autobiography as practiced by the lay preachers after 1650 and incidentally throws light on the place of biographical writing in earlier Puritan literature.

2. Downame, *Guide to Godlynesse,* Epistle Dedicatory.

3. Perkins, *Workes,* II, 650-651.

4. Draxe, *Earnest of our Inheritance,* p. 1.

5. Downame, *Christian Warfare,* pp. 183-184.

6. Sibbes, *Saints Cordialls,* pp. 280-281.

7. Fuller, *Holy State,* pp. 89-90.

8. *Ibidem.*

9. Perkins, *Workes,* III, 431-432.

10. Thomas Goodwin, *Works,* Vol. I, *Preface to the Reader.*

11. Thomas Goodwin, Junior, 'Life,' in Thomas Goodwin, *Works,* Vol. V.

12. Thomas Goodwin, *A Childe of Light Walking in Darknes.*

13. Thomas Goodwin, Junior, 'Life,' in Thomas Goodwin, *Works,* Vol. V.

14. John Fuller, Epistle, in Beadle, *Journal or Diary of a Thankful Christian.*

15. James Janeway, *Invisibles, Realities,* pp. 58-59.

16. Mayo, *Life & Death of Edmund Staunton,* p. 33.

17. Clarke, *Collection of the Lives,* p. 21.

18. Clarke, *Lives of Sundry,* p. 90.

19. Clarke, *Marrow,* p. 126.

20. Clarke, *Lives of Sundry,* pp. 162-163.

21. *Ibidem,* p. 63.

22. Burnet, *Life and Death of Sir Matthew Hale.*

23. Staunton, *Sermon preached . . . at the funerall of . . . Mrs. E. Wilkinson . . . whereunto is added a narrative.*

24. Rowe, *Life and death of Mr. John Rowe,* p. 32.

25. James Janeway, *Invisibles, Realities,* p. 59.

26. Thomas Goodwin, Junior, 'Life,' in Thomas Goodwin, *Works,* Vol. V.

27. Introduction to Alleine, *Life and Death of . . . Joseph Alleine,* pp. 1-4.

28. '. . . understand the true reason of my forbearing personall prayses in the cloze: my text gave me occasion of saying something before, and me thought it handsomer to lay all my stuffe upon the foundation, than to set up a lean-to.' Harris, *Samuels Funerall,* To the Godly Reader, in *Works.*

29. 'Lives,' pp. 127-131, in Clarke, *General Martyrologie,* 1677.

30. 'Life,' in Clarke, *Lives of Sundry.*

31. Catlin, *Life,* in Sibbes, *Works,* ed. Grosart, I, cxxxiv.

32. Fuller, *Worthies,* Cheshire, p. 181.

33. Baxter, 'To the Reader,' in Clarke, *Lives of Sundry.*

34. Ashe, *Living Loves.*

35. 'Lives,' pp. 67-73, in Clarke, *General Martyrologie,* 1677.

36. Bagshaw, *Life and Death of Mr. Bolton.*

37. 'Life,' in Clarke, *Lives of Sundry,* pp. 153-179.

38. 'Life,' in Clarke, *Marrow*, Pt. II, 108-114.
39. Clarke, *Marrow*, Pt. II, 169-196.
40. 'Life,' in Taylor, *Pilgrims Profession*, pp. 159-187.
41. William Gouge, *Recovery from Apostacy*.
42. Gataker, *Abrahams Decease*, pp. 7-8.
43. Calamy, *Saints Transfiguration*, p. 24.
44. Jenkyn, *Shock of Corn*, p. 42.
45. Perkins, *Workes*, II, 671.
46. 'Lives,' p. 177, in Clarke, *General Martyrologie*, 1677.
47. Gataker, *Abrahams Decease*.
48. Clarke, *Lives of Sundry*, p. 34.
49. Rogers, *Seven Treatises*, Entrance into the Book.
50. Rogers and others, *Garden of Spirituall Flowers, passim*. The pages are not numbered. Lewis Baylie's *The Practice of Piety*, third edition, 1613, was another very early and frequently reprinted statement of the Puritan code.
51. Durham, *Life of . . . Robert Harris*, in Clarke, *Collection of the Lives*, p. 281.
52. Gouge, *Of Domesticall Duties*. For the very considerable literature concerning domestic relations, see C. L. Powell, *English Domestic Relations, 1487-1653*, 1917, and L. B. Wright, *Middle-Class Culture in Elizabethan England*, pp. 201-227.
53. Dod, *Plaine and Familiar Exposition of the Ten Commandements*, p. 227.
54. C. S. Lewis, *The Allegory of Love*, 1936; Powell, *English Domestic Relations*.
55. Sibbes, *Saints Cordialls*, p. 188.
56. Rogers, *Seven Treatises*, pp. 579-577 [*sic*].
57. Powell, *Resolved Christian*, pp. 48-49.
58. Perkins, *Workes*, I, 481.
59. *Ibidem*.
60. Sibbes, *A Learned Commentary*, p. 257.
61. Bernard, *Ruths Recompense*, pp. 128-129.
62. Rogers, *Seven Treatises*, pp. 590-591.
63. Downame, *Guide to Godlynesse*, Epistle.

CHAPTER IV

1. 'Lives,' p. 332, in Clarke, *General Martyrologie*, 1677. See also the epistle by Harris to his *Absaloms Funeral*, 1634, in *Works*.
2. Downame, *Christian Warfare*, pp. 339-341. J. E. Spingarn in the introduction to his *Critical Essays of the Seventeenth Century*, 1908, I, xxxvi-xlviii, discusses briefly the trend toward simplicity in pulpit eloquence in the later seventeenth century.
3. Perkins, *Workes*, III, 430.
4. *Ibidem*, II, 670-671.

5. *Ibidem,* II, 381.

6. Gataker, *Abrahams Decease,* p. 10.

7. 'Lives,' p. 67, in Clarke, *General Martyrologie,* 1677.

8. Clarke, *Collection of the Lives,* pp. 33-35.

9. Marshall, 'Life,' in Capel, *Remains.*

10. Clarke, *Lives of Sundry,* p. 135.

11. Clarke, *Collection of the Lives,* p. 311.

12. 'Lives,' p. 163, in Clarke, *General Martyrologie,* 1677.

13. Owst, *Literature and Pulpit in Medieval England.*

14. Mitchell, *English Pulpit Oratory from Andrewes to Tillotson,* gives an account of the training of the preachers in rhetoric, of the conventional form of the sermon, and of the habits and methods of recording sermons by shorthand.

15. *Arte of Prophecying,* in Perkins, *Workes,* II, p. 673 and *passim.*

16. 'Lives,' p. 169, in Clarke, *General Martyrologie,* 1677.

17. *Ibidem,* p. 176.

18. Clarke, *Collection of the Lives,* p. 311.

19. The prefaces prepared by John Preston's editors, Thomas Goodwin, Ball, Sibbes and Davenport, for the posthumous editions of his sermons give particularly striking evidence of the practice of taking sermons down in church by shorthand and of circulating them afterwards in unauthorized written and printed copies.

20. Draxe, *Churches Securitie,* p. 40.

21. Clarke, *Martyrologie,* 1652, p. 91.

22. Clarke, *Collection of the Lives,* p. 282.

23. Conant, 'To the Christian Reader,' in Bernard, *Thesaurus Biblicus.*

24. Bernard, *Faithfull Shepheard,* 1607, pp. 2-13.

25. Bernard, *Ready Way to Good Works,* pp. 4-6.

26. Bernard, *Faithfull Shepheard,* 1607, pp. 75-78.

27. *Ibidem,* pp. 40-41.

28. *Ibidem,* p. 19.

29. *Ibidem,* pp. 65-66.

30. Bernard, *The Isle of Man.* The quotations are from the apology addressed to the reader at the close of the book.

31. Marshall, 'Life,' in Capel, *Remains.*

32. Sibbes, *Works,* I, 53.

33. Marshall, 'To the Reader,' in Capel, *Remains.*

34. Topsell, *Times Lamentation,* p. 391.

35. Thomas Goodwin, *Childe of Light,* To the Reader.

36. *Ibidem,* p. 5.

37. *Ibidem,* p. 81.

38. *Ibidem,* p. 124.

39. *Ibidem,* p. 171.

40. *Ibidem,* p. 114.

41. *Ibidem*, p. 183.
42. *Ibidem*, p. 185.
43. *Ibidem*, p. 113.
44. *Ibidem*, pp. 172-173.
45. Rogers and others, *Garden of Spirituall Flowers*.
46. Preston, *The New Covenant*, p. 181.
47. Downame, *Christian Warfare*, p. 90.
48. Sibbes, *Soules Conflict*, p. 49.
49. Preston, *The New Covenant*, p. 183.
50. 'Life,' in Taylor, *Works*.
51. Taylor, *Three Treatises*, p. 123.
52. *Ibidem*, p. 127.
53. *Ibidem*, p. 128.
54. *Ibidem*, pp. 150-151.
55. J. B. Wharey, *Study of the Sources of Bunyan's Allegories*, 1904; W. Y. Tindall, *John Bunyan, Mechanick Preacher*, 1934.
56. Downame, *Christian Warfare*, Dedicatory Epistle.
57. Taylor, *Chrisrs Combate*, p. 8.
58. Gouge, *Whole-armor of God*, Epistle.
59. Perkins, *Case of Conscience*, To the Godly Reader.
60. Perkins, *Workes* I, [475].
61. Downame, *Christian Warfare*, Dedicatory Epistle.
62. *Ibidem*, pp. 34-35.
63. *Ibidem*, pp. 38-39.
64. *Ibidem*, p. 5.
65. *Ibidem*, p. 120.
66. *Ibidem*, p. 5.
67. *Ibidem*, pp. 129-130.
68. Taylor, *Chrisrs Combate*, p. 9.
69. *Ibidem*, p. 20.
70. *Ibidem*, p. 64.
71. *Ibidem*, p. 96.
72. *Ibidem*, p. 3.
73. *The Pearl of the Gospell*, in Taylor, *Three Treatises*, pp. 18-19.
74. *Ibidem*, p. 20.
75. *Ibidem*, pp. 43-44.
76. Sibbes, *Works*, I, 63.
77. Sibbes, *Soules Conflict*, p. 155.
78. Sibbes, *Works*, I, 63.
79. Sibbes, *Soules Conflict*, p. 26.
80. *Ibidem*, p. 23.
81. *Ibidem*, pp. 98-99.
82. Sibbes, *Saints Cordialls*, p. 366.
83. Sibbes, *Soules Conflict*, p. 33.

84. Sibbes, *Saints Cordialls*, pp. 383-386.
85. *Ibidem*, p. 280.
86. *Ibidem*, p. 174.
87. Sibbes, *Beames of Divine Light*, pp. 74-75.
88. Sibbes, *Saints Cordialls*, p. 157.
89. Sibbes, *Beames of Divine Light*, p. 75.
90. Sibbes, *Soules Conflict*, pp. 542-543.
91. *Ibidem*.
92. Preston, *New Covenant*, p. 63.
93. *Ibidem*, To the Reader.
94. *Ibidem*, p. 30.
95. *Ibidem*, p. 33.
96. *Ibidem*, p. 48.
97. *Ibidem*, pp. 214-215.
98. *Ibidem*, p. 43.
99. *Ibidem*, p. 47.
100. *Ibidem*, p. 104.
101. *Ibidem*, p. 136.
102. Preston, *Saints Daily Exercise*, p. 53.
103. Preston, *Sermons Preached before his Maiestie*, To the Reader.
104. *Ibidem*, pp. 44-45.
105. *Ibidem*, p. 81.
106. *Ibidem*, pp. 86-87.
107. Preston, *Life Eternall*, Epistle Dedicatorie.
108. *Ibidem*, pp. 13-15.
109. *Ibidem*, p. 4.
110. *Ibidem*, p. 9.
111. *Ibidem*, p. 5.
112. *Ibidem*, p. 56.
113. Gouge, *Guide to Goe to God*, Epistle.

CHAPTER V

1. There is an extensive literature concerning the English sects but no adequate treatment of dissent in general in its relation to the Puritan movement as a whole. T. C. Hall discusses the matter illuminatingly but of necessity briefly in his *Religious Background of American Culture*, 1930. W. K. Jordan discusses the sects in relation to toleration in *The Development of Religious Toleration 1603-1640*, 1930. Among the older works on non-conformity, Robert Barclay, *The Inner Life of the Religious Societies*, 1876, is most useful for its descriptive account of the several religious groups. For the distinction between the reformers within the church and the separatists of various sorts, Champlin Burrage, *The Early English Dissenters*, 1912, is authoritative, but

Perry Miller has greatly added to the understanding of the subject in his *Orthodoxy in Massachusetts*, 1933.

2. Burrage, *Early English Dissenters*, I, 68; W. T. Whitley, *History of the British Baptists*, 1923, p. 17.

3. S. E. Morison, *The Puritan Pronaos*, 1936, p. 155, justly observes that the founders of New England were far from being strict Calvinists. He says, indeed, that the first New England Calvinist was Jonathan Edwards.

4. The most authoritative account of Browne is to be found in Burrage, *The Early English Dissenters*, 1912, and *The True Story of Robert Browne*, 1906. See also F. J. Powicke, *Robert Browne*, 1910.

5. Browne, *True and Short Declaration*.

6. H. M. Dexter, *Congregationalism of the Last Three Hundred Years*, 1880, pp. 119-126, and Burrage, *True Story*, p. 30*note*.

7. The best account of Smyth is the biography by W. T. Whitley in his edition of the *Works of John Smyth*, 1915. See also W. H. Burgess, *John Smith the Se-Baptist*, 1911. Jordan, *Development of Religious Toleration, 1603-1640*, analyzes the writings of Smyth and of his immediate followers, Helwys, Busher and Murton, particularly as they concern toleration.

8. *Bright Morning Starre*, Epistle Dedicatory, in Smyth, *Works*, p. 2.

9. *Patterne of True Prayer*, To the Reader, in Smyth, *Works*, p. 72.

10. Whitley, Introduction to Smyth, *Works*, pp. liv-lxviii and 767-769; Burgess, *John Smith*, pp. 71-80.

11. *Christian Advertisements and Counsels of Peace: Also disswasions from the Separatists Schisme*, 1608; *Plaine evidences: The Church of England is apostolicall, the separation schismaticall*, 1610. See also John Robinson, *A Iustification of Separation from the Church of England Against Mr. Richard Bernard his invective, intituled The Separatists Schisme*, 1610, and John Smyth, *Parallels, censures, observations*, 1609.

12. W. H. Burgess, *John Robinson, Pastor of the Pilgrim Fathers*, 1920; Champlin Burrage, *New Facts concerning John Robinson*, 1910.

13. *Propositions and Conclusions*, in Smyth, *Works*, pp. 733-750.

14. Bradford, *History of Plymouth Plantation*, I, 41-42.

15. Robinson, *Works*, edited by Robert Ashton, 1851.

16. The address of Robinson to the Pilgrims on their departure from Holland, attributed to him by Edward Winslow, *Hypocrisy Unmasked*, 1646, quoted by Cotton Mather, *Magnalia*, I, 64 (1853 edition), is probably in large measure apocryphal. See the article on Robinson by Alexander Gordon in *Dictionary of National Biography*. See also Burrage, *New Facts*, p. 17, and Burgess, *John Robinson*, pp. 239-241.

17. Chaderton, *A Fruitfull Sermon*.

18. H. M. Dexter, 'Elder Brewster's Library,' in *Proceedings of the Massachusetts Historical Society*, 2d series, V, 37-85.

19. Bradford, *History of Plymouth Plantation*, I, 3.

20. *Ibidem*, I, 60.

21. *Ibidem*, I, 124.

22. See the excellent analysis of this argument by Miller, *Orthodoxy in Massachusetts*.

23. Castellio, *Concerning Heretics*, translated and edited by R. H. Bainton, 1935; Ferdinand Buisson, *Sébastien Castellion, sa vie et son œuvre*, 1892.

24. Castellio, *Contra libellum Calvini*, in *Concerning Heretics*, edited by Bainton, p. 271.

25. Jordan, *Development of Religious Toleration in England from the Beginning of the English Reformation to the Death of Queen Elizabeth*, pp. 303-365.

26. Acontius, *Satans Stratagems*, Epistle. Acontius' book is analyzed in detail by Jordan, *Development of Religious Toleration*, using the French version. I have used the English translation of the first four books. These present the leading ideas of the work which were of particular interest to Englishmen.

27. Acontius, *Satans Stratagems*, p. 20.

28. *Ibidem*, p. 59.

29. *Ibidem*, p. 55.

30. *Ibidem*, p. 28.

31. *Ibidem*, p. 125.

32. *Ibidem*, p. 91.

33. *Ibidem*, p. 136.

34. *Ibidem*, p. 54.

35. Reprinted in my *Tracts on Liberty*, III, 3-58. Facts about Goodwin are to be found in Thomas Jackson, *Life of John Goodwin*, 1822, written from a sectarian point of view, in David Masson, *Life of John Milton*, 1877-1896, III, 120-122, and in my *Tracts on Liberty*, I, *passim*. A study of the career of Goodwin is, however, an important chapter in the intellectual history of the Puritan Revolution which still remains, and deserves, to be written.

36. I have found no evidence to confirm the assertion of Alexander Gordon in his article on Goodwin in the *Dictionary of National Biography* that Goodwin was actually the translator of *Satanae Stratagemata* as well as the author of the prefatory epistle to the translation.

37. John Goodwin, *Impedit Ira Animum* and especially *Imputatio Fidei*, p. 2.

38. John Goodwin, *Imputatio Fidei*, Epistle Dedicatory.

39. *Ibidem*, Epistle to the London Clergy.

40. *Ibidem*, To the Reader.

41. *Last Booke*, in Smyth, *Works*, II, 752.

42. *Ibidem*, II, 755.

43. *Propositions and Conclusions*, in Smyth, *Works*, II, 735.

44. *Objections: Answered*, p. 74.

45. Busher, *Religions Peace*, p. 2.

46. Haller, *Tracts on Liberty*, I, 42-45.

47. Nicholas, *An Introduction to the Holy Understanding of the Glasse of Righteousnesse*, p. 107.

48. At Basle, 1557, at Antwerp and at Cologne, 1558. See Buisson, *Sébastien Castellion*, II, 365.

49. R. M. Jones, *Spiritual Reformers in the Sixteenth and Seventeenth Centuries*, 1914, p. 243.

50. Randall, editor or translator, *Theologia Germanica*, To the Reader.

51. Jones, *Spiritual Reformers*, pp. 242, 256.

52. Everard's sermons appeared in 1653 as *Some Gospel Treasures Opened* and again in 1657 as *The Gospel-Treasury Opened*. I have used the latter edition.

53. Rapha Harford, 'To the Reader,' in Everard, *Gospel-Treasury Opened*.

54. *Ibidem*.

55. *Ibidem*.

56. 'Approbation' by Tho Brooks and M. Barker in Everard, *Gospel Treasury Opened*.

57. Everard, *Gospel-Treasury Opened*, Pt. ii, p. 18.

58. *Ibidem*, Pt. ii, p. 20.

59. *Ibidem*, Pt. ii, p. 29.

60. *Ibidem*, Pt. ii, p. 176.

61. *Ibidem*, Pt. ii, p. 27.

62. *Ibidem*, Pt. ii, p. 293.

63. *Ibidem*, Pt. ii, p. 29.

64. *Ibidem*, Pt. ii, p. 21.

65. *Ibidem*, Pt. i, pp. 36-37.

66. *Ibidem*, Pt. i, pp. 67-68.

67. *Ibidem*, Pt. i, p. 42.

68. *Ibidem*, Pt. i, p. 43.

69. *Ibidem*; Jones, *Spiritual Reformers*, 242.

70. *Gospel-Treasury Opened*, Pt. i, p. 89.

71. Eaton, *Honey-Combe*, p. 4.

72. *Ibidem*, p. 411.

73. *Ibidem*, p. 467.

74. Saltmarsh, *Holy Discoveries*, Dedication.

75. *Ibidem*, p. 34.

76. *Ibidem*, p. 54.

77. *Ibidem*, pp. 223-224.

78. A critical account of Lilburne, uncolored by the prepossessions which troubled Masson, Gardiner and Morley, is much needed. The article by the late Sir Charles Harding Firth in the *Dictionary of National Biography* and the discussion of Lilburne by T. C. Pease, 1916, in his *The Leveller Movement* are both excellent as far as they go, but each is least good in its treatment of Lilburne's early years and of the influence of religious enthusiasm on him and the other Levellers, particularly in the early stages of the movement for democracy. My own discussion of Lilburne in *Tracts on Liberty* is open to the same criticism.

79. William Pierce, *An Historical Introduction to the Marprelate Tracts*, 1909; *The Marprelate Tracts*, 1911; *John Penry his Life, Times and Writings*, 1923.

80. Prynne is another figure of the Puritan Revolution who deserves closer critical study than he has so far received. Besides the excellent and full article on him in the *Dictionary of National Biography* by Firth, see S. R. Gardiner, ed., *Documents Relating to the Proceedings against William Prynne in 1634 and 1637, with a Biographical Fragment by the Late John Bruce*, Camden Society, 1872, containing a bibliography of Prynne's writings. Bibliographical information is also to be found in E. W. Kirby, *William Prynne: A Study in Puritanism*, 1931.

81. Prynne, *Perpetuitie of a Regenerate Mans Estate*, Epistle.

82. *Ibidem*, p. 410.

83. *Ibidem*, Epistle.

84. Prynne, *Looking Glasse*, Epistle.

85. Prynne, *Church of Englands old Antithesis*, Epistle.

86. Prynne, *Newes from Ipswich*, Epistle.

CHAPTER VI

1. There is no satisfactory modern study of Laud. W. H. Hutton, *William Laud*, 1895, is useful but strongly Anglican. Jordan, *The Development of Religious Toleration in England, 1603-1640*, gives a good account of his struggle to repress Puritan preachers and pamphleteers. Contemporary sources of primary importance, besides Prynne's *Breviate of the Life of William Laud*, 1644, and other controversial writings referred to in these pages, are Laud's own writings (*Works*, 1847-50); the anonymous *A Briefe Relation of the Death and Sufferings of William Laud*, 1644; *The History of the Troubles and Tryal of . . . William Laud, . . . Wrote by himself, during his Imprisonment in the Tower, To which is prefixed The Diary of his own Life*, Vol. I, 1695, Vol. II, 1700; and Peter Heylyn, *Cyprianus Anglicus*, 1671.

2. *Diary*, in Laud, *Works*, III, 131-136.

3. Heylyn, *Cyprianus Anglicus*, p. 52; Dering, *Collection of Speeches*, 1642, p. 5.

4. Clarendon, *History of the Rebellion*, edited by W. Dunn Macray, 1888, I, p. 120.

5. Laud, *History of the Troubles*, pp. 68-69.

6. *Briefe Relation*, p. 23. This popular account of Laud's execution may not, of course, be strictly accurate.

7. Leighton, *Epitome or Briefe Discoverie*.

8. Laud, *Relation of the Conference*, p. 78.

9. Pierre Desmaiseaux, *An Historical and Critical Account of the Life and Writings of Wm. Chillingworth*, 1725, gives a good account of Chillingworth from the eighteenth-century latitudinarian point of view.

10. Quoted by Desmaiseaux, *Life*, p. 2. Wood, *Athenae Oxoniensis*, II, 20.

11. Little has so far been added to the memorable picture of Falkland given by his friend Clarendon in his *History of the Rebellion* and his *Life of Edward Earl of Clarendon*, but see J. A. R. Marriott, *The Life and Times of Lucius Cary, Viscount Falkland*, 1907.

12. Clarendon, *History*, Bk. VII, §220.

13. Quoted from Clarendon, *Life*, in the article on Chillingworth in *Dictionary of National Biography*.

14. Chillingworth, *Religion of Protestants*, Preface.

15. Desmaiseaux, *Life*, p. 372.

16. Quoted by Desmaiseaux, *Life*, *loc. cit.*

17. Chillingworth, *Religion of Protestants*, Preface.

18. *Ibidem*.

19. A partial collection of the writings of Hales appeared in 1659 as *Golden Remains of the Ever Memorable M. John Hales*, and was several times reprinted. The most complete collection is to be found in *The Works of the Ever Memorable Mr. John Hales*, 1765. Pierre Desmaiseaux published an account of Hales, *An Historical . . . Account of the Life and Writings of . . . J. H. . . . , being a specimen of an historical and critical English Dictionary*, 1719.

20. *Letters from the Synod of Dort* in Hales, *Golden Remains*.

21. Letter of Anthony Farindon prefixed to Hales, *Golden Remains*.

22. Hales, *Golden Remains*, pp. 1-25.

23. *Ibidem*, 26-30.

24. *Of Enquiry and Private Judgment in Religion*, in Hales, *Works*, III, 141-166.

25. Hales, *Works*, I, 164.

26. *Ibidem*, I, 177.

27. Hales, *Tract concerning Schisme*, p. 4.

28. *Works*, I, 135-144.

29. *Of Dealing with Erring Christians*, in Hales, *Golden Remains*. Note also the letter by Anthony Farindon in the same work.

30. Cheynell, *Chillingworthi Novissima*.

31. Clarendon, *Life*, I, 175; *History*, Bk. VII, §§230-234; Whitelocke, *Memorials*, p. 70.

CHAPTER VII

1. The documents relating to the punishment of Prynne in 1634 and, together with Bastwick and Burton, in 1637, have been edited by S. R. Gardiner, *Documents Relating to the Proceedings against William Prynne in 1634 and 1637, with a Biographical Fragment by the Late John Bruce*, Camden Society, 1872. I have quoted below from the contemporary popular account of the affair, *A Briefe Relation of Certain Speciall and Most Materiall Passages*, which

appeared in three editions, 1637, 1638, 1641. The last was appended to Prynne's *New Discovery of the Prelates Tyranny,* 1641, and bears some changes and additions. I have indicated in each case to which edition I am referring. Since in each edition *A Briefe Relation* was a partisan journalistic report, it must be taken not as a strictly accurate statement of what happened but as a brilliant example of popular Puritan revolutionary propaganda. Further details concerning the incident are to be found in Bastwick, *Letany,* the second, third and fourth parts, 1637, and *A Just Defence of John Bastwick,* 1645, and in Burton, *A Narration of the Life,* 1643.

2. Burton, *Narration of the Life,* Preface to the Reader.

3. *Ibidem,* p. 1.

4. Burton, *For God, and the King,* pp. 39-40.

5. Burton, *Narration of the Life,* p. 11.

6. Bastwick, *A Just Defence,* pp. 10-11.

7. *Briefe Relation,* 1641, p. 21. In the 1637 edition the appeal is simply to 'the Law of God and man.'

8. *Briefe Relation,* 1641, p. 24.

9. *Briefe Relation,* 1641, p. 30.

10. *Briefe Relation,* 1641, p. 31.

11. *Briefe Relation,* 1637, p. 28.

12. *Briefe Relation,* 1637, pp. 21-22, but the matter enclosed in square brackets was added in the edition of 1641 [p. 64].

13. Bastwick, *Letany,* pp. 5-6.

14. Bastwick, *Just Defence,* p. 11.

15. See above, Chap. V, note 78. The principal contemporary sources concerning Lilburne's early career are his writings of the years 1638-1640 (see below, pp. 432-440); the accounts he gives of himself in *Innocency and Truth Justified,* 1645, *Legall Fundamentall Liberties,* 1649; *A True Relation of the materiall passages in Lieft. Colonell J. Lilburne his Apologeticall Narration,* 1652; and Bastwick, *A Just Defence,* 1645.

16. Pease, *The Leveller Movement;* Haller, *Tracts on Liberty,* I.

17. Denison, *The White Wolfe or, A Sermon Preached at Pauls Crosse, Feb. 11. . . . 1627,* 1627.

18. Heywood, *True Discourse,* 1636.

19. The principal source of information concerning Kiffin is his autobiography which was, however, written late and not published until the nineteenth century; *Remarkable Passages in the Life of William Kiffin,* 1823.

20. Kiffin, *Remarkable Passages,* pp. 2-3.

21. *Ibidem,* p. 7.

22. *Ibidem,* pp. 9-14.

23. Lilburne, *Christian Mans Triall* including *A Worke of the Beast,* 2d edition, 1641.

24. Until recently, though Pease, *Leveller Movement,* pointed out his probably great importance, little was known about Walwyn, and that little was distorted

Notes

if not erroneous. See my *Tracts on Liberty*, I, *passim*; for Walwyn's *Power of Love* see the same work, II, 271-304, and for his *The Compassionate Samaritane*, III, 59-104. He became so important a figure in the Leveller movement and in the pamphlet literature which attended it after 1643 that it is necessary to reserve fuller discussion of him to an ensuing volume.

25. Pease, *Leveller Movement*, pp. 256-257, thinks that *The Humble Petition of the Brownists* was by Walwyn. I have expressed doubt concerning this attribution in *Tracts on Liberty*, I, 126, but am now inclined to agree with Pease. *A New Petition of the Papists* is obviously by the same hand.

26. Crosby, *History of the English Baptists*, I, 164. Contemporary references are found in [John Taylor], *Brownists Conventicle*, 1641, p. 3; Lilburne, *Letter to the Wardens*, 1640, pp. 4, 7; John Taylor, *A Swarme of Sectaries*, 1641, pp. 8-13. See also Tindall, *John Bunyan, Mechanick Preacher*, p. 87.

27. Lilburne, *Letter to the Wardens*, p. 7.

28. *Ibidem*, p. 4.

29. Brook, *Lives of the Puritans*, III, 529, cites Edwards, *Gangraena*, Pt. III, p. 49.

30. For comment upon How and Spencer and an account of the later development of their ideas and practices up to their great flowering in Bunyan, see Tindall, *John Bunyan, Mechanick Preacher*.

31. The beginnings of millenarian enthusiasm are only somewhat slightly treated by Louise Fargo Brown, *Baptists and Fifth Monarchy Men*, 1912.

32. This has been attributed to Knollys by Halkett and Laing, *Dictionary*; by Alexander Gordon in his article on Knollys in the *Dictionary of National Biography*; by the *Catalogue* of the British Museum, and by J. H. Bloom, *English Tracts*, 1922. W. T. Whitley, *Baptist Bibliography*, 1916, and the *Catalogue of the McAlpin Collection* assign it to Kiffin, but he was obviously responsible only for the epistle. The work was printed for William Larner, probably a baptist, later a Leveller and a seller of Leveller books and pamphlets. The second edition of Lilburne's *Christian Mans Triall* with an epistle signed by William Kiffin was also printed to be sold by him in 1641. *A Glimpse* was undoubtedly written by a baptist of some education and literary ability known to Kiffin and regarded by him with respect. This description fits Knollys better than any other person of the time known to me. Baillie, however, in his *Dissuasive*, 1645, pp. 79-80, says, 'The glimpse of Sions glory Preached at a Fast in Holland by T. G. (which common report without any contradiction that I have heard declares to be Thomas Goodwin).' The title-page of a copy of *A Glimpse* which belonged to Grosart is reprinted in the edition of Goodwin's works in Nichol's Standard Divines, Vol. XII. The text of this is identical with that of the title-page of the McAlpin copy except for slight differences in spelling and the addition of the words, 'Briefly layd open in a Sermon, at a general Fast day in Holland, by T. G. And now Published.' The editor, following Grosart, identifies T. G. with Thomas Goodwin, and reprints the

work as positively his. I have been unable to locate this Grosart copy. Neither the British Museum *Catalogue* nor the *Baptist Bibliography* compiled by Whitley, who made use of the copy in the Bodleian, make any reference to T. G. or to Goodwin. It is of course possible that the work was a sermon preached in Holland by someone bearing the initials T. G. and that this was Thomas Goodwin. Goodwin like most Puritans believed in the second coming of Christ and the millennium. Certain sermons of his presenting such ideas, which may have been preached about 1640, were in fact published in 1654 and 1655 by some more enthusiastic hand probably from copies taken down in church and certainly without his authority, namely, *A Sermon of the Fifth Monarchy . . . Preached by Mr. Tho. Goodwin, on Rev. 5. 9, 10,* 1654, and *The World to Come, or, The Kingdome of Christ asserted in two Expository Lectures on Ephes. 1. 21, 22 . . . Preached by Mr. Tho: Goodwin many yeares since, at Antholins, London,* 1655. Goodwin and men of his station did not, however, like the author of *A Glimpse of Sions Glory,* look for the immediate inauguration of Christ's kingdom on earth or identify the saints as the common people. When the more enthusiastic millenarians presently grew dangerous to the revolutionary state, men like Goodwin ranged themselves against them (see Brown, *Baptists and Fifth Monarchy Men,* pp. 16, 20, 26, 46). It seems most unlikely, therefore, that Goodwin had anything to do with *A Glimpse* or with persons like Kiffin and Larner. Baillie, who was eager to discredit his independent opponents, was probably reporting unfounded gossip. Grosart, finally, was easily misled. I suspect his injudicious hand on the title-page reproduced in Nichol's Standard Divines.

33. Knollys, *Life and Death.*
34. *Ibidem,* Epistle.
35. Knollys, *Glimpse of Sions Glory.*
36. Rushworth, *Historical Collections,* II, 788-799.
37. Lilburne, *Innocency and Truth,* p. 8.
38. Lilburne, *Worke of the Beast,* p. 19.
39. Lilburne, *Christian Mans Triall,* p. 2; *Innocency and Truth,* p. 7.
40. Lilburne, *Legall Fundamentall Liberties,* pp. 20-21.
41. *Ibidem.*
42. Nicholas Fuller, *Argument of Master Nicholas Fuller.*
43. Lilburne, *Legall Fundamentall Liberties.*
44. Copy of a Letter in Lilburne, *Innocency and Truth,* pp. 15-17.
45. Kiffin and others, *Walwins Wiles.*
46. Lilburne, *Legall Fundamentall Liberties,* pp. 19-24.
47. *Ibidem,* p. 21.
48. Bastwick, *Just Defence,* p. 15.
49. Lilburne, *Christian Mans Triall,* pp. 1, 15; Rushworth, *Historical Collections,* II, 463-464.
50. Lilburne, *Christian Mans Triall,* p. 12.
51. Bastwick, *Just Defence,* pp. 11, 31.

52. Lilburne, *Letter to the Apprentices.*
53. The details concerning Lilburne's punishment are to be found in his *Worke of the Beast,* except the stamping and the bleeding at the mouth. These are to be found in 'A True Relation,' p. 29, in *Legall Fundamentall Liberties,* and in *Lieft. Colonell J. Lilburne his Apologeticall Narration,* 1652. See also Rushworth, *Historical Collections,* II, 466.
54. Lilburne, *Innocency and Truth,* p. 73.
55. Lilburne, *Letter to the Apprentices.*
56. Lilburne, *Letter to the Wardens.*
57. Lilburne, *Innocency and Truth,* p. 74; *Letter to the Apprentices.*
58. Lilburne, *Innocency and Truth,* p. 74.
59. *Ibidem.*
60. Lilburne, 'True Relation,' in *Legall Fundamentall Liberties.*
61. Lilburne, *Innocency and Truth,* pp. 39-40.
62. Lilburne, *Coppy of a Letter,* p. 14.
63. *Ibidem,* p. 12.
64. *Ibidem,* pp. 16-17.
65. Lilburne, *Come out of her,* p. 25.
66. Lilburne, *Coppy of a Letter,* pp. 1-3.
67. *Ibidem,* p. 14.
68. *Ibidem,* p. 4.
69. See especially Lilburne, *Come out of her* and *Answer to Nine Arguments.*
70. Lilburne, *Answer to Nine Arguments,* p. 2.
71. Lilburne, *Come out of her,* p. 20.
72. Lilburne, *Worke of the Beast,* p. 19.
73. Lilburne, *Come out of her,* p. 26.
74. *Ibidem,* p. 24.
75. *Ibidem,* p. 25.
76. *Ibidem,* p. 32.
77. Lilburne, *Letter to the Wardens.*

CHAPTER VIII

1. For references to Milton's writings I have made use of the Columbia University edition of *The Works of John Milton,* 1931-37, except in the following instances. For Milton's private letters and academic exercises, I have used the translation of Phyllis B. Tillyard, *Milton: Private Correspondence and Academic Exercises,* 1932. For Milton's Latin poems I have used the translations of W. V. Moody, revised by E. K. Rand, in *The Complete Poetical Works of John Milton,* edited by W. V. Moody, 1924. David Masson's *Life of Milton* must remain as the basis and starting point for any later biographical study of Milton in spite of the fact that Masson's critical attitude is, to say the least, obsolete. J. H. Hanford, *A Milton Handbook,* revised edition 1933, provides an excellent digest of information and critical opinion and serves as

a useful guide to the abundant literature about Milton which has appeared in recent years. In dealing with Milton's early career, I have also been much indebted to Hanford, 'The Youth of Milton' in *Studies in Shakespeare, Milton and Donne*, 1925, and to E. M. W. Tillyard, *Milton*, 1930, and to his Introduction and Commentary to Phyllis B. Tillyard, *Milton: Private Correspondence and Academic Exercises*. Mr. Tillyard's *The Miltonic Setting*, 1938, has come to me as this book has been going through the press. I see in it a cogent effort to do for Milton what the present work also attempts in its way, to set Milton's Puritanism in a juster critical and historical perspective. I wish to say, finally, that in taking the view of Milton here presented I have been perhaps most greatly influenced and encouraged by Sir Herbert Grierson's *Cross Currents in English Literature of the Seventeenth Century*, 1929, and his *Milton and Wordsworth*, 1937.

2. D. H. Stevens, *Milton Papers*, 1927.

3. Thomas Gataker, *Abrahams Decease, A meditation on Genesis 25, 8 Delivered at the Funerall of . . . Mr. Richard Stock . . . Together with the Testimonie then given unto him*, 1627. Gataker's *Testimonie* is reprinted in Clarke, *Martyrologie*, 1652. See also Masson, *Life of Milton*, I, 34-35.

4. Rushworth, *Historical Collections*, II, 150-152.

5. Stock, *The Churches Lamentation for the Losse of the Godly*, 1614; reprinted in Clarke, *Marrow*.

6. Quotations are taken from the edition of Gataker's life in Clarke, *Marrow*.

7. Stock, *Learned and Very Usefull Commentary*, pp. 151-152.

8. Professor Ernest W. Brennecke, who is preparing for publication a life of the elder Milton and an edition of his musical compositions, has assured me that his accomplishments as a composer were distinctly higher even than has been supposed.

9. *Second Defence*, in Milton, *Works*, VIII, 119; *Reason of Church Government*, *Works*, III, 235.

10. *Ad Patrem*, ll. 86-89; Moody-Rand translation, in Milton, *Complete Poetical Works*, p. 364.

11. Masson, *Life of Milton*, I, 44-47.

12. Milton, *Elegia Quarta*. See also the two letters to Young, translated by P. B. Tillyard, in *Milton: Private Correspondence*, pp. 5-6, 9, and W. R. Parker, 'Milton and Thomas Young,' *Modern Language Notes*, LIII, 6 June 1938.

13. *Apology*, in Milton, *Works*, III, 297.

14. *Elegia Quarta*, ll. 91-94; Moody-Rand translation, in Milton, *Complete Poetical Works*, p. 333.

15. *Of Reformation*, in Milton, *Works*, III, 49-50. See also *Apology*, in Milton, *Works*, III, 111.

16. *Reason of Church Government*, in Milton, *Works*, III, 242.

17. Letter to Alexander Gill, in P. B. Tillyard, *Milton: Private Correspondence*, p. 8; First Academic Exercise, *ibidem*, p. 53.

18. *Apology*, in Milton, *Works*, III, 297.

19. The formal curriculum pursued at Cambridge in Milton's time is described by Mullinger, *The University of Cambridge*, II, and by Masson, *Life of Milton*. E. M. W. Tillyard has recently reviewed it in the introduction to P. B. Tillyard's translation of Milton's private letters and prolusions, *Milton: Private Correspondence and Academic Exercises*. The most detailed account of the actual teaching that went on at Cambridge in the days of men like Chaderton, Perkins and Preston and of their disciples, the founders of Massachusetts, is to be found in S. E. Morison, *The Founding of Harvard College*, 1935. Milton's academic exercises should be read in the light of this, but the reader should remember that they were written while the Puritan movement at Cambridge was breaking up under pressure from Charles and Laud. That Bacon's influence, as Tillyard suggests, lent strength thus early to the movement for educational reform at Cambridge may possibly be true, but it should be noted that educational reform went hand in hand with Puritanism and that Puritanism in 1625 at Cambridge was about to be overwhelmed. The suppression of the Puritan Lord Brooke's lectureship in history, the establishment of which may well have been suggested to his mind by Bacon, was but part of the general campaign against Puritanism in the university.

20. For the importance of Puritanism at a later stage in furthering the spread of Baconian ideas, see R. F. Jones, *Ancients and Moderns: A Study of the Background of the Battle of the Books*, Washington University Studies, new series, St. Louis, 1936.

21. P. B. Tillyard, *Milton: Private Correspondence*, pp. xxv-xxvi, 53-64.

22. *Ibidem*, pp. 7-8.

23. *Ibidem*, pp. 67-73.

24. See the interesting account of the 'Purposes and Standards' of seventeenth-century Harvard in Morison, *Founding of Harvard College*, pp. 247-251. The persistence of the ideal of training young men for the ministry and for public life in oratory, rhetoric, the Bible, the classics and moral and natural philosophy can be clearly seen as late as the nineteenth century in such a New England college as Amherst, founded with similar purposes and standards at a time when Harvard, it was thought, was straying from the old ways of the godly.

25. *Third Academic Exercise*, in P. B. Tillyard, *Milton: Private Correspondence*.

26. *Seventh Academic Exercise*, in P. B. Tillyard, *Milton: Private Correspondence*, pp. 104-120.

27. See also *Fifth Academic Exercise*, in P. B. Tillyard, *Milton: Private Correspondence*, pp. 81-82.

28. *Elegia Quarta*.

29. *Apology*, in Milton, *Works*, III, 302.

30. *Elegia Prima*. E. K. Rand, "Milton in Rustication," *Studies in Philology*, XIX (1922), 109-135.

31. *Elegia Quinta*.

32. *Elegia Septima.*

33. *Apology,* in Milton, *Works,* III, 305.

34. *Elegia Septima.*

35. *Apology,* in Milton, *Works,* III, 305.

36. *Areopagitica,* in Milton, *Works,* IV, 311.

37. *Reason of Church Government,* in Milton, *Works,* III, 235.

38. *Ibidem,* III, 238.

39. *Sixth Academic Exercise,* in P. B. Tillyard, *Milton: Private Correspondence,* pp. 85-104.

40. *Elegia Sexta,* ll. 55-90; Moody-Rand translation, in Milton, *Complete Poetical Works,* pp. 340-341.

41. *Ad Patrem,* ll. 101-104; Moody-Rand translation, in Milton, *Complete Poetical Works,* p. 364.

42. *Reason of Church Government,* in Milton, *Works,* III, 241.

43. *Seventh Academic Exercise,* in P. B. Tillyard, *Milton: Private Correspondence,* pp. 104-120. The letter appears in the Columbia edition of Milton, *Works,* XII, 320-325.

44. Milton clearly seems to have written 'seasing' in the second draft of his letter as preserved in the Cambridge manuscript and 'seasure' in the first draft; Columbia edition of Milton, *Works,* XII, 321, 324. Masson's reading of 'feasing' in the second draft, *Life of Milton,* I, 245, though interesting is incorrect.

45. *Apology,* in Milton, *Works,* III, 357; *Second Defence, Works,* VIII, 121. See also J. H. Hanford, 'Chronology of Milton's Private Studies,' PMLA, XXXVI (1921), 251-314.

46. P. B. Tillyard, *Milton: Private Correspondence,* p. 15.

47. *Apology,* in Milton, *Works,* III, 358.

48. Letter to Charles Diodati, in P. B. Tillyard, *Milton: Private Correspondence,* p. 14.

49. *Apology,* in Milton, *Works,* III, 357.

50. A. J. Horwood, ed., *A Commonplace Book of John Milton,* Camden Society, 1876. See also Hanford, "Chronology of Milton's Private Studies," PMLA, XXXVI (1921), 251-314.

51. *Reason of Church Government,* in Milton, *Works,* III, 232.

52. *Second Defence,* in Milton, *Works,* VIII, 129.

53. *Apology,* in Milton, *Works,* III, 282.

54. P. B. Tillyard, *Milton: Private Correspondence,* pp. 12-15.

CHAPTER IX

1. Masson, *Life of Milton,* II, 122-126.

2. An account by G. K. Fortescue of Thomason and his collection is given in the preface to the *Catalogue of the Pamphlets, Books, Newspapers, and Manuscripts relating to the Civil War, the Commonwealth, and the Restoration,*

Collected by George Thomason, 1640-1661, published by the British Museum, 1908.

3. Masson gives some account of Hall in his *Life of Milton*, but the most vivid impression of the man is to be got from *Observations of Some Specialities of Divine Providence in the Life of Joseph Hall, Bishop of Norwich, Written with his own hand* in *The Works of the Right Reverend Joseph Hall*, edited by Philip Wynter, 1863, I, xix-xlvii. See also Hall's 'Letter Sent from the Tower to a Private Friend,' *Works*, I, xlviii-lv, and 'Bishop Hall's Hard Measure,' *Works*, I, lvi-lxix. There are biographies of Hall by John Jones, *Bishop Hall, his Life and Times*, 1826, and George Lewis, *Life of Joseph Hall*, 1886.

4. Hall, *Via Media*, in *Works*, IX, 517.

5. Masson, *Life of Milton*, II, 219-222.

6. Thomas Hutchinson, *The History of the Colony and Province of Massachusetts Bay*, edited by L. S. Mayo, 1936, gives an account of this affair and prints, I, 410-413, 'Certain Proposals made by Lord Say, Lord Brooke, and other Persons of quality, as conditions of their removing to New-England, with the answers thereto.'

7. Reprinted in Haller, *Tracts on Liberty*, II, 37-163.

8. Brooke, *Discourse*, in Haller, *Tracts on Liberty*, II, 55-56.

9. Brooke, *Nature of Truth*, pp. 125-126.

10. Brooke, *Discourse*, in Haller, *Tracts on Liberty*, II, 89-91.

11. *Ibidem*, II, 153.

12. *Ibidem*, II, 159.

13. *Ibidem*, II, 150.

14. *Ibidem*, II, 151.

15. *Reason of Church Government*, in Milton, *Works*, III, 232.

16. *Ibidem*, III, 236.

17. *Second Defence*, in Milton, *Works*, VIII, 125.

18. *Mansus*, ll. 80-84; Moody-Rand translation, in Milton, *Complete Political Works*, p. 369.

19. *Facsimile of the Manuscript of Milton's Minor Poems Preserved in the Library of Trinity College, Cambridge*, edited by W. A. Wright, 1899.

20. Edward Philips, *Life*, in L. E. Lockwood, edition of Milton, *Of Education, Areopagitica, The Commonwealth*.

21. *Of Prelatical Episcopacy*, in Milton, *Works*, III, 82.

22. *Of Reformation*, in Milton, *Works*, III, 22.

23. *Of Prelatical Episcopacy*, in Milton, *Works*, III, 82.

24. *Ibidem*, III, 101.

25. *Ibidem*, III, 82.

26. *Of Reformation*, in Milton, *Works*, III, 37-38.

27. *Ibidem*.

28. *Of Reformation*, in Milton, *Works*, III, 63.

29. *Reason of Church Government*, in Milton, *Works*, III, 255.

30. *Of Reformation*, in Milton, *Works*, III, 65.
31. *Reason of Church Government*, in Milton, *Works*, III, 254.
32. *Ibidem*, III, 249.
33. *Ibidem*, III, 223.
34. *Of Reformation*, in Milton, *Works*, III, 2.
35. *Ibidem*, III, 10.
36. *Ibidem*, III, 32-33.
37. *Ibidem*, III, 35.
38. *Reason of Church Government*, in Milton, *Works*, III, 184.
39. *Animadversions*, in Milton, *Works*, III, 139-140.
40. *Of Reformation*, in Milton, *Works*, III, 33.
41. *Animadversions*, in Milton, *Works*, III, 156.
42. *Of Reformation*, in Milton, *Works*, III, 12.
43. *Animadversions*, in Milton, *Works*, III, 162-163.
44. *Ibidem*, III, 164.
45. *Ibidem*, III, 162.
46. *Ibidem*, III, 119.
47. *Apology*, in Milton, *Works*, III, 300.
48. *Ibidem*, III, 348.
49. *Animadversions*, in Milton, *Works*, III, 162.
50. *Of Reformation*, in Milton, *Works*, III, 11-12.
51. *Ibidem*, III, 47-48.
52. *Reason of Church Government*, in Milton, *Works*, III, 231.
53. *Animadversions*, in Milton, *Works*, III, 167.
54. *Reason of Church Government*, in Milton, *Works*, III, 240.
55. *Of Reformation*, in Milton, *Works*, III, 67-69.
56. *Animadversions*, in Milton, *Works*, III, 148.
57. *Reason of Church Government*, in Milton, *Works*, III, 236.
58. *Ibidem*, III, 237-238.
59. *Ibidem*, III, 241.
60. *Apology*, in Milton, *Works*, III, 305.
61. *Animadversions*, in Milton, *Works*, III, 106.
62. *Ibidem*, III, 107-108.
63. *Apology*, in Milton, *Works*, III, 314-316.
64. *Ibidem*, III, 308.
65. *Ibidem*, III, 342.

CHAPTER X

1. *Scripture and Reason Pleaded for Defensive Armes*, 1643, To the Reader.
2. Reproduced in Haller, *Tracts on Liberty*, frontispiece, I.
3. Hunton, *Treatise of Monarchie*, pp. 28-29.
4. Parker, *Discourse concerning Puritans*, To the Reader.
5. Parker, *The Case of Shipmony*, p. 7.

6. Parker, *Observations*, reprinted in Haller, *Tracts on Liberty*, II, 165-213.

7. *Ibidem*, II, 169.

8. *Ibidem*, II, 179.

9. Spelman, *View of a Printed Book*.

10. Ferne, *Resolving of Conscience*.

11. Digges, *Answer to a Printed Book*.

12. I accept B. A. Wright's conclusion that Milton's first marriage in all probability occurred in 1642 and not, as ungrounded tradition has had it, in 1643. *Modern Language Review*, XXVI (October 1931), 383-400.

13. John Goodwin, *Ireland's Advocate*, 1641.

14. John Goodwin, *Anti-Cavalierisme*, reprinted in Haller, *Tracts on Liberty*, II, 217-269.

15. *Ibidem*, II, 221-222.

16. *Ibidem*, II, 236.

17. *Ibidem*, II, 238.

18. *Ibidem*, II, 236.

19. *To the High Court of Parliament: The Humble Remonstrance of the Company of Stationers*, April 1643.

Bibliographical Notes

Pollard and Redgrave, *Short-Title Catalogue* of English printed books prior to 1641, the *Stationers' Register*, the *Catalogue* of the Library of the British Museum, the *Check-List or Brief Catalogue of the Library of Henry E. Huntington*, 1919-20, W. T. Whitley, *Baptist Bibliography*, 1916, and the *Catalogue of the McAlpin Collection of British History and Theology* in the Union Theological Seminary by C. R. Gillett, 1927, supply primary bibliographical information concerning Puritan literature. The *Catalogue of the McAlpin Collection* is particularly valuable, since it offers a special but widely representative selection. The present work is in large measure based upon the McAlpin Collection.

Certain contemporary sources also give valuable help in finding what to read. Samuel Clarke in his successive compilations of biographical material issued after 1650 (see below pp. 423-426) indicates many of the preachers of the generations just preceding whose works were most widely circulated and read. Of great importance is the list of books for a preacher's library recommended by Richard Baxter in 1673 (see above p. 24). Of special interest in confirming the representative character of this list are the lists of books in the libraries of William Brewster in H. M. Dexter 'Elder Brewster's Library,' *Proceedings of the Massachusetts Historical Society*, 2d series, V, 37-85, and of John Harvard in A. C. Potter 'Catalogue of John Harvard's Library,' *Publications of the Colonial Society of Massachusetts*, XXI, 190-230. Interesting but less useful because less selective is the information contained in John Wilkins, *Ecclesiastes*, 1646; William London, *Catalogue of the Most Vendible Books in England*, 1658; and William Crowe, *Exact Collection or Catalogue*, 1663. The preachers themselves, finally, help readers by frequently recommending one another's wares.

Besides the contemporary or early biographies, I have depended for primary biographical information on Thomas Fuller, *The Church History of Britain*, edited by J. S. Brewer, 1848, and *The History of the Worthies of England*, 1662, and on Anthony à Wood, *Athenae Oxoniensis*, edited by Philip Bliss, 1813. I have turned often to the *Dictionary of National Biography*; C. H. Cooper and Thompson Cooper, *Athenae Cantabrigiensis*; John Venn and J. A. Venn, *Alumni Cantabrigiensis*; and Joseph Foster, *Alumni Oxoniensis*. For the general outline of historical events, I have relied upon A. F. Pollard, *History of England from the Accession of Edward VI to the Death of Elizabeth*, 1910; on S. R. Gardiner, *History of England, 1603-1642*, 1883-1884, and *History of the Great Civil War, 1642-1649*, 1893; and, though to a less extent, on W. H. Frere, *History of the English Church in the Reigns of Elizabeth and James I*, 1904, and W. H. Hutton, *The English Church from the Accession of Charles I to the Death of Anne*, 1903. The older historians of non-conformity, for example, Benjamin

Brook, *Lives of the Puritans*, 1813, Daniel Neal, *History of the Puritans*, 1843-44, Robert Barclay, *The Inner Life of the Religious Societies*, 1876, and Henry Martyn Dexter, *Congregationalism of the Last Three Hundred Years*, 1880, are less useful than one might expect. These writers were not, for the most part, interested in the general stream of Puritan thought and expression. They were the chroniclers and apologists of non-conformity and dissent, and much of the information they convey can be found more conveniently elsewhere. This is least true of Barclay. Other writers who have been particularly useful on specific matters are referred to at appropriate points in the notes above. The interpretation of Puritanism here set forth is, however, based mainly on the literature of Puritanism itself. The Puritan books listed below include all those discussed or referred to in these pages together with others but not all others which are also pertinent. The list is, of course, not an exhaustive catalogue. The primary entry of each title represents the edition referred to in the text. Information concerning other editions is drawn either directly from the books or from the sources of information mentioned at the beginning of this note. For convenience of reference, early lives of Puritan saints and the early writings of John Lilburne have been placed under separate headings.

SERMONS AND OTHER WORKS OF EDIFICATION
AND CONTROVERSY

ACONTIUS, JACOBUS. Satans stratagems, or the devils cabinet-councel discovered, 1648.
Anonymous translation of the first four books of Acontius, *Satanae Stratagemata*, 1565.
Reissued with the title, *Darkness Discovered*, 1651.
ADAMS, THOMAS. The workes of Thomas Adams. Being the summe of his sermons, meditations, and . . . discourses, 1629.
Numerous earlier editions of individual sermons.
The works were reissued in Nichol's Standard Divines, 1861-62.
ALSTED, JOHANN HEINRICH. The beloved city, or, the saints reign on earth a thousand yeares, 1643.
Translation by William Burton of Alsted, *Diatribe de mille annis*, 1627; another edition, 1630.
ARCHER, JOHN. The personall raigne of Christ upon earth, 1641.
Other editions, 1642, 1643, 1661 [called the 5th].
BAILLIE, ROBERT. The unlawfulness and danger of limited episcopacie, 1641.
BASTWICK, JOHN. The answer of John Bastwick, . . . To the exceptions made against his Letany by a learned gentleman . . . This is to follow the Letany as a second part thereof, 1637.
———The confession of the faithful witnesse of Christ, 1641.

BASTWICK, JOHN. Elenchus papisticae religionis, . . . 3d edition, 1634.
  Other editions, 1624, 1627.
————Flagellum pontificis, 1641.
————A just defence of John Bastwick, doctor in phisicke, 1645.
————The Letany of John Bastwick, 1637.
————A more full answer of John Bastwick, . . . this is to follow the Letany as a fourth part of it, 1637.
————πραξεις των 'Επισκόπων, sive apologeticus ad praesules Anglicanos, 1636.
————The vanity and mischeife of the Old Letany, or a further answer of John Bastwick, . . . This is to follow the Letany as a third part of it, 1637.
BAXTER, RICHARD. A Christian directory: or, a summ of practical theologie . . . in four parts, . . . III Christian Ecclesiasticks (or Church Duties), 1673.
  Another edition, 1678. In *The Practical Works of Richard Baxter*, edited by William Orme, 1830.
————Reliquiae Baxterianae: or, Mr. Richard Baxter's narrative of the memorable passages of his life and times. Faithfullly published from his own original manuscript, by Matthew Sylvester, 1696.
BAYLIE, LEWIS. The practise of pietie. Third edition. Profitably amplified by the author, 1613.
  Numerous later editions: 11th, 1619; 12th, 1620; 1623; 1624; 16[25?]; 1627; 1630; 1632; 1633; 1635; 1635 [called the 35th]; 1636; 1637; 1638; 1639; 1640.
BAYNES, PAUL. A caveat for cold Christians, 1618.
————The diocesans tryall, 1621.
  Another edition, 1641.
————Christian letters of Mr. Paul Bayne. Replenished with divers consolations, exhortations, and directions, tending to promote the honour of godlinesse. Hereunto is added a fruitfull sermon for the triall of a Christians estate, 1637. An edition with the title, *Holy Soliloquies*, 1618 [called the 2d]; other editions, 1620, 1627. *The Triall of a Christians Estate* appeared separately in 1618.
BEADLE, JOHN. The journal or diary of a thankful Christian, 1656.
Beauty of godly government in a church reformed: or a Platforme of government consonant to the word of truth, The, 1641.
BERNARD, RICHARD. Christian see to thy conscience, or a treatise of the nature, the kinds and manifold differences of conscience, 1631.
————The Faithfull shepheard, 1607.
  Another edition, 1609; another, 'wholy in a manner transposed, and made anew, and very much inlarged,' 1621.
————The Isle of Man: or, the legall proceding in Manshire against sinne, 1627.
  Other editions, 1626, 1628, 1630, 1632, 1634, 1635, 1640 [called the 11th], 1648, 1659, 1683 [called the 16th].
————The ready way to good works, or, a treatise of charitie, 1635.

BERNARD, RICHARD. Ruths recompense: or a commentarie upon the booke of Ruth, 1628.

BOLTON, ROBERT. A discourse about the state of true happinesse, 1631.
Other editions, 1611, 1612, 1614, 1625, 1633, 1636, 1637, 1638 [called the 7th].

————Instructions for a right comforting afflicted consciences, with speciall antidotes against some grievous temptations, 1635.
Other editions, 1631, 1640.

————Mr. Boltons last and learned worke of the foure last things, 1633.

————The saints sure and perpetual guide. Or, a treatise concerning the word, 1634.

————Some generall directions for a comfortable walking with God, 1638.
Other editions, 1626, 1630, 1634.

————Two sermons preached at Northampton at two several assises there, 1639.
Another edition, 1635.

————The workes of the reverend, truly pious, and iudiciously learned Robert Bolton . . . as they were finished by himselfe in his life time, 1641.
Includes 'The Life and death of the Author' by E[dward] B[agshaw] and the funeral sermon by Nicholas Estwick.
Other editions, 1638, 1640.

BRADFORD, WILLIAM. The history of Plymouth Plantation, 1620-1647, edited by W. C. Ford for the Massachusetts Historical Society, 1912.

BRADSHAW, WILLIAM. English Puritanisme. Containeing: the maine opinions of the rigidest sort of those that are called Puritanes in the realme of England, 1605.
Translated into Latin by William Ames, 1640.
Other editions, 1640 [attributed to William Ames], 1660.

BRIDGES, JOHN. A defense of the government established in the church of Englande for ecclesiasticall matters, 1587.

BRIGHTMAN, THOMAS. Apocalypsis Apocalypseos, 1609.
Another edition, 1612. Translated into English with the title, *A Revelation of the Revelation,* Amsterdam, 1615; *The Revelation of St. John,* Leyden, 1616; other editions in English, 1611, 1644.

BRINSLEY, JOHN, *the elder.* The true watch and rule of life, 1611.
Consists of four parts which were also issued separately, the first in 1606, and frequently reissued, separately or together, between 1606 and 1637.

BROOKE, ROBERT GREVILLE, LORD. A discourse opening the nature of that episcopacie, which is exercised in England, 1641.
Another edition, 1642; reprinted in Haller, *Tracts on Liberty.*

————The nature of truth, 1640.

BROWNE, ROBERT. The 'retractation . . .' being 'a reproofe of certeine schismatical persons and their Doctrine touching the hearing and preaching of the Word of God.' Written probably early in the year 1588, since lost, and now first published with a brief account of its discovery by Champlin Burrage, 1907.

BROWNE, ROBERT. A treatise of reformation without tarying for anie, and of the wickedness of those preachers which will not reforme till the magistrate commande or compell them, Middelburgh, 1582.

This work has been consulted in the reprint in Congregational Historical Society, *Transactions*, December 1901, Vol. I.

———A true and short declaration, both of the gathering and joyning together of certaine persons: and also of the lamentable breach and division which fell amongst them, 1584.

This work has been consulted in the reprint in *The Congregationalist*, 1882, Vol. XI.

BURTON, HENRY. Babel no Bethel, 1629.

———The baiting of the popes bull, 1627.

———For God, and the King. The summe of two sermons preached on the fifth of November last in St. Matthews Friday-Streete, 1636.

BUSHER, LEONARD. Religions peace: or, a plea for liberty of conscience, 1646. Another edition, 1614.

Reprinted in *Tracts on Liberty of Conscience*, edited by E. B. Underhill, Hanserd Knollys Society, 1846.

CAPEL, RICHARD. Tentations: their nature, danger, cure. The sixth edition. The fourth part left enlarged by the author, and now there is added his remains to the work of tentations, to which thou hast prefixed an abridgement of the authours life, by Valentine Marshall. 1659.

Remains with 'an abridgement of the authours life' was issued separately in 1658 and appears in *Tentations*, 1659, with a separate title-page bearing the date 1658.

Other editions of *Tentations*, 1633, 1635, 1637.

CARTWRIGHT, THOMAS. Disciplina ecclesiae sàcra Dei verbo descripta. Disciplina synodica ex ecclesiarum quae eam ex verbo dei instaurarunt usu synodis atque libris de eadem re scriptis collecta, et ad certa quaedam capita redacta.

Published in Scott Pearson, *Der Älteste englische Presbyterianismus*, and in Francis Paget, *An Introduction to the Fifth Book of Hooker's Treatise of the Laws of Ecclesiastical Polity*, 1907. Translated as *A Directory of Church-government. Anciently contended for, and as farre as the Times would suffer, practised by the first Non-conformists in the dais of Queen Elizabeth. Found in the study of the most accomplished Divine, Mr. Thomas Cartwright, after his decease*, 1644.

A facsimile reprint, edited by Peter Lorimer, appeared in 1872. Reprinted also in Daniel Neal, *History of the Puritans*, 1837, Appendix IV; and in C. A. Briggs, *American Presbyterianism*, 1885, Appendix.

CASTELLIO, SEBASTIAN. Concerning heretics, whether they are to be persecuted and how they are to be treated. A collection of the opinions of learned men both ancient and modern. An anonymous work attributed to Sebastian Castellio. Now first done into English, together with excerpts from other works of Sebastian Castellio and David Joris on religious liberty, by Roland H. Bainton, 1935.

CHADERTON, LAURENCE. An excellent sermon preached at Paules Crosse the XXVI daye of October 1578, 1578.
Another edition, 1580.

——A fruitfull sermon, upon the 3. 4. 5. 6. 7. & 8. verses of the 12. Chapter of the Epistle of S. Paule to the Romanes, 1584.
Published anonymously and attributed to Chaderton in the *Catalogue* of the British Museum. Other editions, 1586, 1589; reprinted by William Brewster, Leyden, 1618.

CHILLINGWORTH, WILLIAM. The religion of Protestants a safe way to salvation. The Second Edition, 1638.
The 1st edition also appeared in 1638.

CLEAVER, ROBERT. *See* Dod, John.

CROWE, WILLIAM. An exact collection or catalogue of our English writers on the Old and New Testament, either in whole, or in part: whether commentators, elucidators, annotators, at large, or in single sermons, 1663.
Another edition, corrected and enlarged, 1668.

CULVERWEL, EZEKIEL. A treatise of faith. The way to a blessed estate, 1629-30.
Other editions, 1623, 1625, 1633, 1646-48.

DENISON, STEPHEN. The white wolfe or, a sermon preached at Pauls Crosse, Feb. 11. . . . 1627, 1627.

DERING, EDWARD. A brief & necessary instruction, 1572.
Reissued as *A bryefe and necessary catechisme or instruction*, 1583, 1606.

——M. Derings workes. More at large than euer hath heer-to-fore been printed in any one volume, 1597.
Another edition, 1614.

——A sermon preached before the quenes maiestie . . . the 25 day of February . . . , 1569 [1570], 1570 [?]
Eleven later editions before 1604.

DIGGES, SIR DUDLEY. Answer to a printed book, 1642.

——The unlawfulnesse of subjects taking up armes, 1644.

DILLINGHAM, W. Vita L. Chadertoni . . . una cum vita J. Usserii, archiepiscopi Armachani, 1700. Translated by E. S. Shuckburgh, 1884.

DOD, JOHN. A plaine and familiar exposition on the Lords Prayer, 1635.

——A sermon upon the word malt. Preached in the stump of a hollow tree, by the Rev. John Dod, M. A. author of the remarkable and approved sayings, to which is prefixed a brief account of the life of the author, 1777.
Reprinted by John Taylor, *Memorials of the Rev. John Dod*, 1875.

DOD, JOHN *and* CLEAVER, ROBERT. A briefe explanation of the whole book of the Proverbs of Salomon, 1615.
Originally issued in separate parts, of which the earliest recorded in the *Short Title Catalogue* bears the date 1606. Frequently reprinted.

——Ten sermons tending to the fitting of men for the Lords Supper. The six first by J. Dod; the foure last by R. Cleaver, 1609.
Other editions, 1621, 1628, 1632, and 1634; also 1661 with 'The Life and

Death of Master John Dod' 'Collected by C. B. July 17, 1660,' based upon Clarke and Fuller.

DOD, JOHN *and* CLEAVER, ROBERT. A treatise or exposition upon the ten commandements, 1603.

Reissued as *A Plaine and Familiar Exposition of the Ten Commandements,* 1606.

Other editions, 1604, 1606, 1607, 1609, 1615, 1617, 1618, 1622, 1624 [called the 16th], 1629, 1630, 1632, 1635 [called the 19th].

DOWNAME, JOHN. The Christian warfare, 1609.

Other editions, 1604, 1608, 1609, 1612-19 [called the third 'much enlarged and corrected by the author'], 1634.

————A guide to godlynesse, 1622.

Another edition, 1629.

————Lectures upon the foure first Chapters of the Prophecie of Hosea, 1608.

DRAXE, THOMAS. The churches securitie. Togither with the antidote or preservative of ever waking faith, 1608.

————The earnest of our inheritance: together with a description of the new heaven and of the new earth, 1613.

————The worldes resurrection, or the generall calling of the Jewes, 1608.

DYKE, DANIEL. The mystery of selfe-deceiving. Or, a discourse and discovery of the deceitfulnesse of mans heart, 1615.

Other editions, 1614, 1616, 1620 [called the 7th], 1628, 1630, 1634.

EATON, JOHN. The honey-combe of free justification by Christ alone, 1642.

EVERARD, JOHN. The gospel-treasury opened: or the holiest of all unvailing . . . Whereunto is added, the mystical divinity of Dionysius the Areopagite . . . with collections out of other divine authors, translated by Dr. Everard, 1657.

First published as *Some Gospel Treasures opened,* 1653. Another edition, 1659.

FERNE, HENRY. The resolving of conscience, 1642.

FULKE, WILLIAM, *attributed to.* A briefe and plaine declaration, concerning the desires of all those faithfull ministers, that have and do seeke for the discipline and reformation of the Churche of Englande, 1584.

FULLER, NICHOLAS. The argument of Master Nicholas Fuller in the case of Thomas Lad, and Richard Maunsell, his clients, 1607.

Another edition, 1641.

FULLER, THOMAS. The appeal of iniured innocence: unto the religious learned and ingenuous reader. In a controversie betwixt the animadvertor Dr. Peter Heylyn and the author, 1659.

————The church-history of britain; from the birth of Jesus Christ, untill the year 1648, 1655.

Other editions, 1837, 1845, 1868. Contains *History of the University of Cambridge,* which was published separately, 1840.

————The history of the worthies of England, 1662.

Other editions, 1811, 1814.

GOODWIN, JOHN. Anti-cavalierisme, or, truth pleading as well the necessity, as the lawfulness of this present war, 1642.

Other editions, 1642, 1643; reprinted in Haller, *Tracts on Liberty*.

————The butchers blessing, or the bloody intentions of Romish cavaliers against the city of London, 1642.

————Christ lifted up, or, the heads of the chief controverted points, preached by John Goodwin, 1641.

————Impedit ira animum, or animadversions upon some of the looser and fouler passages in a written pamphlet intituled, A Defence of the True Sence and Meaning of the Words of the Holy Apostle . . . by George Walker, 1641.

————Imputatio fidei or a treatise of justification, 1642.

————Irelands advocate: or, a sermon preached upon Novemb. 14, 1641. To promote the contributions . . . for the present reliefe of the Protestants party in Ireland, 1641.

————Os ossorianum, or, a bone for a bishop to pick: being a vindication of some passages in a treatise lately published, called Anti-Cavalierisme, from the impertinent and importune exceptions of Gr: Williams, the author of the Grand Rebellion, 1643.

————The returne of mercies: or, the saints advantage by losses . . . in sundry sermons, 1641.

————Right and might well met. Or, a briefe and impartiall enquiry into the late and present proceedings of the army under the command of his excellency the Lord Fairfax, 1648.

————The saints interest in god, 1640.

————ΘΕΟΜΑΧΙΑ; or the grand imprudence of men running the hazard of fighting against God, in suppressing any way, doctrine, or practice, concerning which they know not certainly whether it be from God or no, 1644.

Reprinted in Haller, *Tracts on Liberty*.

GOODWIN, THOMAS. A childe of light walking in darknes, 1636.

Other editions, 1638, 1643.

————The returne of prayers, 1636.

Other editions, 1636, 1641, 1643, 1651.

————The vanity of thoughts, 1637.

Other editions, 1638, 1643, 1650.

————The works of Thomas Goodwin, 1681-1704.

Reissued with a preface to the reader by Thanckful Owen and James Barron. Volume V contains a life of Goodwin by his son Thomas.

GOUGE, WILLIAM. Gods three arrows: plague, famine, sword, 1631.

Called the 2d edition.

————A guide to goe to God: or, an explanation of . . . the Lords Prayer, 1626.

Another edition, 1636.

GOUGE, WILLIAM. A learned and very useful commentary on the whole Epistle to the Hebrewes . . . being the substance of thirty years Wednesdayes lectures at Black-fryers London, 1655.

————Of domesticall duties, 1622.

Other editions, 1626, 1634.

————The saints sacrifice or a commentarie on the CXVI Psalme, 1632.

————πανοπλια του Θεου: the whole-armor of God or the spirituall furniture which God hath provided to keepe safe every Christian souldier from all the assaults of Satan, 1616.

Other editions, 1619, 1647.

GREENHAM, RICHARD. The workes of the reverend and faithful servant of Jesus Christ M. Richard Greenham, examined, corrected and published: by H[enry] H[olland], 1605.

Other editions, 1599, 1601, 1605, 1612.

See also Rogers, Richard, *The Garden of Spirituall Flowers.*

HALES, JOHN. Golden remains of the ever memorable M. John Hales of Eton College, 1659.

————A tract concerning schisme and schismaticks, 1642.

Other editions, 1642.

————The workes of the ever memorable Mr. John Hales of Eaton. Now first collected together, 1765.

HALL, JOSEPH. Characters of vertues and vices, 1608.

Other editions, 1608; in French 1619, 1634, in verse 1691.

————A common apologie of the church of England: against . . . the Brownists, 1610.

————A defence of the humble remonstrance, against the frivolous and false exceptions of Smectymnuus, 1641.

————Episcopacy by divine right asserted, 1640.

————Heaven upon earth: or, of true peace and tranquillity of minde, 1609.

Other editions, 1606, 1606, 1607, each with two issues; 1819.

————An humble remonstrance to the high court of parliament, 1640.

————A modest confutation of . . . Animadversions upon the remonstrants defense against Smectymnuus, 1642.

————A recollection of such treatises as have been heretofore published and are new revised, corrected, augmented. With addition of some others not hitherto extant, 1617.

Other editions, 1614, 1615, with additions, 1621.

————The remedy of discontentment, or, a treatise of contentation in whatsoever condition: fit for these sad and troubled times, 1645.

4th edition, 1684.

————The shaking of the olive tree. The remaining works of that incomparable prelate Joseph Hall, D.D. late bishop of Norwich. With some specialities of divine providence in his life. Noted by his own hand. Together with his Hard Measure: written also by himself, 1660.

HALL, JOSEPH. A short answer to the tedious vindication of Smectymnuus, 1641.
————The works of the Right Reverend Joseph Hall, D.D. A new edition, revised and corrected, with some additions by Philip Wynter, 1863.

HARRIS, ROBERT. The works of Robert Harris; . . . revised and corrected, and collected into one volume. Whereunto are added two other sermons, 1635.
Includes *Samuels Funerall: or A Sermon preached at the Funerall of Sir Anthony Cope*, 1634.

HENDERSON, ALEXANDER. The unlawfulness and danger of limited prelacie, 1641.

HEYLYN, PETER. Cyprianus Anglicus: or the history of the life and death, of . . . William [Laud] . . . lord archbishop of Canterbury, 1671.

HEYWOOD, THOMAS. A true discourse of the two infamous upstart prophets R. Farnham, weaver, of White-Chappell, and J. Bull, weaver, of St. Butolphs Algate, 1636.

HIERON, SAMUEL. The Christians iournall, 1607.
Another edition, 1609.
————The doctrine of the beginning of Christ, 1606.
Other editions, 1613, 1616, 1626 [called the 13th], 1632, 1635.
————The Sermons . . . formerly collected together by himselfe, and published in one volume in his life time, 1620.
Other editions, 1614, 1620, 1624, 1628, 1629, 1635.

HILDERSAM, ARTHUR. Lectures upon the fourth of John. Preached, at Ashby-Delazouch, 1629.
Other editions, 1632, 1647.

HOOKER, THOMAS. The souls preparation for Christ. Or, a treatise of contrition. Wherein is discovered how God breaks the heart, and wounds the soul in the conversion of a sinner to himself . . . the seventh edition, 1658.
Other editions, 1632, 1635, 1638, 1638, 1643.

HOW, SAMUEL. The sufficiency of the spirits teaching without human learning: or, a treatise tending to prove humane learning to be no help to the spiritual understanding of the Word of God, 1640.
Other editions, 1639, 1644, 1655, 1692.

Humble Petition of the Brownists,.The, 1641.

HUNTON, PHILIP. A treatise of monarchie, 1643.

KIFFIN, WILLIAM. Remarkable passages in the life of William Kiffin: written by himself, and edited from the original manuscript, with notes and additions by William Orme, 1823.

KIFFIN, WILLIAM, *and others*. Walwins wiles: or the manifestators manifested, 1649.

KNOLLYS, HANSERD. Christ exalted: a lost sinner sought, and saved by Christ: Gods people are an holy people, 1646.
————An exposition of the whole book of the Revelation, 1689.
————A glimpse of Sions glory or, the churches beautie specified, 1641.
For the reasons for attributing this work to Knollys, see above pp. 270-271, note 32.

LAUD, WILLIAM. A relation of the conference between William Lawd, . . . and Mr. Fisher the Jesuit, 1639.

Appeared first in White, Francis, *A Replie to Jesuit Fishers answere to certain questions . . . Hereunto is annexed, a Conference of the right R: B: of St Davids with the Same Jesuit*, 1624.

————The history of the troubles and tryal of . . . William Laud, . . . wrote by himself, during his imprisonment in the Tower. To which is prefixed the diary of his own life, Vol. I, 1695; Vol. II, 1700.

————The works of the most reverend father in God, William Laud, 1847-50.

LAUD, WILLIAM, *concerning*. A briefe relation of the death and sufferings of William Laud, the L. Archbishop of Canterbury, 1644.

LAWRENCE, HENRY. Of our communion and warre with angels, 1646.

LEIGHTON, ALEXANDER. An appeal to the parliament, or Sions plea against the prelacie . . . printed the year & moneth wherein Rochell was lost [October 1628].

LEIGHTON, ALEXANDER, *concerning*. An epitome or briefe discoverie . . . of the many and great troubles that Dr. Leighton suffered, 1646.

LONDON, WILLIAM. A catalogue of the most vendible books in England, orderly and alphabetically digested, 1658.

MARPRELATE, MARTIN. The Marprelate tracts 1588, 1589, edited by William Pierce, 1909.

MATHER, COTTON. Magnalia Christi Americana; or the ecclesiastical history of New-England, from its first planting, in the year 1620, unto the year of Our Lord 1698. . . . With an introduction and occasional notes, by the Rev. Thomas Robbins, 1853.

Other editions, 1702, 1820.

MEDE, JOSEPH. Clavis Apocalyptica, 1627.

Another edition, 1632.

MILTON, JOHN. Animadversions upon the remonstrants defence, against Smectymnuus, 1641.

————An apology against a pamphlet call'd A Modest Confutation of the Animadversions upon the Remonstrant against Smectymnuus, 1642.

————Lycidas. First published in Justa Edovardo King naufrago, ab amicis moerentibus, 1638.

————Of prelatical episcopacy, and whether it may be deduc'd from the apostolical times by vertue of those testimonies which are allegd to that purpose in some late treatises: One whereof goes under the name of James Arch-bishop of Armagh, 1641.

————Of reformation touching church-discipline in England: and the causes that hitherto have hindred it, 1641.

————Poems of Mr. John Milton, both English and Latin compos'd at several times, 1645.

————The reason of church-government urg'd against prelaty, 1641.

MURTON, JOHN. Objections: answered by way of dialogue, wherin is proved by the law of God: by the law of our land: and by his maties many testimonies that no man ought to be persecuted for his religion, so he testifie his allegeance by the oath, appointed by law, 1615.

Another edition with the title, *Persecution for Religion Judg'd and Condemn'd*, 1662. See Burrage, *Early English Dissenters*, p. 258.

Reprinted in *Tracts on Liberty of Conscience*, ed. by E. B. Underhill, Hanserd Knollys Society, 1846.

New petition of the papists, A, 1641.

NICHOLAS, HENRY. An introduction to the holy understanding of the glasse of righteousnesse, *ca.* 1575.

Another edition, 1649.

PARKER, HENRY. Animadversions animadverted; or, the observator defended, 1642.

——The case of shipmony, 1640.

——A discourse concerning Puritans, 1641.

——Observations upon some of his majesties late answers and expresses, 1642. Another edition, 1642.

——A petition humbly desired to be presented to his majestie, 1642.

Also published as, *The Danger to England Observed*, 1642.

——The question concerning the divine right of episcopacie, 1641.

——Some few observations upon his majesties late answer, 1642.

——The true grounds of ecclesiasticall regiment, 1641.

PERKINS, WILLIAM. The workes of that famous minister of Christ in the Universitie of Cambridge, Mr. William Perkins, Vol. I, 1616; Vol. II, 1617; Vol. III, 1609.

Armilla Aurea, 1590, appeared in at least three Latin and nine English editions by 1612. A translation of *Armilla Aurea*, called *A Golden Chain*, with twelve other treatises in English, appeared in 1600, followed by editions of *Workes* in 1602 and, in three volumes, in 1608. Numerous later editions appeared, and Perkins was translated into several other languages. There were also numerous editions of individual works. In *Workes* see especially: The Foundation of the Christian Religion; A Golden Chain; A Treatise Tending unto a Declaration; A Case of Conscience; How to Live, and That well; A Graine of Mustard Seed; The True Gaine: More in Worth than All the Goods in the World; A Treatise of Vocations; The Art of Prophecying; The Combate betweene Christ and the Devill; Of the Calling of the Ministerie; Short Survey of the Right Manner of Erecting and Ordering a Family.

See also Rogers, Richard, *Garden of Spirituall Flowers*.

POWELL, GABRIEL. The resolved christian; exhorting to resolution. Written to comfort the faint-hearted, to strengthen the faithfull, to recall the worldling, and to perswade all men, so to run, that they may obtaine, 1603.

Other editions, 1600, 1602, 1603, 1607, 1616, 1617.

PRESTON, JOHN. An abridgement of Dr. Preston's Works, formerly published by Dr. Sibbes, Mr. Davenport, for sermons preached at Lincolns Inn. Mr. Goodwin,

Mr. Ball, for those at Cambridge. Reduced into order, and contracted thus for the comfort and benefit of meaner Christians, who cannot buy, or attend to read the great volumns. By the industry of William Jemmat, 1648.

PRESTON, JOHN. The breast-plate of faith and love . . . The second edition, corrected, 1630.

Issued by Richard Sibbes and John Davenport. Other editions, 1630, 1631, 1632, 1634.

————The doctrine of the saints infirmities, 1637.

Issued by Thomas Goodwin and Thomas Ball. Other editions, 1630, 1636, 1638.

————The golden scepter held forth to the humble, 1638.

Issued by Thomas Goodwin and Thomas Ball. Another edition, 1638.

————Life eternall or, a treatise of the knowledge of the divine essence and attributes . . . The third edition, corrected, 1632.

Issued by Thomas Goodwin and Thomas Ball. Other editions, 1631, 1632, 1633, 1634.

————The new covenant, or the saints portion, 1629.

Issued by Richard Sibbes and John Davenport. Other editions, 1630, 1631, 1633, 1634, 1639 [called the 9th].

————The position of John Preston . . . concerning the irresistiblenesse of converting grace, 1654.

Contains 'An exact Catalogue of all the works of Dr. John Preston.'

————The saints daily exercise, 1629.

Issued by Richard Sibbes and John Davenport. Other editions, 1629, 1630, 1631, 1632, 1633, 1633 [called the 9th], 1634, 1635.

————The saints qualification, 1633.

Issued by Richard Sibbes and John Davenport. Other editions, 1634, 1637.

————Sermons preached before his maiestie; and upon other speciall occasions, 1630.

Issued by Thomas Goodwin and Thomas Ball. Other editions, 1631, 1634, 1637.

————Sins overthrow: or, a godly and learned treatise of mortification, 1633.

Other editions, 1635, 1641.

PRYNNE, WILLIAM. Breviate of the life of William Laud, 1644.

————Canterburies doome, or the first part of a compleat history of the commitment, charge, tryall, condemnation, and execution of William Laud, 1646.

————The church of Englands old antithesis to the new Arminianisme, 1629.

Another edition with the title *Anti Arminianisme*, 1630.

————Divine tragedie lately acted, or a collection of sundry memorable examples of Gods judgements upon Sabbath-breakers, 1636.

————God, no imposter nor deluder, 1629.

Another edition, 1630; also issued as part II of *Anti Arminianisme*, 1630.

————Healthes sicknesse, 1628.

————Hidden workes of darkenes brought to publike light, 1645.

PYRNNE, WILLIAM. Histrio-mastix: The players scourge or actors traegedie, 1633.
———Lame Giles his haultings, 1630.
———A looking glasse for all lordly prelates, 1636.
———A new discovery of the prelates tyranny, 1641.
———Newes from Ipswich, 1636.
———The perpetuitie of a regenerate mans estate, 1626.
    Other editions, 1627.
———A revindication of the anoynting and priviledges of faithfull subjects, 1634.
———A soveraign antidote, 1642.
———The soveraigne power of parliaments, 1643.
———The treachery and disloyalty of papists to their soveraignes, 1643.
———The unlovelinesse of love-lockes, 1628.
PRYNNE, WILLIAM, JOHN BASTWICK *and* HENRY BURTON, *concerning*. A briefe relation of certain speciall and most materiall passages, and speeches in the Starre-Chamber, occasioned and delivered June the 14th 1637 at the censure of those three worthy Gentlemen, Dr. Bastwick, Mr. Burton, and Mr. Prynne, 1637.
    Another edition, 1638; another edition with added matter appeared in Prynne, *New Discovery of the Prelates Tyranny*, 1641.
RANDALL, GILES. The single eye, entituled the vision of God . . . penned by the Learned Dr. Cusanus, and published by . . . Giles Randall, 1646.
———Theologia germanica. Or, mysticall divinite: a little golden manuall briefly discovering the mysteries, sublimity, perfection and simplicity of Christianity, in belief and practise. Written above 250 years since in high Dutch, & for its worth translated into Latine, and printed at Antwerp, 1588, 1648.
ROBINSON, JOHN. Works . . . with a memoir and annotations, edited by Robert Ashton, 1851.
ROGERS, RICHARD. A commentary upon . . . Judges, 1615.
———A garden of spirituall flowers. Planted by Ri[chard] Ro[gers]. Will[iam] Per[kins]. Ri[chard] Gree[nham]. M. M. and Geo[rge] Web[be], 1625.
    Nine editions before 1640 are listed in the *Short-Title Catalogue*, of which the earliest, 1609, is noted as the fifth.
———Seven treatises, containing such direction as is gathered out of holie scriptures, leading and guiding to true happines, both in this life, and in the life to come: and may be called the practise of Christianitie: profitable for all such as heartily desire the same: in the which, more particularly true Christians may learne how to leade a godly and comfortable life every day, 1603.
    5th edition, 1630. An abbreviated version appeared in 1618 and was several times reissued as, *The Practice of Christianitie. Or, an epitome of Seven Treatises.*
RUTHERFORD, SAMUEL. Lex, rex: the law and the prince, 1644.
SAINT-GERMAN, CHRISTOPHER. Dialogus de fundamentis legum Angliae et de conscientia, 1604.

Another edition, 1528. Translated into English as *The Dialogue in English, betweene a Doctor of Divinity, and a Student in the Lawes of England*, 1604; other editions 1528, 1607, 1609, 1613, 1623, 1638.

SALTMARSH, JOHN. Holy discoveries and flames, 1640.

————Poemata sacra, Latinè & Anglicè scripta, 1636.

Scripture and reason pleaded for defensive armes. . . . Published by diverse . . . divines, 1643.

SCUDDER, HENRY. The Christians daily walk in holy securitie and peace, 1627. Other editions, 1631, 1633, 1637, 1652.

SENHOUSE, RICHARD. Foure sermons, 1627.

SIBBES, RICHARD. Beames of divine light. . . . Published according to the doctor his owne appointment subscribed with his hand; to prevent imperfect coppies, 1639.

Dedication signed by John Sedgwick, address 'To the Reader' by Arthur Jackson.

————Bowels opened. . . . Being in part finished by his owne pen in his life-time, and the rest of them perused and corrected by those whom he intrusted with the publishing of his works, 1641.

Dedication signed by T[homas] G[oodwin] and P[hilip] N[ye], 'Epistle to the Reader' by I. Dod.

Other editions, 1639, 1648.

————The bruised reede and smoaking flax, 1630.

Other editions, 1631, 1632, 1635, 1638.

————The complete works of Richard Sibbes . . . edited, with a memoir, by the Rev. Alexander Balloch Grosart, 1862-64.

————The Christians portion, 1637.

Issued by T[homas] G[oodwin] and P[hilip] N[ye]. Another edition, 1638, with an epistle signed by J[eremiah] B[urroughs].

————The excellencie of the gospell above the law, 1639.

Issued by T[homas] G[oodwin] and P[hilip] N[ye].

————A fountain sealed, 1637.

Issued by Thomas Goodwin and Philip Nye.

————A learned commentary or exposition, upon the fourth chapter of . . . Corrinthians, 1656.

Epistle to the reader signed by Simeon Ash, James Nalton and Joseph Church.

————The saints cordials, 1637.

Other editions, 1629, 1658.

————The soules conflict with it selfe, 1635.

Other editions, 1636, 1638.

————The spirituall-mans aime, 1637.

Issued by T[homas] G[oodwin] and P[hilip] N[ye].

Other editions, 1637, 1638, 1656.

SIBBES, RICHARD. Two sermons upon the first words of Christs last sermon, Iohn 14,1, 1637.
Dedication signed by Thomas Goodwin and Philip Nye.
Other editions, 1636, 1637, 1638.

SMECTYMNUUS [Stephen Marshall, Edmund Calamy, Thomas Young, Matthew Newcomen, and William Spurstow]. An answer to a book entituled, An Humble Remonstrance, 1641.
———A vindication of the answer to the humble remonstrance, 1641.

SMITH, HENRY. Micro-cosmo-graphia: the little worldes description: or the map of man. From Latin Saphiks of . . . Henry Smith translated by Ioshua Sylvester.
In Sylvester, Joshua, translator, *Du Bartas His Divine Weekes and Workes*, 1621.
———The sermons of . . . gathered into one volume . . . and the life of Mr. Henry Smith, by Tho. Fuller, B.D., . . . 1657. 2d edition, 1675.
Beginning with the first edition of 1592, collections of Smith's sermons, partial or complete, were repeatedly issued down to the end of the nineteenth century. A single sermon was published in 1590. Fuller's edition was reissued in Nichol's Standard Divines as, *The Works . . . including Sermons, Treatises, Prayers, and Poems with life of the author, by Thomas Fuller, . . . and other biographical notes*, 1867.

SMYTH, JOHN. The works of John Smyth, edited by W. T. Whitley, 1915.

SPELMAN, SIR JOHN. A view of a printed book, 1643.

SPENCER, JOHN. A short treatise concerning the lawfullnesse of every mans exercising his gift as God shall call him thereunto, 1641.

STOCK, RICHARD. A learned and very usefull commentary upon the whole Prophesie of Malachy, 1641.
———A sermon preached at Paules Crosse, the second of November, 1606, 1609.
———A stock of divine knowledge. Being a lively description of the divine nature, 1641.

TAYLOR, THOMAS. Christs combate and conquest: or, the lyon of the Tribe of Judah, vanquishing the roaring lyon, 1618.
Another edition, 1618.
———Christs victorie over the dragon: or, Satans downfall: shewing the glorious conquests of our Saviour for his poore church, against the greatest persecutors, 1633.
———The parable of the sower and of the seed, 1621.
Other editions, 1623, 1634, 1659.
———The progresse of saints to full holinesse, 1631.
Another edition, 1630.
———Three treatises: the pearle of the gospel, the pilgrims profession: and a glasse for gentlewomen to dresse themselves by, 1633.
Another edition, 1625. *The Pilgrims Profession* appeared separately, 1622,

1625. The Pearle of the Gospel and *The Pilgrims Profession* also appeared as *Two Treatises*, 1624.

TAYLOR, THOMAS. The works of that faithful servant of Jesus Christ, Dr. Thom. Taylor, 1653.

Another edition, 1659.

Theologia Germanica. *See* Randall, Giles.

To the high court of parliament: the humble remonstrance of the company of stationers, 1643.

TOPSELL, EDWARD. Times lamentation: or an exposition on the prophet Ioel, 1599.

TRAVERS, WALTER. Disciplina ecclesiae. *See* Cartwright, Thomas.

WALKER, GEORGE. Socinianisme in the fundamentall point of justification discovered, and confuted, 1641.

WALWYN, WILLIAM. The compassionate samaritane, 1644.

————The power of love, 1643.

————Some considerations tending to the undeceiving those, whose judgements are misinformed, 1642.

The Compassionate Samaritane and *The Power of Love* are reprinted in Haller, *Tracts on Liberty*. For the identification of Walwyn as the author of the three tracts listed above, see the same work, Vol. I, Appendix A.

WHATELY, WILLIAM. A bride-bush. Or, a direction for married persons, 1623.

Other editions, 1617, 1619.

————The new birth: or, a treatise of regeneration, 1635.

Other editions, 1618, 1619, 1622, 1628, 1630.

————The oyle of gladnesse. Or, comfort for dejected sinners. First preached in the parish church of Banbury in certaine sermons, and now published in this present treatise, 1637.

————Prototypes, or, the primarie precedent presidents out of the Booke of Genesis, 1640.

WILKINS, JOHN. Ecclesiastes, or, a discourse concerning the gift of preaching as it fals under the rules of art, shewing the most proper rules and directions, for method, invention, books, expression, whereby a minister may be furnished with such abilities as may make him a workman that needs not to be ashamed. . . . The second edition, 1647.

1st edition, 1646; other editions, 1651, 1669, 1679.

LIVES OF THE PURITAN SAINTS

ALLEINE, THEODOSIA, *and others*. The life and death of that excellent minister of Christ Mr. Joseph Alleine, 1672.

Introduction by Richard Baxter. Other editions, 1673, 1677, 1822, 1829.

In Clarke, *Lives of sundry*. See also Charles Stanford, *Joseph Alleine*, 1861.

ASHE, SIMEON. The good mans death lamented. A sermon preached . . . at the funerall of that faithfull servant of Christ Mr. Ralph Robinson, 1655.

In Clarke, *Lives of sundry*.

ASHE, SIMEON. Gray hayres crowned with grace . . . the narrative of the life and death of Mr. Gataker, 1655.
In Clarke, *Collection of the Lives.*

————Living loves betwixt Christ and dying Christians. A sermon preached . . . at the funerall of that faithfull servant of Christ, Mr. Jeremiah Whitaker . . . with a narrative of his exemplary life and death. 2d edition, 1654.
Other editions, 1654, 1656.
In Clarke, *Collection of the Lives.*

BAGSHAW, EDWARD. 'The life and death of Mr. Bolton.' In *Mr. Boltons Last and Learned Worke of the Foure last Things,* 1633. Other editions of the latter work, 1632, 1635, 1639. Also appeared in Bolton, *Workes,* 1641, of which there were other editions in 1640, 1641, in Clarke, *Marrow,* and in Fuller, *Abel Redevivus.*

BALL, THOMAS. The life of the renowned Docter Preston, writ by his pupil, Master Thomas Ball . . . in the year 1628. Now first published and edited by E. W. Harcourt, 1885.
In Clarke, *General Martyrologie,* 1651.

BAXTER, RICHARD. A breviate of the life of Margaret, . . . wife of Richard Baxter. With the character of her mother, truly described in her published funeral sermon, reprinted at her daughters request, called, The Last Work of a Believer . . . also Mr. John How's sermon at Mrs. Baxters funeral, 1681.
In Clarke, *Lives of sundry.*

BELLERS, FULK. Abrahams interment: or the good old-mans buriall in a good old age. Opened in a sermon . . . at the funerall of the worshipfull John Lamotte Esq. . . . Unto which is added a short narrative of his life and death, 1656.
In Clarke, *Lives of sundry.*

BERNARD, NICOLAS. The life & death of the most reverend and learned father of our church Dr. James Usher. . . . Published on a sermon at his funeral . . . and now re-viewed with some other enlargements, 1656.
In Clarke, *Collection of the Lives.*

BIRCHALL, JOHN. The non-pareil, or, the vertuous daughter, surmounting all her sisters: described, in a funerall sermon upon the death of that vertuous lady, Elizabeth Hoyle, late wife of the worshipfull Thomas Hoyle, 1644.

BURNET, GILBERT. The life and death of Sir Matthew Hale, Kt., 1682.
In Clarke, *Lives of sundry.*

BURTON, HENRY. A narration of the life of Mr. Henry Burton. Where-in is set forth the various and remarkable passages thereof, his sufferings, supports, comforts, and deliverances. Now published for the benefit of all those that either doe or may suffer for the cause of Christ. According to a copy written with his owne hand, 1643.

CALAMY, EDMUND. The saints transfiguration: or the body of vilenesse changed into a body of glory, a sermon preached . . . at the funerall of that reverend, and faithful minister of Jesus Christ Dr. Samuel Bolton. . . . With a short account of his Death, 1655.

In Clarke, *Lives of sundry.*

CARTER, JOHN, JUNIOR. The tombstone, or, a . . . monument, of . . . J. Carter . . . (The life of J. Carter, pastor of Bramford . . . in a sermon upon the Solemne Guildday, June 18, 1650.), 1653.

In Clarke, *Collection of the Lives.*

CATLIN, ZACHARY. 'Dr. Sibbs, his life.'

In *The Complete Works of Richard Sibbes,* edited by A. B. Grosart, 1862.

Another edition, edited by J. E. B. Mayor, Cambridge, 1856.

CLARKE, SAMUEL. 'A brief narrative of my life, and of the most remarkable acts of Gods providence in guiding and governing the same.'

In Clarke, *Lives of sundry,* 1683.

CLARKE, SAMUEL, *editor.*

(Note. The following is a list of the biographical collections of Samuel Clarke. The lives of Puritan saints included in each collection are cited in the order in which they occur in the original.)

The marrow of ecclesiastical historie, conteined in the lives of the fathers, and other learned men, and famous divines, which have flourished in the church since Christs time, to this present age, 1650.

2d edition, 1654; 3d edition, 1675. See page with signature b4v for references to the sources of some of the lives included. Contains the lives of:

Edward Dering [abstracted with additions from Dering, *Workes.* See also Fuller, *Abel Redevivus.*]

William Perkins [abstracted with additions from Fuller, *Holy State.* See also Fuller, *Abel Redevivus.*]

William Cowper ['Cowpers Life is written by himself.' See Cowper, *Workes.*]

Robert Bolton ['Boltons Life is written by Mr. Bagshaw.' See Bagshaw, Edward.]

William Whately ['Whatelies Life is written by Mr. Scudder.' See Scudder, William.]

————The second part of the marrow of ecclesiastical history: containing the lives of many eminent christians which have lived since the primitive times to this present age, divided into two books: wherof the first contains the lives of Christian emperors, kings, and soveraign princes: the second contains the lives of christians of an inferiour rank, 1650.

Published with the preceding. Contains the lives of:

Katherine Brettargh ['Collected out of her Life and Death, Printed with two excellent Sermons, preached at her Funeral by two Eminent and godly Divines' (Bk. 2, p. 120). See Harrison, William.]

John Harington, second Lord Harington of Exton ['Collected partly out of my own knowledge, and partly out of Mr. Stocks Sermon at his Funerall, and Dr. Hollands Heroωlogia Anglica' (Bk. 2, p. 130). See Stock, Richard and Holland, Henry.]

John Bruen ['Collected out of that learned and elaborate Work, written of his Life and Death, by Mr. William Hinde' (Bk. 2, p. 205). See Hinde, William.]

CLARKE, SAMUEL. A general martyrologie, containing a collection of all the greatest persecutions which have befallen the church of Christ from the creation to our present times. Whereunto are added the lives of sundry modern divines, 1651. Thomas Cartwright ['Master Dod preached his Funeral Sermon' (*General Martyrologie*, 1677, p. 22).]

Richard Rothwel ['This Life was drawn up by my reverend Friend Master Stanly Gower of Dorcester' (*General Martyrologie*, 1677, p. 74).]

John Preston ['This Life was written by my Reverend Friend Master Thomas Ball of Northampton' (*General Martyrologie*, 1677, p. 114).]

Arthur Hildersam [Hildersam's son Samuel furnished materials for this life from his father's papers (*General Martyrologie*, 1677, p. 124).]

Hugh Clarke ['This Master Hugh Clarke was my father' (*General Martyrologie*, 1677, p. 131).]

John Ball [Materials furnished by John Taylor, Thomas Langley, Simeon Ashe, George Crosse, friends of the deceased (*General Martyrologie*, 1677, p. 155).]

Barnaby Potter

Richard Sedgwick

Julines Herring

John Dod

Robert Balsom

Herbert Palmer

————A Martyrologie, containing a collection of all the persecutions which have befallen the church of England since the first plantation of the gospel to the end of Queen Maries reign. Whereunto are added the lives of Jasper Coligni Admiral of France, who was slain in the massacre of Paris. And of Joane Queen of Navarre, who died of poyson a few dayes before that bloody massacre. Together with the lives of ten of our English divines, famous in their generations for learning, piety, parts, and for their sufferings in the cause of Christ, 1652.

Contains the lives of:

Richard Greenham [abstracted from the Preface by Henry Holland to Greenham, *Workes*.]

Paul Baynes [abstracted from the Preface by William Ames to Baynes, *Diocesans Tryall*.]

William Bradshaw ['This Life was drawn up by my Reverend, Learned and worthy friend Mr. Thomas Gataker of Rederith' (p. 140). Gataker obtained information from Samuel, son of Arthur, Hildersam, and from Bradshaw's son, John. See Gataker, *Life*, p. 137.]

Richard Stock [Taken almost word for word from Thomas Gataker, *Abrahams Decease*.]

Richard Sibbes

Thomas Taylor [may be related to Life in Taylor, *Works.*]

Laurence Chaderton ['Dr. Richard Holsworth, the then Master of Emmanuel, preached his Funerall Sermon, and gave him a large and deserved Commendation,' p. 156.]

CLARKE, SAMUEL. A collection of the lives of ten eminent divines, famous in their generations for learning, prudence, piety, and painfulness in the work of the ministry. Where unto is added, the life of Gustavus Ericson, king of Sueden, who first reformed religion in that kingdome, and of some other eminent Christians, 1662.

Contains lives of:

John Carter [Clarke prints a letter from John Carter, Junior, requesting the publication of this life of his father, which he had already printed. See Carter, *The Tomb Stone.*]

Samuel Crooke [See W. G., 'ΑΝΘΟΛΟΓΙΑ.]

John Cotton [abstracted from Norton, *Abel being Dead.*]

Thomas Hill [adapted from Tuckney, ΘΑΝΑΤΟΚΤΑΣΙΑ.]

William Gouge ['My Reverend Friend Mr. Tho. Gouge, eldest son to this famous Docter,' desired me to insert this Life, amongst these other Worthies contained in this Volume' (p. 125). See Gouge, Thomas.]

Thomas Gataker [abstracted from Ashe, *Gray Hayres*]

James Ussher ['Reverend and Learned Dr. Bernard, who was of my ancient acquaintance above forty years ago in Emanuel College in Cambridge hath written his Life and Death excellent well' (p. 188). See Bernard, Nicholas.]

Richard Capel [adapted from Valentine Marshall's 'Abridgement' in Capel, *Remains.*]

Robert Harris [abstracted from William Durham, *Life.*]

Jane Ratcliffe [abstracted from John Ley, *Patterne of Pietie.*]

Ignatius Jurdaine [abstracted from Ferdinando Nicolls, *Life.*]

Margaret Ducke [adapted from 'a short Relation' by William Gouge, *A Funerall Sermon.*]

Margaret Corbet ['This Life was drawn up by my Reverend and worthy Friend Dr. Henry Wilkinson, principal of Magdalen Hall, Oxon.,' p. 511.]

Elizabeth Wilkinson [abstracted from Edmund Staunton, *A Sermon.*]

————A general martyrologie, containing a collection of all the greatest persecutions which have befallen the church of Christ, from the creation, to our present times; wherein is given an exact account of the Protestants sufferings in Queen Maries reign. Whereunto is added the lives of thirty two English divines. 3d edition, corrected and enlarged, 1677.

Brings together into a single volume lives Clarke had previously published in *A general Martyrologie*, 1651, *A Martyrology*, 1652, and *A Collection*, 1662, but not including those in *Marrow*, 1650. No new lives appeared in this volume.

————The lives of sundry eminent persons in this later age. In two parts, I. Of divines. II of nobility and gentry of both sexes. . . . printed and reviewed by himself just before his death. To which is added his own life, and the lives of the Countess of Suffolk, Sir Nathaniel Barnardiston, Mr. Richard Blackerby, and Mr. Samuel Fairclough, drawn up by other hands, 1683.

The epistle 'To the Reader' is by Richard Baxter.

Among the many lives included in this collection, the following may be especially noted:

Samuel Clarke, *A Brief Narrative of my Life.*

Thomas Wilson by G[eorge] S[winnock].

Samuel Bolton by Edmund Calamy

Richard Vines by Thomas Jacombe

Richard Blackerby

Ralph Robinson [adapted from Simeon Ashe, *The Good mans Death.*]

John Janeway [abridged from James Janeway, *Invisibles, Realities.*]

John Machin by [Henry Newcome], *A faithful narrative.*

Samuel Winter by J. W., *The life and death.*

Richard Mather [based on Increase Mather, *The Life and Death.*]

Joseph Alleine [adapted from Theodosia Alleine and others, *The Life and Death.*]

Edmund Staunton by Richard Mayo, *The Life & Death.*

Samuel Fairclough

Sir Charles Coot ['These things were attested and declared by Faithful Teat, D. D. then Lecturer in Dublin, in his Sermon preached in Christ-Church, May the 14th. Anno Christi, 1642: before the State, and chief of the Army, at the interment of the said Sir Charles Coot,' p. 102.]

John LaMotte by Fulk Bellers, *Abrahams Interment.*

Sir Nathaniel Barnardiston by Samuel Fairclough, Ἅγια ἄξια.

John Row by [John Rowe, the younger], *The Life and Death.*

Sir Matthew Hale [abstracted from Gilbert Burnet, *The Life and Death.*]

Mary Gunter by Thomas Taylor, *The Pilgrims Profession.*

Lady Aliee Lucy by Thomas Dugard, *Death and the Grave.*

Lady Mary Vere by William Gurnall, *The Christians Labour.*

Katherine Clarke by Samuel Clarke, her husband.

Lady Mary, Countess of Warwick by Anthony Walker, *The virtuous woman found.*

Margaret Baxter [abstracted from Richard Baxter, *A Breviate of the Life.*]

Lady Mary Armine by J. D., *A Sermon.*

COLLINGES, JOHN. Par nobile. Two treatises. The one, concerning the excellent woman, evincing a person fearing the Lord, to be the most excellent person: discoursed more privately upon occasion of the death of the right honourable, the Lady Frances Hobart, late of Norwich. . . . The other, discovering a fountain of comfort and satisfaction, to persons walking with God, yet living and dying without sensible consolations . . . at the funerals of the Right Honourable, the Lady Katherine Courten. March 27, 1652. With the narratives of the holy lives and deaths of those two noble sisters, 1669.

CONANT, JOHN. 'To the Christian reader.'

An account of Richard Bernard in Bernard, Richard, *Thesaurus Biblicus*, 1644.

COWPER, WILLIAM. The life and death of the reverend father and faithfull servant of God, Mr. William Cowper. . . . Who departed this Life at Edinburgh, the 15, of February, 1619.

In *The Workes of Mr. William Cowper*, 1629. 'This Discourse was penned by himselfe on the first of January, 1626 [1616?].'

Other editions of *Workes*, 1623, 1626. The *Life* appeared independently in 1619.

In Clarke, *Marrow*, and in Fuller, *Abel Redevivus*.

D., J. A sermon preached at the funeral of Lady Mary Armyne, 1676.

The introduction is by Richard Baxter. In Clarke, *Lives of sundry*.

DERING, EDWARD. 'M. Derings words, spoken on his death-bed at Toby. The 26. of June. 1576.'

In *M. Derings Workes*, 1597.

Other editions of *Workes*, 1590, 1614.

In Clarke, *Marrow*, and in Fuller, *Abel Redevivus*.

DUGARD, THOMAS. Death and the grave: or a sermon preached at the funeral of that honorable and virtuous ladie, the Ladie Alice Lucie, August 17, 1648, 1649.

In Clarke, *Lives of sundry*.

DUNCON, JOHN. The returns of spiritual comfort and grief in a devout soul. Represented (by entercourse of letters) to the Right Honorable, the Ladie Letice, Vi-Countess Falkland, in her life time and exemplified in the holie life and death of the said honorable ladie . . . , 2d edition, enlarged, 1649.

Other editions, 1648, 1653; edited by M. F. Howard, 1908.

DURHAM, WILLIAM. The life and death of that judicious divine, and accomplish'd preacher, Robert Harris, D.D. . . . Collected by a joynt-concurrence of some, who knew him well in his strength, visited him often in his sickness, attended him at his death, and still honour his memory. Published at the earnest request of many, for the satisfaction of some, for the silencing of others, and for the imitation of all, 1660.

In Clarke, *Collection of the Lives*.

ESTWICK, NICOLAS. A learned and godly Sermon preached on the XIX day of December, Anno Dom. MDCXXXI at the funerall of Mr. Robert Bolton, 1633.

FAIRCLOUGH, SAMUEL. Ἅγιοι ἄξιοι or the saints worthinesse and the worlds worthlessnesse, . . . declared in a sermon at the funerall of Sr. N. Barnardiston, 1653.

In Clarke, *Lives of sundry*.

FEATLEY, DANIEL, *and others*. ΘΡΗΝΟΙΚΟΣ. The house of mourning . . . XLVII sermons, preached at the funeralls of divers faithfull servants of Christ by Daniel Featley, Martin Day, Richard Sibbs, Thomas Taylor. . . . And other Reverend Divines . . . , 1640.

Another edition, including fifty-three sermons and the names of Thomas Fuller, John Preston, and Richard Houldsworth on the title-page, 1660.

FORD, SIMON. 'Ησυχια Χρωτιανου, or, a Christians acquiescence in all the products of divine providence: opened, in a sermon . . . preached . . . April the 16, 1664, at the interment of . . . Lady E. Langham, 1665.
In Clarke, *Lives of sundry*.

FULLER, THOMAS. Abel redevivus: or the dead yet speaking. The lives and deaths of the moderne divines. Written by severall able and learned men (whose names ye shall finde in the epistle to the reader.), 1651.
Includes lives of:
Edward Dering [from Clarke, *Marrow*.]
William Perkins [by Fuller but differing from the life in his *The Holy State*.]
William Cowper [from Clarke, *Marrow*.]
Andrew Willet [differing from the life by Peter Smith in Willet, *Synopsis Papismi*, but by the same hand.]
Robert Bolton [from Clarke, *Marrow*.]
William Whately [from Clarke, *Marrow*.]
————The holy state: The profane state, 1642.
Other editions, 1648, 1652, 1663, 1884.
Includes a life of William Perkins.

G., W. 'ΑΝΘΟΛΟΓΙΑ   The Life and death of Mr. S. Crook, 1651.
In Clarke, *Collection of the Lives*.

GATAKER, THOMAS. Abrahams decease. A meditation on Genesis 25,8 delivered at the Funerall of that worthy servant of Christ, Mr. Richard Stock . . . Together with the Testimonie then given unto him, 1627.
In Clarke, *Martyrologie*, 1652.
————Christian constancy crowned by Christ. A funerall sermon. . . . Preached at the buriall of M. William Winter . . . Together with the testimonie then given unto Him, 1629.
————The decease of Lazarus Christs friend. A funerall sermon. . . . Preached at the buriall of Mr. John Parker, 1640.
————The life and death of Mr. William Bradshaw who died Anno Christi, 1618.
In Clarke, *Martyrologie*, 1652.
————Pauls desire of dissolution, and deaths advantage. A sermon preached at the funerall of . . . Mrs. Rebekka Crisp togither with the testimonie then given unto her, 1620.
————Saint Stevens last will and testament. A funerall sermon. . . . Preached at the enterrement of . . . Mris Joice Featly. Together with the testimonie then given unto her, 1638.

GOODWIN, THOMAS, JUNIOR. 'The life of Dr. Thomas Goodwin; compos'd out of his own papers and memoirs.'
In *The Works of Thomas Goodwin*, Vol. V, 1704.

GOUGE, THOMAS. 'A narrative of the life and death of Docter Gouge.'
In Gouge, William, *A Learned . . . Commentary on . . . Hebrews*, 1655.
In Clarke, *Collection of the Lives*.

GOUGE, WILLIAM. A funerall sermon preached by Dr. Gouge . . . at the funeralls of Mrs. Margaret Ducke . . . with a short relation of her life and death, written by a friend, 1646.
In Clarke, *Collection of the Lives*.

———A recovery from apostacy. Set out in a sermon preached in Stepny Church neere London at the receiving of a penitent renegado [Vincent Jukes] into the church, 1639.

GOWER, STANLEY. 'The life of Master Richard Rothwel, who dyed Anno Christi, 1627.'
In Clarke, *General Martyrologie*, 1651.

GURNALL, WILLIAM. The Christians labour and reward; or, a sermon . . . at the funeral of the . . . Lady Mary Vere, 1672.
In Clarke, *Lives of sundry*.

HARFORD, RAPHA. 'To the reader of Dr. Everards sermons.'
An account of John Everard in Everard, John, *Gospell-Treasury Opened*, 1657.

HARRIS, ROBERT. Samuels funerall or a sermon preached at the funerall of Sir Anthony Cope.
In *Works*, 1634-35.
Other editions of the sermon, 1618, 1622, 1626, 1630; of *Works*, 1654.

HARRISON, WILLIAM *and* WILLIAM LEYGH. Deaths advantage little regarded, and the soules solace against sorrow. Preached in two funerall sermons . . . at the buriall of Mistris Katherin Brettergh the third of June 1601. The one by William Harrison . . . the other by William Leygh. . . . Whereunto is annexed, the christian life and godly death, of the said gentlewoman, 1605 [N.S. 1606].
Contains:
A Brief Discourse of the Christian Life and death, of Mistris Katherin Bretterghoult . . . who departed this world the last of May. 1601.
Other editions, 1612, 1634, 1641.

HINDE, WILLIAM. A faithfull remonstrance of the holy life and happy death of J. Bruen, 1641.
Edited and republished by W. Coddington as *The very singular life . . .*, 1799.
In Clarke, *Marrow*.

HOWES, JOHN. Real comforts, extracted from moral and spiritual principles. Presented in a sermon, preached at the funeral of that reverend divine Mr. Thomas Ball . . . upon the 21 day of June, A. D. 1659. With a narrative of his life and death, 1660.

HUGHES, G. The art of embalming dead saints, discovered in a sermon preached at the funerall of Master William Crompton. . . . Usefull observations upon the life and death of Mr. William Crompton, 1642.

JACOMBE, SAMUEL. Moses his death: opened and applyed, in a sermon. . . . At the funeral of Mr. Edward Bright, . . . With some Elegies, 1657.

JACOMBE, THOMAS. Enochs walk and change, opened in a sermon. . . . Febr. 7th, 1653 at the funeral of the reverend Mr. Richard Vines. . . . With a short account of his life and death. 2d edition, 1656.
1st edition, 1656.

JANEWAY, JAMES. Invisibles, realities, demonstrated in the holy life and triumphant death of Mr. John Janeway, 1673.
Other editions, 1674, 1702, 1745, 1854, 1885.
In Clarke, *Lives of sundry*.

JENKYN, WILLIAM. A shock of corn coming in in its season. A sermon preached at the funeral of that ancient and eminent servant of Christ William Gouge, . . . with the ample and deserved testimony that then was given of his life, 1654.
Another edition, 1654.

KILBYE, RICHARD. The burthen of a loaden conscience: or the miserie of sinne: set forth by the confession of a miserable sinner, 1613.
Other editions, 1608, 1613, 1614, 1616, 1618, 1630.

LEY, JOHN. A monitor of mortalitie, in two sermons; . . . occasioned by the death of that hopefull young gentleman John Archer. . . . And by the death of Mistris Harpur, a grave and godly matron, (wife to Mr. Henry Harpur of the City of Chester,) and of the death of their religious daughter Phoebe Harpur, a child of about 12 yeares of age, 1643.
———A patterne of pietie. Or, the religious life and death of Jane Ratcliffe, 1640.
In Clarke, *Collection of the Lives*.

MARSHALL, VALENTINE. 'An abridgement of the authors [Richard Capel] life.'
In Capel, Richard, *Remains*, 1658; also in Capel, *Tentations*, 1659.
In Clarke, *Collection of the Lives*.

MATHER, INCREASE. The life and death of that reverend man of God, Mr. Richard Mather, 1670.
In Clarke, *Lives of sundry*.

MAYO, RICHARD. The life & death of Edmund Staunton, 1673.
In Clarke, *Lives of sundry*.
———Moses in the mount: or, the beloved disciple leaning on Jesus's bosom. Being a narrative of the life and death of Mr. John Murcot. . . . Written by a friend, 1657.

NEWCOME, HENRY. A faithful narrative of the life and death of that holy . . . preacher, Mr. John Machin, 1671.
In Clarke, *Lives of sundry*.

NICOLLS, FERDINANDO. Life and death of Mr. Ignatius Jurdain, 2d edition, 1655.
1st edition, 1640.
In Clarke, *Collection of the Lives*.

NORTON, JOHN. Abel being dead yet speaketh; or, the life & death of that deservedly famous man of God, Mr. John Cotton, 1658.
In Clarke, *Collection of the Lives.*

REYNOLDS, EDWARD. The churches triumph over death. Opened in a sermon preached Septemb. 11. 1660 at the funeral of the most religious and vertuous lady, the Lady Mary Langham, 1662.

ROGERS, RICHARD. Diary.
In *Two Elizabethan Puritan Diaries,* ed. by M. M. Knappen, 1933.

ROWE, JOHN, JUNIOR. The life and death of Mr. John Rowe, 1673.
In Clarke, *Lives of sundry.*

SCUDDER, WILLIAM. 'The life and death of Mr. William Whately.'
In Whately, William, *Prototypes,* 1640.
Another edition, 1647.
In Clarke, *Marrow,* and in Fuller, *Abel Redevivus.*

SIBBES, RICHARD. 'Christ is best: or, a sweet passage to glory. Preached at the funerall of Mr. Sherland . . . Together with the most vertuous life, and heavenly end of that religious gentleman.'
In Sibbes, *The Saints Cordials,* 1637.

SMITH, PETER. 'The life and death of Andrew Willet.'
In Willet, Andrew, *Synopsis Papismi,* Now the fifth time published, 1634.
In Clarke, *Marrow.*

STAUNTON, EDMUND. A sermon preached . . . Decemb:9, 1654, at the funerall of . . . Mrs. E. Wilkinson. . . . Whereunto is added a narrative of her godly life and death, 1654.
In Clarke, *Collection of the Lives.*

STOCK, RICHARD. The churches lamentation for the losse of the godly . . . delivered in a sermon at the funeral of John Lord Harington. . . . Together with a pattern of piety . . . expressed in his life and death, 1614.
In Clarke, *Marrow.*

S[WINNOCK], G[EORGE]. The life and death of Mr. Tho. Wilson, 1672.
In Clarke, *Lives of sundry.*

TAYLOR, THOMAS. 'The pil[g]rims profession or, a sermon preached at the funerall of Mrs. Mary Gunter, . . . To which (by his consent) also is added, a short relation of the life and death of the said gentlewoman, as a perpetuall monument of her graces and vertues.'
In Taylor, *Three Treatises,* 1633.
Other editions, 1622, 1624, 1625.

TUCKNEY, ANTHONY. ΘΑΝΑΤΟΚΤΑΣΙΑ, or death disarmed: and the grave swallowed up in victory. A sermon preached . . . Decemb. 22. 1653. At the publick funerals of Dr. Hill, . . . With a short account of his life and death, 1654.
In Clarke, *Collection of the Lives.*

W., J. The life and death of . . . Dr. Samuel Winter. Edited by J. W., 1671.
In Clarke, *Lives of sundry.*

WALKER, ANTHONY. The virtuous woman found, her loss bewayl'd and character exemplified in a sermon preached . . . at the funeral of . . . Mary, Countess Dowager of Warwick . . . with so large additions as may be stiled the Life of that . . . Lady, 1678.
Other editions, 1680, 1686.
In Clarke, *Lives of sundry*.

WARD, SAMUEL. Diary.
In *Two Elizabethan Puritan Diaries*, ed. by M. M. Knappen, 1933.

W[HISTON], E[DWARD]. The life and death of Mr. Henry Jessey, late preacher of the gospel of Christ in London, 1671.

WHITING, SAMUEL. 'Life of John Cotton.'
In Young, Alexander, *Chronicles of the first Planters of Massachusetts Bay*, 1846.

WILKINSON, HENRY. The hope of glory or Christs indwelling in true believers. . . . As it was set forth in a sermon . . . March 5, 1656 . . . at the funerall of . . . M. Corbet, 1657.
In Clarke, *Collection of Lives*.

THE WRITINGS OF JOHN LILBURNE, 1638–40

IN THE pamphlets dealing with his punishment and imprisonment in 1638-40, Lilburne refers to letters, addresses and petitions which he wrote in those years from gaol. Some of these writings are easily identified with extant publications. Others I have been unable to trace, perhaps for the reason that they were never in fact printed, perhaps for the reason that I have not looked farther. What Lilburne wrote, what he published and what were the immediate circumstances of composition and publication appear, so far as I know, to be as follows:

In his *Letter to the Apprentices*, 10 May 1639, Lilburne speaks of having put forth '3 severall bookes in print.' This statement refers without doubt to *The Christian Mans Triall*, 1st edition 1638; *A Worke of the Beast*, 1638; and *Come out of her my people*, 1639. *The Poore Mans Cry*, written in December 1638 and published in 1639, may not yet have appeared, especially if, as seems likely, it had to be printed in Holland. In his *Letter to the Wardens*, 4 October 1640, Lilburne speaks of his published pleas to the Lord Mayor and Aldermen and to the apprentices, 'which now with foure other Bookes are all in Print.' The latter statement probably means that by that date *The Poore Mans Cry* had reached London. Lilburne also speaks of certain other writings which I have not been able otherwise to identify; viz.

A tract on the 'heavenly *Jerusalm*, or spirituall Syon . . . the compleatnesse, state, and matter of which, I have in part many months agoe described, and illustrated in my answer to W.G. as there you may read,' *Coppy of a Letter . . . to one of his speciall friends*, p. 16. The 'Answer to W.G.' is again twice referred to in *An Answer to Nine Arguments* (pp. 24, 38). This may have been the tract published with the title *Come out of her my people: Or An Answer to the questions of a Gentlewoman*, but there is no definite proof.

A 'Complaint to the . . . Lord Major of the City of London intituled *A Cry for Justice* and the worshipfull Alderman . . . and . . . worthy Citizens published,' *Letter to the Apprentices*. This is referred to in the *Letter to the Wardens* as being in print. It was probably written and published at the same time as, if not just before, the *Letter to the Apprentices*, 10 May 1639, which urges the apprentices to support Lilburne's plea to the Lord Mayor.

The recovery of these and other writings of Lilburne of the years 1638–40 would probably add little to what we already know. The story is clearly outlined in the extant publications. Lilburne was punished for publishing Bastwick's *Letany* and at once put out his account of the affair. He passed directly into an emotional religious crisis, recorded in his next three tracts and probably in other writings which have been lost. He then plunged into a heated quarrel with his keepers, issuing a series of petitions and appeals, some of which have been preserved. Various persons, probably separatist or baptist sympathizers, anonymous or known only by their initials, assisted him to get his writings into print and circulation. William Kiffin, baptist, and William Larner, later a Leveller, who had to do with the republication of *The Christian Mans Triall* and *A Worke of the Beast* in 1641, may almost certainly be said to have helped with the earlier issues of these and other tracts. These were probably sent to Holland to be printed. Though Lilburne denied responsibility for publishing Bastwick's *Letany*, he had obviously been busy among printers in Holland at the time that work was being put into type. He alludes to these activities in his *Letter to the Apprentices* as well as in *The Christian Mans Triall*. In the former he also declares that he has published his griefs 'unto the view of *England, Scotland, Ireland* and *Holland*.' He tells the wardens that he has written more sheets than all his previously published books put together, 'which many moneths agoe I sent into *Holland* to my Printer' (*Letter to the Wardens*, pp. 6-7) and goes on to warn them that 'if there be but a Printing-house in any of the Cities in the Provinces of Holland, I will cause this Letter to be Printed' (*Letter to the Wardens*, p. 8). In the same letter (p. 4), he complains that '*Canterburies* Catchpoles took from me the last yeare at the Custome house, almost two thousand of my Bookes as they came from *Amsterdam*.' Lilburne's baptist and separatist friends were in constant communication with their sympathizers in the Low Countries. It is safe to say that his pamphlets found their way to the press and into the hands of his countrymen by channels much the same as those along which he had himself conducted Bastwick's *Letany* to a similar end. Those pamphlets are listed below in the order in which they would appear to have been written.

The Christian Mans Triall: or a True Relation of the first apprehension and severall examinations of John Lilburne. The second Edition, with an addition. London: printed for William Larner, 1641.

In a marginal note to his *Letter to the Apprentices*, published 1648, Lilburne refers to his 'examination and defence at the Star-Chamber barre &c. called the Christian mans tryall reprinted by William Larnar.' The tract is subscribed by the author's name and dated 'From the Fleete . . . the 12 of March 1637[8].' It is an account of Lilburne's arrest, 11 or 12 December 1637, and of his arraignment and conviction, 13 February 1638. It was no doubt written directly after that event and conveyed into the hands of the prisoner's friends to be printed in March 1638, certainly before Lilburne's punishment 18 April. That it actually appeared in print is, so far as I know, attested only by the statement on the title-page, supported by Lilburne, that this is a second edition. I know of no extant copy of the first edition. 'With an addition' clearly refers to the fact that *A Worke of the Beast*, which had previously been issued separately, was included in the second edition of *A Christian Mans Triall*. In this edition an epistle 'To the Reader', commending the work in the usual baptist vein, is signed by William Kiffin.

A Worke of the Beast or A Relation of a most unchristian Censure, Executed upon John Lilburne, (Now prisoner in the fleet) the 18 of Aprill 1638. With the heavenly speech uttered by him at the time of his suffering. Very usefull for these times both for the encouragement of the Godly to suffer, And for the terrour and shame of the Lords Adversaries . . . Printed in the yeare the Beast was Wounded 1638.

An epistle, 'The Publisher to the Reader', signed F.R., commends the tract in the language of separatist enthusiasm. F.R. has not been identified. The work itself is subscribed 'Iohn Lilburne' as are the rude verses at the end, said by the author to have been composed the day after his punishment. The whole thing must have been written and issued to be printed soon after that event. It was reprinted as an 'addition' to the second edition of *The Christian Mans Triall*, 1641 (see above). A facsimile reprint appears in my *Tracts on Liberty in the Puritan Revolution*.

Come out of her my people: Or An Answer to the questions of a Gentlewoman (professour in the Antichristian Church of England) about Hearing the Publicke Ministers: where it is largely discussed and proved to be sinfull and unlawfull.
Also
A Iust Apologie for the way of Totall Separation (Commonly but falsly called Brownisme) That it is the truth of God, though lightly esteemed in the eyes of the blinde world. *With*
A Challenge to Dispute with them publickly before King and Counsell: to prove whatsoever I said at the Pillery against them. Viz. That the Calling of them all is Jure Diabolo: Even from the Divell himselfe.
By mee John Lilburne. *Close Prisoner in the Cause of Christ* . . .
Printed in the yeare of hope, of Englands purgation, & the Prelates dissolution. Anno 1639.

The brief epistle, '*The Publisher to the Reader*,' unsigned but separatist in spirit, was probably written by Kiffin or some other separatist sympathizer. The moment when Lilburne wrote the tract can be calculated quite exactly. He says that 'upon Thursday, the 17 or 18 of May last' he was 'had before Sir *John Bancks* and Mr. *Littleton*, the Kings Attourney and Soliciter Generall, to be examined what I said at the Pillory' (p. 27). He asked his examiners to convey to the bishops his challenge to dispute with them before the King. 'But their Argument & replication to this my challeng, was: Lay him fast in Iron chains, Armes, and Leggs, coupled together' (p. 27). This was apparently the beginning of Lilburne's 'close' imprisonment. He says in the present tract, 'I have beene lockt up close prisoner about 4 Moneths.' This would indicate that he was writing some time in September, 1638, four months after his appearance before Sir John Banks. He refers to the tract in his *Coppy of a Letter*, written in November, as his 'large epistle to a Citizens wife, and a professour in the Church of England, which long since before the depths of my sorrowes, and the time of my so publique disgracefull and contemptible condition, was my loving friend, though now for my judgment sake (which is the truth) shee with divers others, become as strangers and forraigners to me, which I compiled without either pen or inke in the beginning of my cruell fettered and shackled condition' (p. 9). It appears that this woman had let him know that he was reported to have said that he would as soon hear the devil preach as Dr. Stoughton or M. Walker (p. 3). He denies mentioning these names, gives an account of his spiritual experiences in prison after his punishment, argues that the Church of England is the church of Antichrist and once more challenges Laud and the clergy to public debate. The woman to whom all this is addressed has not been identified. She may perhaps be the 'W. G.' referred to in *Coppy of a Letter*, p. 16, and *Answer to Nine Arguments*, pp. 24, 38. In his *Letter to the Wardens*, p. 4, dated 4 October 1640, Lilburne says that '*Canterburies* Catchpoles took from me the last yeare at the Custome house, almost two thousand of my Bookes as they came from *Amsterdam*.' In the same letter he says that he has four books in print, probably referring to *The Christian Mans Triall* (1st edition), *A Worke of the Beast*, *Come out of her my people* and *Poore Mans Cry*. Of these the two last named were published with the date 1639. We may conclude that either or both of them may have been the printed matter seized at the custom-house and that either or, more probably, both were printed in Holland.

> Coppy of a Letter written by L. C. L. to one of his special friends when he was in his cruell close imprisonment, in the Common Gaole of the Fleet wherein is a large discovery of those soule ravishing Comforts, Ioyes, and Supportations, which he then constantly injoyed, from the Fountaine of all Comfort; Published now for the incouragement of the Saints, cheerfully to suffer afflictions and sorrowes for the sake and cause of their Lord and Master. [*Referred to in these pages as* Coppy of a Letter.]

This was first published by Lilburne in his *Innocency and Truth Justified* . . . *Unto which reply is annext* [see above] . . . *Printed in the Yeare 1645*. It occurs after page 76; its pages are independently numbered 1-21, but under the same title, repeated, viz. '*Innocency and Truth Justified* Let the quintessence of sweetnesse which is the Lord Jesus Christ, be alwayes your delight. London, Printed according to Order by Thomas Paine, 1646.' It is subscribed 'From the Fleet, the place of the sweetest spirituall rejoycings, soul refreshings, inward gloryings, hearty consolations, and heavenly comforts, that ever my inward man was possessor of, or I thinke ever shall so long as I am in this earthly tabernacle, and house of clay, this 11. Moneth called November, *Anno* MDCXXXVIIJ. *Etatis suae* 22. John Lilburne.' It was obviously published in 1645 or 1646 in order that Lilburne in his quarrel of that date with Prynne might avail himself of popular sympathy for his sufferings of 1638-40. On the opening page of the first part of the whole tract he refers to 'this my insuing epistle written in the yeare 1638.' In the course of the epistle itself he alludes to earlier writings, particularly to *Come out of her my people, viz.*

'My Apologie and just and innocent defence to some of my loving Friends I have Latelie made, in which you may read' etc. (p. 5). *Come out of her my people* opens with such a personal defense, 'This by way of *Preface* or *Apology* for my selfe' (p. 7).

'I could fill your eares with the true relation of reall works of wonder indeed . . . but I must be forced to abbreviate my selfe, and leave you to the admiring of that goodnesse, sweetnes, and almightie power, the expressions of which in part, you may not only read in this my epistle to your selfe, but also in my epistle to others of my friends; and my answers to my opposers, but especially in a large epistle to a Citizens wife, and a professour in the Church of England' (p. 9).

'The transcendent glory of this holy Citie, or heavenly *Jerusalem*, or spirituall *Syon* . . . I have in part many months agoe described, and illustrated in my answer to W.G. as there you may read' (p. 16). Perhaps an allusion to *Come out of her my people.*

Coppy of a Letter was written to a woman sympathizer, of what age and name does not appear. Lilburne has heard from her that she is 'one . . . that may enjoy all outward things that heart can desire' (p. 14). He is scarcely acquainted with her; it is 'unknown to me what you are, but onely by sight, and a few speeches long since had before my keeper, and as yet unknown to me where you dwell or abide' (p. 21). She had called on him in prison shortly after his public punishment; 'you say when you were first with me in this my close imprisonment, which was before I was laid in Iron fetters' (p. 8), and 'at the time when you were with me, it was but the beginning of my feast of fat things' (p. 9). She has since prayed for him and written him a letter; 'I have fared the better, and exceedingly felt the strength of the prayers of you and others of the Lords people'

(p. 12); 'Deare and loving friend, your sweet letter I have received' with great comfort (p. 7); 'You desire me to write unto you' (p. 9). The result of the woman's solicitude is this epistle, giving an account of Lilburne's spiritual experience.

An Answer to Nine Arguments: Written by *T.B.* Wherein is plainly from the Scriptures shewed the weaknesse of his Arguments, whereby he undertakes to prove both the Church and Ministery of *England* true; as likewise describing the nature and properties of a true Church and Ministry. Written long since by that faithfull Servant of God and his Countrey, *John Lilburne Leiftenant Collonell*: And now published for further good, by a well-willer to Him and the Truth . . . London. Printed in the yeare of our Lord, 1645.

Frontispiece, portrait engraved by Glover. Thomason entered the date 'Jan. 17th' on this pamphlet. It was published upon Lilburne's return from service in the army and captivity in the hands of the royalists probably to support his claims for the reparations voted him by parliament for the losses he had suffered in 1638-40 but not yet paid. The epistle 'To the Reader' is signed *M.N.*, suggested by the Thomason Catalogue to have been Marchamont Needham, a possible but not certain attribution. M.N. says, 'I thought good to publish to thy view, that which was written by him . . . when he was in the depth of his sorrowes, or rather sufferings, close prisoner in Irons in the Fleet.' T.B., author of the nine arguments Lilburne is refuting, remains unidentified. Lilburne addresses himself first to a 'loving friend' who has reported to him T.B.'s arguments against separa-tion. T.B. is obviously a man; Lilburne begins addressing him directly on page four. The 'loving friend' appears to be a woman; in challenging T.B. to reply to him in writing, Lilburne says, 'otherwise I beleeve and hope that you will loose her' (p. 43). She may have been the citizen's wife addressed in *Come out of her my people* or, more likely, the sympathetic friend to whom he addressed the letter written in November 1638. The exact date of the composition of the *Answer* to T.B. is uncertain. Lilburne twice refers to 'my Answer to W.G.' (pp. 24, 38), which may allude to *Come out of her my people*, probably written the preceding September. He subscribes the tract 'in my most cruell and close imprisonment in Irons . . . John Lilburne. Anno 1638. which to me is the second yeare of Remembrance, and the 21 yeare of my age. From the Fleet the Prelates fiery Furnace.' Appended at the end are some crude verses prefaced by this note: 'These Verses were my meditations one night in my close Imprisonment after the reading of a pamphlet sung in the streets of London, in which I was joyned as a Traytor with the Scots at their first coming into England. The King's first campaign against the Scots took place in the spring of 1639, the first coming of the Scots into England in August, 1640.

The Poore Mans Cry. Wherein Is shewed the present miserable estate of mee Iohn Lilburne, Close prisoner in the Fleet. Also An humble Petition to his Majesties Honorable privy Councill, for maintenance that I famish not . . . Published by a backe friend of the English Popish Prelates, 1639.

In *Come out of her my people* Lilburne says (p. 31) that during his close confinement beginning in May 1638, 'the Warden of the Fleete hath denied me penn, inke and paper, only to write a short petition to the Lords of the Counsell, (in the presence of my Keeper).' This was probably an earlier petition much like the present, which is subscribed 'John Lilburne. Etatis 22' and dated '*December 20. Anno*. 1638.' In it the writer refers to a 'Humble Petition to the Noble Lords . . . which I sent last week to the Wardens of the Fleete, having leave of them for a Scribe to write it' (p. 3). The wardens, disapproving what he had written, 'sent a scribe to me, to draw it over a gaine, and to leave out most of it, especially about my lying in Irons in my sicknesse.' The old woman who tended him delivered the paper to one of the wardens 'upon Tuesday last.' It was not, he avers, submitted to the clerk of the council until 'this present Frydaie morning,' the day on which he was penning the present complaint, as appears from his dating it 'this present Friday . . . commonly called, St. *Thomas-day*.' The petition to the privy council is printed at the conclusion. This was no doubt only one of several such with which Lilburne besieged the authorities for relief. He complains that they 'have used much meanes, that my petitions should not have audience' (p. 12). For references to others see *Letter to the Apprentices*. The publication of this one and the accompanying plea of the author was sponsored by an anonymous sympathizer who supplied an epistle to the 'Courteous Reader' and signed himself 'thy exiled friend and nameless Country-man.' He says, 'I here report it of knowledge: that in all the Popish countries where I have beene, there is not that cruelty now exercised by Bis. anywhere, as here in England. The Prelates in Poland, Spaine, France, are not halfe so vile' (p. 11). This 'backe friend' of the prelates may well have been some exiled separatist abroad who saw to the printing of Lilburne's tract. In his *Letter to the Wardens*, dated 4 October 1640, Lilburne, perhaps referring to *The Poore Mans Cry*, says that he has bequeathed to his executor 'a punctual Anatomie of some part of your matchlesse knavery, villanie, and blood thirstinesse, with a strict Order to put it in Print, with some Marginall Notes to it' (p. 5). These words even to the marginal notes are an exact description of *The Poore Mans Cry*, though that work must already have been in print.

To all the brave, courageous, and valiant Apprentizes of the honourable City of London, but especially those that appertain to the worshipfull Company of Cloth workers, (of which company, if I live I hope to be a Free man.) [*Referred to in these pages as* Letter to the Apprentices.]

This was first published in *The Prisoners Plea for a Habeas Corpus, Or an Epistle writ by L. C. Joh. Lilburne prerogative prisoner in the Tower of London the 4 of Aprill, to the Honourable Mr. W. Lenthall Speaker of the House of Commons . . . unto which he hath annexed his Epistle which he writ to the Prentices of London the 10th of May 1639 when he was like to be murdered in the Tower, by Crumwell and his tirannicall fellow Grandees.*

The Prisoners Plea appeared without imprint or date but was subscribed by Lilburne from the Tower 4 April 1648 and was no doubt printed and circulated in the same year. The address to the apprentices is subscribed 'Iohn Lilburne. From . . . the Fleet . . . the 10th day of this 5 moneth of May, in the yeare of remembrance 1639.' In his *Innocency and Truth*, 1645, he had stated, 'first when I was a prisoner in the Fleet . . . in the height of my extremity, I writ an Epistle in 2 sheets of Paper to the Magistrates of *London*, and one sheet to the prentices thereof, which was thrown among them one day when they were at their recreations in *Moor-fields*, which had like to have occasioned the Bishop of *Canterburies* ruine, for the throwing of which, my maid was taken and carried before Sir *Morris Abbet*, then Lord Mayor of London, where there was witnesse that appeared to justifie the thing to her face, upon which the Lord Mayor committed her to prison without a warrant' (p. 74). After his release, it would seem, Lilburne brought complaint against the Lord Mayor before a committee of the House of Lords. He says that Lord Brooks [Brooke?] and Lord Roberts appeared for him and that the Mayor was ordered to pay the maid ten pounds.

In *Letter to the Apprentices* Lilburne refers to his 'late grievous lamentaced [*sic*] and just complaint to the right honourable the Lord Major of the City of London intituled *A Cry for Justice* and the right worshipfull Aldermen his brethren, and all the rest of the grave and worthy Citizens published and which I have more largely in 3 severall books in print . . . declared and published unto the view of *England, Scotland, Ireland* and *Holland*.' He mentions also 'multitudes of humble petitions' which he has sent 'both to the King and the Nobles, joyntly and severally' together with supplications to friends at The Hague to be submitted to the Queen of Bohemia begging her to intercede for him with her brother, the King of England. None of these petitions, so far as I know, has survived.

A Coppy of a Letter written by John Lilburne, Close Pris[o]ner In the Wards of the Fleet, which he sent to *Iames Ingram* and *Henry Hopkins*, Wardens of the Fleet. Wherein is fully discovered their great cruelty exercised upon his Body. [*Referred to in these pages as* Letter to the Wardens.]

Published without title-page, date or imprint. Subscribed 'honest John Lilburne' and dated 'From your Common and bloody Slaughter-house, called the *Wards* of the *Fleet*, this 4th day of October, 1640.'

Lilburne makes several allusions to other writings. He says that he has left to his executor a 'punctuall Anatomie' of the wardens villainy 'with a strict Order to put it in Print, with some Marginall Notes to it' (p. 5); see *Poor Mans Cry*. He refers to his *Come out of her my people* (p. 6). He writes: 'True it is that your . . . cruelty, made mee the last Yeere . . . cry out to the Lord Major and Aldermen of *London*; also to my Fellow Apprentices, which now with foure other Bookes are all in print, . . . when I had my health . . . I was not Idle, but writ then, and have at command now, more sheetes of paper (which many moneths agoe I sent into *Holland* to my Printer, which the World yet never see) then all my Printed Bookes doe containe' (pp. 6-7).

'Know . . . that if there be but a Printing-house in any of the Cities in the

Provinces of Holland, I will cause this Letter to be Printed that so, (if it be possible) it may be claimed [*sic*] up upon the Posts, and made as publique as the Coblers Sermon, that so you may (if you will) read it in the streets, as you goe to the Parliament house' (p. 8).

To the Honourable House of Commons now assembled in the High Court of Parliament. The humble Petition of Iohn Lilburne Prisoner in the Fleet.

The petition written by Lilburne in 1640. Published in his *Innocency and Truth*, 1645, pp. 66-67.

Index

Index 451

Hildersam, Arthur, 25, 56, 63, 67, 72, 184; career and personal connections, 54, 55; *Lectures upon the Fourth of John*, 56; biographical source, 104

Hildersam, Samuel, 105

Hill, Thomas, 106

Hinde, William, 104; life of John Bruen, 112

History, influence of Puritanism upon the writing of, 100 ff.; interest in, 302, 303

History of Plymouth Plantation (Bradford), 189; excerpts, 187, 190

Holdsworth, Richard, 106

Holland, Henry, 26, 105; quoted, 26, 27; *Herwologia Anglica*, 104

Holland, separatists in, 185 ff., 206, 264

Hollar, Wenceslas, 365

Holy days, 151

Hooker, Richard, *Of the Laws of Ecclesiastical Polity*, 11; defined principles of Anglicanism, 11, 22

Hooker, Thomas, 79, 96, 102, 228; flight to America, 61, 70; *The Soul's Preparation for Christ*, 265; supported by Puritan peers, 331

House of Mourning, The, 102

How, Samuel, 267, 268; *The Sufficiencie of the Spirits Teaching . . .*, 267

Humanism, Renaissance, influence upon political leaders, 330

Humanists, scepticism concerning dogma of predestination, 199; notions concerning atonement, 200

Humble Petition of the Brownists, The, 266

Huntingdon, Henry Hastings, Earl of, 55

Hunton, Philip, *Treatise of Monarchie*, 365

Husband, wife's subordination to, 121

Hutchinson, Anne, 69, 213, 332

Idealism, based on belief in mystic brotherhood of man, 206; democratic, 273; of the Renaissance, 334

Idealists, influence of Platonism, 308

Imagery, 140, 147; extravaganzas of, 150

Immersion, total, 186

Imprisonment, *see* Punishment

Impropriated tithes, society for buying, 80 ff., 230, 231; feoffees for, 81;

Stock involved with, 291; dissolution of feoffees, 230; feoffees reimbursed, 231

Independency, 53, 55; Thomas Goodwin's stand for, 78 f.; preachers active in the cause of, 79; influence, 231

Independents, 16; Puritans rendered into, 17; stand in Westminster Assembly, 174, 192; emergence of, within reform party, 175; part in revolutionary movement, 176; doctrine, 181; part in founding Massachusetts, 192; state of mind which gave importance to radical, 260

Individualism, 97, 120, 268 f.; a menace to reform of church and dominance of clergy, 172; reformers' promotion of, 173 ff., 179, 301, 375; separatism the extreme expression of, 181; a disrupting force, 188; bars to, which Calvinism set up, 193; reaction against predestination and uniformity, 203; freedom of expression and of ideas, 229, 247; conscience the only check, 261; influence of doctrine upon Lilburne, 274; confounds uniformity, 339; Milton's antiprelatical tracts swell stream of, 361

Infallibility, arguments against papal, 238; claim to, a bar to charity and truth, 244

Intellectual freedom, Hales's defense of, 245

Intellectuals, become opponents of authority, 40; *see also* Liberals

Intolerance, failure of Stuarts to realize inexpediency of, 49; confession of futility of, 204; baptists oppose, 205

Ireland, reports of atrocities committed by Catholics, 371

Jackson, Arthur, 67

Jacobs, Henry, 262, 264

James I, petitioned to reorganize church: persecution of nonconformists, 49; effect of persecutions, 50; extravagance and corruption of court, 51; Dod silenced by, 57; pleased by logic of Preston, 71; makes him chaplain to Prince of Wales, 72; on Everard, 208

James, William, 92

Janeway, John, 100; diary, 97

Jemmat, William, 74

454

Index

Marshall, Valentine, quoted, 140
Martyrologie, A. (Clarke), 105
Mary, Queen, 47; seeds of dissent sown in reign of, 176
Massachusetts, noblemen's application for political privilege in; qualification for citizenship, 332 (*see also* New England)
Mather, Cotton, *Magnalia Christi Americana*, 61
Mather, Richard, 79, 132
Mayflower, 188; voyage inspired by ideals common to separatists and Puritans in general, 189
'Mechanick' preachers, 79
Mede, William, *Clavis Apocalyptica*, 269
Medieval tradition, influence over university education, 298
Mendicants, Puritan preachers become essentially, 40
Mennonites, 186
Midgley, Master, 109
Mildmay, Sir Walter, 55; founded Emmanuel College, 20
Millenarians, 17
Millenary Petition, 55
Millennium, saints' expectation of the, 269; Knollys' faith in, 271; hope of arising out of desperation of poor, 271
Milton, John, 9, 21, 88, 124, 133, 137, 167, 218, 256, 287, 334, 337; *Paradise Lost*, 18, 21, 122, 342, 356; works in which his spiritual experience is set forth, 114 f.; *Comus*, 114, 146, 317-21; *Lycidas*, 114, 257, 259, 288, 311, 317, 320, 321-23, 325; excerpt, 356; use of personal confession, 115; ideas on marriage and family, 122, 123, 361; basic contention in argument for Utopia, 127; attack against prelacy, 288, 295, 296, 297, 322, 325, 338-63; what his genius expresses, 288; determination to forgo the pulpit, 288, 293, 295, 296, 313; critics' appraisals of, 289; recognition of own gifts and destiny, 289, 297, 304, 306, 310, 314, 315, 322, 358; Puritanism, 289, 308, 311, 317 f.; 362; family background, 290; early life and influences, 290 ff., 318; conception of the preacher's role, 292,

303; early poems, 293, 294, 301, 310 ff.; relations with Thomas Young, 293, 294, 296, 307, 340; aspiration; purpose, 293, 305, 315, 340, 344; independence of mind and character, 293; at Cambridge, 293, 296 ff.; personal experience that helped to make him a revolutionary shown in spiritual autobiography and other writings, 296; disapproval of scholasticism, 297 ff., 305, 314, 345; Bacon's influence upon, 299, 301; college orations, 300, 303, 311; violence of language, 300, 359; *Naturam non pati senium*, 301; belief that knowledge is power, 304; reading of ancient orators and historians, 307, 315; enjoyment of Ovid, 307; embraces beauty, 308, 317; influenced by Spenser, 309, 311, 318; plans for writing *On the Morning of Christ's Nativity*, 312; relations with Diodati, 312, 319, 321, 341, 343; refuses invitation to remain at Cambridge, defends abandonment of the pulpit, explanation to his father, 313; *Ad Patrem*, 313, 319; years of study after college, 314; flowering of poetic gift, 317 ff.; in Italy, 324, 341; Utopian fervor of antiprelatical tracts, 339, 344 ff.; attitude toward presbyterianism, 339, 342 ff.; attacks upon Bishop Hall, 340, 343 ff., 359; *Animadversions upon the Remonstrants Defence against Smectymnuus*, 340, 344, 359; excerpts, 357; *An Apology against . . . a Modest Confutation . . .*, 340, 344, 358, 359, 361; *Of Prelatical Episcopacy*, 340, 344; *Of Reformation . . . in England*, 340, 344, 356; extraordinary prayer and curse in, 354; *The Reason of Church Government . . .*, 340, 344, 357; returns home to aid fight for liberty, 341; plans for composition of his great poem, 341, 355 f., 358; ideas expressed in tracts, 344 ff.; background for understanding of tracts, 344; personal feelings mingle with zeal for public good, 346, 353, 357; on the ideal commonwealth of England, 346 ff.; exaltation of scripture, 349; belief in the poet's godly function, 355 ff.; famous picture of himself as studious

Prelacy (*Continued*)

Milton's attack upon, 288, 295, 296, 297, 322, 352; clamor for abolition of, root and branch, 324-63; defense of, prepared by Joseph Hall, 325; divinely established in primitive church, 329; attacked by parliamentary leaders, 332 ff.; presbyterianism urged against, 340, 344, 353; overthrow of, a blow at Stuart absolutism, 374

Prelates, Puritan opinion of, 242; war of pamphlets against, 250; as seen by man in the street, 257; Lilburne's outbreak against, 259; church-out Milton, 288-323; accused of unpeopling kingdom, 295; *see also* Bishops

Presbyterianism, conceived upon model of Calvinist church at Geneva, 10; attempts to put into practice suppressed, 11; effect of delay in consummation of Puritanism, 14; rejection of Cartwright's program, 18; minority opposed to, 174; John Goodwin's opposition to, 203; attempt to subject church to a rigid, 297; in Scotland, 324 ff.; England kept from falling into mold of, 325; Milton's attitude toward, 339, 342 ff.; urged against prelacy, 340, 344, 353; promised freedom from repression, 342; expected by Milton to usher in Utopia, 343, 344, 350; *see also* Church government

Presbyterians, compose majority of Westminster Assembly, 16; Puritans rendered into, 17; relation of Puritan presbyterian reformers to sectaries and independents, 174; reaction to intransigent dogmatism of, 196; fanatical agitators, 217

Press, Puritans provide material and market for, 82; a serpent in bosom of spiritual brotherhood, 172; in hands of enemies of government, 218; superstitious reverence for authority of, 222; possibilities for making trouble for government, 223; Prynne advances freedom of, 224; hostility toward prelacy, 225; ignoring or circumventing censorship, 227; Laud's attempt to control, 230; unchecked outpouring of Puritan writings, 231; regulations for control of, 232; Star Chamber's jurisdiction over, 232; influence upon life, 233; ancillary and subordinate to church, 234; Puritans' hold upon; government's machinery for control of, ineffective, 249; difficulty of regulating, 252, 376; turns out evidence of dissent, 262; Utopian dreams appear in popular versions from, 270; publishing attacks upon bishops, profitable, 276; fostered by pulpit, 323; Laud sanctions use of, in defense of prelacy, 325; effect of calling of Long Parliament upon, 326; part in conflict between crown and parliament, 364 ff.; revolutionary, 369; parliament undetermined what to do about, 374; need for reducing to order, 375; *see also* Literature

Preston, John, 55, 56, 57, 61, 67, 69, 70, 77, 78, 102, 111, 131, 209, 219, 294, 298, 334; sermons, 66, 74, 164 ff.; career and connections, 70 ff.; as chaplain to the Prince of Wales, 72, 167; makes personal influence count for the advance of preaching, 72; lecturer at Lincoln's Inn; at Trinity, 73; *Life Eternall*, 74, 168, 170; *The New Covenant*, 93, 152, 164; *The Breast-Plate of Faith and Love*, 93, 152, 166; biographical source, 104; sermon method, 136; quoted, 146, 147; *The Doctrine of the Saints Infirmities*, 152, 167; *The Saints Daily Exercise*, 166; *The Saints Qualification*, 167

Price, Mr., 75, 78, 95

Pride, hazard of, 154, 196

Prince of Wales, *see* Charles I

Printing, ordinance for, 377

Prisons, inadequacy of, 249

Propaganda, through pulpit and press, 6

Proselytizing, separatism puts check upon, 179

Prosperity, a check to revolutionary excitement, 272

Protestantism, reformers determined to restore and purify church, 8; effect of Elizabeth's accession to throne, 8; influence of Book of Discipline, 11; origins of communions, 17; dissent among congregations, 176 ff.; sects become aspects of, 178

Pennsylvania Paperbacks

Pennsylvania Paperbacks continued